CULTIVATING THE MASSES

CULTIVATING THE MASSES

Modern State Practices and Soviet Socialism, 1914–1939

DAVID L. HOFFMANN

CORNELL UNIVERSITY PRESS

Ithaca and London

First published 2011 by Cornell University Press

Printed in the United States of America

Library of Congress Cataloging-in-Publication Data

Hoffmann, David L. (David Lloyd), 1961–
    Cultivating the masses : modern state practices and Soviet socialism, 1914–1939 / David L. Hoffmann.
        p. cm.
    Includes bibliographical references and index.
    ISBN 978-0-8014-4629-0 (cloth : alk. paper)
    1. Public welfare—Soviet Union.   2. Soviet Union—Social policy.
3. Welfare state—Soviet Union.   4. Socialism—Soviet Union.
5. Soviet Union—Social conditions—1917–1945.
I. Title.
    HV313.H64   2011
    361.94709'041—dc22   2011017389

Cornell University Press strives to use environmentally responsible suppliers and materials to the fullest extent possible in the publishing of its books. Such materials include vegetable-based, low-VOC inks and acid-free papers that are recycled, totally chlorine-free, or partly composed of nonwood fibers. For further information, visit our website at www.cornellpress.cornell.edu.

Cloth printing   10 9 8 7 6 5 4 3 2 1

To my son Jonah

Contents

Illustrations

Acknowledgments

One of the topics I researched for my previous book was Soviet family policy, in particular the Stalinist leadership's efforts to strengthen familial obligations beginning in 1936. Previously, scholars had seen Communist Party leaders' efforts to buttress the family as part of their "Great Retreat" from revolutionary values in favor of more traditional institutions and culture. But when I began to look beyond the Soviet Union, I was struck by how virtually all European countries in this period introduced similar policies to strengthen the family and increase the birthrate. I began to see Stalinist family policy as one particular manifestation of an international trend toward state attempts to manage reproduction. My convictions were reinforced when I had a series of conversations in the mid-1990s with my friend Peter Holquist, who was taking a comparative approach to the topic of surveillance. By placing Soviet surveillance in a pan-European context, Peter was able to demonstrate that techniques utilized by both the Reds and the Whites during the Russian Civil War derived from surveillance practices employed by all the major combatant countries in Europe during the First World War.

After further discussion, Peter and I decided to coauthor a book that would analyze Soviet policies on welfare, public health, reproduction, surveillance, propaganda, and state violence in an international context. We felt that such an approach would offer a different perspective on the Soviet system and demonstrate the relevance of Soviet history to an understanding of broader trends in twentieth-century world history. Unfortunately Peter soon became too busy with other projects and was unable to pursue this one. He did, however, contribute to an early draft of the book's first chapter and provide me with materials he had gathered on surveillance and state violence. As my footnotes make clear, I also relied heavily on his published work, particularly in the sections on surveillance (where the pioneering research of Vladlen Izmozik also proved invaluable). Nearly ten years have elapsed since Peter left the project, and in that time my thinking has evolved considerably, which is to say that I alone am responsible for the ideas expressed in this book. Nonetheless, I wish to acknowledge Peter's important early role, and to thank him for subsequently commenting on my chapter drafts. He is both an outstanding scholar and a loyal friend, someone whose enthusiasm, wealth of historical knowledge, and sharp analytical mind have done so much to help not only me but so many scholars in the Russian history field.

Other friends and colleagues have read and commented on my work, and I would like to thank them as well. Of the three referees who read the entire book manuscript, two are no longer anonymous—Michael David-Fox and Lynne Viola. Their reports and that of the third referee proved extremely helpful, both in strongly endorsing the manuscript and in offering incisive criticisms to improve it. Daniel Beer, Frances Bernstein, Aleksa Djilas, Laura Engelstein, Thomas Ewing, Isabel Hull, Yanni Kotsonis, Kenneth Pinnow, Amy Randall, and Susan Gross Solomon all provided excellent feedback on chapters of the book manuscript. I have presented portions of my research at numerous conferences, and I would like to thank those who served as formal commentators on my work—Brian Bonhomme, Norman Naimark, David Shearer, and Ronald Grigor Suny. Early on I presented a chapter at the University of California, Berkeley, and for their comments there I would like to thank Victoria Frede, Henry Reichman, Nicholas Riasanovsky, Yuri Slezkine, and the late Reginald Zelnik, who strongly encouraged me to use my comparative approach as a means to highlight both the common and the distinctive features of Soviet governance. I also presented a chapter at Stanford University, and I would like to thank Holly Case, Stuart Finkel, Andrew Jenks, Nancy Kollmann, Marcie Shore, and Amir Weiner for their comments there. At a symposium on Stalinism held at The Ohio State University, Sheila Fitzpatrick not only delivered the keynote address but provided insightful comments on my paper, which pushed me to distinguish more carefully between Stalinist rule and technocratic administration. I also presented a chapter at the Midwest Russian History Workshop, and I would like to thank all of the participants, especially John Bushnell, Ben Eklof, Diane Koenker, David McDonald, Karen Petrone, David Ransel, Christine Ruane, Mark Steinberg, Charles Steinwedel, Lewis Siegelbaum, and Christine Worobec.

In addition to help from these scholars, I have discussed my research with other friends and colleagues in the field and appreciate the advice and encouragement they have given me. They include Golfo Alexopoulos, Robert Argenbright, Francesco Benvenuti, Peter Blitstein, Frederick Corney, Sarah Davies, Adrienne Edgar, Donald Filtzer, Delia Fontana, Wendy Goldman, Anne Gorsuch, Paul Hagenloh, Igal Halfin, James Harris, Dan Healey, Jochen Hellbeck, Francine Hirsch, Adeeb Khalid, Oleg Kharkhordin, Oleg Khlevniuk, Nathaniel Knight, Stephen Kotkin, Lars Lih, Laurie Manchester, Amy Nelson, Elena Osokina, Donald Raleigh, Jeffrey Rossman, Andrei Konstantinovich Sokolov, Kenneth Straus, Paul Valliere, Mark von Hagen, Elizabeth Wood, and Sergei Zhuravlev.

I feel fortunate to have assembled at The Ohio State University an outstanding group of scholars in the Russian, East European, and Eurasian history field—Nicholas Breyfogle, Mollie Cavender, Theodora Dragostinova, Scott Levi, and Jennifer Siegel. All of them have been model colleagues who have provided a stimulating and congenial setting in which to work. Friends in other fields as well have done much to help me, and in particular I would like to thank Angela Brintlinger, Alice Conklin, Steven Conn, Ted Hopf, David Horn, Robin Judd, Stephanie Smith, Birgitte Soland, and Judy Wu, as well as Christopher Otter, whose broad expertise in European history helped me enormously. Aaron Retish, William Risch, and Tricia Starks, three of my former doctoral students who have since gone on to highly successful academic careers, commented on my book chapters, and I thank them for their suggestions. Current graduate students at Ohio State have also provided me with help and inspiration. In particular, I had many fruitful discussions with Yigit Akin about the historical parallels between the Soviet Union and Republican Turkey, and I benefitted from his bibliographic suggestions as well. I relied on Ian Lanzillotti's expertise on the North Caucasus to understand the myriad of ethnic groups there. Sarah Douglas and John Johnson offered research assistance as I prepared the book manuscript for publication.

I received research support in the form of several travel grants from the Mershon Center and sabbatical leave from The Ohio State University College of Arts and Humanities. I conducted research in a number of archives and libraries, and I would like to thank their respective staffs for their help. In Russia, I worked in the Center for the Preservation of Documents of Youth Organizations, the Central Archive of the City of Moscow, the Central Archive of the Socio-Political History of Moscow, the Russian State Archive of Economics, the Russian State Archive of Socio-Political History, and the State Archive of the Russian Federation. I also conducted archival research in the Public Record Office of the United Kingdom and the Hoover Institution Archives. The libraries I used include the Library of Congress, the National Institute of Health Library, the New York Public Library, the

Ohio State University libraries, the Russian State Library, the Stanford University libraries, the University of Illinois Library, and the Widener Library of Harvard University. Aleksandr Polunov provided expert research assistance in Moscow, and I thank him for all of his help. I also thank my friends Sasha Meissner, Liza Tikhomirova, and Iulia Trubikhina for their hospitality in Moscow over many years.

I wish to express my gratitude to the staff of Cornell University Press. Director John Ackerman vigorously supported the project from its inception and drew on his own expansive knowledge of Russian history to provide astute comments and suggestions. I also thank manuscript editor Karen Laun, copyeditor Jack Rummel, and indexer Judith Kip for their excellent work preparing the book manuscript for publication.

Most of all, I thank my family members for their unfailing love and encouragement. My parents, George Hoffmann and Irene L. Hoffmann, and my sisters, Jill Hoffmann and Karen Hoffmann, have supported me in every way, and I am extremely grateful to them. My wife, Patricia Weitsman, is my partner and soul mate, someone whom I can always confide in and rely on. For this book, she has read and commented on countless chapter drafts, and has discussed my work to allow me to clarify my ideas. More than that, she has helped me persevere through difficult times and has always celebrated my successes. I am extremely grateful for the immeasurable love and happiness she has given me. Finally I wish to acknowledge my children Sarah and Jonah. Their presence has delayed completion of this book considerably. And yet I do not for a moment regret the time I have spent caring for them. On the contrary, they have given my life so much meaning and joy, and I treasure our time together. As they constantly remind me, it would not be fair to do something for one of them and not for the other, and since I have already dedicated a book to Sarah, I dedicate this book to Jonah.

Abbreviations

d., dd.	delo, dela (file, files)
f.	fond (collection)
GARF	Gosudarstvennyi Arkhiv Rossiiskoi Federatsii (State Archive of the Russian Federation)
l., ll.	list, listy (page, pages)
op.	opis' (inventory)
PRO	Public Record Office, U.K.
RGAE	Rossiiskii Gosudarstvennyi Arkhiv Ekonomiki (Russian State Archive of Economics)
RGASPI	Rossiiskii Gosudarstvennyi Arkhiv Sotsial'no-Politicheskoi Istorii (Russian State Archive of Socio-Political History)
RGIA	Rossiiskii Gosudarstvennyi Istoricheskii Arkhiv (Russian State Historical Archive)
TsAOPIM	Tsentral'nyi Arkhiv Obshchestvenno-Politicheskoi Istorii Moskvy (Central Archive of the Socio-Political History of Moscow)
TsKhDMO	Tsentr Khraneniia Dokumentov Molodezhnykh Organizatsii (Center for the Preservation of Documents of Youth Organizations)
TsKhSD	Tsentr Khraneniia Sovremmenoi Dokumentatsii (Center for the Preservation of Contemporary Documentation)
TsAGM	Tsentral'nyi Arkhiv Goroda Moskvy (Central Archive of the City of Moscow)

Introduction

Our children blossom on the living trunk of our life; they are not
a bouquet, they are a wonderful apple orchard. And this orchard
is ours.... Be so kind as to take on this job: dig, water, get rid of
caterpillars, prune out the dead branches. Remember the words of
the great gardener, Comrade Stalin.
—ANTON MAKARENKO, *A Book for Parents,* 1937

People must be cultivated as tenderly and carefully as a gardener
cultivates a favorite fruit tree.
—JOSEPH STALIN, Speech at a reception of metallurgists, 1934

The Stalinist regime was among the most repressive and violent in all
human history. Under Stalin's leadership, the Soviet government carried
out a massive number of deportations, incarcerations, and executions.
Official figures show that in 1937–38 alone the Soviet security police
executed 681,692 people.[1] Yet, paradoxically, at the very moment that
the Soviet government was killing hundreds of thousands of people, it
was engaged in an enormous pronatalist campaign to boost the population. Even as the number of incarcerations and executions grew exponentially, Communist Party leaders enacted sweeping social welfare
and public health measures to safeguard people's well-being. Extensive
state surveillance of the population went hand in hand with literacy campaigns, political education, and efforts to instill in people an appreciation of high culture. Far from seeking to subjugate society and obliterate
people's sense of self, Soviet authorities sought to cultivate educated, cultured citizens who would transcend selfish, petty-bourgeois instincts and
contribute willingly to a harmonious social order.[2] Only by examining the

---

1. Nicolas Werth, "A State against its People: Violence, Repression, and Terror in the
Soviet Union," *The Black Book of Communism: Crime, Terror, Repression,* trans. Jonathan Murphy and Mark Kramer (Cambridge, Mass., 1999), 190–91, 213.
2. For studies that emphasize the productive as well as repressive aspects of Soviet
power, see Stephen Kotkin, *Magnetic Mountain: Stalinism as a Civilization* (Berkeley,

Party leadership's pursuit of both "positive" and "negative" population policies can one fully grasp the character of the Stalinist regime, a regime intent on transforming the socioeconomic order and the very nature of its citizens, and ready to employ unprecedented levels of social intervention to do so.

In this book, I present Soviet social intervention as one particular constellation of modern state practices that arose in conjunction with ambitions to refashion society and mobilize populations for industrial labor and mass warfare. Soviet social policies reflected a new ethos by which state officials and nongovernment professionals sought to reshape their societies in accordance with scientific and aesthetic norms.[3] This rationalist ethos of social intervention first arose in nineteenth-century Europe, and it subsequently prompted welfare programs, public health initiatives, and reproductive policies in countries around the world. Social intervention intensified with the rise of mass warfare. The tremendous mobilizational demands of the First World War in particular impelled the leaders of all combatant countries to expand their use of economic controls, health measures, surveillance, propaganda, and state violence—all of which became prominent features of the Soviet system.

Although the Soviet state exemplified many facets of modern governance, it clearly did not fit the Western European model of modernity, which included nation-states, industrial capitalism, and parliamentary democracy.[4] Soviet leaders repudiated "bourgeois democracy" in favor of

---

1995), 21–22; Jochen Hellbeck, *Revolution on My Mind: Writing a Diary under Stalin* (Cambridge, Mass., 2006), 5–14.

3. Theorists who have highlighted rational social management as a defining feature of modernity include Anthony Giddens, *The Consequences of Modernity* (Stanford, 1990), 53, 83; James C. Scott, *Seeing Like a State: How Certain Schemes to Improve the Human Condition Have Failed* (New Haven, 1998), 4; Zygmunt Bauman, *Modernity and the Holocaust* (Ithaca, 1991), 12–18. Some historians of Stalinism have counterposed "modernity" and "neo-traditionalism," but these two approaches are in fact complementary. Neo-traditionalism refers to the selective use of traditions to mobilize people, and this practice was characteristic of modern mass politics; David L. Hoffmann, "European Modernity and Soviet Socialism," in *Russian Modernity: Politics, Knowledge, Practices*, ed. Hoffmann and Yanni Kotsonis (New York, 2000), 247. Neo-traditionalism can also refer to traditional social networks that continue to function within modern, industrial society; Andrew G. Walder, *Communist Neo-Traditionalism: Work and Authority in Chinese Industry* (Berkeley, 1986).

4. As scholars have noted, Western European countries themselves often did not fit this idealized model of modernity; see Björn Wittrock, "Modernity: One, None, or Many? European Origins and Modernity as a Global Condition," *Multiple Modernities*, ed. Shmuel N. Eisenstadt (New Brunswick, 2002), 34–35.

an authoritarian, noncapitalist system, which they claimed to rule in the interests of the working class. As the first socialist state, the Soviet Union posed an enormous ideological challenge to the capitalist world. Contemporaries, whether for or against the Soviet system, saw it as an anomaly when compared to the West. But for the purposes of historical analysis, it is problematic to posit Western modernity as the norm against which all other political systems are measured. Recent theorists have introduced the concept of "multiple modernities," an approach that acknowledges divergent trajectories of development in the modern era.[5] This approach provides two major analytical advantages. First, it avoids the ethnocentrism of modernization theory, particularly its assumption that all countries will eventually converge on the Western ideal of liberal democracy and free-market capitalism. Second, it leads us to consider both the commonalities and differences of modern political systems. By examining the Soviet system within this comparative framework, I seek to delineate both its general and distinctive features and to explain why Soviet social intervention assumed such an extreme character.

The modern state practices and new technologies of social intervention that developed across the world assumed very different forms in particular social, political, and ideological settings. In the Soviet case, I explain such differences by analyzing its historically conditioned particularities, which included but were not limited to Marxist-Leninist ideology. Also significant were the social and political conditions in which prerevolutionary Russian professionals developed their ideas and practices, borrowing from Western European thought but also drawing on their own concerns with battling the autocracy, uplifting the masses, and renovating Russian society. Russian disciplinary traditions had a strong nurturist orientation, one that meshed well with Marxism and indeed helps account for many Russian intellectuals' embrace of Marxism in the first place. Although I acknowledge the importance of ideology to the Soviet system, I avoid a reified view of Marxism and instead see it as one of a range of transformational ideologies and agendas. Though Marxism-Leninism was enshrined as the official ideology of the Soviet Communist Party, it did not provide a blueprint for the new social order that Party leaders endeavored to build.

5. Shmuel N. Eisenstadt, "Multiple Modernities," in *Multiple Modernities*, 1–3. For work that applies this concept to Russian history, see S. A. Smith, *Revolution and the People in Russia and China: A Comparative History* (Cambridge, 2008), 5–6; Michael David-Fox, "The Intelligentsia, the Masses, and the West: Particularities of Russian-Soviet Modernity," *Crossing Borders: Modernity, Ideology, and Culture in Soviet Russia* (Pittsburgh, forthcoming).

As I will demonstrate, many Soviet social policies were formulated and enacted by non-Marxist professionals who shared a similar agenda of rational social reordering.[6]

I also explore the place of historical contingency in the development of the Soviet system, as well as the interplay between ideological goals and political circumstances. The Soviet state was formed at a moment of total war, and wartime institutions and practices of mobilization became the building blocks of the new political order. State interventionist practices developed across Europe during the First World War, but in constitutional democracies they were subordinated to the preexisting order once the war was over. In the Soviet Union, these practices became institutionalized without any traditional or legal constraints. The revolutionary origin of the Soviet state also meant that there were fewer limits on the ambitions of political leaders in their quest to reshape society. Indeed the form of the Soviet government—a dictatorship that functioned extrajudicially and acknowledged no moral claims beyond its own authority—meant there were no checks on state power. So even though state interventionism expanded throughout Europe and in countries around the world, it assumed a particularly virulent form in the Soviet case.

Refashioning Society

The origins of modern state interventionism may be found in cameralist thought of the early modern era. Cameralist thinkers were the first to analyze systematically the connection between a state's military power and the economic capacity of its population. They argued for a greater state role in fostering a productive society, as a means to expand wealth and increase tax revenues. While cameralist regulations and economic inducements were intended primarily to generate increased revenue for the sovereign and his army, some cameralist thinkers articulated their ideal of an orderly society in terms of the "common good," a term that came to play an autonomous role in cameralist writings. By the late seventeenth century, central European rulers had adopted a range of cameralist policies,

---

6. Kenneth Pinnow stresses that the approach of Russian social scientists merged well with the scientism of Bolshevism. He writes, "It was not just ideology but the assumptions and conceptual tools that signify the social realm that shaped the interventions and activities of the state and its investigators." Kenneth M. Pinnow, *Lost to the Collective: Suicide and the Promise of Soviet Socialism, 1921–1929* (Ithaca, 2010), 11.

for example, constructing poorhouses in Austria and Prussia to ensure the profitable employment of the lower classes.[7]

The ambition to refashion society expanded with the eighteenth-century French Enlightenment, whose thinkers sought to apply science and reason to the organization of human society. The notion of radically restructuring society—in fact the very idea of society as a discrete realm of human existence—had been inconceivable within a traditional religious imaginary, that is, within a worldview that saw God as the sole arbiter of worldly affairs.[8] But Enlightenment thinkers questioned both the existence of God and the sanctity of tradition. And if there were no God to manage society, then should not humankind construct its own rational social order? If there were no heaven above, should not people seek to create a heaven on earth—a perfect society, with liberty, equality, and prosperity for all? While it was not until the nineteenth century that utopian thought and social science would flourish, the Enlightenment offered both a challenge to traditional ways and a model of social science that could constitute and act on the social realm. In other words, the social world came to be seen as of humankind's own making rather than as something preordained or fixed, and social sciences offered a means to refurbish it.

At the end of the eighteenth century, the French Revolution demonstrated that the existing social and political order could indeed be refashioned. The Revolution thus represented not only a change of political regime but a radical break with conventional notions about the social order and the possibility of remaking it. In the wake of the French Revolution, the social sciences enjoyed greatly enhanced authority. The overthrow of the monarchy displaced the traditional conception of power as a unitary political will. In addition to replacing the sovereign with the ideal of popular sovereignty, "cutting off the king's head" cleared the way for a new conception of power—one constituted by regimes of truth. These regimes of truth, elaborated in the nineteenth century by those in the legal profession, medical profession, and social sciences, gained enormous authority, in part because they were purportedly rational and objective. Whereas the

---

7. George Steinmetz, *Regulating the Social: The Welfare State and Local Politics in Imperial Germany* (Princeton, 1993), 63, 112.

8. As Keith Baker writes, "Society could only appear as a representation of collective human existence once the ontological link between the Creator and the created was broken, which is to say when human existence seemed no longer to depend...upon the maintenance of a divinely ordained and instituted order of relations among beings." Keith Michael Baker, "A Foucauldian French Revolution?" *Foucault and the Writing of History*, ed. Jan Goldstein (Cambridge, Mass., 1994), 195–96.

Terror of the French Revolution came to symbolize the excesses of popular sovereignty, social science disciplines were thought to form an important bulwark to mob rule, given that their authority rested on impartiality and reason.[9]

During the nineteenth century, the emergence of new disciplines (demography, social hygiene, psychology) and new technologies of social intervention (censuses, housing inspections, mass psychological testing) greatly heightened the ambitions of reformers to eliminate social problems and refashion society. In order not to lose sight of human agency, I emphasize that professionals, government bureaucrats, and politicians across the political spectrum sought and were in turn themselves influenced by these new forms of knowledge and interventionist practices. The amassing of social statistics, for example, made social problems more legible and emboldened professionals and government officials to propose comprehensive solutions.[10] Epidemiology swelled the faith of public health officials in the revelatory powers of science and the problem-solving ability of modern medicine. The dizzying pace of modernization in the late nineteenth and early twentieth centuries itself fueled the ambitions of reformers, who felt the optimism of seemingly limitless human progress mixed with unease about a world changing so profoundly that even more radical solutions were needed.[11]

The impulse to restructure society also stemmed from a widespread sense that European industrialization and urbanization had destroyed the organic unity of traditional societies. In order to recover the mythical social harmony of the past and overcome the atomization of the modern world, social thinkers of various stripes—socialists, fascists, Nietzscheans, even liberals—envisioned a more collectivist society and a new human psychology that would befit modern industrial civilization. Marxism was distinguished by its emphasis on violent proletarian revolution as the means to overcome class divisions, but it was by no means unique in combining Enlightenment rationalism with "Romantic Anticapitalism" in a quest for a new, harmonious social order.[12]

9. Ibid., 194, 205.

10. James Scott emphasizes legibility as a precondition of state intervention and points out that by the mid-nineteenth century, governments were engaged in extensive undertakings to count and classify their populations; Scott, *Seeing Like a State*, 183.

11. Detlev Peukert, "The Genesis of the 'Final Solution' from the Spirit of Science," in *Reevaluating the Third Reich*, ed. T. Childers and J. Caplan (New York, 1993), 238; Peukert, *The Weimar Republic: The Crisis of Classical Modernity* (New York, 1993), 187.

12. Katerina Clark, *Petersburg: Crucible of Cultural Revolution* (Cambridge, 1995), 16–17. The term *Romantic Anticapitalism* was first used by György Lukás and later

The problem of social renovation had particular urgency for the Russian intelligentsia at the end of the nineteenth century. Lagging behind Western European countries in industrial development, Russia had a primarily peasant population with high rates of illiteracy, infectious disease, and infant mortality. The country was ruled by the repressive and ineffectual tsarist autocracy, which in the late imperial period, resisted social and political reforms. The intelligentsia, itself largely excluded from power, opposed the autocracy and assumed a moral obligation to help the population. In fact, the intelligentsia's own self-identity revolved around this self-appointed mission. It was in this context that Russian professionals developed their ideas and practices, including their penchant for Lamarckian approaches to biosocial issues. Blaming the wretched condition of the peasant masses on the oppressive social and political environment, they sought to uplift and improve the people, and placed their faith in the transformative powers of science and culture. In this sense, the Russian intelligentsia's disciplinary orientation and reformist goals mirrored those of professionals in other developing countries. And like their non-Western counterparts, Russian professionals hoped to avoid the pitfalls of Western European modernity, even as they promoted economic, social, and cultural modernization.

The Revolution of 1905 both energized and frightened liberal professionals in Russia. Although the creation of representative institutions and the easing of censorship offered a more promising climate in which to pursue their work, many professionals were appalled by the class hatred and violence unleashed by the revolution. They continued to oppose the autocracy and to seek the creation of a genuine civic order in which the educated elite could lead the country toward modernity, but they also feared the instability that might come with liberation. To guard against another outburst of unrest among the lower classes as well as to buttress the increasingly shaky moral order, some liberal professionals focused on criminal deviance and other social pathologies, and sought to establish their disciplinary authority over the population.[13] Even more than doctors and social scientists in Western Europe, Russian professionals simultaneously possessed enormous hopes for social transformation and persistent

developed by Michel Löwy. Clark cautions that Romantic Anticapitalism was not so much a movement as a formula to account for the ideas of a range of European intellectuals who critiqued capitalist society, especially its individualism, alienation, and commodification of culture.

13. Laura Engelstein, *The Keys to Happiness: Sex and the Search for Modernity in Fin-de-Siècle Russia* (Ithaca, 1992), 4–13.

fears about social degeneration and chaos. Specialists in the human sciences selectively applied biomedical theories of social decline in a way that lent scientific authority to moral fears and allowed them to prescribe coercive measures to remove deviant individuals from the body social.[14] And while most members of the Russian intelligentsia detested the tsarist autocracy, many of them sought a strong, progressive state that would maintain social order and push through reforms in the absence of a broad base of popular support or well-developed civic institutions.[15]

The more radical members of Russia's intelligentsia placed their hopes in a revolutionary transformation of Russian society. These radicals followed the left Hegelian tradition of German idealism that maintained a belief in the progression of history toward human liberation—a progression they might facilitate by inspiring the masses to rise up against the old order. But lest the radical intelligentsia be regarded as anomalous, one should note that members of the intelligentsia across the political spectrum shared a deep dissatisfaction with the tsarist system and saw social and political change as not only necessary but imminent. Radicals such as the Bolsheviks were not the only ones with an ideological agenda. Professionals, members of voluntary organizations, and even reform-minded tsarist bureaucrats had a vision of the type of society they wished to create and the type of citizen they hoped would inhabit it.[16]

Many Russian radicals were drawn to Marxism, given its allegedly scientific basis, its critique of capitalism, and its emphasis on environmental factors in the transformation of human consciousness. The particular context in which Marxism took root was one in which members of the Russian intelligentsia fought to overcome a despotic tsarist bureaucracy and to uplift the downtrodden masses. To view Marxism as an ideology artificially imposed on Russia ignores the reasons it was adopted and the fact that non-Marxist Russian intellectuals in many ways shared Marxists' understandings of Russia's problems as well as their eagerness to create a new political and social order.

14. Daniel Beer, *Renovating Russia: The Human Sciences and the Fate of Liberal Modernity, 1880–1930* (Ithaca, 2008), 7–11.

15. On Russia's longstanding statist traditions and their influence on "intelligentsia-etatist modernity," see David-Fox, "The Intelligentsia, the Masses, and the West."

16. See, for example, Yanni Kotsonis, *Making Peasants Backward: Agricultural Cooperatives and the Agrarian Question in Russia, 1861–1914* (New York, 1999), 94–95, on agronomists' plans "to transform a population they believed could not conceive of transforming itself."

Mass Politics and Mass Warfare

To explain why aspirations to reshape society were increasingly taken on by state actors, I emphasize the rise of mass politics and mass warfare. In an age of popular sovereignty, political leaders had to meet the needs and interests of the people, and they came to see the population as a source of legitimacy to be served. And in an era of mass warfare, state power and national security depended more clearly than ever on the labor and military capacity of the population. Particularly during the First World War, government leaders in all combatant states sought to regulate people's health, welfare, and reproduction so as to safeguard their countries' "human capital" and "military manpower." They also established extensive surveillance networks to monitor their populations, as well as internment camps to remove "enemy aliens" and "unreliable" ethnic groups from the body social.

The First World War marked a watershed in Russian as well as European history. Up to that point, the tsarist autocracy had largely eschewed modern practices of social intervention. But wartime mobilizations, national security concerns, widespread epidemic diseases, and massive social displacements required the Russian government to augment state control. Government policies included both positive and negative population measures, ranging from public health and welfare to surveillance and deportations. When, for example, locally based physicians proved unable to cope with the millions of war wounded and the spread of epidemic diseases, the tsar finally agreed in 1916 to the creation of a state Ministry of Health—similar to countries throughout Europe that created ministries of health in the wake of the First World War. Also during the war the tsarist government deported nearly 1 million ethnic minorities from regions near the front, again mirroring wartime deportations and internments in other combatant countries.

When the tsarist autocracy was overthrown in February 1917, the Provisional Government continued to expand state responsibility for the population's welfare in ways that anticipated policies of the Soviet government. It established ministries of health, state welfare, and food supply, and placed many professionals in the positions of leadership they had so long desired. Politically, however, the Provisional Government failed to win a broad base of support among the country's lower classes. Soldiers, peasants, and workers had their own revolutionary agendas that included an end to the war, immediate land redistribution, and workers' control of factories, none of which the Provisional Government delivered. As soldiers deserted from the front, peasants seized land in the countryside, and workers pledged loyalty to the soviets, Provisional Government officials became disillusioned with the masses for refusing to conform to liberal ideals of patriotism and civic consciousness. Increasingly the Provisional Government resorted to coercive means of governance—for example, the use of military force to requisition grain—that anticipated later Soviet practices.[17]

When the Bolsheviks took power in October, they adopted many wartime practices. Soviet state building, then, followed the trends already generated during the First World War, including state economic control, oversight of the population's health and welfare, surveillance, and the use of state violence against "alien elements." The Soviet system was founded not only in the absence of traditional institutional constraints (parliaments, courts, and property rights) but also against the backdrop of a bloody civil war, in which total mobilization of people and resources continued. Even after the Bolsheviks (renamed Communists in 1918) defeated the White armies, their grasp on power remained somewhat tenuous as they battled peasant uprisings, sought to establish control over the periphery of the country, and faced "capitalist encirclement" from hostile foreign nations. Although Lenin pushed through an economic liberalization in 1921, he and other Party leaders took no steps toward political relaxation. On the contrary, they maintained vigilance and perpetuated Communist Party dominance over a highly centralized state apparatus. State agencies such as the Commissariat of Health, the Commissariat of Welfare, and the security police continued, as did wartime surveillance and concentration camps, now permanent features of the Soviet state. Whereas the First World War's other combatant countries stepped back from total war practices at the conclusion of the war, the Soviet government institutionalized these practices as building blocks of the new state system.

Building Socialism

Once in power, the Communists enshrined Marxism-Leninism as their government's official ideology and set about constructing socialism. But never before in history had there been a socialist state, and Marxism-Leninism provided no blueprint for how to create one. Communist Party members shared the goals of eliminating capitalism and industrializing the country, but they debated how to proceed and at what tempo. Their tasks were all the more daunting given the country's overwhelmingly peasant population

---

17. Peter Holquist, *Making War, Forging Revolution: Russia's Continuum of Crisis, 1914–1921* (Cambridge, Mass., 2002), 109–11.

and underdeveloped economic infrastructure. Various Party factions put forward programs for creating and administering the new socialist society. The so-called Workers' Opposition argued for workers' participatory democracy with elected representatives in charge of the economy. A faction led by Lev Trotsky advocated revolutionary progress based on hierarchy, discipline, and the militarization of labor. Lenin rejected both of these models in favor of a gradualist approach—technocratic governance combined with the limited capitalism of the New Economic Policy (NEP).[18]

With their common goals of modernizing and rationalizing Russian society, some Party leaders and many non-Party specialists favored technocracy. A strong state bureaucracy, backed by the expertise of engineers and agronomists, could direct a technocratic transformation of the country and establish a productive economic and social order. But many Communists detested the gradualism and limited capitalism of the New Economic Policy and advocated a revolutionary advance toward socialism. Moreover, Stalin and others deeply distrusted "bourgeois specialists" and wished instead to empower the working class. Opposed to the ideal of technocracy was a strong promethean strain within the Communist Party—a belief that unleashing workers' creative energies would propel the country forward. Freed from the shackles of capitalist exploitation, workers were no longer limited by technical considerations and could break the bounds of time itself.[19]

In a shift at the end of the 1920s that he called the "Great Break," Stalin rejected NEP gradualism and technocracy in favor of a revolutionary leap forward. He and his fellow leaders outlawed free trade, implemented a planned economy geared for rapid industrialization, and embarked on a brutal collectivization campaign that included the deportation or dispossession of several million peasants labeled kulaks. The Great Break also entailed widespread anti-intellectualism, as Marxist radicals persecuted non-Party specialists, and social science thought was made to conform more rigidly to the Party line. Simultaneously, show trials of engineers and economists crushed the pretensions of some non-Party specialists who hoped to achieve a greater role in policy formation. These measures made clear that the Communist Party would remain preeminent, and that

18. On Lenin's attempts to reconcile populism and technicism, and his ultimate adoption of a technicist approach, see David Priestland, *Stalinism and the Politics of Mobilization: Ideas, Power, and Terror in Inter-war Russia* (New York, 2007), 63, 88–89.

19. According to a 1930s Soviet slogan, workers could "Fulfill the Five-Year Plan in Four Years." On the Party leaders' understanding of time and the revolutionary transcendence of it, see Stephen Hanson, *Time and Revolution: Marxism and the Design of Soviet Institutions* (Chapel Hill, 1997).

revolutionary progress would not be impeded by technocratic constraints.[20] The Soviet system under Stalin, then, was not a technocracy. Stalin and his fellow leaders asserted the primacy of Party truth over scientific truth, and they prioritized the training of a new technical elite of proletarian origin to replace "bourgeois specialists."[21]

At the same time, Stalinist industrialization remained heavily dependent on non-Party economists and engineers.[22] More generally Party officials received support from liberal professionals who welcomed the opportunity to apply their specialized knowledge on a large scale through a centralized state network. Communist officials and non-Party specialists shared a belief in the rational management of the population, a reliance on statistics to represent society, and a highly medicalized language to depict social problems and interventionist solutions. While social scientists had to make their disciplines conform to Marxism-Leninism, their concepts, knowledge, and data informed and enabled the transformational aspirations of Party leaders.[23] Many statisticians proved eager to participate in a rational reordering of society and provided the social and economic data on which Party leaders based their policies.[24] Sociologists and criminologists offered an analytical framework that concretized the threat of social contagion and prescribed the coercive removal and reform of deviant constituencies.[25] With the Great Break, Party officials subordinated the efforts

20. Kendall E. Bailes, "The Politics of Technology," *American Historical Review* 79: 2 (April 1974): 448–54.

21. Sheila Fitzpatrick, "Stalin and the Making of a New Elite," *The Cultural Front: Power and Culture in Revolutionary Russia* (Ithaca, 1992). The tension between science and Party orthodoxy, however, reemerged in the 1940s and 1950s, particularly after Stalin's death; Yuri Slezkine, *The Jewish Century* (Princeton, 2004), 306, 331. See also Ethan Pollock, *Stalin and the Soviet Science Wars* (Princeton, 2006).

22. In 1931, the chaos of the First Five-Year Plan impelled Stalin to reestablish the authority of engineers and adopt a more technocratic approach; I. V. Stalin, *Sochineniia* (Moscow, 1946–1952), 13: 56–61.

23. On the Soviet Union as "a new type of scientific state," see Francine Hirsch, *Empire of Nations: Ethnographic Knowledge and the Making of the Soviet System* (Ithaca, 2005), 312–13. Hirsch concludes that the Communist Party looked to ethnographers, anthropologists, and sociologists for scientific precepts to shape social development, but that it also forced these experts "to recast their own fields to reflect the Marxist-Leninist understanding of the world."

24. Despite the arrest of several Gosplan specialists in 1929, leading statisticians such as Stanislav G. Strumilin continued to play a vital role in economic planning, and subsequent directors of the Central Statistical Administration adhered to their vision of social statistics as an objective enterprise. See Alain Blum and Martine Mespoulet, *L'anarchie bureaucratique: Pouvoir et statistique sous Staline* (Paris, 2003), 111–16.

25. Beer, *Renovating Russia*, 202–3.

of sexologists and antialcohol specialists to the goal of building socialism, but they incorporated their aims of sexual control and temperance into this larger project.[26] Building socialism was not only indebted to specialists, in many respects it realized their dreams of refashioning the social order, albeit in an extremely brutal manner.

To pursue this agenda of social transformation, Party leaders employed wartime practices already institutionalized within the Soviet system. They thus used state economic controls, public health measures, surveillance, and excisionary violence to shape their vision of a productive, healthy society minus the "harmful elements" of the old order. Indeed transformational ambitions and interventionist practices were mutually reinforcing. Social redesign was premised on a conception of human society as malleable and on technologies of social intervention to effect such a transformation, while the attempt to create a new society in itself legitimated interventionist practices.

When Party leaders launched their "socialist offensive" at the end of the 1920s, not only did they rely on wartime practices, they conceived of industrialization and collectivization as a military campaign, a momentous battle to eliminate capitalism and peasant backwardness. This battle included the establishment of a completely state-run economy, similar to a wartime economy, where the Soviet government controlled all resources and directed them into heavy industry. Collectivization "brigades" deported "class enemies" and forced other peasants to join collective farms. On the industrialization "front," Soviet officials exhorted workers to construct steel mills, automobile factories, and armament plants in record time. Responding to a severe famine in 1932–33, Party leaders introduced further measures of social control, including an internal passport system, coupled with a moderated pace of industrialization.[27]

By 1934 Party leaders believed that they had won the battle, and at the Seventeenth Party Congress—"the Congress of Victors"—Stalin declared that socialism had been built.[28] For Stalin and other Party leaders, the

26. Frances L. Bernstein, *The Dictatorship of Sex: Lifestyle Advice for the Soviet Masses* (DeKalb, 2007), 190–92; Kate Transchel, *Under the Influence: Working-Class Drinking, Temperance, and Cultural Revolution in Russia, 1895–1932* (Pittsburgh, 2006), chapter 6. On continuities in the cultural realm, see Michael David-Fox, "What Is Cultural Revolution?" *Russian Review* 58: 2 (April 1999): 181–201.

27. For further discussion, see R. W. Davies, *Crisis and Progress in the Soviet Economy, 1931–1933* (London, 1996).

28. I. V. Stalin, "Otchetnyi doklad XVII s"ezdu partii o rabote TsK VKP(b)," *Sochineniia* 13 vols. (Moscow, 1946–52), 13: 308–9.

elimination of capitalism amounted to nothing less than a new epoch in world history. With the triumph of collectivized agriculture and a state-run economy, they believed that they had crossed the Rubicon and entered the land of socialism. The fact that they had weathered the 1932–33 crisis only added to their sense that they had passed through a period of intense struggle and emerged victorious on the other side. Elsewhere I have argued that the purported attainment of socialism had enormous implications for Soviet ideology and culture.[29] It also had ramifications for Party leaders' social policies, contributing to a further escalation of excisionary violence to eliminate "once and for all" the "anti-Soviet elements" who continued to oppose the Soviet state.

With rising international tensions in the late 1930s, and particularly the seeming inevitability of a decisive struggle between fascism and socialism, the search for enemies within the Soviet Union became even more intense.[30] Not only criminals and former kulaks but members of diaspora nationalities became targeted by the Soviet security police as the Stalinist leadership sought to neutralize potential fifth columnists in the event of war. The late 1930s were also characterized by an increasing militarization of Soviet society that influenced social programs, for example, in the realm of physical culture where paramilitary skills were increasingly emphasized. The "building of socialism" occurred at a specific historical conjuncture, an era of industrial mobilization and mass warfare, and its character reflected not only the institutionalization of wartime practices but the mounting foreign threat and Soviet preparation for war.

Overview of Chapters

This book contains five chapters. In the first chapter I trace the rise of social welfare policies, first in Western Europe and then in Russia. I pay particular attention to the new forms of social science knowledge that led reformers to reconceptualize the population as a social entity to be rationally managed. I also discuss the connection between welfare and warfare, and how the rise of mass warfare impelled state officials to intervene more

29. David L. Hoffmann, *Stalinist Values: The Cultural Norms of Soviet Modernity, 1917–1941* (Ithaca, 2003).

30. Amir Weiner, "Nature, Nurture, and Memory in a Socialist Utopia: Delineating the Soviet Socio-Ethnic Body in the Age of Socialism," *American Historical Review* 104: 4 (October 1999): 1114–55.

actively in the newly constituted social realm. In particular the tremendous mobilizational demands of the First World War overrode any attempts to limit the role of the state, and the need for a physically fit population to prosecute the war increased authorities' concern for the well-being of their populations. The Soviet government was established at this moment of amplified state intervention, and its leaders claimed to rule in the name of the lower classes. Accordingly, Soviet officials expanded the scope of state welfare, building on trends begun during the First World War and culminating in the 1930s when virtually all economic and social functions were assumed by the state.

In chapter 2, I examine public health programs. In part as a result of the rise of epidemiology, doctors around the world in the late nineteenth century reconceived health as a social rather than individual problem, and they sought to centralize health care and regulate people's behavior and hygiene. During and immediately after the First World War, countries throughout Europe created ministries of health that vastly expanded the state role in public health and hygiene. From this perspective, the Soviet public health system—a highly centralized system that treated disease as a social rather than an individual phenomenon—was not so much the product of socialist ideology as the culmination of ideas and techniques of social medicine, techniques whose implementation was made more urgent by the First World War and Civil War. In its early years, the Soviet government faced an enormous public health crisis, as epidemics ravaged the country. With no restraints on state power, the Commissariat of Health institutionalized a set of highly interventionist practices to monitor and advance the health of the population.

In chapter 3, I discuss state attempts to control reproduction. In the 1930s, the Soviet government outlawed abortion and offered financial rewards to women with seven or more children. Sometimes seen as communist social engineering, these policies were common to many countries in the interwar period. Soviet pronatalist policies, then, might be better understood as a new form of population politics, based on demographic studies and the ambitions of political leaders to manage their populations. At the same time, I highlight the distinctive features of Soviet reproductive policies. In other countries, the emphasis on women's maternal role meant their exclusion from the workforce. The Soviet construction of gender was quite different in that it emphasized women's roles as both mothers and workers.

In chapter 4, I consider another dimension of increased government intervention—surveillance and propaganda. The Soviet state had an immense apparatus for monitoring and swaying the "political moods" of the population.

The particular techniques of surveillance, such as perlustration of letters, were practiced by governments throughout Europe during the First World War. Similarly the leaders of all combatant countries engaged in extensive propaganda campaigns to secure the loyalty and fighting will of their citizens. The Soviet government continued and expanded surveillance and propaganda efforts and made these practices permanent features of governance. In fact, it used these tools not only to monitor political opposition but to try to transform people's consciousness and create the New Soviet Person.

In chapter 5, I analyze excisionary violence—attempts by state actors to remove segments of the population deemed harmful to the whole. European colonialism was an arena where state officials deployed systems of categorization and technologies of excisionary violence, including concentration camps. The physical removal of groups from the population began to be practiced within Europe itself during the First World War. The British government, for example, ordered the internment of "enemy aliens," while the Austro-Hungarian government interned certain national minorities within its empire. The tsarist government interned roughly 600,000 "enemy aliens" and deported up to 1 million citizens (ethnic Poles, Germans, Jews, and Muslims) from border regions in 1915. During the Russian Civil War, both sides relied on concentration camps to remove "hostile" groups from the population, and the Soviet government continued these practices throughout the 1920s and 1930s, particularly during collectivization and the Great Purges. Excisionary violence and concentration camps, then, were not the invention of Soviet leaders. However, they did employ state violence in distinctive ways. In other countries, governments carried out internments as limited wartime security measures, whereas the Soviet government used excisionary violence to restructure society during peacetime. Despite similarities in technologies of state violence, the scale and objectives of Soviet violence were far more extreme.

Social scientific knowledge, aspirations to reshape society, and wartime technologies of social intervention were all necessary preconditions for Soviet state violence. The actualization of excisionary violence resulted from the form of the Soviet state and the decisions of Party leaders. The Soviet state was a dictatorship, one with a highly centralized bureaucratic apparatus that had institutionalized many wartime practices. Party leaders, with their utopian ambitions and claims to history making, acknowledged no limits on their authority and operated with no constitutional or legal constraints. When they wielded the unchecked power of the Soviet state to pursue their designs, the consequence was state intervention on an unprecedented scale.

1 Social Welfare

> The science of policing consists, therefore, in regulating everything
> that relates to the present condition of society, in strengthening and
> improving it, in seeing that all things contribute to the welfare of the
> members that compose it.
> —JOHANN VON JUSTI, *General Elements of Policing*, 1768

> Social security for all workers who suffer the loss of labor capacity
> or unemployment must be a matter of the state.
> —ALEKSANDR VINOKUROV, *Social Security (from Capitalism to
> Communism)*, 1921

Social welfare in its most basic sense refers to provision for the well-being of society's members, particularly those in need such as the sick, the elderly, and the unemployed. Among the programs commonly associated with welfare are poor relief, disability and unemployment aid, and old age pensions. Welfare, however, can also refer to a broader range of social intervention and regulation designed to improve urban living conditions, order social practices, and inculcate productive behavioral norms—all to ensure the rational conduct of everyday life and the purposeful deployment of human resources. Welfare in this broader sense goes beyond financial assistance to include social work, slum renovation, urban planning, public health, factory inspections, and efforts to school the lower classes in norms of efficiency and hygiene.

Traditional explanations for the rise of the welfare state present it as a by-product of industrialization and urbanization, particularly as the result of labor organizers' and radicals' demands that allegedly compelled state leaders to provide for people in need. Research on state welfare programs, however, has undermined these interpretations. Industrialization in the United States sparked no national welfare initiatives; the first extensive welfare program was created much later with the 1935 Social Security Act.[1] Moreover, European welfare programs were proposed and implemented not

---

1. Theda Skocpol, *Protecting Soldiers and Mothers: The Political Origins of Social Policy in the United States* (Cambridge, MA., 1992), 5–13. Skocpol points out that the

by radicals but by liberal or conservative politicians and bureaucrats. Working-class organizations did not push for, and in some cases even opposed, welfare proposals as they agitated instead for higher wages.[2] Although a desire to preempt unrest or to win working-class votes did motivate some politicians in the second half of the nineteenth century, state responsibility for social welfare resulted from a more general reconceptualization whereby officials and nonstate professionals came to see the conservation of the social whole as dependent on the welfare of its members. Also important was a concern of state officials with maintaining the economic and military capacity of their populations. The term *welfare state* was first used by Sir William Beveridge in the 1940s as an explicit contrast to the Nazi "warfare state." But already in the late nineteenth century, the state role in welfare had expanded dramatically. And particularly during the interwar period, welfare and warfare were intimately connected, as government leaders implemented welfare programs to ensure the war-readiness of their populations.[3]

The Russian case provides a striking example of the catalytic impact of the First World War on the development of state welfare programs. Russia had lagged behind most countries of Western Europe in state responsibility for social welfare. But with the First World War the Russian state greatly expanded its role in providing for the population's well-being, first through parastatal organizations and later via state institutions. Following the October Revolution, Soviet leaders inherited many of the programs of the wartime tsarist and provisional governments. They soon expanded these programs and decreed a comprehensive system of pensions, disability benefits, and unemployment relief. Initially Soviet welfare benefits existed mostly on paper, but with the establishment of the Stalinist planned economy in the 1930s, the Soviet state not only commandeered all available resources but took on responsibility for virtually all workers' needs, including food supply, housing, and full employment. Soviet social provision, then, emerged not as an attempt to ameliorate the negative effects of capitalism, but rather as part of Party leaders' attempt to construct a modern, industrial, noncapitalist economy. More than a social safety net, Soviet welfare was to be part of a rational and productive economic order,

---

only prior national government welfare benefits in the United States were pensions for Civil War veterans.

2. Ibid., 23–24; James E. Cronin, *The Politics of State Expansion: War, State, and Society in Twentieth-Century Britain* (New York, 1991), 37, 42–43. See also Peter Baldwin, *The Politics of Social Solidarity: Class Bases of the European Welfare State, 1875–1975* (New York, 1990).

3 Mark Mazower, *Dark Continent: Europe's Twentieth Century* (New York, 1999), 103, 298–99.

one directed by the state allegedly in the interests of the laboring classes. The Soviet system, with its requirement that everyone perform "socially useful labor," is also an example of how welfare in interwar Europe was expanded as a set of reciprocal obligations between the state and its citizens, rather than as a means to protect the dignity of individuals.

Before turning to welfare in Russia and the Soviet Union, I will trace the origins of social welfare concerns and policies more generally, beginning with some features of cameralist thought in early modern Europe and proceeding to developments in social science in the nineteenth century. The social sciences helped to delineate a social realm, distinct from political and economic spheres, and offered a means to study and act on a range of seemingly interconnected problems, such as indigence, degeneracy, crime, and working-class unrest. The delineation of the social realm and the emergence of "the social question" in nineteenth-century Western Europe were essential precursors to social welfare programs, as well as to various forms of social intervention to be discussed throughout this book.

Cameralism, Social Science, and the Origins of Welfare

Political leaders had always ruled over people, but they had not always conceived of themselves as ruling over a population. Only at a particular moment in history did leaders become overwhelmingly concerned with their populations as a resource to be cultivated. The roots of the welfare state lay in the early modern period, when state officials began to scrutinize the population and its productive capacity. In particular, cameralist thinkers in the sixteenth and seventeenth centuries studied the relationship between the state's economic and military power and the size and productivity of its population. Unlike earlier thinkers who had focused on territory as the fundamental object of governance, cameralists concentrated on the population and material goods. This reorientation implied aims that went beyond control of territory to include maximizing wealth and ensuring the population's ability to produce goods and multiply in number. Such ideas also implied a need for knowledge of people and resources, and an administrative apparatus to produce this knowledge and elevate economic production. Throughout the seventeenth century, cameralist thinkers promoted these new goals of government and further analyzed the possibilities for state efforts to raise the productive capacity of the population.[4]

4. Michel Foucault, "Governmentality," *The Foucault Effect: Studies in Governmentality,* ed. Graham Burchell, Colin Gordon, and Peter Miller (Chicago, 1991), 93–96.

State concern with infant mortality illustrates rulers' new understanding of the population as a resource. By the mid-eighteenth century, social thinkers had generated an extensive literature on infant mortality and its costs to the state. One commentator, describing high mortality rates in foundling homes, decried the fact that such a high percentage of human "forces" had died before having been "made useful to the state."[5] Eighteenth-century Russian rulers expressed similar concerns about "human capital" and acted to expand the population through improved infant care. In 1712, Peter the Great issued a decree that deplored infanticide and that ordered construction of foundling homes for illegitimate children in every province. Under Catherine the Great, Russian foundling homes attempted to train abandoned children to be productive subjects.[6]

Cameralist thought convinced many European rulers that their political and military power depended not only on their ability to collect taxes, but on the overall economic prosperity of the population they ruled. This realization underlay efforts to police societies, enhance their productive capacities, and systematize governmental administration in a way that would encourage economic development.[7] The desire to maximize productive capacity also prompted political thinkers to focus on the human body and utilization of its productive and reproductive capacities. What has been termed "an anatomo-politics of the human body" began in the seventeenth century with efforts to discipline and extract labor from workers by integrating them into systems of efficient economic controls.[8] Eighteenth-century physiocratic thinkers further elaborated these views and described the state not only as the beneficiary of wealth, but as an instrument to increase wealth by governing social relations in a way to intensify production. An expanded notion of policing was articulated, for example, by the German economic thinker Johann von Justi, who wrote, "The aim of policing is to make everything that composes the state serve to strengthen and increase its power, and to likewise serve the public welfare."[9]

5. As cited in Jacques Donzelot, *L'invention du social: Essai sur le déclin des passions politiques* (Paris, 1984), 9.

6. David L. Ransel, *Village Mothers: Three Generations of Change in Russia and Tataria* (Bloomington, 2000), 8–17, 31.

7. On the cameralist handbooks and law codes of seventeenth-century German states and eighteenth-century Russia, see Marc Raeff, *The Well-Ordered Police State: Social and Institutional Change through Law in the Germanies and Russia, 1600–1800* (New Haven, 1983).

8. Michel Foucault, *History of Sexuality* (New York, 1980), 139–40.

9. Donzelot, *L'invention du social,* 7. See also Ursula Backhaus, "Johann Heinrich Gottlob von Justi (1717–1771): Health as Part of a State's Capital Endowment," *The*

Eventually the narrow fiscal interests of cameralist thinkers were super-seded by broader objectives of improving society for its own sake. Politi-cally, this emphasis on social amelioration stemmed from new principles of sovereignty introduced by the American and French revolutions. The French Revolution deposed the king and took from him the ancient notion of sovereignty and linked it with popular will. In the name of popular sov-ereignty, social resources were levied and deployed on an unprecedented scale.[10] Not only did this democratization of sovereignty greatly amplify state power, it also meant that the state, no longer an instrument of the monarch, now was to serve the people and provide for their betterment. While monarchical regimes throughout the nineteenth century contested this new political order, the principle of popular sovereignty nonetheless posed a challenge that traditional regimes had to address. As countries moved fitfully toward this new benchmark, no longer was the popula-tion seen as merely a resource to state ends. Instead political thinkers in-creasingly saw the state and its citizens as having mutual obligations to serve one another. The cameralist police state—society at the service of the state—was gradually replaced by the welfare state—the state at the service of society.

Economic and social changes also contributed to the widening realm of social concern. Industrialization and urbanization presented a host of new social problems, highly visible given their concentration in burgeon-ing cities. A range of nongovernment actors, from religious evangelists and temperance workers to urban planners and labor organizers, while motivated by different philosophies, became concerned with common is-sues of housing, hygiene, industrial accidents, alcoholism, unemployment, and poverty. Given the importance of corporeal labor to the industrial economy, the bodily health of workers was also of interest to merchants and industrialists. And despite liberals' attempts, particularly in Britain, to limit state regulation, government officials saw a need to ameliorate social conditions and safeguard their populations. Indeed, to the extent that the urban poor were seen as a source of crime, degeneracy, and disease that could infect all society, social provision seemed a national necessity.[11]

Beginnings of Political Economy: Johann Heinrich Gottlob von Justi, ed. Jürgen Georg Backhaus (Heidelberg, 2009), 171–95.

10. Keith Michael Baker, "A Foucauldian French Revolution?" *Foucault and the Writ-ing of History*, ed. Jan Goldstein (Cambridge, Mass., 1994), 204–5.

11. My focus here is on the broader conceptual shifts behind the rise of state welfare programs. For an analysis that examines both theoretical issues surrounding welfare and the details of welfare initiatives down to the municipal level in Germany, see George

This newly emerging prophylactic ethos applied to political unrest as well. If popular sovereignty extended solicitous concern to all citizens, it simultaneously extended the realm of potential threats. After 1848, state leaders became concerned not just with outright rebels but with the working class as a source of opposition or even revolution. While labor in the abstract was productive and noble, those actually engaged in it were increasingly viewed as a menace. Moreover, socialist ideology posed a challenge to the established order and cast labor as the new foundation of political legitimacy. Eventually this challenge would contribute in Britain to "gas and water socialism"—housing acts, old-age pensions, and other reforms—and in Germany to old age, sickness, and unemployment insurance, championed by Bismarck to wean workers away from the growing Social Democratic Party.[12] But even prior to these state welfare initiatives, the threat of labor unrest brought "the social question" to the fore.[13]

To address these concerns, state officials now sought to study and categorize their subjects, in the belief that knowing "the population" would make it possible to improve their conditions, diminish their restlessness, and strengthen their character. The result of these efforts was the delineation of a social realm distinct from political and economic spheres. By the mid-nineteenth century, social thinkers not only conceived of the population as a discrete entity, they came to view the social realm as an arena for intervention. As Mary Poovey writes, "These two developments—the aggregation of distinct populations and the conceptual disaggregation of the social domain—were intimately connected, for identifying the problems that afflicted the nation involved isolating the offending populations, abstracting from individual cases the general problems they shared and devising solutions."[14]

Social science provided the means to know the population, so the development of social science disciplines was central to concern for social welfare. The idea of a science of society originated with Enlightenment thinkers' belief that science be used to reorder the human world and guide

---

Steinmetz, *Regulating the Social: The Welfare State and Local Politics in Imperial Germany* (Princeton, 1993).

12. Michael Sullivan, *The Development of the British Welfare State* (New York, 1996), 4–8; Steinmetz, *Regulating the Social,* chapter 5.

13. Donzelot, *L'invention du social,* 14.

14. Mary Poovey, *Making a Social Body: British Cultural Formation, 1830–1864* (Chicago, 1995), 4, 8.

the construction of a rational social order.[15] But it was only in the nineteenth century that the concern with "society" and new disciplines for making it legible combined to produce the social realm. The social realm emerged when a variety of problems were grouped together and acted on by a body of governmental officials and qualified personnel in fields of medicine, social work, demography, urban planning, and social hygiene.[16] Social science itself encompassed two significant components: a model of science deemed applicable to human affairs; and the definition of the social field, which provided a specific view of society and the nature of social processes to which the scientific model could be applied.[17] Societies were increasingly conceived as entities that could be mapped statistically, reordered and cultivated, and administered scientifically by experts who stood above the rights of individuals or the interests of specific social groups.

The impact of social science on social welfare policies is perhaps best illustrated by the enormous influence of social statistics, a type of knowledge that reflected and in turn reinforced reformers' desire to act on the social realm. Already in the seventeenth century cameralists had speculated on the need for a quantitative understanding of the population.[18] By the first half of the nineteenth century, statistical research had become professionalized, and governments had begun to regularize the collection of population data.[19] Once people and social phenomena had been classified and enumerated, government officials and professionals came to conceptualize social issues in a new way. Whereas poverty had previously been viewed as the failings of isolated individuals, the compilation of statistics presented poverty as a social problem that called out for state action to make the impoverished into productive citizens. Industrial accidents, which previously were considered random phenomena that resulted from individual

15. For Condorcet, the power of Newtonian science to explain the natural world demonstrated the potential of social science to understand and reshape the human world. See Keith Michael Baker, *Condorcet: From Natural Philosophy to Social Mathematics* (Chicago, 1975).

16. David G. Horn, *Social Bodies: Science, Reproduction, and Italian Modernity* (Princeton, 1994), 3–11.

17. Baker, *Condorcet*, x.

18. In the 1680s Gottfreid Leibniz in Prussia and William Petty in Britain advocated the creation of central government statistical offices to gather data on the population; Ian Hacking, *The Taming of Chance* (Cambridge, 1990), 18–19.

19. Ibid., 2–3. In the Napoleonic era, government administrators developed departmental statistics, whose explicit purpose was to present a homogeneous vision of the national territory and its people; Marie-Noëlle Bourguet, *Déchiffrer la France: La statistique départementale à l'époque napoléonienne* (Paris, 1988).

error, also came to be seen as regular and predictable events once statistics had been compiled. Governments began to increase factory regulation and require employers to obtain insurance to cover accidents.[20]

As a new form of knowledge, social science data were not always immediately comprehensible. Clearly statistics revealed a great deal about society, but it was only through the invention and application of statistical techniques that their meaning was revealed. The techniques developed by statisticians determined the ways in which disciplinary specialists used data to understand social phenomena. One technique was that of correlation—finding the characteristics that occurred in conjunction with phenomena, and perhaps caused them to happen. The 1832 cholera epidemic in France proved to be something of a watershed both in terms of statistical analysis and of social understandings of disease. Statistics on cholera deaths showed a clear correlation between poor housing conditions and high mortality. Even before advances in epidemiology provided a clearer understanding of the disease, statistical correlations led government officials to see unclean housing as a cause of cholera and to take action to regulate sanitation.[21]

Another statistical technique to make sense of the new mass of numbers was determining the mean. In the 1830s and 1840s, Adolphe Quetelet developed the concept of the average man, based on his discovery that population statistics had a regular distribution around the mean. This step took something abstract—there was no real-life "average man"—and made it seem real, a postulated reality against which people would be measured.[22] Those who fell below this norm were then labeled substandard or even deviant (a deviation from the norm). The establishment of norms for people's physical development also set a mark for improvement. The founder of eugenics, Francis Galton, classified people in quartiles around a statistical median, and advocated interference in reproduction to make statistical gains in the qualities of a race or population.[23] Quetelet's concept of the

20. Horn, *Social Bodies*, 35–37.

21. Paul Rabinow, *French Modern: Norms and Forms of the Social Environment* (Cambridge, Mass., 1989), 31–39. See also François Delaporte, *Disease and Civilization: The Cholera in Paris, 1832,* trans. Arthur Goldhammer (Cambridge, Mass., 1986).

22. Hacking, *The Taming of Chance,* 107–9. On Quetelet's reception in Russia (translations of his works appeared in Russian in 1865–66), see Irina Paperno, *Suicide as a Cultural Institution in Dostoevsky's Russia* (Ithaca, 1997), 66–67.

23. Hacking, *Taming of Chance,* 168–69; Rabinow, *French Modern,* 327. At the end of the nineteenth century, Émile Durkheim took the model of the physiological mean and applied it to ethics and behavior; Hacking, *Taming of Chance,* 172.

average man also replaced the enormous diversity of individuals with a set of social laws and regularities. This displacement of the liberal political subject in turn shifted the focus toward the collective and its overall well-being.[24]

Statistical thinking, then, had important implications both for understandings of social welfare and for the ambitions of social scientists and policymakers to improve it. The impulse for statistical studies and social intervention was of course utilitarian, and in some cases philanthropic. People such as Quetelet wanted to improve the conditions of the working masses, and they tried to do so by discovering the statistical laws that governed disease, crime, and indigence in order to alter the conditions under which the laws applied.[25] As a result there were real improvements to social welfare, such as slum renovation and poor relief. But such work also increased government interference in people's lives, and led to greater enforcement of behavioral norms.

Social statistics and social science more generally contributed to the ideal of technocracy—the scientific management of society. The appeal of technocracy derived in part from the idea that it was objective and could therefore present solutions that would be above debate. In reality, social science could be highly subjective, because social statistics were generated only for categories assumed to be significant (such as ethnicity and income level), and were correlated only according to preconceptions about causality (such as the link between alcoholism and crime). Moreover, social science disciplines were often employed in a highly normative way that set standards of behavior against which people were then judged. But far from recognizing the limitations and biases of their analysis, most social scientists believed in the power of their tools to understand and solve social problems as never before.

To many political leaders, technocracy also suggested an appealing alternative to the complexities of coalition politics and democratic reform.[26] Particularly given the sharp class antagonisms of the nineteenth century, a technocratic approach to social problems offered a welcome alternative to partisan politics as well as a means to serve the good of the whole.

24. François Ewald, *L'État providence* (Paris, 1986), 146; Bruce Curtis, "Surveying the Social: Techniques, Practices, Power," *Histoire sociale/Social History* 35 (2002): 95–97. See also Theodore M. Porter, *The Rise of Statistical Thinking, 1820–1900* (Princeton, 1988).

25. Hacking, *Taming of Chance*, 118.

26. See Charles Maier, "Between Taylorism and Technocracy: European Ideologies and the Vision of Industrial Productivity in the 1920s," *Journal of Contemporary History* 5:2 (1970): 27–61.

Throughout much of the nineteenth-century, liberalism had been able to criticize power from outside. But, as liberalism and bourgeois societies became increasingly established, many of the intransigent problems they were supposed to resolve stubbornly remained. As one historian of Germany writes, "The mingled hostility and anxiety towards organized labor and criminality (which were often conflated), as towards servants and prostitutes (also often conflated) was the product of a bourgeois disenchantment with its own success. The degree and speed of this success only increased the degree of disenchantment, for it sharpened the sense of what stood to be lost."[27] Traditional liberal approaches and philanthropic efforts to aid individuals no longer seemed adequate to address social problems. Science and technocracy offered an alternative model. Developments such as the rise of statistics and modern medicine made the scientific study and management of society seem possible for the first time. Some social thinkers believed that all human activity could be reorganized on a rational, scientific basis.[28]

In France, for instance, government officials and social thinkers gravitated toward technocracy and increasingly privileged the social whole over the individual. Reform groups from Social Catholics to nonrevolutionary socialists sought to regulate space and eliminate social problems using scientifically derived norms. These activists argued that society, not the individual, should be the focus of their efforts, and they increasingly turned to the state, rather than the church or industry, as the regulator of social relations. By 1900 the doctrine of solidarism—the idea that the social whole was greater than its individual parts—emerged from this intellectual ferment. Proponents of solidarism argued that the interdependence of all people meant that they should cooperate based on scientific norms regarding the division of labor and the exchange of services. For the French sociologist Frédéric Le Play, "the task of social science...involved not only investigating how society with all its conflicts and antagonisms was constituted, but also—and more importantly—fashioning the social machinery to return society to its natural state of class harmony."[29] New forms of solidarity and technocratic oversight were to mitigate class antagonisms

27. David Blackbourne, "The Discreet Charm of the Bourgeoisie," *The Peculiarities of German History*, ed. Blackbourne and Geoff Eley (New York, 1984), 216.

28. Elisabeth Domansky, "Militarization and Reproduction," *Society, Culture and the State in Germany, 1870–1930*, ed. Geoff Eley (Ann Arbor, 1996), 430.

29. Sanford Elwitt, *The Third Republic Defended: Bourgeois Reform in France, 1880–1914* (Baton Rouge, 1986), 23. For further discussion, see Rabinow, *French Modern*, 169–70, 185–86.

and forestall revolution, and in this sense, solidarism represented a middle course between liberalism and Marxism.

In Britain, the Fabian Society (founded 1884) similarly emphasized collectivism and scientific management. Borrowing from positivist philosophical thought, Fabian leader Sidney Webb championed the role of a technocratic elite that could restore social harmony by representing the interests of the collective. In contrast to Marxists, Fabian socialists argued that the state should not be smashed but rather be used as an instrument of social change, relying on the expertise of government bureaucrats.[30] Fabian thinkers were particularly interested in welfare programs to combat poverty, because they viewed the poor as a wasted societal resource. British social thought more generally came to focus no longer on individual failings (as had been true under the workhouse system), but on scientific reform and welfare programs to protect the overall social organism.[31] A disparate coalition of public men and government officials took up the cause of so-called national efficiency. This efficiency group argued that "men and women formed the basic raw material out of which national greatness was constructed: hence, they argued, the statesman had a duty to see that these priceless resources were not squandered through indifference and slackness." Unlike humanitarian social reformers, moved by pity, or labor activists, demanding justice for their class, efficiency advocates took pride in their detached, scientific approach to social problems. In place of the messy politics of party and interest, they espoused the principle of administration as science, as practiced by knowledgeable experts.[32]

In Germany in the 1890s, scientific social work took an expansive, "transindividual" approach to various problems. Scientific social workers relied on the criteria of the natural sciences "to redefine and relocate whole sectors of the social question into the field of 'nature.'" Through this biologization of the social, these specialists claimed that the solution to social problems lay in the realm of experts. In contrast to traditional poor relief, scientific social work was bureaucratized and professionalized, in that it relied on established categories and procedures, and drew on the expertise of doctors and trained social workers. Moreover, it surveyed the entire population with an emphasis on prophylactic rather than reactive

30. Sullivan, *Development of the British Welfare State*, 13–15.

31. Bentley Gilbert, *The Evolution of National Insurance in Great Britain* (London, 1966), 13–14, 26, 98.

32. G. R. Searle, *The Quest for National Efficiency: A Study in British Politics and Political Thought, 1899–1914* (Berkeley, 1971), 60, 62, 82, 85.

treatment of social problems.[33] Social reformers at this time insisted that if Germany were to become a world power the German government must go beyond the existing poor law. Alongside scientific social work, state officials began to establish maternal and infant care centers, public health agencies, and housing inspectorates. These new welfare institutions sought to educate both poor and well-off families in scientific methods of child raising and home improvement.[34]

As described above, social science made recalcitrant social problems seem more comprehensible and perhaps solvable. Medical advances vastly expanded doctors' understanding of contagion and raised hopes that all major diseases could soon be eradicated. Innovations in education and psychology seemed to promise that ignorance and deviance could be eliminated. As Detlev Peukert argues, the new network of social science theories and methods, combined with new social welfare institutions and practices, led professionals "to claim to be able to provide comprehensive solutions to all 'social questions.'"[35] Peukert goes on to note that the dramatic advances in economic production, transportation, and communications of the late nineteenth and early twentieth centuries fed the technocratic utopianism of reformers and undercut traditional sources of meaning (such as religion) that might have challenged the authority of science.[36]

The ambitions of early twentieth-century officials and reformers to solve social problems led to an ever-broadening horizon for state intervention. Programs to improve social welfare extended far beyond old-age pensions and poor relief. Architects and city planners promoted government housing projects and urban renewal programs to improve the living environment. Educators sought to raise productive citizens, and criminologists endeavored to reform criminals. Psychologists and social workers tried to correct asocial behavior. And eugenicists sought to eradicate the genetic causes of abnormality. To effect and enforce social reform, government officials further

33. Steinmetz, *Regulating the Social*, 44, 198–202.

34. David Crew, "The Ambiguities of Modernity: Welfare and the German State from Wilhelm to Hitler," *Society, Culture, and the State in Germany, 1870–1930*, ed. Geoff Eley (Ann Arbor, 1996), 323.

35. Detlev Peukert, "The Genesis of the 'Final Solution' from the Spirit of Science," *Reevaluating the Third Reich*, ed. T. Childers and J. Caplan (New York, 1993), 238.

36. Peukert, "Genesis," 238; Detlev Peukert, *The Weimar Republic: The Crisis of Classical Modernity*, trans. Richard Deveson (London, 1991), 187. In his critique of Peukert, David Crew argues that he overemphasizes the utopianism of reformers and underplays the ruptures of the First World War, which created a desperate need for social reconstruction that underlay the radicalism of Weimar programs and the extreme interventionism of the Nazis. See Crew, "Ambiguities of Modernity," 325–26.

developed disciplinary mechanisms, from school timetables and hygiene in-struction to housing inspections and army training camps, all marked by hierarchical supervision and individual scrutiny to inculcate new behaviors. Welfare came to be understood as a broad effort to reform and educate the lower classes in the rational conduct of everyday life, not only to overcome social problems but to maximize the efficiency and harmony of society.[37]

The statization of welfare—the process by which state agencies displaced religious charities and philanthropic organizations as the purveyors of social provision—was neither uniform nor unilinear. The timing of government welfare programs varied considerably from one country to another and even, to the extent that municipal governments administered welfare, from one city to another. In many instances nongovernment professionals and social reformers rather than government officials took the lead in identifying and addressing social problems.[38] And even as state officials developed welfare programs in the late nineteenth and twentieth centuries, private charities ex-panded their fields of operation alongside government programs. Moreover, Jürgen Habermas has argued that with the rise of the welfare state, "state and society penetrate each other and bring forth a middle sphere of semi-public, semiprivate relationships ordered by social legislation."[39] While the general trend was toward identification of social problems and government action to ameliorate living conditions, the actualization of each country's welfare programs occurred within a particular social and political structure, and at a specific historical conjuncture. It is therefore necessary to describe the setting in which Russian and Soviet welfare programs took shape.

The Social Realm in Russia

The Russian Empire, throughout the nineteenth century, remained a much more agrarian, and a much less urban and literate society than the coun-tries it measured itself against: Britain, France, and increasingly toward the

37. Crew, "Ambiguities of Modernity," 323.

38. In Argentina, for example, welfare programs at the national level emerged only in the 1940s and were an outgrowth of much earlier welfare initiatives organized by philan-thropists, feminists, immigrant societies, and public health professionals; Donna J. Guy, *Women Build the Welfare State: Performing Charity and Creating Rights in Argentina, 1880–1955* (Durham, 2009), 4–5.

39. Jürgen Habermas, *The Structural Transformation of the Public Sphere: An Inquiry into a Category of Bourgeois Society,* trans. Thomas Burger (Cambridge, Mass., 1989), 231.

end of the nineteenth century, Germany. By all objective indices, Russia was less modern than these countries. Equally significantly, Russia's corps of public and official specialists themselves viewed Russia as lagging behind the rest of Europe. This relationship vis-à-vis "advanced" countries was crucial. First, it allowed for a well-developed current of thought among certain professionals and bureaucrats that Russia might avoid the pitfalls of those societies that had already experienced industrialization and urbanization. Their misgivings about modern society were less a carryover of traditional attitudes than a conscious repudiation of certain aspects of liberalism and industrial capitalism. Second, when Russia increasingly began to implement forms of specialist intervention, especially after 1905, it did so after its preferred models had themselves developed critiques of modern industrial society. Thus Russian professionals and reformers could harness these ideas as part of "an anticipatory critique of institutions not yet endowed with the authority of an established order."[40]

Although Russian elites defined their country in relation to Western Europe, their situation was therefore more analogous to the one faced by elites in other less-developed countries, where political and intellectual leaders also sought their own paths to modernity. Romanian intellectuals, for example, similarly believed that they could learn from Western Europe's problems and modernize their country in a way that would avoid negative social effects of industrialization.[41] In Japan, a new generation of bureaucrats became convinced that their state had to do more to manage and mobilize human resources, and in 1906, they organized the Japanese Home Ministry's Local Improvement Campaign that stressed hard work and economic growth.[42] The same year the Constitutional Revolution in Iran cleared the way for parliamentary leaders to undertake modernizing reforms. Iranian intellectuals, alarmed by the disorder of industrialization and urbanization, in turn pushed for a modern society based on education, order, and discipline. Lacking a broad base of social support, they looked

40. Laura Engelstein, "Combined Underdevelopment: Discipline and the Law in Imperial and Soviet Russia," *American Historical Review,* 98:2 (April 1993): 344.

41. Maria Bucur, *Eugenics and Modernization in Interwar Romania* (Pittsburgh, 2002), 64.

42. Sheldon Garon, *Molding Japanese Minds: The State in Everyday Life* (Princeton, 1997), 6–11, 352–54. After the First World War, the Japanese Ministry of Education conducted "daily life improvement campaigns," and was assisted by the nongovernmental League for Daily Life Improvement that dictated norms for diet, hygiene, work habits, and housing.

to the state to impose their vision of a modern, rational order.[43] Russia's professionals harbored a remarkably similar aspiration to overcome backwardness through scientific reform and state intervention. In the late imperial period, however, the tsarist government resisted reform efforts and restricted the influence of professionals and intellectuals.

The only institutions through which Russian professionals were allowed to address social concerns were the *zemstvos,* local self-governing bodies that employed a range of specialists, from physicians and teachers to engineers and agronomists.[44] Transposing broader European sociological paradigms, zemstvo professionals came to rely increasingly on statistics as a means to study social phenomena. Translations of Quetelet had appeared in Russia in 1865–66, and occasioned wide commentary in the contemporary press and professional journals.[45] By the late nineteenth century, zemstvo statisticians had compiled a large body of economic, agricultural, and demographic data. And in 1897, after several abortive attempts, the Russian Empire conducted its first modern universal census of the entire population (modern in the sense that its goal was demographic and not fiscal).

Statistical studies helped to define a newly perceived labor problem in Russia, discussions of which were often couched in terms of the labor situation in Britain and France. An early statistical study by N. S. Veselovskii, in 1848, demonstrated the horrendous living conditions of the capital's poor. His article advanced what was for Russian readers a novel explanation for workers' poverty—their predicament was the product of a specifically social situation, rather than the result of St. Petersburg's topographical or climatic conditions. While studies increasingly demonstrated the concentration of poverty and disease in certain sectors of the population, most tsarist officials continued to view such problems as police issues and prescribed a combination of repression and religious edification. By contrast, a group of doctors affiliated with the Archive of Legal Medicine

43. Cyrus Schayegh, "Sport, Health, and the Iranian Middle Class in the 1920s and 1930s," *Iranian Studies,* 35:4 (fall 2002): 342–43. Much like Russian liberal professionals under the Soviet regime, the Iranian intelligentsia disliked the autocratic character of Reza Shah's regime after his 1921 coup, but they enthusiastically contributed their technocratic expertise to his program of modernizing reforms. See Schayegh, " 'A Sound Mind Lives in a Healthy Body': Texts and Contexts in the Iranian Modernists' Scientific Discourse of Health, 1910s–1940s," *International Journal of Middle East Studies,* 37 (2005): 168.

44. See Terence Emmons and Wayne S. Vucinich, eds., *The Zemstvo in Russia: An Experiment in Local Self-Government* (New York, 1982).

45. Paperno, *Suicide as a Cultural Institution,* 67.

and Social Hygiene (founded in 1865) criticized this traditional approach. As Reginald Zelnik writes, "The doctors came to see social conditions as fundamental, and followed these observations to more radical conclusions," insisting that only an explicit social policy could lead to improvements in the population's health and welfare. By the 1870s, the tsarist police moved toward "support of the full application of state power to a formal program of labor-oriented social welfare, one that would extend beyond the emergency role of 'fireman' that the government had been playing for so many years."[46]

States' roles in social welfare, however, depended not only on new perceptions of social problems, but on the character of the states themselves. In Britain, where liberal ideology was most firmly established, the state's role remained limited prior to the First World War. By contrast, Imperial Germany inherited from Prussia what one scholar terms "a tradition of government activism and state-led modernization, which gave its state an unusual degree of self-confidence and public recognition."[47] The Russian autocracy, while it had led the reforms of the 1860s and 1870s, became an obstacle to social reform under the last two tsars, Alexander III and Nicholas II. The conservatism of these two autocrats thwarted the efforts of professionals and reform-minded bureaucrats alike.

The conservative character of the tsarist state in turn shaped the outlook of Russian professionals and their disciplines. Russian professionals came to resent a regime that refused to allow them to employ their expertise and skills. They viewed the autocracy as the principle obstacle to a more healthy and productive modern society. Many social reformers thus were antigovernment not so much because they wished to limit the role of the state, but because they felt that the existing government was not competently employing the state as an effective tool for social transformation. These professionals were less concerned with professional autonomy than with securing state sponsorship of their projects.[48]

Given their keen awareness of the country's relative backwardness, educated Russians believed they had a special role to overcome it. Yet above them they confronted a despotic autocrat, and below them they faced the benighted masses. Laura Engelstein has described how the Russian

---

46. Reginald E. Zelnik, *Labor and Society in Tsarist Russia: The Factory Workers of St. Petersburg, 1855–1870* (Stanford, 1971), 92, 381.

47. Steinmetz, *Regulating the Social*, 106.

48. John F. Hutchinson, *Politics and Public Health in Revolutionary Russia, 1890–1918* (Baltimore, 1990), xix–xx. See also Nancy M. Frieden, *Russian Physicians in an Era of Reform and Revolution, 1856–1905* (Princeton, 1981).

intelligentsia's political impotence and sense of social obligation fused into a powerful sense of mission: "At the top of the social scale, the educated few were largely excluded from political power and resented their own position as objects of an oppressive, custodial regime. Below them they confronted the mass of the common folk, no less politically disenfranchised, but also culturally and economically deprived. This popular mass aroused in its social superiors a feeling of apprehension mixed with a strong sense of moral obligation and collective guilt."[49] The particular position of Russian professionals helps explain their unusually strong commitment to reforming both the political and social order.

The fact that the Russian intelligentsia blamed the tsarist regime, and not peasants and workers themselves, accounts for a longstanding feature of Russia's professional and disciplinary cultures. The more virulent strands of biologistic and racialist thought had difficulty finding firm purchase in Russian culture and Russian disciplines. Sociologists and anthropologists refused to attribute the backwardness of the peasantry to any inherent flaw, instead stressing the heritage of serfdom and the autocracy's failure to carry out meaningful reform.[50] As a consequence, Russian specialists across the disciplinary spectrum tended not to embrace the more essentialized and deterministic form of biologized thinking so pronounced among the Italian school of Cesare Lombroso, or the followers of Ernst Haeckel in Germany. Russian criminologists, for example, emphasized sociological reasons (or the interaction between biology and social conditions) to explain crime rather than adopting biological determinism.[51] This disciplinary tradition was significant, for many prerevolutionary specialists, such as the leading psychologist Vladimir Bekhterev, continued to shape their disciplines into the Soviet period. The pronounced Lamarckian strain in Soviet science thus was not solely a product of Marxism, but also carried

49. Laura Engelstein, *The Keys to Happiness: Sex and the Search for Modernity in Fin-de-Siècle Russia* (Ithaca, 1992), 129–30.

50. In addition, the boundary between metropole and colony was much less clear-cut in the Russian Empire, a contiguous land empire, than in other European empires, and the practice of racially differentiating imperial subjects correspondingly less. See Willard Sunderland, "Russians into Yakuts? 'Going Native' and the Problems of Russian National Identity in the Siberian North," *Slavic Review* 55:4 (1996): 806–25.

51. Engelstein, *The Keys to Happiness*, 137. See also Daniel Beer, *Renovating Russia: The Human Sciences and Liberal Modernity, 1880–1930* (Ithaca, 2008). Russian naturalists developed an analogous position when they incorporated Darwin's thought into their disciplines; see Daniel Todes, *Darwin without Malthus: The Struggle for Existence in Russian Evolutionary Thought* (New York, 1989).

over traditions from Russian disciplines as they had developed in the pre-revolutionary period.

By the turn of the twentieth century, then, a complex of disciplines had come to describe and delineate the social realm in its Russian form. Textbooks on such subjects as administrative law and statistics explicitly noted the shift in those fields toward a greater emphasis on social issues.[52] By 1909, a Russian encyclopedia defined the three fields for study of the population: population theory, population statistics, and population politics. The encyclopedia defined "population politics" (*politika naseleniia*, from the German *Bevölkerungspolitik*) as the field "which is engaged in solving those problems of social life which flow from [statistical] facts and their regularity, and in particular, relating to questions of government intervention in that sphere."[53] This definition highlights again Russian professionals' enthusiasm for state intervention to raise Russia to the level of more developed countries and to employ those countries' previous experiences to leap beyond them. Members of the intelligentsia shared a sense of mission and a sense of urgency in their quest to address the social welfare needs of the masses and to refurbish Russia's social order.

Warfare and Welfare

While the scope and character of social welfare programs varied considerably from one country to another, military considerations in the late nineteenth and early twentieth centuries pushed political actors toward a greater state role to guarantee the well-being and military preparedness of their populations. The rise of popular sovereignty and the concomitant move toward universal male conscription made the bodily health of the population a matter of national security. In an age of mass warfare, a large and healthy population represented a vital resource for waging war and competing militarily. Casualties of war also spurred state welfare initiatives to care for war widows and the war wounded. The First World War acted as the most significant catalyst for a dramatic increase in state intervention specifically because of the enormous mobilizational demands of the war and the need to field mass armies of healthy soldiers. Even prior to the war, however, European political leaders and military planners focused

52. V. F. Deriuzhinskii, *Politseiskoe pravo: Posobie dlia studentov,* 3rd ed. (St. Petersburg, 1911), 14–16.

53. *Bol'shaia entsiklopediia Iuzhakova* (St. Petersburg, 1904–1909), s.v. "naselenie."

increasingly on the fitness of their populations and on state welfare measures to improve it.

The increased state role as guarantor of social welfare testified to the new and more expansive ways in which national security had come to be defined. No longer was war solely the affair of political and military elites. It now embraced the entire people, and the stakes of warfare rose correspondingly. States no longer fought simply for slices of territory but to defend their citizens. Imperial rivalries also fueled concerns with the robustness of the population.[54] Some politicians expressed these concerns in terms of national or racial degeneration. In 1900 the Earl of Roseberry, a leader of the British Liberal Party, declared, "An Empire such as ours requires as its first condition an Imperial Race—a race vigorous and industrious and intrepid. Health of mind and body exalt a nation in the competition of the universe. The survival of the fittest is an absolute truth in the conditions of the modern world."[55] Fabian leader Sidney Webb echoed these concerns the following year when he asked, "What is the use of an Empire if it does not breed and maintain…an Imperial race?" He criticized the condition of Britain's urban poor ("stunted in education, a prey of intemperance, huddled and congested") and prescribed a minimum level of education, sanitation, and living standards for all manual workers.[56]

Between 1880 and 1914, a number of European countries in addition to Australia, New Zealand, and Brazil launched social spending programs. These programs included public pensions for the elderly, and partly contributory, partly public-funded social insurance.[57] In France, concern about depopulation and degeneration, especially in contrast to the fecundity and vitality of Germany, grew immediately out of the Franco-Prussian War. Anxieties about French national decline led to a range of reform proposals, from antialcohol campaigns to eugenic societies.[58] For their part, German social reformers argued that the government had to promote the health and welfare of the population if Germany were to become a world

---

54. As will be discussed in chapter 5, colonial rule itself contributed to technologies of social control. But as James Scott notes, "Virtually all the initiatives associated with the 'civilizing missions' of colonialism were preceded by [state officials'] comparable programs to assimilate and civilize their own lower-class populations." Scott, *Seeing Like a State*, 378.

55. As quoted in Gilbert, *Evolution of National Insurance*, 72–73.

56. As quoted in ibid., 77. On concerns with degeneration, see Daniel Pick, *Faces of Degeneration: A European Disorder, c. 1848–c.1918* (Cambridge, 1989).

57. Skocpol, *Protecting Soldiers and Mothers*, 4–5.

58. See Robert A. Nye, *Crime, Madness, and Politics in Modern France: The Medical Concept of National Decline* (Princeton, 1984).

power, and many conservatives, including Chancellor Otto von Bismarck, adopted this position.[59] The German parliament passed a series of social insurance laws from 1881 onward that created a basic system of social security, and by the beginning of the First World War, an elaborate system of means testing, legal norms, and bureaucratized provision had vastly expanded the scope of state intervention.[60] The German state also employed youth welfare officers, housing inspectors, and public health workers to oversee the population. These officials provided advice even for "healthy" families to educate them in caring for the body and managing the home and household economy.[61]

Some British politicians, including Prime Minister David Lloyd George, greatly admired the German welfare system.[62] Their interest was prompted in part by military setbacks during the Boer War. General John Frederick Maurice blamed the British army's difficulties defeating a ragtag group of Boer farmers on a lack of physical fitness among young working-class men. Citing rejection rates of up to 60 percent of recruits in some cities, he labeled poor physical health "a national danger" and attributed it to deleterious environmental conditions of working-class life.[63] In 1903, the British government appointed its Interdepartmental Committee on Physical Deterioration to study the effects of poverty, malnutrition, and disease on the population's physical condition. The committee focused particularly on the unhealthy living conditions of the lower classes and recommended a larger state role to regulate the urban environment, feed needy schoolchildren, establish school medical inspections, encourage exercise, and teach mothers proper child care. In the next few years the government adopted its first welfare measures by instituting state-sponsored meals for needy schoolchildren and medical services in schools. Between 1908 and 1911 the British government extended its welfare policies to include limited forms of old age pensions, unemployment assistance, and national health insurance.[64]

59. Hermann Beck, *The Origins of the Authoritarian Welfare State in Prussia: Conservatives, Bureaucracy, and the Social Question, 1815–1870* (Ann Arbor, 1995), 257.

60. Peukert, *Weimar Republic*, 130.

61. David F. Crew, *Germans on Welfare: From Weimar to Hitler* (New York, 1998), 5.

62. Lloyd George travelled to Germany in 1908 to study the social insurance system there, and he returned filled with enthusiasm for pensions and unemployment insurance. See Gilbert, *Evolution of National Insurance*, 266, 291–92.

63. Ibid., 83–84. See also PRO Parliamentary Papers vol. XXXII, Microfiche 110.279, 1–9.

64. PRO Parliamentary Papers vol. XXXII, Microfiche 110.279, 23; Gilbert, *Evolution of National Insurance*, 88–117, 225–26, 268, 291.

Russian poor relief evolved from traditional administration by parish almshouses to a system of government oversight of punitive workhouses in the 1830s.[65] Already in the early nineteenth century, imperial family charities provided limited poor relief. Alexander I founded the Imperial Philanthropic Society in 1802, and the Department of the Institutions of Empress Maria (founded in 1828) ran 862 charitable, medical, and educational establishments by 1904. Funding for these agencies came partially from the state and the imperial family, as well as from private sources.[66] By the 1890s, Russian elites came to see indigence more as a social problem than as an individual failing, and the newly founded Guardianship of Work Assistance (under the patronage of Empress Aleksandra Fedorovna) coordinated the poor relief and vocational training of private charities.[67]

At this time some Russian officials and social critics argued for a comprehensive system of poverty relief. The 1891 famine in particular demonstrated the inadequacy of the existing patchwork of private and imperial family charities. Alexander III created a commission in 1892 to reform public assistance, and the commission, which studied European poor law, concluded that poor relief was the responsibility of the state and that it should be administered through strict legal norms. Within the government, however, there was no consensus as to whether the central bureaucracy, local government, or the church should be in charge of relief, so the commission's recommendations came to naught. Even following the Revolution of 1905, which greatly heightened the Russian nobility's concern with poverty as a source of crime and unrest, no consensus concerning state welfare was reached, and relief remained in the domain of private, municipal, and imperial-family charities.[68]

In towns across Russia, local nobles and philanthropists founded social aid organizations in the late imperial period. The Russo-Japanese War and

65. Joseph Bradley, *Muzhik and Muscovite: Urbanization in Late Imperial Russia* (Berkeley, 1985), 267–69.

66. Adele Lindenmeyr, *Poverty Is not a Vice: Charity, Society, and the State in Imperial Russia* (Princeton, 1996), 75. In a similar way, the imperial family of Japan subsidized private charity and relief organizations. See Garon, *Molding Japanese Minds*, 48.

67. Bradley, *Muzhik and Muscovite*, 309–13.

68. Lindemeyr, *Poverty Is not a Vice*, 72–93; Bradley, *Muzhik and Muscovite*, 318–22. Russian soldiers' substandard performance in the 1904–5 Russo-Japanese War also raised concerns about the physical "degeneration" of the population. The Main Military Sanitary Administration blamed the "conditions in which commoners live" for soldiers' poor physical condition. See Joshua Sanborn, "Drafting the Nation: Military Conscription and the Formation of a Modern Polity in Tsarist and Soviet Russia, 1905–1925" (Ph.D. diss., University of Chicago, 1998), 362.

the 1905 Revolution prompted the formation of many such organizations, as local leaders sought to care for wounded veterans and the widows and orphans of soldiers, as well as to defuse social unrest by providing material aid and moral guidance to the poor. The Taganrog Philanthropic Council, for example, was formed in December 1905 with the simple purpose of helping "those in need." It operated a range of programs, including a number of milk kitchens to improve the nutrition and health of young children. Local donors provided most of the council's funding, but national charities and the city council also contributed money.[69] Also following the 1905 Revolution, local notables in Borovichi founded the Society to Aid the Physical and Moral Development of Children and Adults. The goal of the society was "to combat the decline in morality among children and adults and to care for the welfare of orphans," and it opened nurseries and kindergartens for needy children.[70]

While these welfare societies were organized and funded by local philanthropists, they often came under nominal government control. The Borovichi Society, for example, fell under the jurisdiction of the Ministry of Internal Affairs and was obliged to file annual reports regarding its activities and budgets, though it received no money from the tsarist government.[71] The Ministry of Internal Affairs had a Department of People's Health and Social Welfare within its Main Administration of Local Economic Affairs.[72] Government oversight of private charities represented a step toward state welfare, but it was far short of a comprehensive, state-funded system. Poor relief remained in the hands of philanthropic societies and imperial-family charities until the downfall of the tsarist regime.

The one area where state assistance did take hold prior to the First World War was in aid to soldiers and their families. Beginning in 1877, during the Russo-Turkish War, assistance was provided to soldiers' families under the same principles as poor relief—based on need, peasants could petition for funds from the district zemstvo. During the unprecedented military mobilization of the 1904–5 Russo-Japanese War, local poor relief funds proved insufficient and the state treasury had to supplement local funds. In 1908 members of the Duma argued that assistance to war widows was

69. GARF f. 1795, op. 1, d. 4, l. 1. Also in 1905, the Black Sea Shipowners' Society of Mutual Insurance was founded to insure workers in the case of accident; GARF f. 4100, op. 1, d. 95, ll. 77–83.

70. GARF f. 1795, op. 1, d. 10, ll. 3–4.

71. The society raised money through donations, lotteries, and a buffet at the town's movie hall. GARF f. 1795, op. 1, d. 10, ll. 3–11.

72. GARF f. 1795, op. 1, d. 10, l. 1.

a state obligation and awarded them pensions based not on economic need but rather on the rank of their dead husbands. After several more years of debate the Duma passed another law in 1912 that removed demonstrable need from consideration of aid given to soldiers' families; accordingly every soldier's wife and child received a food allowance paid by the state treasury.[73] The same year, in the wake of the Balkan Wars, the Ottoman government decreed a monthly allowance for soldiers' families.[74]

One other step toward the formation of state welfare in Russia occurred in the area of social insurance. As early as 1866 a law required manufacturers to set up factory hospitals, though this requirement was not enforced. The first social insurance law in Russia was passed in 1893 and provided protection against work-related illness and injury through the creation of insurance funds with equal contributions from workers and employers. And in 1912 the Health and Accident Insurance Law passed by the Duma guaranteed benefits in cases of work-related accidents, illness, maternity, or death of the head of a household, and again these benefits were funded by contributions from workers and employers. While seemingly comprehensive, the law contained so many exclusions that only 23 percent of Russia's industrial workers were actually covered.[75]

The First World War provided enormous impetus for the expansion of state welfare programs. In countries throughout Europe, including Russia, the massive problems of wartime injuries, dislocations, and hunger prompted enlarged state welfare efforts. Government leaders felt a particular responsibility to the huge number of World War I invalids and war widows.[76] In addition to this growing need, there was an increased sense of national interest in maintaining people's welfare, given the correlation between recruits' physical robustness and military power. In a 1917 memorandum, the German general staff stated bluntly that "the power and well-being of a state have their foundation in the number and physique of

73. Emily Pyle, "Village Social Relations and the Reception of Soldiers' Family Aid Policies in Russia, 1912–21" (Ph.D. diss., University of Chicago, 1997), 3–5. See also Iu. V. Aleksandrovskii, *Zakony o pensiiakh nizhnim voinskim chinam i ikh semeistvam (1867–1913 gg.)* (St. Petersburg, 1913).

74. Nicole A. N. M. van Os, "Taking Care of Soldiers' Families: The Ottoman State and the Muinsiz alle maasi," *Arming the State: Military Conscription in the Middle East and Central Asia 1775–1925*, ed. Erik J. Zürcher (New York, 1999), 97.

75. Bernice Q. Madison, *Social Welfare in the Soviet Union* (Stanford, 1968), 19–20.

76. See for example, Crew, *Germans on Welfare*, 5; Leo Grebler and Wilhelm Winkler, *The Cost of the War to Germany and Austria-Hungary* (New Haven, 1940).

its population."[77] The First World War also marked the enormous expansion of government regulation, as the mobilizational needs of mass warfare seemed to necessitate extended state control in the name of national security. It was under the aegis of war that state welfare became both enlarged and increasingly institutionalized.

Most combatant countries expanded state welfare, including veterans benefits, old-age pensions, accident and disability insurance, and aid to mothers and children. The Italian government during the First World War initiated state welfare programs for the first time. It created the Commissariat for Civilian Assistance and Propaganda, as well as the Ministry for Military Relief and War Pensions.[78] Ottoman state aid to soldiers' families, initiated at the time of the Balkan Wars, was put into practice on a large scale during the First World War.[79] The French government authorized state welfare payments to every needy family whose breadwinner had been drafted into the army.[80] The British government systematized pensions and veterans' benefits with the Pensions Act of 1916, which replaced private pension funds and philanthropy with a Ministry of Pensions.[81] It also passed unemployment insurance legislation in 1920, which reflected the new assumption by both legislators and citizens that it was the government's responsibility to provide a minimum level of subsistence to all people.[82]

In Russia the outbreak of World War I sharply increased the scale of social problems. Philanthropic societies multiplied in response, but their efforts proved woefully inadequate to the spiraling welfare needs of the population. In August 1914, local activists in many regions formed committees to aid soldiers' families. Within a few months, these committees

77. Erich Ludendorff, *The General Staff and Its Problems: The History of the Relations between the High Command and the German Imperial Government as Revealed by Official Documents*, trans. F. A. Holt (New York, 1920), vol. 1, 202.

78. Paul Corner and Giovanna Procacci, "The Italian Experience of 'Total' Mobilization 1915–1920," *State, Society, and Mobilization in Europe during the First World War*, ed. John Horne (New York, 1997), 229; Francesca Lagorio, "Italian Widows of the First World War," *Authority, Identity, and the Social History of the Great War*, ed. Frans Coetzee and Marilyn Shevin-Coetzee (Providence, 1995), 182.

79. Yigit Akin, "The Ottoman Home Front during World War I: Everyday Politics, Society, and Gender" (Ph.D. diss., The Ohio State University, 2011), chapter 3. Akin demonstrates that state aid was provided as part of a set of mutual obligations between the government and its citizens, rather than as a safety net for those in need.

80. Jean-Jacques Becker, *The Great War and the French People,* trans. Arnold Pomeraus (Dover, N.H., 1985), 17–19.

81. Arthur Marwick, *Britain in the Century of Total War: War, Peace, and Social Change, 1900–1967* (Boston, 1968), 124.

82. Bentley B. Gilbert, *British Social Policy, 1914–1939* (Ithaca, 1970), 32.

THE BOOSTER

Fig. 1. British welfare poster, 1930. Arms labeled "national interest" lift an infant labeled "child welfare." Poster identification number UK 1543, Poster Collection, Hoover Institution Archives.

came under the auspices of imperial-family charities, though in part they continued to be administered and funded locally.[83] In mid-August the Ministry of Internal Affairs proposed that provincial governors organize

83. GARF f. 6787, op. 1, d. 113, ll. 7–16.

committees to aid soldiers' families, and it pronounced that these should be under the Committee of Grand Duchess Elisaveta Feodorovna.[84] Tsarist authorities also directed that philanthropic organizations concentrate their efforts on helping the families of those serving in the army.[85] To coordinate war relief efforts, the governor of Omsk Province created a special committee to oversee the local work of the Red Cross, the Omsk Philanthropic Society, the town orphanage, various church charities, and other preexisting, nongovernment relief organizations.[86] Thus while welfare continued to be provided by nominally nongovernmental organizations, these local societies increasingly came under the tutelage of the Ministry of Internal Affairs, local government, and quasi-governmental charitable organizations of the imperial family.

As World War I continued, even governmental coordination of relief efforts and funds from imperial family charities proved insufficient to meet burgeoning welfare needs. The charitable organizations of the imperial family quickly exhausted the donations solicited at the beginning of the war, and they then proceeded to expend all the proceeds from a lottery begun in December 1914.[87] Between 1914 and 1916, the Novgorod Department of the Committee of Grand Duchess Elisaveta Fedorovna spent thousands of rubles caring for the war wounded, orphans, and refugees. The Tula and Viatka departments also increased their expenditures sharply in 1915 and 1916 as the number of war victims swelled.[88] The Borovichi Society found itself inundated with orphans and desperately appealed for more money from Grand Duchess Tat'iana Nikolaevna in 1915.[89] In Voronezh the city duma and provincial zemstvo found it necessary to allocate thousands of rubles to war victims and their families to cover the needs that philanthropic societies could not meet. Even this money proved insufficient as the Voronezh relief committee became overwhelmed caring not only for the families of soldiers but for the huge number of refugees fleeing the war zone. The committee also reported that many of its volunteers were away during the summer months, so that it had few people and resources to draw on.[90]

84. GARF f. 6787, op. 1, d. 113, l. 1.
85. GARF f. 1795, op. 1, d. 5, l. 8.
86. GARF f. 6787, op. 1, d. 113, ll. 1–4.
87. RGIA f. 1253, op. 1, d. 94b, ll. 19, 41, 82.
88. RGIA f. 1253, op. 1, d. 69, ll. 2–14.
89. GARF f. 1795, op. 1, d. 10, ll. 18–19.
90. RGIA f. 1253, op. 1, d. 8, l. 29; GARF f. 1795, op. 1, d. 9, l. 67. On the huge demands of refugee relief, see also RGIA f. 457, op. 1, d. 527, ll. 38–41.

This report highlights the weakness of voluntary societies in dealing with such widespread social problems. The First World War made clear not only a vital state interest in maintaining the health of the population, but also the need for a permanent staff and state-funded institutions to provide welfare on a mass scale. Very similar problems arose in wartime Germany where benevolent organizations held primary responsibility for aid to wounded soldiers and war refugees. Not only did philanthropic groups have inadequate resources for the enormous task of war relief, but they proved unsystematic in their distribution of aid. War widows in some regions and towns received much more assistance than those in others. In response, relief to war victims was rapidly bureaucratized, as first nation-wide organizations and eventually the national government absorbed local volunteer groups and set norms for the administration of pensions.[91]

Initially, the war seemed to provide a way out of the impasse between the Russian intelligentsia and the state. The tsarist autocracy was forced to rely increasingly, if reluctantly, on public and professional organizations. In fact, wartime needs resulted in not only state mobilization of society, but what may be termed society's self-mobilization for total war.[92] In Russia, as in other combatant countries, professional and civic organizations rushed to help mobilize and care for the population. Zemstvo leaders from localities around the country agreed to form the All-Russian Union of Zemstvos, which later joined with the All-Russian Union of Towns, to work on a nationwide scale. These public organizations established food distribution centers, disinfection points, hospitals, and bathhouses for soldiers and refugees. Professional activists—in zemstvos, professional unions, and other organizations—viewed the war as an opportunity to realize their longstanding aspirations to modernize and rationalize Russian society.[93] While public organizations came to take over the care of various

91. Robert Weldon Whalen, *Bitter Wounds: German Victims of the Great War, 1914–1939* (Ithaca, 1984), 90–99.

92. Michael Geyer, "The Militarization of Europe, 1914–1945," *The Militarization of the Western World*, ed. John Gillis (New Brunswick, N.J., 1989), 75–80. Geyer uses the term *para-statal complex* to describe the network of semistate, semiautonomous structures that mobilized social resources for the war effort; see Michael Geyer, "The Stigma of Violence," *German Studies Review* 15: 1 (winter 1992): 84. Philanthropic associations in early Republican Turkey similarly "functioned in the ambiguous area between the realm of public and private." See Ayse Bugra, "Poverty and Citizenship: An Overview of the Social-Policy Environment in Republican Turkey," *International Journal of Middle East Studies* 39 (2007): 38.

93. Aaron Retish, *Russia's Peasants in Revolution and Civil War: Citizenship, Identity, and the Creation of the Soviet State, 1914–1922* (Cambridge, 2008), 31–33. See also

welfare and social causes, they received much of their funding from the imperial government. The government created the Supreme Council for the Care of Soldiers' Families and Families of the Wounded and Dead, staffed jointly by members of the bureaucracy and public organizations and headed by the Empress Aleksandra Fedorovna. By September 1915, the imperial government had assigned almost half a billion rubles for soldiers' families, or nearly 1,200,000 rubles a day.[94] Similarly, care for war invalids was originally entrusted to an ad-hoc commission headed by another member of the imperial family, the princess Ksenia Aleksandrovna. By 1916, this responsibility passed to the All-Russian Union of Towns and the All-Russian Union of Zemstvos, which assigned 15 million rubles to this cause in 1916 alone.[95]

In addition to the demands of wartime mobilization, the war itself caused unexpected social disruptions. Russia's defeats and retreats, especially in the first half of 1915, created a veritable wave of refugees. By 1917, the number of refugees is estimated to have been 5 million individuals. At first, refugees were cared for by a commission chartered by Grand Duchess Tat'iana Nikolaevna, but public organizations criticized the Tat'iana Commission's ineffective handling of aid. Liberal professionals cited the refugee crisis to assert their own expertise to solve social problems.[96] In September 1915 Tsar Nicholas II established the Special Council for the Organization of Refugees staffed jointly by government bureaucrats and representatives of the public organizations. Between the summer of 1915 and October 1917, the government allotted more than 600 million rubles for refugee care.[97]

Pirogovskii s"ezd vrachei i predstavitelei vrachebno-sanitarnykh organizatsii zemstv i gorodov (Petrograd, 1916), 37–38; William Gleason, "The All-Russian Union of Zemstvos and World War I," *The Zemstvo in Russia,* ed. Emmons and Vucinich, 365–82; Alessandro Stanziani, "Discours et pratiques sociales de l'économie politique: Économistes, bureaucrates et paysans a l'époque de la 'grande transformation' en Russie, 1892–1930" (Ph.D. diss., Écoles des hautes études en sciences sociales, 1995). On civic efforts to aid soldiers' families, see RGIA, f. 1253, op., d. 8, ll. 2–14, 21, 29, 31–38.

94. Pyle, "Village Social Relations," 3–6, 157–59; RGIA f. 1253, op. 1, d. 69, ll. 4–9, 12–14, 26.

95. *Pirogovskii s"ezd,* 26.

96. Peter Gatrell, *A Whole Empire Walking: Refugees in Russia during World War I* (Bloomington, 1999), 33–41, 95.

97. A. N. Kurtsev, "Bezhentsy pervoi mirovoi voiny," *Voprosy istorii* 8 (1999): 98–113. See also RGIA, f. 1322, op. 1, d. 13, ll. 47–54, on government assignment of nearly 65 million rubles to various provincial authorities to cover refugee needs, April–September 1916. The Special Council for Discussing and Coordinating Food Supply (formed 1915) similarly brought together members of government ministries and public organizations, and assumed responsibility for supplying grain to the entire population as well as the army; Peter

The refugee issue highlights a significant difference between new social welfare programs and previous philanthropic concerns. Aid to refugees was cast not as charity but as a civic right entailing obligations to the state. In January 1916, the interior minister requested that provincial governors employ refugees in agricultural labor. Increasingly, government aid to refugees was tied to labor mobilization in sectors of the economy critical for the war effort. By the summer of that year, more than 250,000 refugees, in addition to more than 600,000 prisoners of war, were employed in agriculture, primarily on large estates.[98] By late March 1917, the Special Council for the Organization of Refugees issued guidelines "on measures for enlisting refugees in agricultural labor." (The same day, it also issued guidelines on the monthly sums to be allotted for supporting refugee kindergartens, day schools, and shelters.)[99] Aid to soldiers' families similarly became tied to punitive measures against families of military deserters, who were to be denied such support or, in extreme cases, were to have their property confiscated.[100] Public officials explicitly endorsed the shift from philanthropy to a model of civic rights and state obligations. One doctor at the 1916 Pirogov Congress, a convention of leading zemstvo physicians, explained that the care of invalids, having passed to the Union of Zemstvos and the Union of Towns, "should be organized from an all-state perspective; it should not only have a philanthropic character."[101]

With the fall of the Russian autocracy in February 1917, the possibilities to reorganize the bureaucracy and expand state welfare increased further still. Leaders of the Provisional Government restructured the bureaucracy along more functional lines and according to the principle of state responsibility for social welfare. On May 5, 1917, the Provisional Government created the Ministry of State Care, and on the very same day it established the Ministry of Labor and the Ministry of Food Sup-

Holquist, *Making War, Forging Revolution: Russia's Continuum of Crisis, 1914–1921* (Cambridge, Mass., 2002), 26.

98. RGIA, f. 1282, op. 1, d. 1165, prilozhenie 2, l. 330; *Ekonomicheskoe polozhenie Rossii nakanune velikoi oktiabr'skoi sotsialisticheskoi revoliutsii: Dokumenty i materialy,* ed. A. L. Sidorov and A. M. Amfimov (Moscow, 1967) vol. 3, 33.

99. RGIA, f. 1322, op. 1, d. 13, ll. 101, 112–15; Kurtsev, "Bezhentsy pervoi mirovoi voiny," 110.

100. *Osobyi zhurnal soveta ministrov* no. 205 (March 27, 1915); Pyle, "Village Social Relations," 167–71. For analogous Austro-Hungarian measures, see Holger Herwig, *The First World War: Germany and Austria Hungary, 1914–1918* (London, 1997), 232.

101. *Pirogovskii s"ezd,* 26.

ply.[102] All three new ministries were institutional expressions of the ideal that the state was obligated to look after the welfare of its citizens. The timing of the establishment of similar ministries in other combatants suggests that the Provisional Government was following a common European trajectory. The Austrian government established both a Ministry of Social Welfare and a Ministry of Food Supply in mid-1917, at virtually the same time as Russia's Provisional Government. And the British government created a Ministry of Pensions in late 1916, as well as founding a Ministry of Health and passing the Housing and Town Planning Act immediately after the war.[103]

The newly appointed Russian minister of state care D. I. Shakhovskoi appealed to former bureaucrats of imperial-family charities to continue and broaden their welfare work by joining the new ministry and fulfilling "one of the most important state needs."[104] In a subsequent speech, Shakhovskoi stated, "The Ministry of State Care is still young and it needs to observe closely and learn from the West how to organize the matter of relief.... This should be approached as a state-societal [*gosudarstvennoe-obshchestvennoe*] matter."[105] A Ministry of State Care report in August 1917 characterized "the uncoordinated activity of existing philanthropic societies and committees" as unable to provide for "the welfare of the crippled and poor" and as "an unproductive expenditure of national resources." It concluded that the operations and resources of existing philanthropic committees should be transferred to the Ministry of State Care to ensure "the unification of activity and more systematic character of providing aid to the needy."[106] In accordance with this decision, the Provisional Government on August 25, 1917, established a commission to transfer the activities and resources of all philanthropic committees and societies to the Ministry of State Care.[107]

Many Russians sought an expanded state role as the chaos of war and revolution simultaneously impeded relief operations and made them more

---

102. N. P. Eroshkin, *Istoriia gosudarstvennykh uchrezhdenii dorevolutsionnoi Rossii* (Moscow, 1968), 351. See also William Rosenberg, "Social Mediation and State Construction(s) in Revolutionary Russia," *Social History* 19:2 (1994): 169–88.

103. Marwick, *Britain in the Century of Total War*, 121–25.

104. "Khronika," *Vestnik vremennogo pravitel'stva* 56 (May 17, 1917).

105. GARF f. 6787, op. 1, d. 28, l. 10.

106. GARF f. 6787, op. 1, d. 102, ll. 1–9. Another government report denounced the tsarist government for having left aid to crippled veterans to the "arbitrary, unsystematic" work of philanthropic societies; GARF f. 6787, op. 1, d. 28, l. 7.

107. GARF f. 6787, op. 1, d. 7, l. 1. The transfer of philanthropic organizations' assets had already begun in July; see *Zhurnaly zasedanii vremennogo pravitel'stva* 133 (July 16, 1917): 7.

urgent.[108] At a congress of war wounded, a delegate named A. I. Kislov called for state aid to those crippled in the war. "On the ruins of the old regime, there are arising in Russia new forms of state [*gosudarstvennost'*] and new civic organizations, though not estate forms as in prerevolutionary times, but on the basis of professional and corporative interests. We, the victims of the war, represent a special corporate group with its own special needs and tasks."[109] In response to the demands of injured veterans, the Provisional Government established the Temporary State Committee for Aid to War Invalids as part of the Ministry of State Care on June 29, 1917.[110] The Ministry of State Care subsequently guaranteed pensions to all those crippled in the war, regardless of rank, and drew up eight categories of pensions to be awarded, depending on the degree to which veterans had lost their labor ability.[111] The ministry also increased the amount of food aid to soldiers' families, and specified that this aid would be provided to a soldier's wife, children under fifteen years of age, and parents (if they were no longer able to work).[112]

The Provisional Government's Ministry of Labor also enacted welfare measures. The ministry contained the Department of Social Insurance, and it took steps to systematize workers' insurance. In May 1917 the Ministry of Labor sent a circular to factory inspectors advising them of the need, "given the new social-political conditions," to revise the June 1912 insurance laws so that all workers would be covered in case of illness, accident, disability, or old age.[113] The ministry proceeded to collect information from each workers' insurance fund on operations since 1912 in order to devise a more comprehensive approach. It also noted the need to study "the experience of insurance in Western European states" in order to develop a "broader plan for the organization of social insurance."[114] As a result of these efforts, the Provisional Government drew up extensive guidelines on the conditions and amounts of benefits to the unemployed, sick, injured, and retired.[115]

---

108. Even prior to 1917, war victims came to expect state aid. See the 1916 letters of wounded soldiers and their families demanding expedited pensions; RGIA f. 1253, op. 1, d. 53, ll. 5, 11, 45–49.

109. GARF f. 6787, op. 1, d. 28, l. 9.

110. GARF f. 6787, op. 1, d. 28, ll. 40–41.

111. GARF f. 6787, op. 1, d. 28, l. 1.

112. GARF f. 6787, op. 1, d. 101, l. 1.

113. GARF f. 4100, op. 1, d. 83, l. 2.

114. GARF f. 4100, op. 1, d. 83, l. 9.

115. GARF f. 4100, op. 1, d. 83, ll. 15–22.

The First World War, then, triggered a vast expansion of the state's role in providing for the population's welfare. This expansion was particularly dramatic in Russia, where the tsarist autocracy reluctantly increased social intervention in response to an enormous array of wartime problems. The autocracy also permitted the intelligentsia a greater role in public affairs, which resulted in the emergence of a parastatal complex—a union of government institutions and public organizations to mobilize for the war effort and aid citizens in need. Imperial family charities were increasingly superseded by "special councils" that brought together tsarist bureaucrats and zemstvo professionals. With the overthrow of the autocracy in February 1917, specialists found themselves with an unfettered opportunity to shape social policy. Under their influence, and faced with a wartime crisis of economic and social disintegration, the Provisional Government moved decisively toward full state responsibility for social welfare. Because the Provisional Government lasted less than a year, it did not survive long enough to put many of its initiatives into practice. This task would fall to the Soviet government.

The Soviet Welfare State

A number of factors shaped the Soviet welfare state. As described above, the Russian intelligentsia's social concerns were informed by nineteenth-century social science and an ethos of rational social reordering to ameliorate the living conditions of the lower classes. Non-Party professionals were to play a central role in generating the knowledge on which Party officials based social policies. Also crucial was the historical conjuncture in which Soviet welfare took shape. The First World War and Civil War resulted in an enormous array of people in need—refugees, disabled soldiers, war widows—who required large-scale state aid. Moreover, the First World War demonstrated to political leaders around the world that the physical well-being of their populations was critical to their countries' military manpower and national defense. Finally, Marxist-Leninist ideology strongly influenced the distribution of welfare benefits, as Soviet officials prioritized the needs of Red Army soldiers and industrial workers, while they denied benefits to those labeled class enemies.

Party leaders relied heavily on the knowledge and expertise of non-Party specialists to identify social problems and implement welfare programs. While most liberal professionals opposed the Bolshevik takeover, many nonetheless jumped at the opportunity provided by the Soviet government to apply their knowledge to social problems. Social statisticians,

for example, who under the tsarist regime had been confined to local zemstvo work, saw the Revolution as their chance to address problems on a
national scale and to promote a rational reordering of society based on
science.[116] In June 1918, leading statistician P. I. Popov proposed to Lenin
the formation of a national statistical bureau, and the following month
the Soviet government opened its Central Statistical Administration, popu-
lated largely by zemstvo statisticians and tsarist-era specialists.[117] Despite
political differences, Party leaders and liberal experts shared a common
belief in the scientific management of society and a common goal of modernization. Indeed, the Bolsheviks desperately needed social science knowledge of a society that they now presumed to rule.[118] Liberal professionals
provided that knowledge through their statistical studies of social welfare
problems and their service in the burgeoning state bureaucracy.[119]

As had been true under the Provisional Government, bureaucrats under
the Soviet regime, including Party officials and non-Party professionals
alike, operated on the principle that social welfare was a responsibility of
the state, and that it could be best provided through centralized, expert administration. Within days of taking power, Bolshevik leaders proclaimed
comprehensive social insurance for all hired laborers.[120] One year later,
in October 1918, the Soviet government issued its statute "On the Full
Social Security of Laborers," which outlined the entire welfare system,
including institutional structure, benefits, and financing. It guaranteed
benefits to all those who worked and did not exploit the labor of others.
Benefits included aid to the disabled, those unemployed through no fault
of their own, pregnant women and new mothers, and homeless children.

---

116. Alain Blum and Marine Mespoulet, *L'anarchie bureaucratique: Pouvoir et statistique sous Staline* (Paris, 2003), 35–38.

117. Alessandro Stanziani, "Les sources démographiques entre contrôle policies et
utopies technocratiques: Le cas russe, 1870–1926," *Cahiers du monde russe* 38:4 (1997):
474–75.

118. Francine Hirsch describes a parallel phenomenon in Soviet governance of national
minorities, where Lenin relied on Sergei Ol'denburg and other ethnographers at the Academy of Sciences who, despite their political opposition to the Bolsheviks, were willing to
serve the Soviet state to pursue their own agenda—"using scientific knowledge to turn Russia into a modern state." Francine Hirsch, *Empire of Nations: Ethnographic Knowledge
and the Making of the Soviet Union* (Ithaca, 2005), 21–22.

119. See, for example, A. N. Vinokurov, ed., *Sotsial'noe obespechenie v Sovetskoi
Rossii: Sbornik statei k s"ezdu sovetov* (Moscow, 1919). On the role of non-Party profes-
sionals in the Central Statistical Administration's Department of Moral Statistics, see
Kenneth M. Pinnow, *Lost to the Collective: Suicide and the Promise of Soviet Socialism*
(Ithaca, 2010), 143–52.

120. Madison, *Social Welfare in the Soviet Union*, 50–51.

The statute specified the creation of special institutions to provide for war invalids and pensions for those who had lost their ability to work. Workers' disability and unemployment benefits were to be administered through state-run social insurance funds financed solely by employers' contributions. In the case of self-employed artisans and peasants, benefits were to be paid by mutual aid cooperatives funded by members' contributions.[121]

Soviet journalists heralded the new welfare statute as leaving far behind the social insurance systems of Germany and Britain.[122] The leader in charge of administering welfare assistance, Commissar Aleksandr Vinokurov, contrasted what he described as the Soviet government's rational and just system of social insurance with the exploitative and ineffectual system that had existed under the tsarist government. He emphasized that the old system served only the interests of capitalists and landowners, forcing workers to fund insurance with their own money. Other officials similarly emphasized the differences between the Soviet system's comprehensive welfare benefits and the hodgepodge of humiliating and inadequate charity aid offered to workers under capitalism.[123]

As Bolshevik leaders took control of the government bureaucracy, they sought to centralize power as well as to institute new principles. They renamed all government ministries "commissariats," so the Ministry of State Care became the Commissariat of State Care, with the designated functions of providing for "war invalids, their families, the elderly, [parentless] minors, and the preservation of mothers and children."[124] In April 1918 the Soviet government gave this branch of the bureaucracy a new appellation—the Commissariat of Social Security (Komissariat sotsial'nogo obespecheniia), with the following departments: Preservation of Maternity and Children; Orphanages; Security of Minors Charged with Socially Dangerous Acts; Medical; Pensions and Assistance, including the Security of Invalids, Widows, and the Elderly; War Wounded; Finance; Publications.[125]

121. GARF f. A-482, op. 35, d. 30, ll. 75–83. See also D.I. Guttsait and I. K. Ksenofontov, *Sistematicheskii sbornik po sotsial'nomu obespecheniiu: Deistvuiushchee zakonodatel'stvo po voprosam gosudarstvennogo obespecheniia krest'ianskoi obshchestvennoi vzaimopomoshchi i kooperatsii invalidov* (Moscow, 1926).

122. *Zhurnal Narodnogo Komissariata sots. obespecheniia* 2 (December 1918): 5.

123. A. Vinokurov, *Sotsial'noe obespechenie (ot kapitalizma k kommunizmu)* (Moscow, 1921), 4–8; Madison, *Social Welfare in the Soviet Union,* 49–50. See also L. V. Zabelin, *Teoreticheskie osnovy sotsial'nogo strakhonvaniia* (Moscow, 1926).

124. E. L. Skandova, ed., *Vysshie organy gos. vlasti i organy tsen. upravleniia RSFSR (1917–1967 gg.)* (Moscow, 1970), 438.

125. GARF f. A-413, op. 2, d. 1, l. 16.

The Soviet government continued the process, uncompleted by the Provisional government, of assuming control of the resources and services of philanthropic organizations. Through a series of decrees issued in the spring and summer of 1918, Soviet leaders renamed all relief organizations, hospitals, orphanages, and other philanthropic agencies, and placed them under the authority of the Commissariat of Social Security.[126] For example, in July 1918 a decree transferred all property and assets of the St. George Committee for aid to wounded veterans to the Commissariat of Social Security. The decree transferred its personnel as well and stated that, with the exception of the two or three leaders of the committee (who were simply fired), all personnel would become employees of the commissariat and work establishing labor *artels,* or collectives, to employ and provide for wounded veterans.[127] Similarly the Commissariat of Social Security abolished the Union of War Wounded in April 1918, stating, "The matter of the social security of war wounded, as a function of the state, must be in the hands of state authority." It transferred all resources of the union to the Soviet government.[128] The commissariat also decreed an end to all lotteries (previously a common means to raise money for charities) and established the state as the sole collector and distributor of relief.[129]

Although the centralizing and statizing thrust of these policies continued the course begun by the Provisional government, the Soviet government was distinguished by the explicit class-orientation of its programs, which privileged the lower classes and discriminated against former members of the nobility and bourgeoisie. The 1918 Soviet constitution deprived rights to those deemed class enemies—private traders, clerics, former tsarist police officials, White army personnel, and those who hired labor. This deprivation encompassed all rights of citizenship, including the right to receive pensions or any other public assistance.[130] Commissariat of Social Security directives emphasized that housing and material aid should be guaranteed to "all children of the poor," and specified that needy families should receive aid only after their social origin had been verified.[131] Commissar

126. GARF f. A-413, op. 2, d. 1, l. 5.

127. GARF f. A-413, op. 2, d. 1, l. 29.

128. GARF f. A-413, op. 2, d. 1, ll. 9–10. Members of the Union of War Wounded did in fact lobby the Soviet government to promote their own cause; see GARF f. A-413, op. 2, d. 8, l. 31.

129. GARF f. A-413, op. 2, d. 1, l. 14.

130. Golfo Alexopoulos, *Stalin's Outcasts: Aliens, Citizens, and the Soviet State, 1926–1936* (Ithaca, 2003), 2–3.

131. GARF f. A-413, op. 2, d. 74, l. 58.

Vinokurov also explained the takeover of philanthropic organizations as in part a means to free welfare institutions from the control of "parasitic elements," and he warned that many welfare institutions employed people from formerly privileged classes who should be purged.[132]

The context in which the Commissariat of Social Security began its work militated for an ever-greater state role. The casualties of the First World War meant that literally millions of war wounded, war widows, and refugees desperately required assistance. At the Commissariat of Social Security's first congress, in July 1918, Vinokurov underscored the tremendous demand for welfare programs. "As a result of bloody foreign and domestic wars, millions of the population have been left disabled and in need of social aid.... These conditions call out for the establishment of relief for the population on a broad state-social scale [*v shirokom gosudarstvennom sotsial'nom masshtabe*]." He went on to highlight the needs of war victims and their families, of the disabled, and of mothers and children.[133] Vinokurov noted that state welfare would require huge expenditures: billions of rubles for disabled veterans, 40 million rubles per month for the families of those killed in wars, and 500 million rubles in pensions to retired government employees in the first half of 1918 alone. To help pay for these relief efforts he proposed that the assets of émigrés be seized and transferred to the Commissariat of Social Security. He also announced a class-based policy to review the pensions paid to former tsarist bureaucrats with the aim of terminating these payments and channeling the money instead to disabled workers and orphans. He added that all physically able people were obliged to work and that aid was only for the needy.[134]

Commissariat of Social Security officials gave particular attention to disabled veterans and studied the programs of other European countries in order to devise policies to provide for them. In 1918, one of the commissariat's representatives, Dr. Brodskii, studied aid to the war wounded in Austria and Germany. Based on his report, commissariat officials concluded, "The matter of aid to invalids of the world war represents a subject of exceptional importance for states... [which] are all trying in one way or other to resolve the problem of how to return the mass of disabled people to the ranks of the laboring classes of the population." The report

132. GARF f. A-413, op. 2, d. 1, l. 11; *Pervyi Vserossiiskii s"ezd komissarov sotsial'nogo obespecheniia* (Moscow, 1918), 1.

133. *Pervyi Vserossiiskii s"ezd*, 1.

134. Ibid., 1–4, 25–26.

noted that in Austria the Ministry of Social Welfare ensured the material well-being of the war wounded, and the Ministry of Labor arranged work for them, including through a system of training invalids to do handicraft labor.[135] The Soviet government similarly sought to grant the war wounded not only assistance, but some sort of labor they could fulfill. At the July 1918 Commissariat of Social Security congress, delegates emphasized the importance of "the restoration of the labor ability of disabled veterans." They expressed a concern not only for recovering the productive capacity of the injured, but also, in keeping with Soviet ideology, the importance of socially productive labor for personal fulfillment. The congress resolved to create special homes for war invalids and craft schools to train them for labor.[136]

The widespread starvation, disease, dislocation, and casualties caused by the Civil War further added to the number of those in need of state welfare, and the Soviet government felt a particular obligation to assist Red Army veterans. In August 1918 it issued a decree, "On the Security of Red Army Soldiers and their Families," that granted pensions to soldiers who were fully or partially disabled and to the families or orphans of any soldiers killed in service.[137] From 1920 to 1922 the Commissariat of Social Security devoted a huge amount of time and resources toward the administration of aid to Civil War disabled veterans and the families of those serving in the Red Army.[138] In addition to meeting the needs of wounded soldiers and their families, the Soviet government sought to provide for noncombatants who suffered losses during the war. At the second congress of the Commissariat of Social Security in April 1921, delegates resolved that state aid should be offered to all "victims of counterrevolution." Their resolution reported that many people lacked basic food and shelter, and it also noted the "enormous political significance" of aid, because state relief

135. GARF f. A-413, op. 2, d. 176, l. 29. The German government also expended enormous resources after the war to provide for the 6 million people who were disabled veterans and their family members or dependent survivors of the dead; Whalen, *Bitter Wounds,* 16.

136. *Pervyi Vserossiiskii s"ezd,* 18–25.

137. GARF f. A-413, op. 2, d. 8, ll. 20, 27. The explanatory notes attached to the decree acknowledged that this policy was simply a more generous version of the June 1912 tsarist decree that had guaranteed pensions to the war wounded and war widows.

138. GARF f. 4085, op. 12, d. 40, ll. 28–29; *Materialy narodnogo komissariata sotsial'nogo obespecheniia* (Moscow, 1922), vol. 3, 6–33. A December 1921 circular stressed the urgency of providing aid to veterans and the families of Red Army soldiers who resided in famine areas; 62–63.

"won support for Soviet power of even the most backward elements of the population."[139]

While the Soviet government from its inception aspired to a comprehensive welfare system and created one in theory, it lacked the resources to put this system into practice during the first decade of its existence. Given the horrendous devastation and economic collapse caused by the Civil War, the Soviet government had virtually no revenues with which to address the escalating welfare needs of millions of disabled, displaced, unemployed, and starving citizens. From 1917 to 1921, social insurance existed mostly on paper. Nationalization of industry meant that the government became the sole employer of industrial workers and was thus responsible for social insurance funds to cover disability and unemployment. But with many factories closing due to shortages of materials and fuel, little revenue was generated for social insurance. Those enterprises that remained open were obligated to pay up to 28 percent of their payroll into the state social insurance fund, and even this money covered only a fraction of unemployed and disabled workers in need.[140] At the Third All-Union Trade Union Congress in 1920, Commissar of Labor Vasili Schmidt acknowledged that the principle of comprehensive social insurance had no basis in reality and promised that government welfare obligations would be fulfilled but only after the economic situation improved.[141]

The introduction of the New Economic Policy marked a retreat not only on the economic front but in the area of government welfare provision. Commissariat of Social Security officials admitted that they lacked the resources to provide relief to all needy citizens. A 1921 commissariat report stated that in "the current transitional period" it was impossible to guarantee the social welfare of all people, so that priority had to be given to the "leading groups of the population (workers and Red Army soldiers), and to the weakest social elements (cases where the family provider has died, been mobilized, or is an invalid)." The report reaffirmed that in the future social welfare would be extended to "other groups in the population, in accordance with state resources."[142] The Soviet government lacked the money even to cover leading industrial workers, so—in violation of the principle that Soviet welfare benefits were a right rather than a charity—it

139. GARF f. 4085, op. 21, d. 27, l. 25. On state famine aid to peasants in 1921, see Retish, *Russia's Peasants*, 255–59.

140. Madison, *Social Welfare in the Soviet Union*, 51. See also A. Vinokurov, ed., *Sotsial'noe obespechenie v Sovetskoi Rossii*.

141. Margaret Dewar, *Labour Policy in the USSR* (London, 1956), 70.

142. GARF f. 4085, op. 12, d. 27, l. 15.

often denied payments to disabled workers with savings or other income. Benefits, if paid at all, did not amount to workers' total salary as stipulated but rather were a percentage of regular earnings.[143]

In 1923, the Commissariat of Social Security again announced that its expenditures had to be reduced and that the Soviet government would guarantee aid only to "those who lost their health defending the state— invalids of the war and families of Red Army soldiers." It stated that peasants in need would have to rely on mutual aid and that invalids not covered by the government would have to work in self-supporting production artels. It concluded that "as a result of six years of war...we have about six million victims [war invalids]. It is clear that this enormous mass of people...cannot be entirely covered by state social security."[144] As economic production and government revenues gradually recovered, the Soviet government was able to increase social welfare expenditures. Social insurance payments roughly doubled between 1924 and 1927. And that year the Soviet government reiterated the principles of comprehensive disability coverage and benefits equal to full salary, though it added the clause, "except in cases of acute shortage of insurance funds." Throughout the 1920s and even into the 1930s, numerous letters and complaints reveal that a large number of people who qualified for disability benefits did not receive them.[145]

Rising unemployment throughout the 1920s placed additional strains on the Soviet state welfare system. While in theory all unemployed workers were entitled to unemployment benefits equal to their full salaries, in practice the Soviet government lacked the money to cover such benefits. Already in October 1921 a government decree restricted unemployment relief to workers at state-run factories who had three or more years' experience. This decree stipulated that benefits for skilled workers would be set at the minimum local wage and one-third to one-half of that for unskilled workers. Any unemployed worker who refused an offer of employment

143. GARF f. 4085, op. 12, d. 316b, l. 5; Madison, *Social Welfare in the Soviet Union*, 52. See also *Polozhenie po poriadke vydachi edinovremennykh posobii i vozmeshcheniia uteriannogo zarabotka chlenam artelei promyslovoi kooperatsii, prizyvaemym v RKKA* (Moscow, 1938), 2.

144. *Sotsial'noe obespechenie za piat' let: 30 apr. 1918 g.—30 apr. 1923 g.* (Moscow, 1923), 25–32. For subsequent (unrealized) plans to extend state social insurance to the peasantry, see *Biulleten' Rossgosstrakha* 10:3 (June 5, 1927): 4–5.

145. Andrea Chandler, *Shocking Mother Russia: Democratization, Social Rights, and Pension Reform in Russia, 1990–2001* (Toronto, 2004), 32, 36; Dewar, *Labour Policy in the USSR*, 108.

would have their benefits cut off.[146] In practice, the Soviet government could not even afford this reduced level of unemployment compensation, as the number of unemployed workers continued to swell. In 1924 Soviet cities registered 1.3 million unemployed persons, and by 1927 urban unemployment reached 2 million.[147]

Ten years after the October Revolution the ambitious social welfare program of the Soviet government remained largely unfulfilled. The principle of employer-funded, state-administered, comprehensive social insurance for workers was still in place, but the high demand for state assistance combined with a dearth of resources meant that it was far from being realized. The Soviet Union in the 1920s remained a poor, agrarian country. It was only during the Soviet industrialization drive of the 1930s that the Soviet government took control of and expanded economic resources in a way that permitted it to establish a functioning welfare system. And the context in which Soviet industrialization took place—the abolition of capitalism and the establishment of a state-run, planned economy—had enormous implications for the scope and form of the Soviet welfare state.

The First Five-Year Plan marked the Stalinist leadership's attempt to harness all available human and natural resources and direct them to the economic and social transformation of the country—something they saw as vital to national defense and progress toward socialism. The plan called for dramatic increases in industrial capacity, particularly in steel production and other heavy industry. More than that, it represented an effort to rationalize economic life in accordance with Marxist principles that sought to abolish market economic relations and the private ownership of the means of production. The planned economy coupled with collectivization meant the replacement of small-scale (supposedly inefficient) producers and the chaos of the free market with large-scale, state-run industry and agriculture. The Soviet planned economy thus corresponded to welfare in the broad sense of the rationalization of everyday life so as to maximize individuals' productivity and contribution to the commonweal.[148]

The First Five-Year Plan did mobilize the Soviet Union's large reserves of labor and in fact eliminated unemployment completely. The industrialization drive created tremendous labor demand, as factory directors and

146. Dewar, *Labour Policy in the USSR*, 111–12.

147. V. Danilov, "Krest'ianskii otkhod na promysly v 1920-kh godakh," *Istoricheskie zapiski* 94 (1974): 104–5; *Na agrarnom fronte* 4 (1927): 38.

148. Stephen Kotkin, *Magnetic Mountain: Stalinism as a* Civilization (Berkeley, 1995), 20.

construction site managers hired as many workers as possible in order to fulfill exorbitant quotas. The size of the industrial workforce doubled from 1928 to 1932, and in Moscow alone the industrial workforce grew from 186,500 to 433,900.[149] By 1930, unemployment had disappeared entirely, thus obviating the need for unemployment relief. Soviet officials abolished unemployment benefits as no longer necessary in an economy where all adults were employed, indeed where all adults were compelled to perform "socially useful labor."[150] Full employment, then, was not established as part of a welfare-state safety net in the contemporary sense of the phrase, but rather was achieved in the spirit of welfare during the interwar period when leaders sought to safeguard and harness their populations' productive capacity. Not only did the planned economy seem to represent the more effective deployment of labor, but full employment eliminated a number of social problems that had been associated with high Soviet unemployment during the 1920s.[151]

Also during the First Five-Year Plan, the Soviet government greatly expanded social welfare benefits for industrial workers. Previously Soviet pensions were not granted based on old age; elderly workers could collect pensions only if they became disabled and unable to work. At the end of the 1920s, industrial workers began to receive old-age pensions (at age fifty-five for women and sixty for men, provided they had worked twenty-five years).[152] In addition Soviet authorities increased social insurance funds for industrial workers, and following Stalin's denunciation of wage leveling in 1931, the Soviet government began to offer even higher disability benefits for shock workers and those with long work tenure.[153] At the same time, due to the continuing labor shortage, Soviet authorities

149. A. I. Vdovin and V. Z. Drobizhev, *Rost rabochego klassa SSSR, 1917–1940 gg.* (Moscow, 1976), 97; A. A. Tverdokhleb, "Chislennost' i sostav rabochego klassa Moskvy v 1917–1939 gg.," *Vestnik Moskovskogo universiteta* ser. 9, 1 (1970): 24.

150. See the end of this chapter for further discussion of the obligation to work. On forced labor, see O. V. Khlevniuk, "Prinuditel'nyi trud v ekonomike SSSR, 1929–1941 gody," *Svobodnaia mysl'* 13 (1992): 73–84.

151. On the connection between high unemployment and prostitution, see GARF f. 4085, op. 12, d. 37, l. 32; N. B. Lebina and M. V. Shkarovskii, *Prostitutsiia v Peterburge (40-e gg. XIX v.–40-e gg. XX v.)* (Moscow, 1994). For further discussion of high unemployment and its social costs in the 1920s, see William J. Chase, *Workers, Society, and the Soviet State: Labor and Life in Moscow, 1918–1929* (Urbana, 1987).

152. Chandler, *Shocking Mother Russia*, 30.

153. In his speech, "New Conditions—New Tasks of Economic Construction" (June 23, 1931), Stalin blamed wage leveling for high labor turnover. I. V. Stalin, *Sochineniia* 13 vols. (Moscow, 1946–52), vol. 13, 56–58.

denied disability benefits to workers who suffered only a minor loss in work capacity in order to induce them to keep working.[154]

During the First Five-Year Plan, the Soviet government began to administer social insurance through state-run trade unions. This process culminated in 1933 with the transfer of "all resources of social insurance" from the Commissariat of Labor (which was abolished at this time) to the All-Union Council of Trade Unions. Henceforth, workers received disability benefits through the trade union office in their factory.[155] Trade unions at this time also began to grant other types of aid, including pay for maternity leave, health resort visits, education stipends, and emergency assistance to workers unable to pay for the funeral of a family member.[156] As state-controlled institutions, Soviet trade unions did not negotiate on behalf of workers regarding wages and working conditions, but in the 1930s they did acquire this new role administering social welfare benefits.[157]

The shift of welfare resources and responsibilities to trade unions meant both a prioritizing of industrial workers' needs (over those of other social groups) and a diminished role for liberal professionals in the administration of welfare benefits. With the "Great Break" at the end of the 1920s, the place of non-Marxist specialists within the Soviet system overall became much more tenuous, as they came under attack in a range of disciplines. At the same time, the industrialization and collectivization drives marked an attempt to modernize Soviet society, partially along the lines that liberal professionals had long sought. While opposed to class militancy and state violence, many liberal professionals nonetheless welcomed the replacement of the old, backward way of life with a modern, industrialized world. Non-Party professionals played a role building this new society, serving as engineers, architects, and urban planners (as well as doctors, demographers, and educators as will be discussed in subsequent

154. Madison, *Social Welfare in the Soviet Union,* 57–58. The number of industrial accidents and injuries indeed multiplied during the First Five-Year Plan; GARF f. 5475, op. 13, d. 171, l. 96; op. 14, d. 67, l. 20.

155. GARF f. 7062, op. 1, d. 83, l. 1; G. S. Simonenko, ed., *Sotsial'noe strakhovanie v SSSR: Sbornik ofitsial'nykh materialov* (Moscow, 1971), 16–18; *Biulleten' VTsSPS* 1–2 (1934): 2.

156. Sergei Zhuravlev and Mikhail Mukhin, *"Krepost' sotsializma": Povsednevnost' i motivatsiia truda na sovetskom predpriiatii, 1928–1938 gg.* (Moscow, 2004), 162–64; Janucy K. Zawodny, "Twenty-six Interviews with Former Soviet Factory Workers," Hoover Institution Archives, I/2, I/9, II/13, II/18.

157. Never independent under the Soviet system, trade unions at the end of the 1920s lost any authority to represent workers' interests; Diane Koenker, *Republic of Labor: Russian Printers and Soviet Socialism, 1918–1930* (Ithaca, 2005), 245–59.

chapters). They thus continued to promote social welfare in the broader sense of establishing an efficient and rational way of life.

Soviet urban planners such as Leonard Sabsovich and Konstantin Melnikov drew up blueprints for well-lit and orderly streets, wide squares and boulevards, and community-oriented parks and housing complexes. They endeavored to eliminate the chaos and congestion of large cities in order to improve efficiency and also to restore harmony and interconnectedness to people's lives.[158] Professionals influenced the projects of Party leaders who paid particular attention to urban renewal in Moscow. At the recommendation of Moscow Party chief Lazar Kaganovich, the Central Committee ordered a plan for the reconstruction of the city, with Stalin reportedly overseeing the work of architects and urban planners. As part of the reconstruction plan (completed in 1935), Soviet authorities began to bulldoze the maze of market stalls and old wooden housing north of the Kremlin in order to replace them with expansive squares, wide streets, and high-rise concrete buildings.[159] Non-Party professionals also served as housing inspectors, criticizing dwellings that did not meet their standards of hygiene and design.[160] Although Soviet urban administrators hailed reconstruction efforts as a uniquely socialist project that would eliminate the fetid slums spawned by capitalism, their counterparts in capitalist countries pursued very similar programs of urban renewal, demolishing slums in favor of spacious housing, parks, and public baths.[161]

Soviet architects' and urban planners' elaborate designs often lacked the funds to be realized. The planned economy placed Party leaders in control of virtually all the country's economic resources, but they dictated that most of these resources be invested in heavy industry, leaving severe shortages in housing. Compounding the problem was the fact that the state planning agency Gosplan had substantially underestimated the rate of urbanization that would accompany the industrialization drive, and city councils had not been allocated enough money for large-scale

158. S. Frederick Starr, "Visionary Town Planning during the Cultural Revolution," *Cultural Revolution in Russia, 1928–1931,* ed. Sheila Fitzpatrick (Bloomington, 1978), 208–11. See also Anatole Kopp, *Town and Revolution: Soviet Architecture and City Planning, 1917–1935,* trans. Thomas E. Burton (New York, 1970).
159. F. E. Ian Hamilton, *The Moscow City Region* (London, 1976), 39. See also *Moskva rekonstruiuretsia: Al'bom diagramm* (Moscow, 1938).
160. GARF f. 9226, op. 1, d. 6, ll. 3–4, 16; I. Kokshaiskii, "Obespechenie kommunal'nym blagoustroistvom otdel'nykh sotsialnykh grupp naseleniia g. Moskvy," *Kommunal'noe khoziaistvo* 19/20 (1931): 44–47.
161. I. S. Romanovskii, *Moskva sotsialisticheskaia* (Moscow, 1940), 28–30; Mazower, *Dark Continent,* 89–90.

housing construction.[162] While Moscow's population doubled from 2 to 4 million people during the 1930s, the city added only 4 million square meters of housing and remained an estimated 46 million square meters short.[163] Given the severe housing shortage, industrial commissariats and factory administrations took on responsibility for housing their workers. Directors of heavy industry plants in particular commanded far more resources than city councils and began to devote millions of rubles each year to housing construction. Throughout the country, factory administrators built thousands of workers' residences to house members of their rapidly expanding workforces.[164]

Factory directors also began to provide food and clothing for their workers. Even with food rationing, Soviet stores in the 1930s often lacked the most basic staples. In August 1930, fifty Moscow factories initiated a system of closed distribution whereby they provided food and clothing in shops open only to workers at those factories. By the end of the year, this system of "closed workers' cooperatives" had spread to industrial enterprises around the country.[165] At the Central Committee Plenum of December 1930, Party leaders endorsed this system as a model for food distribution, and factory managers across the country subsequently organized "departments of worker provisionment" to procure and distribute goods.[166] Given the deficiencies of the food supply network, enterprise directors even established their own agricultural and livestock-raising operations in order to ensure a steady flow of food to their workers.[167] In this manner, state enterprises assumed responsibility for the most basic functions of workers' well-being.

The result of these developments was a further expansion of state provision, going far beyond typical social welfare functions such as

162. TsAGM f. 150, op. 5, d. 36, l. 57.

163. TsAGM f. 126, op. 10, d. 47, l. 16; John Hazard, *Soviet Housing Law* (New Haven, 1939), 16; *Statisticheskii spravochnik po zhilishchno-kommunal'nomu khoziaistvu g. Moskvy* (Moscow, 1939), 9–10.

164. RGAE f. 7622, op. 1, d. 251, l. 2; TsAGM f. 176, op. 4, d. 4, ll. 15–16; TsAOPIM f. 468, op. 1, d. 102, ll. 58, 72.

165. Amy Randall, *The Soviet Dream World of Retail Trade and Consumption in the 1930s* (New York, 2008), chapter 1. On closed stores for the Party elite, see Sheila Fitzpatrick, *Everyday Stalinism, Ordinary Life in Extraordinary Times: Soviet Russia in the 1930s* (New York, 2000), 55–56, 97.

166. Julie Hessler, *A Social History of Soviet Trade: Trade Policy, Retail Practices, and Consumption, 1917–1953* (Princeton, 2004), 178–79.

167. RGAE f. 7676, op. 1, d. 610, l. 33; TsAGM f. 1289, op. 1, d. 861, l. 3; GARF f. 7952, op. 3, d. 560, l. 37.

unemployment relief and pensions. While workers still had to pay for food and housing, they received guaranteed rations and living quarters subsidized by the state. This expanded state role in provision of food and housing was a direct consequence of Party leaders' decision to outlaw free trade and establish a planned economy. State control of all economic resources allowed them to prioritize funding for industrial enterprises and their workers. The distribution of funding was directed by Gosplan through industrial commissariats and ultimately through state-run factories. The fact that state enterprises began to supply workers' food and housing had the effect, over time, of tying workers to their place of work.[168] State responsibility for workers' welfare, both through state-run enterprises and state-run trade unions, became a permanent feature of the Soviet system.

Despite factory directors' efforts to guarantee their workers food and housing, living standards fell sharply during the First Five-Year Plan, and only gradually began to recover during the Second Five-Year Plan. Millions of new workers from the countryside crammed into communal apartments or into hastily constructed residences and barracks that lacked indoor plumbing and adequate heat.[169] Though workers did not starve, as many peasants did in 1932–33, their diets deteriorated as supplies of meat and vegetables dwindled.[170] Workers' misery points to a fundamental contradiction of the Soviet project—though allegedly prioritizing workers' well-being, Soviet leaders created horrendous living and working conditions in their rush to industrialize the country. Although workers were guaranteed food through their factories' closed shops, their living standards fell precipitously nonetheless. Between 1928 and 1937, the real wages of Moscow workers fell by more than one-third.[171] As Party leaders channeled virtually all resources into building steel mills, living conditions, even in Moscow, suffered severely.[172]

168. On high rates of labor turnover that declined somewhat by the mid-1930s, see RGASPI f. 17, op. 116, d. 30, l. 82; Ia. Kats, "Tekuchest rabochei sily v krupnoi promyshlennosti," *Plan* 9 (1937): 21.

169. TsAGM f. 214, op. 1, d. 122, l. 9; *Biulleten' Narkomata kommunal'nogo khoziaistva* 6 (1935): 96; V. V. Ermilov, *Byt rabochei kazarmy* (Moscow/Leningrad, 1930), 13.

170. RGASPI f. 17, op. 114, d. 255, l. 33; d. 256, l. 68; *Trud*, July 2, 1931, 1; E. A. Osokina, *Ierarkhiia potrebleniia: O zhizni liudei v usloviiakh stalinskogo snabzheniia, 1928–1935 gg.* (Moscow, 1993), 23.

171. A. A. Tverdokhleb, "Material'noe blagosostoianie rabochego klassa Moskvy v 1917–1939 gg." (Ph.D. diss., Moscow State University, 1970), 331–32, 360–61.

172. On the food supply priority assigned to Moscow and other large industrial cities, see Osokina, *Ierarkhiia potrebleniia*, 16.

What made their decline in living standards tolerable for many industrial workers was the fact that they received priority over all other social groups. Soviet state provision during the first half of the 1930s was administered on a highly differentiated, class basis. Given the extreme scarcity of food, housing, and material goods, Party leaders expanded state provision for some and further restricted it for others. "Class alien elements," already denied social insurance benefits, now could not work in state enterprises, join trade unions, or live in state-owned housing. And when food rationing was introduced in 1929, these people were also denied ration cards.[173] Industrial workers, on the other hand, received top priority for food rations, housing, and other benefits, including disability insurance and health care.[174]

Prior to 1936, the Soviet welfare system excluded those labeled bourgeois. But the new constitution issued that year extended all rights, including the right to work and the right to receive old age and disability pensions, to all Soviet citizens.[175] This shift was not an act of generosity on the part of Party leaders but rather a reflection of their belief that they had eliminated the bourgeois classes. In their minds, the abolition of private property and capitalism meant the end of the bourgeoisie. The forcible expropriation of the properties of NEPmen and kulaks, combined with labor camp terms for many of them, had either reformed or removed from society these "class alien elements." Politburo member Viacheslav Molotov, speaking at the Eighth All-Union Congress of Soviets, justified the new constitution's extension of rights by declaring that alien social origin no longer prevented people from loyally serving the Soviet government.[176] Soviet welfare policy thus evolved in accordance with Party leaders' ideologically informed understanding of historical progress. Once they had eliminated capitalism and its agents, they shifted from a class-based, discriminatory framework to a universalized social welfare system.

Not only did the Soviet government extend welfare benefits to the entire population, it also continued to broaden the scope of benefits. The 1936 Constitution ensured all Soviet citizens the right to security in old age, so that white collar workers as well as industrial workers began to

---

173. Alexopoulos, *Stalin's Outcasts*, 28–29.

174. *Ekonomicheskoe stroitel'stvo* 7/8 (1930): 17–19. On ration categories, see also R.W. Davies, *The Soviet Economy in Turmoil, 1929–1930* (Basingstoke, 1989), 289–98; Osokina, *Ierarkhiia potrebleniia*, 15–24.

175. *Istoriia sovetskoi konstitutsii: Sbornik dokumentov, 1917–1957* (Moscow, 1957), 356–58; *Sovetskaia iustitsiia* 19 (1936): 6.

176. *Pravda*, November 30, 1936, 2.

receive pensions upon retirement.[177] While still short of resources in the mid-1930s, the Commissariat of Social Security was paying pensions to the elderly and handicapped. It also operated an extensive network of invalid homes and training centers for the disabled, a network that the government continued to expand throughout the rest of the decade.[178] During the Second Five-Year Plan, Party leaders sought to increase the availability of food and housing as well. In September 1935, the Central Committee decreed an end to food rationing.[179] Enterprise administrators continued to maintain special stores for their employees, though ration coupons were no longer required. And factory directors continued to construct housing as well, so that the housing shortage eased slightly.[180]

By the late 1930s, the Soviet system had become one version—an authoritarian and all-encompassing version—of the welfare state, where the government assumed all functions of providing for the population. It guaranteed workers a job, retirement pension, sickness and disability insurance, free health care, and subsidized food and housing. There had been no master plan for the creation of the Soviet welfare state, but neither was the establishment of the Soviet welfare system coincidental. Party leaders embraced a broad concept of social welfare whereby the government would guarantee workers' wellbeing. They envisioned a modern, industrialized economy, administered by the Soviet state so as to fashion a rational and productive society, a vision shared by many non-Party specialists.[181] Stalin and his supporters in the Party leadership

177. Nikolai Aleksandrovich Semashko, *Pravo na sotsial'noe obespechenie* (Moscow, 1938), 23–34; Madison, *Social Welfare in the Soviet Union*, 57. See also I. V. Khokhlachev and S. Shcherbin-Samoilov, *Uchet i otchetnost' po gos. sotsial'nomu strakhovaniiu* (Moscow, 1940). Elderly peasants were to be supported by their collective farms and were not included in the Soviet pension system until 1964.

178. RGAE f. 1562, op. 18, d. 53, ll. 5, 11–12; M. A. Shaburov, *Sovetskaia vlast' obespechila schastlivuiu i spokoinuiu starost'* (Moscow, 1937), 28. For further discussion of Soviet welfare benefits, see Maria Cristina Galmarini, "'Right to be Helped': Welfare Policies and Notions of Rights at the Margins of Soviet Society (1917–1950)" (Ph.D. diss., University of Illinois, forthcoming).

179. *Resheniia Partii i pravitel'stva po khoziaistvennym voprosam: Sbornik dokumentov za 50 let, 1917–1966 gg.* (Moscow, 1967–1985), vol. 2, 547.

180. Tverdokhleb, "Material'noe blagosostoianie," 307–8, 454, 484; Osokina, *Ierarkhiia potrebleniia*, 39.

181. Nikolai Bukharin and E. Preobrazhensky depicted the future Soviet economy and society as "a well-order machine." N. Bukharin and E. Preobrazhensky, *The ABC of Communism*, trans. E. and C. Paul (London, 1969), 118. Non-Party statisticians saw the Revolution as their chance to build a rational social order based scientific knowledge; Blum and Mespoulet, *L'anarchie bureaucratique*, 35. On specialists, see also Alessandro

espoused the violent expropriation of "bourgeois elements" and the establishment of a planned economy as the means to realize this vision, as well as to eradicate capitalism and mobilize resources for national defense.

Because state control of the economy was so central to the expansion of Soviet welfare, it is worthwhile placing the Soviet planned economy within the broader context of international economic thought of the interwar period. The fact that the Soviet welfare system took shape within a noncapitalist, state-run economy made it distinctive, both in the scope of government intervention and in the overtly ideological nature of its policies. But a large state role in the economy was not unique to the Soviet Union, and in fact Party leaders borrowed heavily from the German World War I economic model. During the war, the governments of all major combatants had expanded state economic control, with the German government going as far as universal labor conscription in late 1916.[182] Future Bolshevik planning enthusiast Iurii Larin had greatly admired Germany's wartime economy as an example of how a state could mobilize social resources, and he wrote a series of influential articles lauding the "centralized direction" and planning of the German economy.[183] Once in power, Party leaders had little theoretical guidance for constructing a socialist economy, given that Marx had provided only the vaguest outline of how to organize economic life after a successful proletarian revolution. Lenin, who had been inspired by Larin's articles, adopted an approach to state planning

Stanziani, *L'économie en revolution: Le cas russe, 1870–1930* (Paris, 1998); Kendall E. Bailes, *Technology and Society under Lenin and Stalin* (Princeton, 1978).

182. Lewis H. Siegelbaum, *The Politics of Industrial Mobilization in Russia, 1914–1917: A Study of the War-Industries Committees* (London, 1983), x–xi. On Britain's Defense of the Realm Act, which gave the government power to control key sectors of the economy, see Keith Laybourn, *The Evolution of British Social Policy and the Welfare State* (Keele, 1995), 186. On Germany, see Geyer, "The Militarization of Europe, 1914–1945," and Gerald D. Feldman, *Army, Industry, and Labor in Germany, 1914–1918* (Princeton, 1966). The German government and the Russian Provisional Government established grain monopolies during the war and even deployed military units to requisition grain, as did the Austrian government; Lars T. Lih, *Bread and Authority in Russia: 1914–1921* (Berkeley, 1990), 83, 128; Holquist, *Making War,* 33, 96. The Ottoman government similarly founded a central food supply apparatus; van Os, "Taking Care of Soldiers' Families," 102.

183. E. H. Carr, *The Bolshevik Revolution,* vol. 2 (London, 1952), 359–60. Menshevik leader Vladimir Groman, who was to play a major role in Gosplan during the 1920s, followed Larin's reports closely and became a strong proponent of economic planning; Holquist, *Making War,* 38–39. Russia's own wartime economy included the War-Industries Committees, modeled on German war boards and the British Ministry of Munitions; Siegelbaum, *The Politics of Industrial Mobilization,* 48–49.

consciously based on the German wartime model.[184] Trotsky promoted economic planning even more vigorously and pushed for the establishment of Soviet economic planning organs (Vesenkha and Gosplan).[185]

Soviet leaders' enthusiasm for state economic planning was part of a more general move toward government economic control in the wake of the First World War. Many progressive economists in the United States saw government coordination and planning as necessary to meet the challenges of the modern industrial era. Economist Thorstein Veblen believed that wartime regulatory agencies could be used after the war in order to rid American capitalism of wastefulness caused by profit-seeking. He and his follower Stuart Chase called for strong state economic intervention guided by experts as a means to improve the material welfare of the population and promote social peace. Both admired Soviet economic planning, and Chase traveled to Moscow in 1927 where he praised the Soviet state planning agency.[186] Rexford Tugwell, future member of Franklin Roosevelt's New Deal brain trust, accompanied Chase on his trip and credited Soviet economic planning for the country's stabilization. Following the onset of the Great Depression, Tugwell went further in his praise for the Soviet system and wrote that "the future is becoming visible in Russia."[187]

With the launching of the Five-Year Plans and the Soviet Union's rapid industrial progress, worldwide interest in the Soviet planned economy grew more intense. Following the visit of a Soviet economic delegation, the Turkish government in 1933 announced its own Five-Year Plan, largely based on the delegation's recommendations for industrial development.[188] Nazi officials took great interest in Soviet economic planning and saw themselves in intense competition to match the pace of Soviet

---

184. Lenin labeled the German wartime economy "state capitalism," what he saw as the last line of defense of the capitalist order, and stated that, by contrast, the Soviet planned economy would be an instrument for the transition to socialism; Carr, *The Bolshevik Revolution*, 361.

185. Ibid., 364–74.

186. David Engerman, *Modernization from the Other Shore: American Intellectuals and the Romance of Russian Development* (Cambridge, Mass., 2003), 155–62. During the Great Depression, Chase called for a National Planning Board that would issue "ukases" (from the Russian word *ukaz*) on public works, old age pensions, and agricultural regulation (all of which were partially realized in the New Deal).

187. Peter G. Filene, *Americans and the Soviet Experiment, 1917–1933* (Cambridge, Mass., 1967), 198–99. See also Maurizio Vaudagna, "A Checkered History: The New Deal, Democracy, and Totalitarianism in Transatlantic Welfare States," *The American Century in Europe*, ed. R. Laurence Moore and Maurizio Vaudagna (Ithaca, 2003): 219–42.

188. Erik J. Zürcher, *Turkey: A Modern History*, rev. ed. (New York, 2004), 206.

development.[189] Previously most Russian intellectuals had looked to "the West," but now the flow of ideas seemed to go in the opposite direction. The Soviet Union was no longer just an inspiration for revolutionary socialists—it also represented a new economic archetype with which capitalist leaders had to contend.

Of course what boosted the Soviet model's allure was the fact that its success coincided with a grave crisis of the capitalist order. The failings of classical economic liberalism in the face of the Great Depression compelled many social thinkers to search for alternatives. The Great Depression also reinforced sentiments that new forms of economic and social organization were required in the machine age. While in most countries factories lay idle and workers suffered unemployment, in the Soviet Union hundreds of new factories were being built and all workers had a job. The Soviet planned economy offered a way forward—a purposeful deployment of human resources that would allegedly allow workers to enjoy the fruits of their own labor. That the Soviet government, in theory, protected the welfare of workers at the same time that it marshaled the country's resources, enhanced its appeal even further. In other countries too, state economic intervention was matched by the expansion of government welfare programs. Some political leaders proposed welfare programs specifically to forestall unrest or to confront the economic exigencies of the era. This had been true of Prime Minister David Lloyd George's 1919 warning that "the State" needed to solve the British housing shortage to counter the threat of Bolshevism.[190] And in fact the British government subsidized the construction of 1.5 million housing units for workers during the interwar period.[191]

In addition to more immediate political concerns, state officials in many countries expanded welfare to safeguard what they saw as their country's human capital. The Japanese government, for example, replaced the preexisting mélange of private charities with state programs. In 1920 the Japanese Home Ministry created the Bureau of Social Affairs to handle poor relief, veterans' assistance, and children's welfare, and in 1938 the Japanese war cabinet formed the Ministry of Health and Welfare.[192] Particularly

189. Hitler's 1936 memorandum on the German Four-Year Plan (announced later that year) stated that Germany must take the same economic planning measures as Russia in order to prepare for war; J. Adam Tooze, *The Wages of Destruction: The Making and Breaking of the Nazi Economy* (New York, 2006), 222–23.

190. PRO Cab 23/9 War Cabinet 539, 4–5.

191. Laybourn, *Evolution of British Social Policy*, 202.

192. Garon, *Molding Japanese Minds*, 49–58.

during the 1930s, military preparedness weighed heavily in the decisions of many countries' leaders to expand welfare.

In contrast to the welfare state after 1945, welfare provision during the interwar period was not justified in terms of the protection of individual or human rights. The international consensus in defense of human rights emerged only as a reaction to Nazism and the Second World War. Instead what motivated authorities prior to the war was a desire to defend against the degeneration of the population, the nation, or the race.[193] Anxiety about degeneration dated from the late nineteenth century, but it took on an increasingly social Darwinist cast with the rising international tensions of interwar Europe. Some commentators and political leaders saw the reinvigoration of their population as necessary for their country to assert or defend itself in an increasingly hostile world. Welfare programs, then, were primarily a tool to maintain the vitality of the collective, rather than a means to preserve the dignity of individuals.

The fact that the Soviet Union, as well as several other countries, required all citizens to work helps to illustrate this point. From 1930 on, the Soviet government guaranteed everyone a job, but it also denied the right not to work. Labor was therefore both a right and an obligation. Refusal to perform "socially useful labor" could result in arrest and confinement to a labor camp. In a similar vein, the Italian government in 1927 issued a work charter that declared labor to be the "social duty" of all citizens.[194] The Weimar constitution contained an article that stated, "Every German has the moral obligation, his personal freedom notwithstanding, to exercise his mental and physical powers in a manner required by the welfare of all."[195] The Nazi regime implemented a more coercive program to induce everyone to work. During the 1938 Reich Campaign against the Work-shy, Nazi authorities rounded up those not gainfully employed and imprisoned them in labor camps.[196]

193. Mazower, *Dark Continent*, 103, 298–99.

194. Horn, *Social Bodies*, 40. While it did not act on the idea, the British government's 1904 Inter-Departmental Commission on Physical Deterioration had concluded that the government might have to set up "labour colonies" in which to incarcerate people "incapable of independent existence up to the standard of decency which it imposes." See PRO Parliamentary Papers, 1904, Microfiche 110.279, 85.

195. Quoted in Peukert, *Weimar Republic*, 131.

196. Lisa Pine, *Nazi Family Policy, 1933–1945* (New York, 1997), 118. Nazi officials described those incarcerated as "alien," "socially unfit," and characterized by their "inability to be useful to the life of the community" (120).

According to this ethos, most fully realized in authoritarian regimes, states had to provide for the welfare of their citizens, while their citizens were compelled to contribute to the collective and the state. The expansion of state welfare programs was part of this set of reciprocal responsibilities between citizens and the state, based on the idea that the well-being, and perhaps even the survival, of each was inextricably linked.[197] State welfare in interwar Europe was predicated on trends discussed earlier in this chapter—notions of the common good, the rise of popular sovereignty, social science, and the social realm. But the welfare programs instituted in various countries were not an automatic extension of prior developments. Instead they were forged by the political, economic, and military exigencies of the interwar conjuncture.

Even within this general interwar trend toward state intervention to safeguard the social body and mobilize for war, particular strands of nineteenth-century social thought were adopted in some countries and rejected in others. Liberal democratic governments, while focused on maintaining the nation's collective strength, instituted welfare programs open to all citizens. Fascist governments emphasized the defense of the nation and the race, reserving welfare benefits for their majorities, while persecuting ethnic and racial minorities. Soviet leaders rejected biological and racial criteria as the basis for social welfare programs. Instead, they implemented a class-based system that privileged workers and excluded "bourgeois elements," until the time when, according to official ideology, the bourgeoisie no longer existed and welfare benefits could be universalized.

The Soviet system, then, was not the logical extreme of the European welfare state. Soviet welfare programs were one version of welfare-state policies, following general principles of the rational ordering of society and state-responsibility for the population's well-being, but also adhering to a class-based ideology. The Soviet welfare state was also shaped by Party leaders' rejection of private property and free market capitalism. In the context of an entirely state-run economy and extremely rapid industrialization, the Soviet state created the equivalent of a wartime economy, where the state took control of all resources and also, through state-run

197. In contrast to the tsarist government, which traditionally defined subjects in relation to their sovereign and estate, the Soviet government defined citizens in relation to the state and the social whole. See Pinnow, *Lost to the Collective*, 14; Yanni Kotsonis, "'No Place to Go': Taxation and State Transformation in Late Imperial and Early Soviet Russia," *Journal of Modern History* 76 (September 2004): 575–77.

enterprises, assumed full responsibility for workers' provision and welfare.

The Soviet system thus provided one answer to the "social question" that had arisen in nineteenth-century Europe. It eliminated unemployment, compelled all citizens to perform socially useful labor, guaranteed workers affordable food and housing, and ended class antagonism through the violent expropriation of the bourgeoisie. It also created a planned economy that mobilized the country's natural and human resources to accelerate industrial development and bolster military strength. It accomplished what Soviet leaders believed to be a rational reordering of society to ensure economic productivity and social harmony. At the same time it was not a technocratic regime that placed scientific organization above ideological goals. Whereas technocrats elsewhere asserted their nonpolitical technical competence, in the Soviet Union specialist intervention was explicitly a political endeavor, geared to furthering the country's progress toward socialism and communism.

2 Public Health

War is a stern taskmaster. . . . It has forced us to face our man-power
problem with the close intensity which only a struggle for national
existence can evoke. It has compelled us to take stock of the health
and physique of our manhood; this stock-taking has brought us
face to face with ugly facts and—one hopes—awoken us from the
half-hearted complacency with which in the past we have treated our
most important national asset, the health of the nation.
—Report by the British Ministry of National Service, 1919

The human species . . . will once more enter into a state of radical
transformation, and, in its own hands, will become an object of
the most complicated methods of artificial selection and psycho-
physical training. . . . Man will become immeasurably stronger, wiser
and subtler; his body will become more harmonized, his movements
more rhythmic, his voice more musical.
—LEV TROTSKY, *Literature and Revolution*, 1924

The Soviet health care system was considered one of the defining features
of Soviet socialism. Shortly after coming to power in 1917, the Bolsheviks
instituted a highly centralized state health system based on principles of social medicine. These principles, articulated at the Eighth Communist Party
Congress in 1919, included free and universal health care, improved nutrition and sanitation, prevention of contagious diseases, and treatment of
"social diseases (tuberculosis, venereal diseases, alcoholism, and the like)."[1]
Soviet officials approached health as a state concern, one that justified extensive services and intervention to guarantee the bodily capacity of the
population. The Soviet health care system contrasted sharply with the array
of private, philanthropic, and zemstvo medical services of the tsarist era.

At first glance, one might assume that this new type of centralized state
health care system was the product of socialist ideology. Soviet socialism,

---

1. As quoted in Mark Field, *Soviet Socialized Medicine* (New York, 1967), 59–60.

with its militant anticapitalism and concern for the welfare of the working class, certainly lent itself to state-run social medicine. Yet it is difficult to establish socialist ideology as the sole or even primary impetus for the Soviet health care system. Lenin and other Bolshevik leaders did not have well-developed ideas about health care prior to the October Revolution. At the Russian social democratic congress in 1903, for example, delegates made only general proclamations about the need to improve workers' health through the amelioration of factory conditions.[2] As late as the summer of 1917 the Bolsheviks had only general proposals concerning expanded medical care for workers, and these proposals differed little from those of other political parties. Instead, non-Party physicians active in zemstvo medicine provided the ideas and much of the leadership in the establishment of Soviet health care.[3]

If we place Soviet medicine in comparative context, we cast further doubt on the uniqueness of state-run social medicine to socialist ideology. Many capitalist countries instituted very similar health care principles and practices at the same historical moment as did the Soviet Union. Social medicine and centralized state health care were part of more general trends away from individualist approaches to health and toward state-administered preventative medicine. Throughout Europe, and in countries around the world, expert interventions and state management of society became increasingly accepted in the late nineteenth century and emerged full-blown during the First World War.

Soviet health care is best understood by placing it in this broader framework that includes the rise of social medicine and the dramatic expansion of the state's role as guarantor of public health. To demonstrate that Soviet health policy reflected these more general trends, I will discuss the rise of social medicine, the establishment of state ministries of health, and the concrete mechanisms by which medical ideas and techniques were transmitted during the interwar period. Although Soviet public health reflected approaches common to other countries, it also had a number of distinctive features. As historians of medicine have demonstrated, similar ideas and practices could take different forms depending on the political, social, and disciplinary context in which they were applied.[4] The strong nurturist

2. Don K. Rowney, *Transition to Technocracy: The Structural Origins of the Soviet Administrative State* (Ithaca, 1989), 83–84.

3. John F. Hutchinson, *Politics and Public Health in Revolutionary Russia, 1890–1918* (Baltimore, 1990), 162, 185–95.

4. Susan Gross Solomon, "Circulation of Knowledge and the Russian Locale," *Kritika* 9:1 (winter 2008): 9–26. Solomon points out that the international circulation of

tradition in Russian social science, reinforced by Marxist ideology, resulted in an emphasis within Soviet public health on environmental factors. The highly politicized character of Soviet medicine was also significant, particularly during the First Five-Year Plan. And Soviet physical culture, under the influence of international trends, became increasingly militaristic by the late 1930s, though it also manifested distinctive Soviet principles regarding gender and ethnicity.

Social Medicine and the State

Social medicine is an approach to medical care that emphasizes public health and hygiene, prevention and control of communicable diseases, and universal health services. The rise of social medicine in the late nineteenth and early twentieth centuries reflected new conceptions of society—the social body—and new developments within medicine itself, including epidemiology and social hygiene. References to the social body date from the writings of ancient Greek philosophers, but beginning in the nineteenth century corporeal metaphors became commonly used to support new technologies of social intervention throughout Europe.[5] Social science disciplines such as economics and sociology, and later anthropology and criminology, shifted the traditional metaphoric relationship between the individual and the social body to an argument that there existed an actual correlation between the two. With the growing authority of science, and of physiology in particular, corporeal metaphors came to pervade discussions of how to organize and improve societies. A range of nineteenth-century social thinkers, such as Herbert Spencer and Adolphe Quetelet, invoked the social body as part of their analysis.[6] And the identification of very real linkages between social problems and biological and physiological specializations intensified in the late nineteenth century. To take the example of epidemiology, when medical professionals learned about the spread of tuberculosis in the 1880s, government officials and doctors alike adopted a more collectivist and interventionist approach to disease prevention and hygiene. Epidemiologists called for medical surveillance,

---

knowledge can lead not only to the evolution of ideas depending on the political and social context but to changes in the context itself based on the importation of new ideas.

5. David G. Horn, *Social Bodies: Science, Reproduction, and Italian Modernity* (Princeton, 1994), 14–25.

6. Theodore M. Porter, *The Rise of Statistical Thinking, 1820–1900* (Princeton, 1986), 56, 68.

public hygiene programs, and other technocratic strategies to control the spread of diseases.[7] Thus the health or sickness of individuals came to represent a threat to the larger body social in a way it had not for the body politic.[8]

Representing all individuals in society as a single body reduced them to a passive aggregate and justified highly normative assessments of people's work habits, sexual behavior, and personal hygiene.[9] These judgments were directed in particular against the urban lower classes and were used to justify greater government control.[10] Corporeal metaphors also invited the utilization of physiological concepts to describe function and hierarchy in society. Once government officials, social reformers, and urban planners had identified the functions served by parts of the social body, they felt confident in prescribing measures to improve those parts in ways that would benefit the whole.[11] Science as such was not responsible for these practices; rather, science provided a paradigm for practices that states employed in pursuing political ends. Increasingly, toward the end of the century, a consensus developed that the health and welfare of the population was best protected by enforcement of behavioral norms dictated by experts, and that these norms were clearly a matter of state interest and ultimately national security.

Of course, public health concerns predated the nineteenth century. Governments in Europe took an array of actions against the plague, beginning with quarantines imposed by Mediterranean cities in the fourteenth century. By the seventeenth and eighteenth centuries, French authorities created health boards that cordoned off towns, fumigated possessions, and

7. A 1890s diagnostic test for tuberculosis revealed that 95 percent of the German population had traces of the bacillus; P. Weindling, *Health, Race, and German Politics between National Unification and Nazism, 1870–1945* (Cambridge, 1989), 163. Weindling notes that even some "liberals" became strong advocates of state intervention (155).

8. Mary Poovey, *Making a Social Body: British Cultural Formation, 1830–1864* (Chicago, 1995), 7–8. Poovey traces modern British use of the term *social body* to Adam Smith's phrase "great body of the people" referring to the laboring poor. By the late nineteenth century, "social body" came increasingly to displace the earlier understanding of a "body politic."

9. Ibid., 74–86.

10. Gareth Stedman Jones argues that views of the poor shifted from a model of "demoralization" in the 1860s to one of "degeneration" in the 1880s; Gareth Stedman Jones, *Outcast London: A Study in the Relationship between Classes in Victorian Society* (New York, 1984), chapter 16.

11. Paul Rabinow, *French Modern: Norms and Forms of the Social Environment* (Cambridge, Mass., 1989), 10–11.

occasionally razed entire neighborhoods.[12] Following cameralist principles about the importance of a large and healthy labor force, the Swedish government in the 1760s began to establish hospitals and oversee assistance for the sick, while at the same time Austrian physicians developed plans for a medical police to safeguard the population's health as an economic resource.[13] But the late nineteenth century marked a new epoch in public health, characterized by dramatic advances in bacteriology and rapid expansion of government health interventions. In France the government assumed a particularly prominent public health role, due to republican ideology of the Third Republic, the prestige of Louis Pasteur, and the influence of solidarism.[14] Government health officials in late-nineteenth-century Germany also extended their reach, for example when they founded state sanatoria and administered public health campaigns in the battle to prevent and treat tuberculosis.[15]

To political leaders and social reformers throughout Europe, medical science and technocratic health management offered a means to improve the vigor of the population. Social medicine and social science more generally, as elaborated by experts and enforced by government bureaucrats, represented a superordinate authority that provided incontestable solutions to social problems. Moreover, politicians throughout Europe increasingly came to value the population's health as an important economic and military resource. When, for example, in late-nineteenth-century France the rejection rates of military recruits reached as high as 60–75 percent in some regions, French social thinkers and political leaders sought ways to stem the physical "degeneration" of the population.[16]

The rise of public health in imperial Russia followed a similar path to, and indeed was heavily influenced by, developments in other European countries. After visiting medical centers in Amsterdam and Paris, Peter the Great opened Russia's first hospital in 1706 and brought Dutch doctors to provide instruction there.[17] Catherine the Great drew on European

12. Peter Baldwin, *Contagion and the State in Europe, 1830–1930* (New York, 1999), 559–60.

13. Karin Johannisson, "The People's Health: Public Health Policies in Sweden," *The History of Public Health and the Modern State*, ed. Dorothy Porter (Amsterdam, 1994), 167; Dorothy Porter, "Introduction," *History of Public Health*, 6.

14. Matthew Ramsey, "Public Health in France," *History of Public Health*, 70–77.

15. Weindling, *Health, Race, and German Politics*, 177–78.

16. William H. Schneider, *Quality and Quantity: The Quest for Biological Regeneration in Twentieth-Century France* (Cambridge, 1990), 16.

17. Tricia Starks, *The Body Soviet: Propaganda, Hygiene, and the Revolutionary State* (Madison, 2008), 41. Prior to Peter the Great, the Muscovite government had a small

models in establishing institutions of public health, and she also laid the legislative foundations for policing public behavior and moral standards.[18] In the nineteenth century, Russian physicians followed Western European physicians who emphasized social medicine. In fact, the first holder of the chair of hygiene at Moscow University was a Swiss-born doctor, Friedrich Erismann, who throughout his 1869–96 career in Russia stressed that disease was a social problem. The majority of Russian doctors shared this view, which fit well with the ethos of the 1860s intelligentsia, committed as they were to social welfare and science.[19] Erismann's wife, Nadezha Suslova, and many other Russian doctors had populist political leanings and sought to combine medicine with social action to improve the lives of the peasantry.[20]

A strong tradition of socially oriented zemstvo medicine developed in the latter part of the nineteenth century. Many zemstvo doctors, including most prominently Dmitrii Zhbankov, the executive director of the Pirogov Society (the leading organization of zemstvo physicians), opposed private medical practice and instead advocated socially oriented medicine. S. N. Ignumnov stated at the 1910 Pirogov Congress that a zemstvo doctor is "a physician sociologist who has the broad masses of the population for the object of his study and activity, and not a physician-individualist who is interested only in a particular sick organism."[21] Although zemstvo physicians' social orientation paralleled that of other European doctors, the situation in Russia was complicated by their opposition to the tsarist autocracy and their conviction that health care was best administered through community medicine. In other European countries, the attitudes and programs of state health officials and socially oriented physicians tended to complement each other, but in Russia government bureaucrats and

---

Apothecary Department (Aptekarskii Prikaz), one of more than 130 departments or chancelleries established in the course of the seventeenth century; see Peter B. Brown, "Bureaucratic Administration in Seventeenth-Century Russia," *Modernizing Muscovy: Reform and Social Change in Seventeenth-Century Russia,* ed. Jarmo Kotilaine and Marshall Poe (New York, 2004), 57–78.

18. Laura Engelstein, *The Keys to Happiness: Sex and the Search for Modernity in Fin-de-Siècle Russia* (Ithaca, 1992), 85. See also John T. Alexander, "Catherine the Great and Public Health," *Journal of the History of Medicine* 36:2 (1981): 185–204.

19. Engelstein, *Keys to Happiness,* 174.

20. Elizabeth A. Hachten, "Science in the Service of Society: Bacteriology, Medicine, and Hygiene in Russia, 1855–1907" (Ph.D. diss., University of Wisconsin, 1991), 255–62.

21. John F. Hutchinson, "Who Killed Cock Robin? An Inquiry into the Death of Zemstvo Medicine," *Health and Society in Revolutionary Russia,* eds. Susan Gross Solomon and John F. Hutchinson (Bloomington, 1990), 9–11.

zemstvo physicians remained highly distrustful of one another. Tsarist officials were suspicious of any nonstate programs—indeed the zemstvos were
virtually the only outlet for any local initiative—and zemstvo physicians,
far from seeing the autocracy as a possible ally in the battle to improve
public health, saw the tsar and his bureaucrats as an impediment to the
population's well-being.[22]

Within the tsarist government, however, sentiment was building for
the establishment of some sort of state health administration. In 1836 the
Ministry of Internal Affairs had created its medical department, which
established a system of provincial medical boards.[23] In the second half of
the nineteenth century, a group of bureaucrats in the Ministry of Internal
Affairs' medical department argued for an independent ministry of health.
And following an embarrassing discussion of conditions in Russia at the
1885 International Sanitary Conference, a Russian commission on the improvement of sanitary conditions recommended a separate government
health administration. In both cases, leaders of the Ministry of Internal
Affairs opposed an independent ministry of health and blocked these proposals.[24] But this sentiment remained and would eventually come to fruition during the First World War.

At the same time a new breed of physicians emerged who shared zemstvo physicians' orientation toward social medicine but who sought more
professionalized and less populist avenues through which to practice it.
One spokesperson for this new orientation, A. N. Sysin, depicted the ideal
sanitary physician as a technical specialist, similar to engineers and town
planners, who would benefit the common people through large-scale, tech-
nically advanced programs, rather than through the daily clinical contact
of zemstvo physicians.[25] A leading Russian bacteriologist, Il'ia Mechnikov,
pressed for bacteriological and epidemiological measures as the most effective means of combating disease. By the 1890s bacteriology and epidemiology flourished as fields in Russia, and physicians increasingly adopted
technocratic approaches in their practices.[26]

22. See Samuel C. Ramer, "The Zemstvo and Public Health," *The Zemstvo in Russia:
An Experiment in Local Self-Government,* eds. Terence Emmons and Wayne S. Vucinich
(Cambridge, 1982), 279–314.
23. Rowney, *Transition to Technocracy,* 25–26; Hachten, "Science in the Service of
Society," 41.
24. Hutchinson, *Politics and Public Health in Revolutionary Russia,* 82.
25. Hutchinson, "Who Killed Cock Robin?" 9–11.
26. Hachten, "Science in the Service of Society," 269, 288, 340.

Many of these physicians were trained in epidemiology and saw the efforts of zemstvo physicians in individual villages as powerless to combat the spread of epidemics across entire regions of the country. The cholera epidemic of 1892–93 demonstrated the inadequacy of community efforts, and the central government empowered sanitary commissions to override the control of provincial and zemstvo health authorities. In the epidemic's aftermath, Pirogov Society members themselves proposed more sweeping programs for hygiene education, factory medicine, and epidemiological research.[27] Centralized coordination of health programs continued to gain ground in the early twentieth century. In 1910, physicians founded a nongovernmental organization called the All-Russian League for the Fight against Tuberculosis, modeled on nationwide organizations in other countries such as the National Tuberculosis Association in the United States. Members of the league saw a need, particularly given the tsarist autocracy's inaction, to combat infectious disease on a nationwide level.[28]

By the late nineteenth and early twentieth centuries, then, physicians and public health officials in Russia and elsewhere had come to see a need for centralized health care, and many advocated a greater role for the state. Throughout the world, state health programs expanded dramatically at this time. In Egypt, administrators began to view the population's physical wellness as a state objective and increased the state's role in public health.[29] In response to an outbreak of smallpox in the South Pacific, the New Zealand Central Board of Health was created in 1876, and by 1901 it was expanded into a ministry of health. Several Latin American countries established national departments of health and hygiene within their ministries of internal affairs, including Argentina in 1880, Brazil in 1897, and Chile in 1918. Administrators in Thailand similarly founded the Division of Public Health within the interior ministry in 1918.[30]

The First World War dramatically increased both the number of health problems and the awareness of the need to maintain a healthy population

---

27. Nancy M. Frieden, *Russian Physicians in an Era of Reform and Revolution, 1856–1905* (Princeton, 1981), 158–59.

28. Michael Z. David, "The White Plague in the Red Capital: The Control of Tuberculosis in Russia, 1900–1941" (Ph.D. diss., University of Chicago, 2007), chapter 3.

29. Khaled Fahmy, "Medicine and Power: Towards a Social History of Medicine in Nineteenth-Century Egypt," *Cairo Papers in Social Science* 23:2 (summer 2000), 22. Fahmy writes that with this concern for public health, the state "became more active and intrusive than it had ever been in the long history of Egypt."

30. Milton I. Roemer, *National Health Systems of the World*, vol. 2 (Oxford, 1991), 81–82.

for the sake of military power. In March 1917 the British War Cabinet issued a memorandum on "The Urgent Need for a Ministry of Health."[31] In April 1918 a memorandum from Minister of Reconstruction C. Addison reiterated the need for a centralized government department of health, stating that "without such a Ministry we are fighting with divided forces against the evils which menace the nation's health."[32] With the added impetus of the worldwide influenza epidemic at this time, the British government finally established a ministry of health in 1919.[33] In a number of other countries, ministries of health were created to provide coordinated state administration of health programs on a nationwide scale. In France, for example, the first cabinet-level ministry of health was created in 1920; it grew out of government involvement in health and public hygiene during World War I.[34] Shortly after its establishment in 1920, the Turkish National Assembly founded the Ministry of Health.[35] Doctors in newly independent Romania lobbied for a ministry of health, which the Romanian government established 1923.[36]

In Russia just prior to World War I, officials again proposed a centralized state health administration. G. E. Rein, the head of the Ministry of Internal Affairs' Medical Council, submitted a report to the tsar in 1910 that argued that cholera and other epidemics cost the state thousands of lives, financial resources, international prestige, and the people's trust. And at subsequent meetings of a commission he chaired on reform of the Medical Council, Rein demonstrated the economic costs of epidemics and argued that disease weakened the army and the state. The Rein Commission's report issued in 1912 advocated the creation of a powerful ministry of health that would centralize state health care, expand medical research, standardize medical practices, and promote hygiene education. Rein's proposals

31. PRO CAB 23/2, War Cabinet 115, Appendix I.

32. PRO CAB 24/49, GT 4399, 2. Looking ahead to the end of the war, Addison warned especially of the danger of epidemic disease that could follow the return of demobilized soldiers.

33. Roemer, *National Health Systems of the World*, 81; Richard A. Soloway, *Demography and Degeneration: Eugenics and the Declining Birthrate in Twentieth-Century Britain* (Chapel Hill, 1990), 152.

34. Schneider, *Quality and Quantity*, 120. See also Ramsey, "Public Health in France," 89.

35. Ayca Alemdaroglu, "Politics of the Body and Eugenic Discourse in Early Republican Turkey," *Body and Society* 11:3: 68.

36. Maria Bucur, *Eugenics and Modernization in Interwar Romania* (Pittsburgh, 2002), 190–91. On Germany, see P. Weindling, *Epidemics and Genocide in Eastern Europe, 1890–1945* (Oxford, 2000), 138.

provoked some opposition and were not acted on immediately. Leaders of the Ministry of Internal Affairs feared a loss of their authority to a rival ministry. And zemstvo physicians, while they shared many of Rein's ideas, distrusted the autocracy and resisted the establishment of a central ministry of health. Nonetheless, both within and outside the government a growing number of doctors, bacteriologists, and urban planners saw a need for a centralized state health administration and ultimately would provide leadership when such an administration was created.[37]

The First World War generated a strong impetus to proceed with centralized state health administration. Faced with problems on a vast scale—wounded soldiers, refugees, hunger, epidemics—health officials and specialists pushed even harder for coordinated state health efforts. By the end of 1915, thirty-nine provinces in the Russian Empire had outbreaks of epidemic diseases (primarily typhus and typhoid). Even a number of liberal physicians who had previously opposed centralization began to support state coordination of antiepidemic measures.[38] Military officers created the Sanitary and Evacuation Section within the army to organize medical care, hygiene measures, and steps against the spread of infectious diseases. This section also had the authority to order pharmaceutical companies to produce medicines needed for health care in the army.[39] In 1916, Rein finally persuaded the Council of Ministers and Tsar Nicholas II to approve a ministry-level Main Administration for State Health Protection.[40] Because the tsarist autocracy collapsed just a few months later, the Main Administration did not have time to be realized under the tsarist government. But under the Provisional and Soviet governments, this idea of a central state health administration would come to fruition.

Following the overthrow of the autocracy in February 1917, zemstvo physicians elected representatives to form the Central Medical-Sanitary Council. This body provided democratic coordination of health policy without state interference in doctors' practices. In August 1917 the council reaffirmed its principles of social medicine, including an emphasis on preventative medicine and free universal health care.[41] Although council members hoped to minimize state interference in medical practice, they acknowledged that many localities lacked sufficient resources to deal with

37. Hutchinson, *Politics and Public Health*, 88–100; Hutchinson, "Who Killed Cock Robin?," 12, 17–19.
38. Hutchinson, *Politics and Public Health*, 120, 148.
39. GARF f. A-482, op. 1, d. 1, ll. 18–20.
40. Hutchinson, "Who Killed Cock Robin?," 16.
41. GARF f. A-482, op. 1, d. 1, l. 33.

epidemics and called for state aid from the Ministry of Internal Affairs. They also recognized the need for a "unified central organ of state sanitary statistics" in order to coordinate the gathering of information on the spread of disease.[42]

After the October Revolution, members of the Central Medical-Sanitary Council refused to recognize Soviet power, and the Soviet government confiscated their property and abrogated their authority.[43] In its place, Soviet leaders in December 1917 established the Council of Medical Boards, which united representatives of all government offices that dealt with health care.[44] In May 1918, at a congress of medical personnel, Z. P. Solov'ev, the chair of the Council of Medical Boards and future deputy commissar of health, gave a speech entitled, "The Tasks and Organization of the People's Commissariat of Health." He argued, "It is necessary to create a united central organ of the Commissariat of Health which will lead all medical-sanitary-veterinary affairs." He stressed that the commissariat should be invested with wide-ranging authority to oversee all health institutions, medical research, and prophylactic health measures. The congress endorsed all of his recommendations.[45]

On July 11, 1918, the Soviet government founded the Commissariat of Health and placed "all medical and sanitary affairs under its authority."[46] To accompany the decree, a government report explained that the Council of Medical Boards had proven unable to cope with the health problems precipitated by "the war, economic collapse, and resulting malnutrition and emaciation of the population." It emphasized the need for coordinated state action to fight epidemics, purify drinking water, improve sanitation, and provide health care for "the broad mass of the population." The report added that the commissariat faced an enormous organizational task of destroying the "old, diluted-with-liberalism, bureaucratic medical-sanitary organs" and replacing the "counterrevolutionary face" of zemstvo health organizations with Soviet medicine.[47] In this way, the creation of a

42. GARF f. A-482, op. 1, d. 1, ll. 31, 40.

43. GARF f. A-482, op. 1, d. 1, l. 2.

44. E. L. Skandova, ed. *Vysshie organy gos. vlasti i organy tsen. upravleniia RSFSR (1917–1967 gg.)* (Moscow, 1970), 443. Many commissariats, including those of education, transportation, and welfare, had departments of health; GARF f. A-482, op. 1, d. 2, l. 5.

45. GARF f. A-482, op. 1, d. 83, ll. 28–29.

46. GARF f. A-482, op. 1, d. 2, l. 2. The decree also allotted 25 million rubles to fight cholera, authorized the commissariat to take emergency measures to combat the epidemic, and ordered it to issue semiweekly reports on the spread of the disease.

47. GARF f. A-482, op. 1, d. 2, l. 5. A second accompanying report noted that some commissariats had opposed the creation of an independent Commissariat of Health, because they were loathe to relinquish their authority in health matters; l. 19.

centralized state health administration also served to consolidate Soviet power in the medical sector.

The process of bureaucratic consolidation did not proceed entirely smoothly. In response to Lenin's inquiry about the formation of the Commissariat of Health, Commissar Nikolai Semashko reported in August 1918 that the medical departments of the commissariats of Internal Affairs, Education, Labor, and Social Security had been united under the Commissariat of Health. But he went on to complain that the health and sanitation officials of the Commissariat of War and of the Commissariat of Transportation and Communication were refusing to subordinate themselves to the Commissariat of Health.[48] In response the Council of People's Commissars ordered all health and sanitation personnel of the War Commissariat to submit to the Commissariat of Health, though in a subsequent memorandum Semashko continued to condemn military-sanitary departments for operating independently, as well as for poorly coordinating the evacuation of injured soldiers from the front.[49]

A Commissariat of Health report in the fall of 1918 indicated progress on the centralization of health care. It noted that the commissariat had taken control of all health care facilities, and that antiepidemic measures were being carried out more systematically than had previously been possible.[50] The establishment of the Commissariat of Health also led to central control over local health care administration. Initially following the October Revolution, the Soviet government had pushed local soviets to handle health problems, but they lacked the resources and expertise to accomplish much. In late 1918 and 1919, the Commissariat of Health began to exert direct control over local health care—registering physicians and allocating money to hospitals without going through local soviets.[51]

Another step toward centralized state health care was taken when the Soviet government nationalized all pharmacies in December 1918.[52] Soviet health officials had argued for nationalization based on their assessment

48. GARF f. A-482, op. 1, d. 27, l. 15.

49. GARF f. A-482, op. 1, d. 26, ll. 117, 119.

50. GARF f. A-482, op. 1, d. 2, l. 64. On the centralization of Soviet health care, see also Neil Weissman, "Origins of the Soviet Health Administration: Narkomzdrav, 1918–1928," *Health and Society in Revolutionary Russia*, 97–102.

51. Rowney, *Transition to Technocracy*, 86–87.

52. GARF f. A-482, op. 1, d. 4, l. 107. Already in May 1918 the Congress of Medical Workers had resolved that pharmacies should be nationalized and that the state should control the production and distribution of all medicine; d. 83, ll. 23–24.

that privately owned pharmacies "completely fail to fulfill the task" of providing medicine to the population. They added that extreme shortages of medicine had spurred sharp price increases and that nationalization was needed to control prices.[53] We see here the way that anticapitalist ideology merged well with the statist orientation of health care officials. Faced with a public health catastrophe, Bolshevik officials and non-Party specialists alike found for-profit and privately administered medical treatment to be inadequate if not immoral. They believed instead in the necessity of centralized state health care administered in the interests of the population as a whole.

In the Soviet Union the trend toward state intervention in public health was magnified further by the Civil War. Along with the death and destruction of the Civil War came widespread hunger and disease. Between 1918 and 1920, Soviet officials registered 5 million typhus cases (3 million of which resulted in deaths), and estimates of total typhus cases were much higher. Although less severe than the typhus epidemic, typhoid, cholera, and malaria also took a toll on the population, and for the period 1916 to 1923 there were an estimated 10 million deaths due to famine and disease.[54] The Commissariat of Health in 1918 ordered that doctors report every case of infectious disease within twenty-four hours; these data were compiled and discussed every five days by a special commission on infectious diseases. In 1920, the Central Statistical Administration assembled tables by province on the number of deaths every month due to each infectious disease, and it compared these figures with zemstvo statistics on disease for 1913.[55]

In 1918 the Commissariat of Health established a list of rules on the treatment of typhus and cholera victims. These rules covered everything from the extermination of bedbugs and lice in the clothing of the ill to the control of travelers in epidemic regions and the disposal of corpses.[56] The Commissariat of Health also created commissions to deal with epidemics

53. GARF f. A-482, op. 1, d. 4, ll. 3–7. For further discussion, see Mary Schaeffer Conroy, *The Soviet Pharmaceutical Business during the First Two Decades (1917–1937)* (New York, 2006).

54. Starks, *Body Soviet*, 48–49. On the typhus epidemic, see also Robert Argenbright, "Lethal Mobilities: Bodies and Lice on the Soviet Railroads, 1918–1922," *Journal of Transport History* 29:2 (September 2008): 259–76.

55. RGAE f. 1562, op. 18, d. 1, ll. 1–158. The Central Statistical Administration made an effort to collect and use prerevolutionary zemstvo statistics, and its journal praised the work of prerevolutionary statisticians as "a bright incarnation of the genius of national creativity." See *Vestnik statistiki* 2 (1919): 111.

56. GARF f. A-482, op. 1, d. 5, ll. 4–7.

Fig. 2. Soviet antityphus poster, 1921. "The Red Army crushed the White-guard parasites Iudenich, Denikin, and Kolchak. A new menace has advanced on it—the typhus louse. Comrades, fight contagion and exterminate the louse." Poster identification number RU/SU 11, Poster Collection, Hoover Institution Archives.

and famine.[57] The Commission for Aid to Starving People established "medical-nutrition points" at train stations where famine victims were arriving. It dictated procedures to medically examine, cleanse, and evacuate starving children from famine regions.[58] With the Civil War raging, Soviet doctors similarly had to treat ill and wounded soldiers in assembly-line fashion. Again, they developed procedures to handle this enormous patient load, with a multitude of disinfection and sanitation regulations.[59] The extensive state health restrictions established during the Civil War helped shape the highly centralized and interventionist character of the Soviet health system.

The majority of rank-and-file doctors, steeped in the community-based ethos of zemstvo medicine, initially opposed the Soviet government and its centralizing policies. At a conference of the Pirogov Society in June 1918, delegates denounced the centralization of health care, warning that it would crush local initiative. At the same time, they acknowledged their need for state financial aid and recommended antiepidemic measures very similar to those pursued by the Commissariat of Health.[60] For his part, Semashko in 1918 praised zemstvo medicine for its accomplishments in the "democratization" of health care. But he also noted that however much zemstvo physicians had tried to help the poor, that under conditions of private philanthropy that health care would remain uncoordinated and insufficient.[61] Gradually most zemstvo doctors became reconciled to Soviet state health care and worked in its institutions. Despite their initial hostility, even most leaders of the Pirogov Society came to see the Bolsheviks as allies in their efforts to abolish private medicine and establish free and universal health care, to prevent epidemics, and to promote sanitary education. At a Moscow meeting of Pirogov Society members in May 1919, participants resolved, "The basic principles of public medicine have remained vibrant, even in the new political and social conditions. As a matter of fact, the so-called Soviet medicine has assumed the same organizational forms and is seeking the same goals, which always constituted the essence of public medicine."[62]

57. GARF f. A-482, op. 1, d. 268, l. 6; V. Z. Drobizhev, *U istokov sovetskoi demografii* (Moscow, 1987), 86–87.

58. GARF f. A-482, op. 11, d. 79, l. 6.

59. RGAE f. 1562, op. 21, d. 27, ll. 3–6; GARF f. A-482, op. 1, d. 26, l. 258.

60. GARF f. A-482, op. 1, d. 20, ll. 5–7.

61. GARF f. A-482, op. 1, d. 2, ll. 71–72.

62. As cited in Peter F. Krug, "Russian Public Physicians and Revolution: The Pirogov Society, 1917–20" (Ph.D. diss., University of Wisconsin, 1979), 219.

A number of zemstvo physicians went on to play a crucial role in establishing the Soviet health care system. Solov'ev, who led the founding the Commissariat of Health, was somewhat exceptional in that he had been both a Pirogov Society board member and a Bolshevik Party member before the Revolution.[63] Most zemstvo doctors were not Bolsheviks, but many of them nonetheless became leading Soviet health officials, including A. N. Sysin, D. K. Zabolotnyi, L. A. Tarasevich, and E. I. Martsinovskii.[64] In addition, Pirogov board member Petr N. Diatroptov became the head of the Commissariat of Health's scientific-medical council.[65] Nikolai F. Gamaleia, a leading prerevolutionary bacteriologist, served as director of the Leningrad vaccination institute under the Soviet government, and A. V. Mol'kov, former president of the Pirogov Commission for Popular Hygiene Education, directed the Soviet Institute for Social Hygiene in the 1920s.[66] Virtually none of the leaders of the Commissariat of Health's Tuberculosis section had been Party members before the Revolution, and instead had been members of the All-Russian League for the Fight against Tuberculosis.[67] One physician, E. M. Konius, stated explicitly that Soviet medicine, with its emphasis on prophylactic measures and social hygiene, had its roots in prerevolutionary social medicine.[68]

The structure of the Soviet health care system, then, reflected a number of currents: the anticapitalism and statism of Bolshevik ideology; the centralizing prerogative in the fight against epidemics raging in the country; and zemstvo physicians' belief in social medicine, with an emphasis on free, universal health care, preventative medicine, sanitation, and hygiene.[69] The Commissariat of Health also signaled the culmination of a more general shift in government bureaucracy. Not only did it provide the centralized, uniform administration of health care that was lacking under the tsarist autocracy, it also represented the triumph of specialist administration. The

63. *Great Soviet Encyclopedia* (New York, 1980), vol. 24, 307–8.

64. Hutchinson, *Politics and Public Health*, 187.

65. *Bol'shaia meditsinskaia entsiklopediia* (Moscow, 1928), vol. 9, 154–55.

66. Frances Lee Bernstein, "'What Everyone Should Know about Sex:' Gender, Sexual Enlightenment, and the Politics of Health in Revolutionary Russia, 1918–31" (Ph. D. diss., Columbia University, 1997), 137.

67. David, "The White Plague in the Red Capital," chapter 3.

68. E. M. Konius, *Obshchestvennaia i kul'turno-prosvetitel'naia rabota meditsinskogo personala po okhrane materinstva i mladenchestva*, ed. V. P. Lebedeva (Moscow, 1928), 7–8.

69. Hutchinson concludes that the Commissariat of Health "owed much more to Russian precedent and tradition than to Bolshevik ideology." Hutchinson, *Politics and Public Health*, 202.

limited public health supervision under the tsarist government was housed in the Ministry of Internal Affairs and administered by nonspecialist bureaucrats and lawyers. In other words, the tsarist bureaucracy, although authoritarian, was not specialist. By the end of the imperial era, however, the upper ranks of the bureaucracy had become increasingly professionalized and specialized, and the First World War led to even greater influence of experts.[70] Under the Soviet government, specialists were promoted into positions of bureaucratic authority, and in the Commissariat of Health, physicians assumed administrative control. In addition, the generalist administrations of the tsarist bureaucracy (most importantly the Ministry of Internal Affairs) were subdivided into operationally specialized commissariats.[71] The formation of the Commissariat of Health thus marked the triumph of expert and state oversight of public health.

Social Hygiene

In his book on contagious disease in nineteenth and early twentieth-century Europe, Peter Baldwin distinguishes between two different etiologies that guided preventative strategies: contagionism (a view of disease as spread by direct or indirect contact) and environmentalism (a focus on environmental factors that permitted the spread of disease). Contagionism prompted cordons and quarantines to stop the circulation of carriers, whereas environmentalism relied on sanitation and upgraded living conditions to prevent illness. Many scholars of public health have assumed that a nation's political system and culture determined which of these preventative strategies held sway, seeing, for example, German authoritarian traditions as dictating an interventionist, quarantinist approach and British liberalism as militating instead for an environmentalist strategy that protected individual liberties.[72] Baldwin, however, challenges this assumption. He argues that the prophylactic steps taken by national governments cannot be explained simply on the basis of political system. Instead, he sees a constellation of factors including geo-epidemiological concerns, administrative

70. Daniel T. Orlovsky, "Professionalism in the Ministerial Bureaucracy on the Eve of the February Revolution of 1917," *Russia's Missing Middle Class: The Professions in Russian History*, ed. Harley D. Balzer (Armonk, N.Y., 1996), 270–71.

71. Rowney, *Transition to Technocracy*, 186–87.

72. See Erwin H. Ackerknecht, "Anticontagionism Between 1821 and 1867," *Bulletin of the History of Medicine* 22:5 (September—October 1948): 565–68.

structures, and commercial interests as influencing public health policies, which shifted over time even within the same political system.[73]

Soviet public health policies provide a striking case with which to test Baldwin's argument. Certainly the Soviet political system was an authoritarian dictatorship with no regard for individual liberties. Yet Soviet officials strongly favored an environmentalist over a quarantinist approach to contagious disease. True, when epidemics were raging during the Civil War, authorities did resort to quarantines, but these measures only confirm Baldwin's point about the shifting nature of governments' prophylactic steps. Overall the Soviet government, despite its authoritarian character, emphasized hygiene, nutrition, lifestyle, and other environmental factors, thus supporting Baldwin's argument. The reasons for this environmentalist orientation, however, go beyond the geo-epidemiological, structural, and commercial considerations highlighted by Baldwin. We need also consider Russian disciplinary traditions and revolutionary politics to account for Soviet health care policies.

In his 1919 article "The Tasks of Public Health in Soviet Russia," Commissar Semashko stressed sanitation, prevention, and "free and widely accessible medical help."[74] Semashko's focus was social hygiene—a field of public health that understood disease as a condition of society as much as a condition of the body. Emphasizing the social environment and prevention over clinical medicine and treatment, social hygienists viewed health as a sociological as well as a biological issue. According to Semashko, Soviet physicians needed to be "as much at home in sociology as in biology, as much interested in preventing illness as curing it."[75] The tenets of hygiene, prophylaxis, and free health care became the guiding principles of Soviet public health.

Though Semashko sought to distinguish Soviet health care from capitalist medicine, his ideas on social hygiene actually drew heavily on foreign models and prerevolutionary traditions. He and other Russian physicians were inspired by late-nineteenth-century German public health pioneers

---

73. Baldwin, *Contagion and the State*, 12, 242–43. Baldwin also points out that some environmentalist techniques could actually be more interventionist than quarantinist measures (535).

74. Reprinted in William G. Rosenberg, ed., *Bolshevik Visions: First Phase of the Cultural Revolution in Soviet Russia* (Ann Arbor, 1990), 148–49.

75. N. A. Semashko, "Sotsial'naia gigiena, ee sushchnost', metod, i znachenie," *Sotsial'naia gigiena* 1 (1922): 5–11, as quoted in Susan Gross Solomon, "Infertile Soil: Heinz Zeiss and the Import of Medical Geography to Russia, 1922–1930," in *Doing Medicine Together: Germany and Russia between the Wars*, ed. Solomon (Toronto, 2006), 267.

such as Alfred Grotjahn.[76] While the principles of social hygiene were already strong among zemstvo physicians, the Commissariat of Health under Semashko's leadership institutionalized these ideas as the guiding force of Soviet medicine.[77] Semashko himself assumed a newly created professorship of social hygiene at Moscow State University, as well as the editorship of a new journal entitled *Social Hygiene*. By 1923 there were departments of social hygiene at the leading universities, and the State Institute of Social Hygiene was founded to coordinate and standardize social hygiene research throughout the country.[78] Russian epidemiologists and bacteriologists were forced to work with social hygienists (as they had in the prerevolutionary period) and to acknowledge the importance of social conditions in their research. In his 1922 reports for the League of Nations Health Section, leading immunologist Lev Tarasevich listed the following as the chief causes of epidemics in Russia: "poor and insufficient nourishment; dirt due to a shortage of soap and linen; cold in the houses; overcrowding in the houses; a highly unsatisfactory method of railway travelling; a shortage of sanitary and medical appliances."[79] Even Soviet bacteriologists highlighted the importance of lifestyle and diet to explain the spread of infectious disease.[80]

The prominence of social hygiene illustrates that while Soviet health care followed international trends toward social medicine and prophylaxis, it also retained distinctive features based on Russian disciplinary culture. Whereas in many countries the focus on sanitation and social work gave way by the end of the nineteenth century to bacteriology and sanitary engineering, Soviet health specialists in the 1920s continued to privilege social factors over the bacteriological causes of disease. Soviet

76. Starks, *Body Soviet*, 47. See also Weissman, "Origins of the Soviet Health Administration."

77. According to Stefan Plaggenborg, Semashko, who in 1917 returned with Lenin from exile in Switzerland, was shocked by Russia's unsanitary conditions after having lived for years in Western Europe, and this added to the urgency with which he pursued improvements in hygiene; Stefan Plaggenborg, *Revolutionskultur: Menschenbilder und Kulturelle Praxis in Sowjetrussland zwischen Oktoberrevolution und Stalinismus* (Köln, 1996), 85–87.

78. Solomon, "Infertile Soil," 267.

79. As quoted in Solomon, "Infertile Soil," 268. Tarasevich had helped organize the Union of Zemstvos' mass immunization campaigns during the First World War and went on to found the Institute for Serum and Vaccine Control, which became a prominent institute of the Commissariat of Health. See Elizabeth A. Hachten, "How to Win Friends and Influence People: Heinz Zeiss, Boundary Objects, and the Pursuit of Cross-National Scientific Collaboration in Microbiology," in *Doing Medicine Together*, 168–69.

80. Solomon, "Infertile Soil," 268.

social statistician E. I. Iakovenko, for example, approvingly contrasted Soviet public health officials' sociological approach to epidemics with the Kochian approach of German bacteriologists.[81] Of course, both social hygienists and bacteriologists agreed that fresh air, pure water, a clean living environment, and bodily cleanliness were essential to disease prevention, and both sought to improve health through state intervention. But given the predominance of nurturist thinking in Russian disciplinary thought, social hygiene triumphed over bacteriology and general hygiene in the 1920s, and specialists approached disease as more a social than a biological phenomenon. Soviet social hygienists employed a range of social scientific methodologies (anthropometry, demography, and anamnesis) to uncover the social causes of disease.[82]

The end of the Civil War marked a shift in health care from a defensive approach (fighting epidemics) to an offensive campaign to create healthy labor and living conditions. The Soviet government, however, lacked the resources to realize its ambitions for an expanded and centralized health care system. In 1922 the Commissariat of Health transferred funding of most medical facilities to local governments, which themselves lacked resources and were forced to curtail health services.[83] Soviet physicians relied on dispensaries to provide health care. According to the dispensary method, doctors were supposed not only to treat patients' symptoms but to inspect homes and factories in order to advise people on proper hygiene, safety, and diet.[84] The dispensary method had been invented in eighteenth-century Britain, and zemstvo physicians in late-nineteenth-century Russia had used it widely, particularly members of the All-Russian League for the Fight against Tuberculosis, who placed dispensaries at the center of their

81. Ibid., 268.

82. Susan Gross Solomon, "The Expert and the State in Russian Public Health: Continuities and Changes Across the Revolutionary Divide," *The History of Public Health and the Modern State,* ed. Dorothy Porter (Amsterdam, 1994), 194–203. The picture is more complicated than presented here. General hygienists and bacteriologists were rival groups who pursued their research using different means (sanitary statistics and laboratory research, respectively). See Susan Gross Solomon, "Social Hygiene and Soviet Public Health, 1921–1930," *Health and Society in Revolutionary Russia,* 175–76.

83. GARF f. 4085, op. 12, d. 169, l. 26; Weissman, "Origins of the Soviet Health Administration," 108. The Soviet government even reversed its previous ban on lotteries to allow local governments to raise money for health care; *Biulleten'* (Narkomzdrav) July 15, 1922, 1.

84. Christopher Burton, "Medical Welfare during Late Stalinism: A Study of Doctors and the Soviet Health System, 1945–1953" (Ph.D. diss., University of Chicago, 2000), 28–29.

efforts.[85] This approach corresponded with the limited resources available for health care but was also in keeping with the principles of social hygiene—a focus on social conditions, prophylaxis, and the inculcation of hygienic norms.

Commissariat of Health officials also sought to improve the population's health through propaganda to promote bodily and domestic hygiene. Such efforts were common to public health campaigns in countries around the world in the late nineteenth and early twentieth centuries. Health officials in Germany, for example, admonished people to clean their body, clothing, and bedding, to control nose-blowing, spitting, and coughing, and to minimize contact between family members.[86] Commissariat of Health publications instructed Soviet citizens in extreme detail how to clean various parts of their body, as well as their clothes and bed linens. The Red Army included in its regulations a statement that "each serviceman is obligated to follow stringently the rules of personal hygiene, the first and most fundamental rule of which is cleanliness of the body and clothing." The regulations also required that soldiers wash their hands before eating and brush their teeth both morning and night. Textbooks on school hygiene similarly emphasized "a regimen of cleanliness" and underscored the role of the school doctor in instructing both children and parents in proper bodily hygiene.[87] Social hygienists conducted surveys to gather data on the population's progress, for example checking to make sure that workers at a Leningrad factory had three or more pairs of underwear.[88] Health inspectors at one Moscow barracks found that workers shared toothbrushes or had none at all, and they launched a campaign for dental hygiene.[89] Surveys and inspections acted as didactic as well as data-gathering devices. One questionnaire asked workers dozens of questions

85. Starks, *Body Soviet,* 51.

86. Weindling, *Health, Race, and German Politics,* 226–27. Within this general trend toward greater state interference to promote hygiene, there were differences from one country to another. In nineteenth-century Britain, for example, health inspectors established rules to protect privacy in accordance with liberal principles. See Christopher Otter, *The Victorian Eye: A Political History of Light and Vision in Britain, 1800–1910* (Chicago, 2008), 123–32.

87. *Za zdorovyi kul'turnyi byt: Sbornik statei* (Moscow/Leningrad, 1931), 39; M. S. Malinovskii and E. M. Shvartzman, *Gigiena zhenshchiny,* 3rd ed. (Moscow/Leningrad, 1935), 3–4, 12–13, 34–35; A. V. Mol'kov, ed., *Shkol'naia gigiena* (Moscow/Leningrad, 1937), 22, 163.

88. *Gigiena i zdorov'e* 20 (1936): 12–13.

89. *Klub* 10 (1929): 39–40. For further discussion of dental hygiene, see Starks, *Body Soviet,* 173–75.

about their "hygienic habits"—whether they had their own towel, how often they bathed and brushed their teeth, how frequently they changed their bedding, and so forth.[90] Workers who filled out these questionnaires were thereby made to reflect on their daily routine and to compare it with implicit norms.

Public health officials in the Soviet Union and elsewhere viewed the home as the principal site for disease prevention. Housing inspections in Western Europe predated the late nineteenth century, though at this time municipal governments began to apply new methods of inventory and surveillance. The Parisian government, for example, assembled files on every residential building in the city, recording each death by contagious disease, and in 1893 created sanitary departments to inspect apartments.[91] By the interwar period, inspections had undergone a process of professionalization and routinization, as social workers in countries throughout Europe began to intervene in the homes of problem families. In Italy, for example, a range of experts from physicians and social workers to the members of fascist women's organizations visited homes to carry out inspections and recommend changes. Their focus was on issues of hygiene, diet, childraising, and "rationalization" of the households.[92]

Although purportedly scientific and objective, medical interventions in the home also entailed the value judgments of experts regarding the lifestyle and morality of the people they sought to reform. The writings of Soviet doctors, though politically favoring workers, reflected the revulsion of educated medical personnel when they observed lower-class housing. Ia. Trakhtman condemned the population's "unculturedness" and "darkness." He went on, "We live in filth, and are untidy and unfastidious. Because of this we get sick and die from infectious diseases, many of which no longer occur among cultured peoples."[93] Medical specialists condemned peasants' living conditions even more stridently. One Soviet commentator noted that peasants inhabited dark huts "without windows" and slept on beds covered with such "soot and dirt that every parasite and microbe lives in clover."[94] Soviet medical personnel in Kazakhstan, despite their scientific awareness of germs, similarly identified Kazakh nomads'

90. GARF f. 7952, op. 3, d. 387, ll. 3–9. I thank Tricia Starks for bringing this questionnaire to my attention.

91. David S. Barnes, *The Making of a Social Disease: Tuberculosis in Nineteenth-Century France* (Berkeley, 1995), 112–20.

92. Horn, *Social Bodies*, 114.

93. *Gigiena i sots. zdravookhranenie* 4/5 (1932): 58.

94. *Za zdorovyi kul'turnyi byt*, 23.

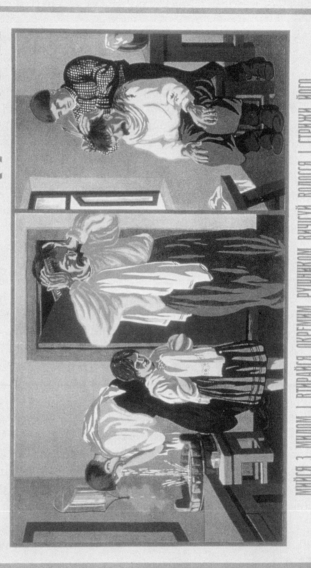

Fig. 3. Soviet hygiene poster, 1920s. "Cleanliness is the guarantor of health." Poster identification number RU/SU 940, Poster Collection, Hoover Institution Archives.

lifestyle and customs as the conduit or even the cause of disease.[95] These critiques illustrate the way that experts grafted scientific explanations onto their preexisting disdain for the lifestyles of the lower classes and national minorities.

In comparison to specialists in Western European countries, however, Soviet doctors tended to be less harsh in their judgments. Some British government officials blamed their population's physical deterioration on tenement dwellers—"persons usually of the lowest type, steeped in every kind of degradation and cynically indifferent to the vile surroundings engendered by their filthy habits."[96] French inspectors in working-class slums similarly passed moral judgment on the poor, and portrayed their foul odors and filth as part of an overall repulsive environment that bred disease.[97] Soviet health inspectors, by contrast, found fault with living conditions rather than with the inherent qualities of workers, peasants, and national minorities. In keeping with the Russian intelligentsia's traditions, Soviet public health officials believed that socioeconomic improvement and education would uplift and humanize the masses.

To enforce sanitary housing norms, the Commissariat of Health set up an extensive system of housing inspections. During the 1920s it formed "health cells" in housing units to assist sanitary doctors conducting inspections and enforcing regulations.[98] In Moscow by 1935, fifty-eight "housing sanitation inspectors," ninety-two doctors, and several hundred assistants worked full-time inspecting the city's housing. They had the authority to order hygienic improvements and institute "sanitary measures" in any housing they deemed unclean. Soviet housing inspectors also had the authority to fine any resident who did not maintain adequate hygiene in their apartment or building.[99] The Workers and

95. Paula Michaels, *Curative Powers: Medicine and Empire in Stalin's Soviet Central Asia* (Pittsburgh, 2003), chapter 6. See also Cassandra Cavanaugh, "Backwardness and Biology: Medicine and Power in Russian and Soviet Central Asia, 1868–1934" (Ph.D. diss., Columbia University, 2001).

96. PRO Parliamentary Papers, Microfiche 110.279, 23 (Inter-Departmental Commission on Physical Deterioration, 1904). On the range of theories in Britain regarding the spread of disease, see Michael Woroboys, *Spreading Germs: Disease Theories and Medical Practice in Britain, 1865–1900* (Cambridge, 2000).

97. Barnes, *The Making of a Social Disease*, 112–22. Barnes concludes that the lower classes, already seen as uncivilized and politically dangerous, by 1900 were classified as a biological threat as well.

98. Starks, *Body Soviet*, 67–68.

99. GARF f. 9226, op. 1, d. 6, ll. 3–4, 16.

Peasants' Inspectorate also carried out inspections of housing, hospitals, resorts, and schools.[100]

In addition to Soviet officials, unofficial housing inspectors visited homes and ordered improvements. At a 1935 conference of the Main Sanitation Inspectorate of the Commissariat of Health, one delegate reported that in Western Europe and the United States nongovernmental organizations played a crucial role assisting government inspectors in the upgrading of hygienic housing conditions.[101] The Soviet government adopted this approach when Commissar of Heavy Industry Ordzhonikidze initiated the wife-activist (*obshchestvennitsa*) movement, whereby women volunteers taught workers about hygiene and inspected their living quarters. At the All-Union Conference to found the movement in 1936, Ordzhonikidze announced that these women would bring "cleanliness and order" to workers' residences and cafeterias.[102] The wife-activist movement was a means to mobilize the labor of elite women to improve workers' health and hygiene. Soviet authorities referred to the wives of factory directors and engineers as "a large cultural force," and "an enormous cultural army [which] will bring order to workers' apartments."[103]

The Soviet government's reliance on women as unofficial housing inspectors reflected gender stereotypes that cast the home as a feminine domain. In fact, Soviet hygiene propaganda more generally emphasized the part of women in establishing a hygienic and healthy home. While men were depicted as having little or no role in the domestic sphere, women were shown preparing healthy meals, caring for small children, and providing a clean home environment.[104] The attempt to refashion the populace into a healthier, more efficient, and more rational society required the inculcation of new norms of health and hygiene, and in the domestic sphere Soviet authorities assigned this task to women.

100. GARF f. 8009, op. 3, d. 4, ll. 2–4; f. 4085, op. 12, d. 385, l. 104. On inspections, see also TsAGM f. 552, op. 1, d. 72, ll. 45–6, 67; GARF f. 9226, op. 1, d. 6, l. 19.

101. GARF f. 9226, op. 1, d. 6, ll. 39–40.

102. *Vsesoiuznoe soveshchanie zhen khoziaistvennikov i inzhenerno-tekhnicheskikh rabotnikov tiazheloi promyshlennosti: Stenograficheskii otchet* (Moscow, 1936), 8. On the founding of the movement, see also RGASPI f. 17, op. 120, d. 255, ll. 14–16; GARF f. 7709, op. 6, d. 2, ll. 126–29.

103. GARF f. 5451, op. 20, d. 22, l. 2; RGASPI f. 17, op. 120, d. 255, ll. 2–3. See also Robert Maier, "Die Hausfrau als Kul'turtreger im Sozialismus: Zur Geschichte der Ehefrauen-Bewegung in den 30er Jahren," *Kultur im Stalinismus*, ed. Gabriele Gorzka (Bremen, 1994), 39–45.

104. Starks, *Body Soviet*, 66.

4. Чистое, светлое жилище—защита от чахотки (туберкулеза).
Дайте доступ в ваше жилище солнечному свету
и свежему воздуху.

Издательство Наркомздрава

Fig. 4. Soviet antituberculosis poster, 1920s. "A clean, bright dwelling is protection from tuberculosis. Allow sunlight and fresh air into your home." Poster identification number RU/SU 1198.2, Poster Collection, Hoover Institution Archives.

Extensive inspection efforts did not mean that Soviet living conditions were in fact hygienic. During the industrialization drive, the Soviet leadership channeled virtually all resources into building factories. Housing conditions therefore deteriorated at the very moment when rapid urbanization necessitated their expansion and improvement. As many urban residents found themselves living in overcrowded communal apartments, rat-infested barracks, and unheated shacks and mudhuts, hygienic standards fell.[105] Lacking the resources to expand and improve housing,

105. David L. Hoffmann, *Peasant Metropolis: Social Identities in Moscow, 1929–1941* (Ithaca, 1994), 136–41.

Soviet officials ordered even more regulations and interventions to safeguard the health of the population. One Moscow inspector noted that the housing in his district consisted primarily of unclean and overcrowded barracks, and he recommended an increase in the number of inspectors and fines in order to improve the situation.[106]

With its focus on environmental factors, the field of social hygiene extended beyond bodily and domestic cleanliness to include antialcohol and antismoking campaigns. Medical personnel in the Soviet Union and elsewhere linked alcohol and tobacco to illness and degeneration.[107] Soviet specialists claimed that alcohol played a large role in the spread of venereal disease, and they asserted that smoking spoiled the appetite and harmed the nervous system.[108] Participants in a 1925 Commissariat of Labor conference on alcohol attributed illnesses, accidents, and declines in worker productivity to drunkenness.[109] In an effort to reduce alcohol consumption, Soviet officials waged a protracted (and largely ineffective) campaign against drinking.[110] Temperance workers in other countries had long conducted similar campaigns, but whereas they often invoked religion, in the Soviet Union the opposite was true. Soviet officials depicted religion and religious holidays as abetting drunkenness, and they often combined antireligious and antialcohol propaganda.[111]

Commissariat of Health officials also blamed poor diet and a lack of vitamins for health problems and deficient physical development.[112] Already in 1919, the Central Statistical Administration collected figures on

106. GARF f. 9226, op. 1, d. 6, l. 18.

107. Studies in France, for example, indicated that alcohol made the body more susceptible to tuberculosis and linked both alcohol and tobacco to the "degeneration of the French population." See Barnes, *The Making of a Social Disease*, 138–41, 162–63; Schneider, *Quality and Quantity*, 15.

108. M. S. Maslinovskii and E. M. Shvartsman, *Gigiena zhenshchiny*, 3rd ed. (Moscow/Leningrad, 1935), 26–28; *Gigiena i zdorov'e rabochei i krest'ianskoi sem'i* 16 (1926): 10. For more on Soviet antismoking campaigns, see Starks, *Body Soviet*, 178–83.

109. GARF f. 7062, op. 1, d. 15, l. 1.

110. RGASPI f. 17, op. 114, d. 255, l. 66; *Pravda*, December 22, 1937, 2; TsAGM f. 1289, op. 1, d. 173, l. 1. For further discussion, see Laura L. Phillips, *Bolsheviks and the Bottle: Drinking and Worker Culture in St. Petersburg, 1900–1929* (DeKalb, 2000); Kate Transchel, *Under the Influence: Working-Class Drinking, Temperance, and Cultural Revolution in Russia, 1895–1932* (Pittsburgh, 2006).

111. Starks, *Body Soviet*, 185–86. On antireligious propaganda, see William Husband, *"Godless Communists": Atheism and Society in Soviet Russia, 1917–1932* (DeKalb, 2000), and Daniel Peris, *Storming the Heavens: The Soviet League of the Militant Godless* (Ithaca, 1998).

112. GARF f. A-482, op. 1, d. 806, l. 243; *Gigiena i sanitariia* 2 (1936): 3–9. The 1904 British Inter-Departmental Commission on Physical Deterioration blamed a poor diet (and British housewives' "incurable laziness and distaste for the obligations of domestic

"the influence of current nutritional conditions on disease rates."[113] In the 1920s, Soviet nutritionists used statistical methods and laboratory studies, based on German techniques, to set nutritional norms.[114] Nutritional deficiencies, however, proved unavoidable during the food shortages and famine that followed collectivization. Given food supply problems, Soviet officials sought to determine the minimum sustainable caloric intake for workers and the most efficient ways to provide (and ration) food.[115] Food cleanliness also presented a challenge, given the underdeveloped Soviet food distribution system. The State Sanitation Inspectorate created a special department for food sanitation, which focused on "the battle with dirt and vermin in food products."[116]

While the spirit of social hygiene continued to guide public health policies throughout the Soviet period, the social hygiene movement met its demise during the Great Break of the late 1920s. The attack on non-Party specialists that the Great Break entailed included criticism of non-Party health specialists, particularly those who held apolitical, technocratic views. Many zemstvo-era physicians who helped found and lead the Commissariat of Health were targeted due to their lack of Marxist credentials. Social hygienists in particular suffered, because their focus on poor socioeconomic conditions as the cause of diseases implicitly deprecated the Soviet government's efforts to improve living conditions during its first decade in power.[117] Moreover, with the launch of the First Five-Year Plan, industrialization took precedence over issues of health, hygiene, and living conditions.

The attack on specialists and the field of social hygiene led to changes in personnel. Though most continued their research, some non-Party health officials were replaced by "Red" specialists—Party members who had received medical training in the Soviet era and whose allegiance was not in question. Moreover, the Soviet government in this period cut funding for social hygiene research and shifted money to clinical services, especially to serve the industrialization drive. The new sanitary physician was supposed

life") for a deterioration in the population's health; PRO Parliamentary Papers, Microfiche 110.279, 39–40.

113. RGAE f. 1562, op. 18, d. 1, ll. 25–28.

114. Mol'kov and Semashko, Sotsial'naia gigiena, 204–7.

115. One study held up the German wartime economy as a model, and for the Soviet Union advocated "the creation of a harmoniously developed national economy independent of capitalist encirclement." E. Khmel'nitskaia, Voennaia ekonomika Germanii, 1914–1918 gg. (Moscow-Leningrad, 1929), 235.

116. GARF f. 9226, op. 1, d. 43, ll. 1–2. See also Rabotnitsa i krest'ianka 1 (1936): 11.

117. Solomon, "The Expert and the State," 206–8.

to be an expert in industrial safety and sanitary technology, not in social criticism.[118] Commissar Semashko, the champion of social hygiene, was replaced in 1930. The new commissar of health, Mikhail Vladimirskii, although he had worked before the Revolution in the Moscow provincial sanitary organization, deemphasized social hygiene and no longer made a distinction between preventative and clinical medicine.[119]

In the spirit of the First Five-Year Plan, Soviet health officials began to emphasize the practical utility of medicine to treat industrial workers, rather than more general hygiene measures that would improve the health of the entire population. Vladimirskii called doctors, in their role safeguarding workers' health, "builders of the socialist economy" and went on to declare that all health care workers "have become participants in the Bolshevik charge.... We begin in the factory shop, where health preservation becomes part of the production plan."[120] Dispensaries serving geographic areas were eclipsed by "health points" in factories to care for workers. Similar medical services were supposed to be offered to peasants on collective farms, but most resources went instead to industrial enterprises. Health specialists still aspired to comprehensive care, including a focus on hygiene and nutrition, but they prioritized industrial workers.[121] Government expenditures on health care and hygiene similarly privileged industrial workers.[122] Although comprehensive in its approach, Soviet health care during the First Five-Year Plan was far from universal.

Public health in this period changed from an apolitical, theoretically oriented field into a more politicized and practical program to achieve Soviet goals of industrialization and social transformation. These goals themselves, however, embodied the larger ambitions of many technocratic thinkers. As discussed in the introduction, the Great Break inaugurated a more politicized, revolutionary attempt to achieve a fully rationalized and modernized society. Although non-Party specialists and their gradualist methods were cast aside during the Great Break, their goals of a healthy, modern society were not. Scientific health care and hygiene remained

118. Ibid., 206–8.
119. *Bol'shaia meditsinskaia entsiklopediia*, vol. 5, 150.
120. *Gigiena i sotsialisticheskoe zdravookhranenie* 1 (1932): 2.
121. Ibid., 1 (1932): 16–17; 6 (932): 39; Burton, "Medical Welfare during Late Stalinism," 34–36.
122. RGASPI f. 607, op. 1, d. 7, l. 45; RGAE f. 1562, op. 18, d. 33, ll. 8–11. On the Soviet government's Sanitary Minimum for factories, see Christopher M. Davis, "Economics of Soviet Public Health, 1928–1952," *Health and Society in Revolutionary Russia*, 162.

important, though they were subordinated to the Party's mission of industrialization.

Following the purported attainment of socialism in 1934, Soviet public health once again assumed a more universal character. Believing that bourgeois classes had been "liquidated," Party leaders began to treat all members of society as important contributors to the socialist order. The 1936 Constitution guaranteed all Soviet citizens free medical care. And the Third Five-Year Plan (1938–1941) substantially increased outlays for health care, including for the construction of hospitals and clinics available to everyone.[123] In the late 1930s, Soviet officials redoubled their efforts to track the spread of disease, and the Central Statistical Administration compiled data on every illness and death for each administrative district.[124] The Commissariat of Health once again focused on sanitation and disease prevention, as its officials sought to improve hygiene in rural areas through the regulation of drinking water and the construction of bath houses.[125]

Developments in Soviet public health, then, largely paralleled those in social welfare. Drawing on prerevolutionary intelligentsia traditions, Soviet officials and physicians sought to uplift the masses by improving their health and living conditions. In particular, Commissar Semashko and many non-Bolshevik specialists who became Soviet officials prioritized social hygiene and preventative medicine. Their universalized approach was first hampered by a lack of resources and then supplanted during the First Five-Year Plan with a policy that prioritized industrial workers and neglected the health care needs of the rest of the population. Once Party leaders declared that socialism had been built, they returned to a more universal approach to public health—one that sought, through free medical services and hygiene programs, to improve the health of the population as a whole.

123. Burton, "Medical Welfare during Late Stalinism," 36–38. Burton explains that during the Fourth Five-Year Plan (1946–1950) the Soviet government continued to work toward universal health care and prioritized the expansion of services to rural areas (39, 105–8).

124. GARF f. 9226, op. 1, d. 1, ll. 20–28; RGAE f. 1562, op. 18, dd. 44–52. See also the formerly classified statistics on causes of death in the late 1930s; RGAE f. 1562 s.ch., op. 329, d. 392, ll. 2–22.

125. *Gigiena i zdorov'e*, 1936 no. 24, 10–11. Despite these efforts, health conditions remained substandard, particularly in rural areas; RGAE f. 1562 s.ch., op. 329, d. 407, ll. 2–9; GARF f. 7062, op. 1, d. 123, l. 1; TsAGM f. 552, op. 1, d. 11, ll. 21–23.

To return to the frame of analysis with which I began this section, the Soviet government, despite the fact that it was a dictatorship, favored an environmentalist over a quarantinist approach to disease prevention, a fact that validates Baldwin's critique of views that correlate quarantinism with political authoritarianism. In arguing for explanations of preventative strategies that go beyond political systems, Baldwin highlights factors such as geo-epidemiology, and even suggests that quarantinism in the face of epidemiological threats shaped authoritarian political traditions rather than the other way around.[126] But the Soviet government, despite facing a greater threat from epidemic disease than any other European country, did not permanently adopt quarantinist measures, and instead favored an environmental approach that would safeguard public health through improved hygiene, nutrition, and rationalized lifestyles. This environmentalist orientation is explained by Russian disciplinary traditions forged in the social context of imperial Russia, where the intelligentsia championed the cause of the downtrodden masses and sought to uplift them through social amelioration. Also crucial was the revolutionary political change that brought the radial intelligentsia to power, thrusting aside monarchical conservatism and installing an ideology of social transformation and equality.

The Soviet case was in some ways unique within Europe, but it was not at all anomalous when compared with other late-developing nations such as Mexico, Iran, and Turkey. In those countries, health professionals harbored a similar ethos, seeking to modernize their societies by improving the health and living conditions of the masses.[127] As in Russia, physicians in Mexico and Iran felt a sense of inferiority and national shame when they compared their countries' rates of infectious disease with those of "civilized" nations. And they saw science and medicine as the means to effect a sociocultural transformation that would simultaneously modernize their societies and alleviate the suffering of peasants and workers. In fact, Mexican revolutionary hygienists even shared Soviet physicians'

---

126. Baldwin, *Contagion and the State*, 563.

127. Katherine E. Bliss, "For the Health of the Nation: Gender and the Cultural Politics of Social Hygiene in Revolutionary Mexico," *The Eagle and the Virgin: Nation and Cultural Revolution in Mexico, 1920–1940*, ed. Mary Kay Vaughan and Stephen E. Lewis (Durham, 2006), 197; Amir Arsalan Afkhami, "Defending the Guarded Domain: Epidemics and the Emergence of an International Sanitary Policy in Iran," *Comparative Studies of South Asia, Africa, and the Middle East* 19:1 (1999): 122; Ceren Gulser Ilikan, "Tuberculosis, Medicine, and Politics: Public Health in Early Republican Turkey," (M.A. thesis, Bogazici University, 2006), 81.

ideological orientation, blaming the church and capitalism for the population's ignorance and poor health, and extending health care to the lower classes in the name of equality.[128] In late-developing countries, then, health professionals' crusade for modernization and social progress accompanied their efforts to protect the population's health, and led them to embrace environmental approaches to disease prevention.

Foreign Influences on Soviet Health Care

The parallels between public health policies in the Soviet Union and other countries may be explained partly as a consequence of similar concerns and ways of thinking: government leaders had come to conceive of their populations' health as a vital resource, and modern medicine had proven the need to tackle health threats on a social level. But the similarities in health care also resulted from the mechanisms specialists developed to circulate medical knowledge and techniques. By the interwar period, medicine had acquired a truly international character due to extensive scholarly exchanges, publications, and international conferences. Through these means Soviet doctors and health officials absorbed approaches to public health from colleagues abroad.[129]

To foster contacts and cooperation with foreign medical specialists, the Commissariat of Health established the Department of Foreign Information in February 1921. Its purpose was to inform people in Western Europe and the United States about the progress of Soviet health care, to gather information on developments in Western medicine, and to facilitate contacts between Soviet and foreign medical researchers.[130] Over the next two decades, the department tracked ideas and practices of health

128. Bliss, "For the Health of the Nation," 198, 203; Cyrus Schayegh, "'A Sound Mind Lives in a Healthy Body': Texts and Contexts in the Iranian Modernists' Scientific Discourse of Health, 1910s-1940s," *International Journal of Middle East Studies* 37 (2005): 167–68. Medical professionals in colonial India were similarly attracted to science and medicine as the means to modernize their society. But the fact that Western medicine was the domain of colonial administrators led native physicians to seek their own brand of modern medicine that selectively incorporated Hindi ideas and traditions; David Arnold, *Science, Technology, and Medicine in Colonial India* (New York, 2000), 16–17.

129. Members of the Academy of Sciences also visited Germany, Britain, and France to observe the organization and workings of research institutes there; Loren R. Graham, "The Formation of Soviet Research Institutes: A Combination of Revolutionary Innovation and International Borrowing," *Social Studies of Science* 5:3 (August 1975): 314.

130. GARF f. A-482, op. 35, d. 8, l. 9.

practitioners in other countries. It issued reports on the British health care system, the structure of the French Ministry of Health, the principles of U.S. health care (with emphasis on sanitation, children's health, and preventative medicine), the administration of health care in Japan, and the health care practices established by the Danish Ministry of Hygiene and the German Ministry of Health.[131] To aid the collection of data on foreign health care, the department maintained offices abroad. The office in London, for example, wrote daily reports on public health activities, including about a government commission on diet and health, public lectures on the importance of sunlight, exhibitions on housing sanitation, and publications on factory safety.[132]

Department of Foreign Information bureaucrats also facilitated (and monitored) exchanges between Soviet and foreign doctors. They arranged trips abroad for Soviet doctors and invitations for foreign medical personnel to visit the Soviet Union. They also kept copies of all correspondence between Soviet and foreign health specialists, and collected reports from Soviet doctors who had travelled abroad.[133] This system of information collection permitted the Soviet government to keep tabs on foreign exchanges and interactions, but it also helped to circulate foreign medical ideas and practices. The director of the Rostov State Microbiology Institute, for example, reported on his trip to a scarlet fever conference in Konigsberg and a medical institute in Berlin. In addition to recording the names of the German researchers he met, he also described German procedures for the prevention and cure of scarlet fever.[134] The department also worked to propagandize abroad the achievements of Soviet health care. One non-Party Soviet doctor, following a visit to Britain, wrote a health official there to express his concern that no one in Western Europe acknowledged the positive accomplishments of the Soviet government in health and education. He concluded, "The Bolsheviks are now the only strong party which can save (and already saved) Russia and with her also Europe from anarchy, starvation, and mob rule."[135]

Under the auspices of the Department of Foreign Information, Soviet doctors attended international medical conferences. These conferences

131. GARF f. A-482, op. 35, d. 1, ll. 10–42.

132. GARF f. A-482, op. 35, d. 144, ll. 213–38, 314–30.

133. GARF f. A-482, op. 35, d. 52, ll. 111–96. This correspondence also illustrates the department's role arranging the procurement of medicines from abroad and acquiring foreign medical publications.

134. GARF f. A-482, op. 35, d. 340, l. 24.

135. GARF f. A-482, op. 35, d. 8, l. 8.

covered a range of health issues, from the 1925 International Malaria Conference in Rome to the 1930 International Mental Hygiene Congress in Washington.[136] The department's hygiene bureau sent delegates to twelve conferences in 1935 alone, as well as to semiannual meetings of the Bureau of Social Hygiene in Paris. Soviet specialists returned from these conferences with new ideas and techniques on hygiene and health care.[137] The Commissariat of Health also hosted foreign scholars at Soviet conferences—for example, a delegation of German doctors at the 1925 All-Russian Congress on Venereal Disease in Kharkov.[138]

International organizations provided another avenue through which new medical principles and practices reached the Soviet Union. The International Red Cross had been operating in Russia since before the Revolution.[139] The Soviet government's consolidation of medical personnel and property following the Revolution led mistakenly to confiscation of Red Cross property by Soviet officials. At the end of April 1918, the Soviet government corrected this mistake and affirmed that "all prerogatives of the Russian Red Cross as a division of the International Society of the Red Cross are preserved."[140] Not only did the Soviet government allow the Red Cross to operate as an independent entity, but it also drew on its expertise during the Civil War and into the 1920s.[141]

The American Relief Association (ARA) provided both famine aid and medical care to millions of Soviet citizens from 1921 to 1923.[142] The association's Medical Division gave supplies and guidance to more than five thousand hospitals and clinics around the country. It also administered 8 million vaccinations and crusaded for sanitation to stop epidemics. ARA administrators even contemplated a vast delousing campaign of the entire Volga region to combat typhus, but instead settled for a network of ambulatories, dispensaries, "sanitary trains," and disinfecting stations to prevent the spread of the disease. They also initiated and supervised the purification of drinking water and the disinfection of famine relief stations.

136. GARF f. A-482, op. 35, d. 138, l. 4; d. 314, l. 10.

137. GARF f. A-482, op. 35, d. 604, l. 1.

138. GARF f. A-482, op. 35, d. 162, l. 22. See also, Susan Gross Solomon, "The Soviet-German Syphilis Expedition," *Slavic Review* 52:2 (summer 1993): 204–32.

139. On the Red Cross, founded in 1863 in Geneva, see Milton I. Roemer, "Internationalism in Medicine and Public Health," *History of Public Health*, 409.

140. GARF f. A-482, op. 1, d. 1a, l. 36.

141. GARF f. A-482, op. 1, d. 26, l. 93; *Revue internationale de la Croix Rouge* 63 (1924): 190.

142. See Bertrand M. Patenaude, *The Big Show in Bololand: The American Relief Expedition to Soviet Russia in the Famine of 1921* (Stanford, 2002).

American specialists, then, introduced a range of techniques, equipment, and supplies to aid Soviet antiepidemic efforts.[143]

The League of Nations also influenced Soviet health care and provided ideas for the prevention of epidemic diseases. In 1922 the league held an international conference in Warsaw on the threat of infectious disease in Russia. League health officials portrayed the typhus epidemic there as an international problem that required supranational action to safeguard European health and stability. Conference participants called for 1.5 million British pounds to create a string of delousing stations in Russia and Ukraine.[144] Though the league's funding proved insufficient, its commission nonetheless visited Russia, Ukraine, and Belorussia to conduct an epidemiological study and to hold courses for Soviet doctors on the prevention of disease. The commission reported that the typhus epidemic in the Soviet Union was being spread by people fleeing famine areas and recommended the control of population movement (though it acknowledged that this would be impossible).[145] By 1923, the League of Nations Epidemiological Commission had placed a permanent representative in Moscow, who distributed foreign medical books to doctors there. The same year a delegation of Soviet doctors attended the league's international sanitation courses in Britain, the Netherlands, and Switzerland.[146] Semashko welcomed aid from the League of Nations Health Organization (as well as from other foreign groups such as the Rockefeller Foundation), and he attended the league's hygiene conference in Geneva in 1923.[147]

The international connections enjoyed by Soviet specialists taught them new approaches to public health and instilled in them an appreciation for foreign medical care.[148] The publishers of Soviet medical journals frequently included translations of foreign articles and made comparisons with health conditions and treatments in other countries. To take just one example, an article entitled "The Fight with Tuberculosis in Germany" published in 1926 explained that medical personnel there had found a connection between social conditions, including inferior

143. Harold H. Fisher, *The American Relief Administration in Russia, 1921–1923* (New York, 1943), 20–24.

144. Weindling, *Epidemics and Genocide,* 168–69.

145. GARF f. A-482, op. 35, d. 40, ll. 46, 81–82.

146. GARF f. A-482, op. 35, d. 46, ll. 3–4, 8. See also d. 644, ll. 95–104 on a 1935 League of Nations conference on hygiene.

147. Weindling, *Epidemics and Genocide,* 171.

148. See, for example, A.V. Mol'kov and N.A. Semashko, eds., *Sotsial'naia gigiena: Rukovodstvo dlia studentov-medikov,* vol.1 (Moscow/Leningrad, 1927), 148–55.

housing, and the spread of tuberculosis. It concluded that Soviet doctors too must understand tuberculosis "not only as an infectious but also a social disease."[149]

Although some imported ideas influenced Soviet public health policy, others did not take root. Racial pathology was largely rejected by Soviet health care specialists, despite the prominence of the field in other countries, especially Germany. A group of Soviet specialists led by Nikolai Kol'tsov founded the Russian Society for the Study of Racial Pathology and the Geographical Distribution of Disease in 1928. Kol'tsov, however, did not provide a precise definition of race and called for research on climate, nutrition, and social life, as well as genetics, to understand disease patterns. Within three years the society had largely died out. As Susan Gross Solomon explains, Russian pathologists, with a few exceptions, had never taken much interest in racial pathology. They concentrated instead on environmental factors, including climate, economics, and work conditions. When they did discuss race, they generally denied that it played any role in the distribution of disease.[150] Soviet specialists' rejection of racial pathology reflects the fact that racialized and biologized thinking did not fit with Russian disciplinary traditions or with Marxism, both of which emphasized environmental explanations over biological ones. In other cases, Soviet health officials did not so much reject ideas of foreign specialists as modify them in accordance with their own disciplinary orientation. Soviet sanitary statisticians were eager to be part of the international health care community, but they favored a different classificatory system for illness that emphasized social etiology far more than did the standard international system.[151]

---

149. *Gigiena i zdorov'e rabochei i krest'ianskoi sem'i* 18 (1926): 13. The article also noted that the United States and Britain had special labor colonies for those with tuberculosis where they could work without the risk of infecting others. Government reports also frequently compared disease rates in the Soviet Union with those in other countries; GARF f. 8009, op. 3, d. 214, ll. 4–30.

150. Solomon, "Infertile Soil," 265–66. By contrast, German medical reports on the eastern front during the First World War depicted Jews as the source of epidemics and stated that disease prevention and cleanliness could only be achieved if the Jews were replaced by another race; Weindling, *Epidemics and Genocide,* 102.

151. See Susan Gross Solomon, "Les statistiques de santé publique dans L'Union Soviétique des Années vingt: Coopération internationale et tradition nationale dans un cadre post-révolutionnaire," *Annales de Démographie Historique* 84 (1997): 19–44. Ian Hacking writes that as countries around the world became statistical, they did so in their own ways; Ian Hacking, *The Taming of Chance* (Cambridge, 1990), 17.

A similar pattern of modified borrowing occurred in Soviet studies on health and labor. The importance of corporeal labor to industrial production prompted an international movement to study and protect labor capacity, the value of which was sometimes expressed in baldly economic terms. One French eugenicist of the interwar period, Sicard de Plauzoles, developed a mathematical formula that computed each individual's value to society by taking their lifetime economic productivity and subtracting their lifetime maintenance costs.[152] With a similar mentality, a leading Soviet eugenicist, Aleksandr Serebrovskii, complained that the First Five-Year Plan's figures on natural resources had "completely left out the tabulation of the biological quality of the population."[153] And Commissar Vladimirskii, in his article "The Struggle with Illness Provides New Resources for Industry," calculated that workers' illnesses would cost the Soviet economy more than 2 billion rubles in 1930.[154] To ensure the health and efficiency of industrial workers, "labor hygienists" conducted surveys on topics ranging from the effect of industrial toxins to the proper posture for workers.[155] They also monitored industrial accidents and recommended increased safety measures, workplace cleanliness, and added mechanization of industrial processes.[156] Labor hygienists and their safety measures sometimes came under attack for impeding advances in industrial output.[157] Party leaders' rush to industrialize thus overrode many safety concerns, though in principle Soviet labor policy sought to protect workers' health.[158]

In addition to overseeing the health and safety of workers, labor hygienists studied ways to maximize productivity. In special laboratories, efficiency experts conducted physiological research to determine optimal

152. Schneider, *Quality and Quantity,* 179–80.
153. As quoted in Mark B. Adams, "Eugenics in Russia, 1900–1940," in *Health and Society in Revolutionary Russia,* 216.
154. M. Vladimirskii, "Bor'ba s zabolevaemosti dast promyshlennosti novye resursy," *Na fronte zdravookhraneniia* 13–14 (1930), as cited in Davis, "Economics of Soviet Public Health," 162. Since the early 1920s, commissariat officials, including Deputy Commissar Solov'ev, had linked the population's health to labor capacity and economic output; GARF f. A-482, op. 11, d. 58, ll. 44–53; Field, *Soviet Socialized Medicine,* 62.
155. Mol'kov and Semashko, *Sotsial'naia gigiena,* 250–51; S. I. Kaplun, *Obshchaia gigiena truda* (Moscow/Leningrad, 1940).
156. *Gigiena truda* 3 (1934): 24; 4: 3–5.
157. Lewis H. Siegelbaum, "Okhrana Truda: Industrial Hygiene, Psychotechnics, and Industrialization in the USSR," *Health and Society in Revolutionary Russia,* 235–40.
158. Some coal mines, for example, had annual accident rates of 650 for every 1,000 workers; RGAE f. 1562 s.ch., op. 329, d. 407, ll. 52–58.

labor techniques for industrial workers. Their studies went far beyond questions of lighting and ventilation within factories to address "biological and socioeconomic" influences on workers' performance.[159] The leading journal on these issues, *Labor Hygiene,* kept Soviet specialists apprised of the latest European studies on industrial physiology, technology, accident prevention, and efficiency. For example, studies of "leucocytosis in exercise," and "the relative fatigue recovery value of different carbohydrate blends," from the British *Journal of Industrial Hygiene* were published in summary form.[160]

Soviet efficiency experts also examined psychological effects of industrial labor and ways to minimize neurological stress. A leading Soviet psychologist, Aron Zalkind, wrote in 1930 that "socialist construction requires the maximal, planned use of all sciences connected with questions of human psycho-neurology." He sought to upgrade the labor performance of "the working masses" (something he termed "production psycho-neurology") through psychological, motor-skills, and pedalogical research.[161] Soviet industrial psychology was part of a broader international movement. In the early 1920s psychotechnical institutes were established in Britain, France, Germany, Italy, Poland, and Japan, as well as in the Soviet Union. In fact, an international psychotechnical congress to create a unified terminology for the psychotechnical movement was held in Moscow in 1931. The new subdisciplines of industrial psychology and aptitude testing became part of more general attempts to replace the chaos of the free market with the rational deployment of personnel.[162]

Soviet efficiency experts' efforts to maximize productivity were also apparent in the image of the human-machine hybrid. The machine was perhaps the most salient symbol of progress and perfectibility, and for some it became a model for human transformation.[163] A number of nineteenth-century European thinkers argued that the body, like the machine, was a motor that converted energy into mechanical work. They believed that

159. *Gigiena truda* 1 (1934): 13; 5: 27–29.
160. Ibid. 3 (1934): 93.
161. A. B. Zalkind, ed., *Psikhonevrologicheskie nauki v SSSR: Materialy I Vsesoiuznogo s"ezda po izucheniiu povedeniia cheloveka* (Moscow, 1930), 5–8. See also *Gigiena truda* 5 (1934): 30–32.
162. Anson Rabinbach, *The Human Motor: Energy, Fatigue, and the Origins of Modernity* (New York, 1990), 274–78.
163. Toby Clark, "The 'New Man's' Body: A Motif in Early Soviet Culture," *Art of the Soviets: Painting, Sculpture, and Architecture in a One-Party State, 1917–1992*, eds., Matthew Cullerne Bown and Brandon Taylor (New York, 1993), 36.

society should conserve, deploy, and expand the energies of the laboring human body, and harmonize bodily movements with those of the machine. By the 1890s "the science of work" had emerged as a field, and in the twentieth century this scientific approach to the laboring body pervaded parliamentary debates, sociological treatises, liberal reform programs, and socialist tracts.[164]

Some Soviet leaders adopted this ideal of human beings as machines, whose labor would be deployed rationally in order to maximize the productivity of society as a whole. In 1923, Nikolai Bukharin urged the creation of "qualified, especially disciplined, living labor machines."[165] Filmmaker Dziga Vertov wrote, "The New Man, free of unwieldiness and clumsiness, will have the light, precise movements of machines."[166] The ideal of the machine-man was popular among German thinkers of the interwar period as well, but it took a much different form than in the Soviet Union. The German version of the machine-man was associated with militarism in the aftermath of the First World War. Ernst Jünger wrote of a new breed of machine men who were "fearless and fabulous, unsparing of blood and sparing of pity—a race that builds machines and trusts to machines, to whom machines are not soulless iron, but engines of might."[167] The Soviet version of the machine-man, by contrast, had no militaristic connotation and was instead connected to the ideal of labor. Aleksei Gastev, the leading Soviet Taylorist, developed ideas on human automation to enhance labor productivity. At his Central Institute of Labor in Moscow, he studied the physiological aspects of labor and trained workers to perform more efficiently. Gastev's ultimate goal was the symbiosis of man and machine, in which workers would adopt the rhythm and efficiency of factory equipment and become robotlike producers with perfectly disciplined minds and bodies.[168]

164. Rabinbach, *Human Motor*, 2–8.

165. As quoted in Clark, "The 'New Man's' Body," 36.

166. Dziga Vertov, "The New Man," (1922) *Kino-Eye: The Writings of Dziga Vertov*, ed. Annette Michelson, trans. Kevin O'Brien (Berkeley, 1984), 7–8, as quoted in Peter Fritzsche and Jochen Hellbeck, "The New Man in Soviet Russia and Nazi Germany," *Beyond Totalitarianism: Stalinism and Nazism Compared*, ed. Michael Geyer and Sheila Fitzpatrick (Cambridge, 2009), 316.

167. Ernst Jünger, *Copse 125: A Chronicle from the Trench Warfare of 1918* (New York, 1988), 21, as quoted in Fritzsche and Hellbeck, 310.

168. Richard Stites, *Revolutionary Dreams: Utopian Vision and Experimental Life in the Russian Revolution* (Oxford, 1989), 152–54. On the ideas of Platon Kerzhentsev, a Soviet efficiency expert who sought to "introduce scientific principles not only into

Gastev's ideas, while very influential, did not take hold without considerable opposition. Many labor hygienists feared that Gastev placed efficiency before the safety and health of workers.[169] Even more fundamentally, many workers and Left Communists opposed Gastev's Taylorist methods as capitalist exploitation. Lenin strongly supported Gastev and the creation of the Central Institute of Labor in 1920, and justified his approach by arguing that "it is necessary to grasp all the culture which capitalism has left and build socialism from it."[170] Gastev's ideas clearly triumphed only during the early 1930s, when the industrialization drive necessitated optimal labor productivity and the rapid training of millions of former peasants for industrial labor.[171]

Although Party leaders' main concern during the First Five-Year Plan was labor for the sake of industrial production, the Soviet ideal of labor was not purely utilitarian. According to Soviet ideology, labor helped people achieve personal fulfillment. In the words of Ordzhonikidze, labor was "a matter of honour, a matter of glory, a matter of valour and heroism."[172] Perfecting workers' labor capacity was a means not only to higher productivity but an end in itself—a part of workers' realization of their full potential as human beings and Soviet citizens. Publicity surrounding Stakhanovites called attention to the production records of these hero-workers but also to their transformation into cultured, edified citizens.[173] Soviet doctrine regarding labor, therefore, paralleled efforts in other countries to improve efficiency but went beyond these ventures to extol labor's role in reshaping people's thinking and behavior.

We see, then, both commonalities and differences between public health in the Soviet Union and other countries. The international circulation of ideas on public health in many ways influenced Soviet health care during the 1920s and 1930s. Foreign specialists introduced antiepidemic measures, including vaccinations, quarantines, and disinfection techniques. Soviet health officials eagerly adopted many foreign methods of disease

---

man's economic activity or production but into all organized activity or work," see Stites, *Revolutionary Dreams*, 155–59.

169. Siegelbaum, "Okhrana Truda," 226–27.

170. Kendall E. Bailes, *Technology and Society under Lenin and Stalin: Origins of the Soviet Technical Intelligentsia, 1917–1941* (Princeton, 1978), 50–52.

171. Hoffmann, *Peasant Metropolis*, 78–79.

172. *Labour in the Land of Socialism: Stakhanovites in Conference* (Moscow, 1936), 64.

173. RGASPI f. 17, op. 120, d. 251, l. 238; *Rabotnitsa i krest'ianka* 6 (1936): 11; *Kul'turnaia rabota profsoiuzov* 5 (1938): 48. See also Lewis H. Siegelbaum, *Stakhanovism and the Politics of Productivity in the USSR, 1935–1941* (Cambridge, 1988), chapter 6.

prevention and treatment. At the same time, imported theories and practices often took on a distinctively Soviet form or were rejected entirely. Soviet physicians favored social conditions to explain the spread of disease,
and they largely rejected racialized medical thought. Labor hygienists and
industrial psychologists sought to train Soviet workers for maximum efficiency, but they also viewed labor as an uplifting enterprise that would
transform the human psyche and help fashion the New Soviet Person.[174]
Soviet health programs therefore reflected both the international circulation of ideas and the ideological and disciplinary particularities of the
Soviet Union. A similar combination of foreign influences and Soviet dis-
tinctiveness characterized physical culture as well.

Physical Culture and Its Militarization

Physical culture was another means by which Soviet officials sought to
cultivate a healthy and fit population. During the interwar period, physical culture programs received enormous attention in the Soviet Union and
in countries around the world. As with public health programs more generally, the Soviet government tracked physical culture activities in other
countries. Commissariat of Health specialists saw physical exercise as a
way to maintain people's bodily health and labor capacity. But physical
culture was also of interest to military officers in the Soviet Union and
elsewhere, as it represented a form of military preparation. Initially Soviet physical culture was portrayed primarily as a means to promote the
healthy development of people's minds and bodies, and to enhance their
labor capacity. By the late 1930s, however, it assumed an increasingly militaristic tone and, in many instances, became a form of paramilitary training, based on the examples of other countries.

Already in the late nineteenth century sports programs had served as a
type of paramilitary training to endow young men with physical strength
and a sense of political unity.[175] Team sports promoted cooperation and
solidarity, and group gymnastics in particular synchronized the movements
of participants, seeming to unify people in body and spirit. Organized gymnastics in many countries had national unity as their explicit goal. Friedrich

174. For further discussion of the New Soviet Person, see chapter 4.
175. Physical culture programs in Europe were first publicized in the 1820s and became
widely promoted by the late nineteenth century; Frances Lee Bernstein, *Dictatorship
of Sex: Lifestyle Advice for the Soviet Masses* (DeKalb, 2007), 153.

Ludwig Jahn founded the nineteenth-century German gymnastics movement in order to promote German unification. This movement combined group exercises with walks in the countryside to recapture the wholeness and purity of rural life and to overcome the alienation and decadence of the city.[176] Like the German *Turnen* societies, the Czech *Sokol,* and the Scandinavian gymnastics movements of the nineteenth century, Russian gymnastics were introduced to enhance national solidarity. The first Russian gymnastics club was founded following defeat in the Crimean War, and in 1874 Petr Lesgaft, the "father" of Russian gymnastics, instituted a Prussian model of gymnastics training into the Russian military.[177] Tsarist authorities also borrowed the idea of the Boy Scouts, founded by Colonel Robert Baden-Powell after the Boer War to provide physical and paramilitary training to British boys. The Russo-Japanese War had revealed the poor physical condition of Russian recruits, and it prompted tsarist officers, who had observed the Boy Scouts in Britain, to form the first scout troop in Russia in 1909. By 1917 there were fifty thousand boys and girls in scout troops that existed in 143 Russian towns.[178]

On the eve of the First World War, the tsarist government sought to promote additional physical fitness programs. In January 1914, the Council of Ministers issued a directive on "the physical development of the Russian Empire's population." Noting that "a majority of European powers...are spending large monetary resources on the proper bodily upbringing of school-age youth" as preparation for military service, the directive outlined steps to provide government coordination and funding for Russian physical culture. It argued that physical culture programs would guarantee the health and strength of the younger generation and would also ensure

176. George L. Mosse, *The Nationalization of the Masses: Political Symbolism and Mass Movements in Germany from the Napoleonic Wars through the Third Reich* (New York, 1975), 50, 78.

177. James Riordan, *Sport in Soviet Society: Development of Sport and Physical Education in Russia and the USSR* (Cambridge, 1977), 19–20. The Russian Sokol gymnastics movement that arose in the 1880s was modeled on the Czech movement and had an explicit pan-Slavist ideology; also see ibid., 35. For a more comprehensive discussion of physical culture and leisure activities in tsarist Russia, see Louise McReynolds, *Russia at Play: Leisure Activities at the End of the Tsarist Era* (Ithaca, 2003).

178. Joshua Sanborn, *Drafting the Russian Nation: Military Conscription, Total War and Mass Politics, 1905–1925* (DeKalb, 2002), 133–34; Riordan, *Sport in Soviet Society,* 35–36; I. V. Kudiashov, ed., *Istoriia, teoriia i praktika skautizma: Organizatsionnye voprosy: Dokumenty i materialy* (Arkhangelsk, 1992), 36–37, 50–51. After the Revolution, scout organizations were labeled bourgeois and disbanded, but in 1922 the Soviet government created a similar (though coed) organization—the Pioneers—that taught children physical fitness, discipline, patriotism, and outdoor survival skills.

that youth were "made morally healthy."[179] Once the war began, the tsarist government's Temporary Council on Physical Development and Sport subsidized sport clubs and sought to require all schools to institute military training classes. General V. N. Voeikov assumed the title of head observer of the Physical Development of the Population of the Russian Empire, and in 1915 he convinced the tsar to allocate roughly 13 million rubles for youth physical culture programs.[180]

In most countries, physical culture in the wake of the First World War assumed even more militaristic tones. In Republican Turkey, for example, leader Mustafa Kemal Atatürk pushed for physical culture based on a German model, and youth sports clubs took on a very clear military function.[181] By contrast, Soviet leaders depicted physical culture as a means to expand people's labor capacity and prepare them to participate in the construction of socialism. A 1920 government decree entitled, "On the Physical Upbringing of the Juvenile Population," stated that "it is essential for the laboring population to have physical and mental strengths in order to move forward on the path of socialist construction." The decree called for physical activities in all schools, extracurricular athletic programs (including for preschool children), and the overall expansion of physical culture in everyday life.[182] Semashko called physical culture "one of the principal links to labor and to work ability."[183] Official reports touted physical culture as a means to teach peasants to work rationally and effectively.[184] Studies on labor productivity showed that workers who did physical exercises at the start of the workday and during breaks were more productive than workers who did not.[185] One physical culture expert, K. Mechonoshin, argued that exercise would instill in youth an appreciation of labor's importance and would increase work efficiency.[186]

Beyond the practical aim of increasing the population's labor capacity, physical culture offered a means to transform people's attitude toward

179. *Osobyi zhurnal Soveta Ministrov* 1 (January 3, 1914): 1–6.

180. Sanborn, *Drafting the Russian Nation*, 136.

181. Yigit Akin, "'Not Just a Game': Sports and Physical Education in Early Republican Turkey (1923–1951)" (M.A. thesis, Bogazici University, 2003), 129–30, 136.

182. GARF f. A-482, op. 11, d. 58, l. 19.

183. N. A. Semashko, *Novyi byt i polovoi vopros* (Moscow/Leningrad, 1926), 15.

184. GARF f. A-482, op. 11, d. 58, l. 9.

185. *Gigiena i sotsialisticheskoe zdravookhranenie* 4/5 (1932): 27–30.

186. K. Mechonoshin, "Fizicheskoe vospitanie trudiashchikhsia," *Fizicheskaia kul'tura* 3–4 (1923): 2–3, as cited in Plaggenborg, *Revolutionskultur*, 81.

work. New fields of labor gymnastics and labor sports were developed by Soviet physical culture specialists in the 1920s.[187] Soviet physical culture pageants combined labor and sports images in an allusion to Marx's prophesy that work would become pleasurable.[188] The renowned Soviet theater director Vsevolod Meierhold, in his 1922 lecture entitled "The Actor of the Future and Biomechanics," argued that the actor "will be working in a society where labor is no longer regarded as a curse but as a joyful, vital necessity."[189] In order to prepare workers and actors alike for continuous, efficient, and aesthetic labor, Meierhold prescribed a regimen to perfect the body. He argued that when "gymnastics and all forms of sport are both available and compulsory, we shall achieve the new person who is capable of any form of labor."[190] Physical culture, then, offered a means to transform work into a recreational, fulfilling, and joyous enterprise.

To promote fitness, Soviet specialists first sought to develop methods of physical conditioning. The Institute of Physical Culture in Moscow scientifically determined training techniques through physiological observation and experimentation.[191] Laboratory research by Soviet physiologists also established norms for exercise and leisure. One such study determined that "active leisure" in the form of rhythmic exercises was the most efficient way to restore the body's energy and labor ability.[192] Physiologist S. I. Kaplun linked "proper leisure" with high labor productivity, citing both physiological studies (on the nervous system and blood circulation) and industrial productivity experiments.[193] Semashko in 1926 recognized the need for leisure "to cleanse" the bodily organism "from the harmful substances which accumulate in it as a result of work."[194] And Commissariat of Health officials, noting that working-class children were not as healthy as peasant children, recommended

187. Plaggenborg, *Revolutionskultur*, 80.

188. Clark, "The 'New Man's' Body," 40.

189. Vsevolod Meierhold, "The Actor of the Future and Biomechanics," in *Meierhold on Theatre*, ed. Edward Brown (New York, 1969), 197–98.

190. Ibid., 200.

191. GARF f. A-482, op. 11, d. 58, l. 27.

192. *Gimnastika na predpriiatiak i proizvoditel'nost' truda* (Moscow, 1936), 25. Studies on labor productivity showed that workers who did physical exercises at the start of the workday and during breaks were more productive than workers who did not; *Gigiena i sotsialisticheskoe zdravookhranenie* 4/5 (1932): 27–30.

193. Kaplun, *Obshchaia gigiena truda*, 91–92.

194. Semashko, *Novyi byt*, 15.

"excursions, walks, and other means of natural health improvement" for children.[195]

The Soviet government also emphasized physical culture as a bulwark against decadence. Lenin himself recommended "healthy sport—gymnastics, swimming, excursions, physical exercises," concluding that "in a healthy body there is a healthy spirit."[196] In contrast to traditional leisure activities (which might include drinking, card playing, and other vices), Soviet leisure was to be part of a balanced lifestyle that improved the health and vitality of the human organism. A 1926 Komsomol resolution stressed physical culture as a means to divert young people from the evil influences of alcohol and prostitution.[197] And one Soviet commentator, after observing sporting exercises, contrasted their "freshness, vibrancy, and healthy strength," to the decadence of "Americanized dances."[198] A Soviet health journal emphasized that proper leisure could revitalize the human organism as effectively as sleep and restore energy to "the human machine."[199] Soviet officials advocated the division of daily life into equal eight-hour segments of work, sleep, and leisure. This approach, also common to Fordism and international workers' movements, reflected not only an interest in leisure to maintain workers' health but also in the comprehensive ordering of everyday life.[200]

Physical culture also served the Soviet government's larger aspiration to restore social harmony and remake humankind. Since before the Revolution, physical fitness had been linked to mental development and a harmonious personality. Nineteenth-century social critic Vissarion Belinsky had written that "the development of mental capacity corresponds to that of the health and strength of the body," and he advocated gymnastics and Russian folk games to develop "a harmonious personality."[201] Soviet officials

---

195. GARF f. A-482, op. 11, d. 19, l. 68; d. 58, l. 8. A 1934 report claimed that Germans spent weekends in the countryside absorbing fresh air and sunshine, and that these activities promoted good health; GARF f. 7876, op. 2, d. 153, l. 5.

196. K. Tsekin, "Lenin o morale i voprosakh pola," *Komsomol'skii byt: Sbornik*, ed. O. Razin (Moscow/Leningrad, 1927), 20.

197. Riordan, *Sport in Soviet Society*, 107.

198. A. Gvozdev, "Postanovka 'D. Ye.' v 'Teatre imeni Vs. Meyerkhol'da,'" *Zhizn' isskustva* 26 (June 24, 1924): 6, as cited in Katerina Clark, *Petersburg: Crucible of Cultural Revolution* (Cambridge, Mass., 1995), 162. For further discussion of Soviet prescriptions for youth activities, see Anne Gorsuch, *Youth in Revolutionary Russia: Enthusiasts, Bohemians, Delinquents* (Bloomington, 2000).

199. "Otdykh i son," *Gigiena i zdorov'e rabochei i krest'ianskoi sem'i* 21 (1926): 2.

200. For further discussion of Soviet leisure, see Starks, *Body Soviet*, 70–79.

201. V. G. Belinsky, *Izbrannye pedagogicheskie sochineniia*, vol. 2 (Moscow/Leningrad, 1948), 76, as quoted in Riordan, *Sport in Soviet Society*, 43. In nineteenth-century Britain the field of psychophysiology also stressed the link between the physical and mental

also saw physical culture as a means to cultivate harmonious individuals who would contribute to the perfect society. A 1919 report on children's well-being explained that a healthy body also meant a "healthy spirit," and it went on to link a proper physical upbringing with "the harmonious development of the individual."[202] A 1920 Commissariat of Health report entitled "The Tasks of Physical Culture" stated that "medicine, with all its scientific discoveries, is not in a position to create the new individual." It went on to argue that of all means available ("new social conditions, cultural enlightenment work, a new upbringing, sanitary-hygiene measures"), physical culture "has nearly the most important place" in creating "an individual with the harmonious development of mental and bodily strengths."[203]

While its officially stated purpose remained preparing people for socialist construction, Soviet physical culture also acquired a paramilitary dimension. The population's physical condition was of concern to Red Army officers who compiled and analyzed statistics on the height and weight of all recruits.[204] Red Army physicians examined all recruits using elaborate procedures, including laboratory testing for diseases, vision and hearing checks, and psychological and neurological observation.[205] The data from these examinations were then carefully compiled and analyzed. With these and other statistics, Soviet statisticians tracked the "physical development of youth" and correlated physical characteristics with specific regions and nationalities.[206] They also tabulated data on the reasons that recruits were rejected, including for diseases such as tuberculosis and malaria, nervous disorders, and disabilities such as deafness.[207]

During the Civil War compulsory physical education had been instituted in schools, and the Central Board of Universal Military Training had taken over and expanded existing gymnastic societies and sport clubs to

condition; Bruce Haley, *The Healthy Body and Victorian Culture* (Cambridge, Mass., 1978), 23. Russell Trall, a British gymnastics advocate in the 1850s, claimed that "people naturally stupid" could be made "comparatively intelligent" through gymnastic exercise; Harvey Green, *Fit for America: Health, Fitness, Sport, and American Society* (New York, 1986), 183.

202. GARF f. A-482, op. 11, d. 19, l. 77.
203. GARF f. A-482, op. 11, d. 58, l. 8.
204. RGAE f. 1562, op. 21, d. 434. The Red Army also conducted its own censuses of the entire population; see dd. 120, 356.
205. RGAE f. 1562, op, 18, d. 54, l. 6.
206. RGAE f. 1562, op. 18, d. 38, ll. 4–5; d. 54, ll. 11–26.
207. RGAE f. 1562, op. 18, d. 40, ll. 1–8.

ensure the physical preparedness of youth.[208] In 1920 the Soviet government created commissions to oversee physical culture in schools and to establish preschool physical culture programs.[209] Soviet authorities also founded "Houses of Physical Culture"—centers that were to promote physical exercise in a "scientifically instructive" manner, including supervised activities, lectures, and exhibits.[210] In July 1925 the Communist Party Central Committee renounced noncompetitive physical culture activities (previously proposed as a socialist alternative to bourgeois sports) and mandated a more competitive approach to sports and physical culture.[211] It also declared physical culture to be "a method of educating the masses (inasmuch as it develops will power and builds up team work, endurance, resourcefulness and other valuable qualities)."[212] At the Sixteenth Party Congress in 1930, Stalin called for the younger generation to be trained to defend the country from foreign attack, and the same year the Soviet government further centralized and prioritized physical culture with the founding of the All-Union Physical Culture Council. The following year the Komsomol launched a physical training program called "Prepared for Labor and Defense of the USSR."[213]

By the late 1930s, foreign physical culture programs increasingly influenced Soviet policies and contributed to their militarization. As was true of public health programs, Soviet officials made a conscious effort to monitor and emulate the physical education initiatives of other countries. The Soviet government hired foreign trainers to teach Soviet athletes and prepare them for international competitions in the 1930s.[214] The Soviet Committee on Physical Culture and Sport had an international relations division that researched and wrote regular reports on physical training taking place in Europe, North America, and Japan. A report on sports in fascist countries stated that in Nazi Germany "the entire nation must do physical exercises. The physical perfection of men and women is extremely important to the state, and no one has the right to refuse the obligation to

208. Riordan, *Sport in Soviet Society,* 69–76; Sanborn, *Drafting the Russian Nation,* 371–74. See also Plaggenborg, *Revolutionskultur,* 70–71.

209. GARF f. A-482, op. 11, d. 58, ll. 19–20.

210. GARF f. A-482, op. 11, d. 40, l. 81.

211. Robert Edelman, *Serious Fun: A History of Spectator Sports in the USSR* (Oxford, 1993), 34.

212. *Izvestiia tsentral'nogo komiteta RKP*(b), July 20, 1925, as quoted in Riordan, *Sport in Soviet Society,* 106.

213. Bernstein, *Dictatorship of Sex,* 188; Riordan, *Sport in Soviet Society,* 122.

214. Barbara Keys, "Soviet Sport and Transnational Mass Culture," *Journal of Contemporary History* 38:3 (July 2003): 420.

develop their body and fortify their health."[215] Government reports and articles in the press covered topics such as French athletic clubs, Japanese swimmers' training techniques, international cross-country ski races, foreign soccer tournaments, and the 1936 Olympic Games in Berlin.[216] These reports kept Soviet officials informed about the physical and military preparedness of other countries, and also transmitted methods that could be applied in the Soviet Union.

To take one example, Soviet officials observed and emulated foreign initiatives that promoted physical culture among women. They translated articles from American journals on how to incorporate athletic events into women's higher education.[217] The All-Union Physical Culture Council in 1934 lauded the benefits of physical fitness among German women and argued that female athletics created "well-developed young women, who also produce healthy and robust children." In language that echoed Nazi ideology, it concluded that "this rapid transformation of the race, without a doubt, must be attributed to physical education.... [German leaders] have understood that only physical culture may sustain and increase the capital of the health of the nation."[218] Within two years the Soviet government convened a conference that launched new programs to promote physical culture among women.[219] Unlike the essentialist Nazi gender order, however, the Soviet gender order stressed women's roles as both mothers and workers, and cultivated their physical fitness to enhance their performance of both roles. Soviet physical culture programs and youth organizations, including both the Young Pioneers and Komsomol, were distinct in that they were coeducational. This fact reflected the (oft-violated) Soviet ideal of gender equality and an equal role for women to play in building socialism.

In addition to highlighting the physical benefits of athletic programs, Soviet reports on physical culture abroad stressed its disciplinary and patriotic aspects. One report on Germany stated that "only physical education can bestow the following qualities proclaimed by National Socialism: a sense of discipline, order, and subordination; a sense of solidarity, courage, decisiveness, and the ability to make quick decisions when circumstances demand it; endurance, and readiness for self-sacrifice." The same

215. GARF f. 7576, op. 2, d. 153, ll. 2–3.
216. GARF f. 7576, op. 2, d. 245, ll. 2–6; *Fizkul'tura i sport* 1 (1937): 14; 2: 4, 12; 13: 15; GARF f. 7576, op. 2, d. 183, l. 117.
217. See, for example, GARF f. 7576, op. 2, d. 210, ll. 1–10.
218. GARF f. 7576, op. 2, d. 153, l. 5.
219. GARF f. 7576, op. 14, d. 2, l. 1.

Fig. 5. French Ministry of War poster, 1918. "Preparation of French Youth for Military Service." Poster identification number FR 611, Poster Collection, Hoover Institution Archives.

report noted that the German government focused on young people and oriented them toward self-discipline and "the spirit of Adolf Hitler." It also cited a German article that claimed Hitler had "restored the pride of the German people," and that gymnastics societies had helped develop this pride.[220]

Officials of the Soviet Committee on Physical Culture and Sport underscored that other countries used physical education as military preparation, and they argued that the Soviet Union should do the same. Reports in 1934 and again in 1938 concluded that under the Nazi dictatorship "sport has become an integral part of preparation for war."[221] The head of the Komsomol, Aleksandr Kosarev, warned in 1936 that rightwing governments in Germany, Poland, Italy, and Japan had conducted "an intensified militarization of youth," and he called on the Komsomol to prepare young people to defend their country.[222] In a 1937 speech to Komsomol activists of the Dinamo Sports Club, an official of the Committee on Physical Culture and Sport criticized the lack of attention to military aspects of sport and called for gymnastics that were less like ballet and more like military training.[223]

In the years leading up to the Second World War, Soviet physical culture indeed took on an increasingly militaristic character. In 1935 a civil defense pamphlet stated that "to be prepared for defense means to be physically healthy," and it emphasized the importance of shooting contests, gymnastics, swimming, and cycling, as well as training in the use of gas masks and bayonets.[224] In June 1936 the Politburo approved the formation of the Committee for Physical Culture and Sport, which gave priority to combat sports.[225] A Politburo resolution in November 1939 further strengthened

220. GARF f. 7576, op. 2, d. 153, ll. 3–4. A 1931 British government report on physical training programs in Sweden, Czechoslovakia, and Germany also noted the "political ends" to which the programs were used, but nonetheless recommended them, arguing that "their beneficial effect on physique and morale is undoubted." PRO LAB 18/25.

221. GARF f. 7576, op. 2, d. 153, ll. 3–4; d. 201, l. 64. The second report stated that Germany sent teams to international sport competitions to try to prove the superiority of the Nazi regime and the "northern race."

222. A. Kosarev, *Otchet TsK VLKSM Desiatomu Vsesoiuznomu s"ezdu leninskogo komsomola* (Moscow, 1936), 28–34.

223. TsKhDMO f. 1, op. 23, d. 1268, l. 3.

224. M. Likhachev, *Byt' gotovym: Rabota oboronnoi sektsii sel'soveta* (Leningrad, 1935), 26–28. The pamphlet's preface explained that fascist Germany planned a "crusade" against the Soviet Union and that Japanese fascists conspired to grab territory in eastern Siberia (3).

225. RGASPI f. 17, op. 3, d. 978, l. 130. The same year the British government established the National Advisory Council for Physical Fitness and provided grants for recreational facilities and fitness programs; PRO ED 136/76.

the Prepared for Labor and Defense of the USSR movement with additional physical education programs in schools, physical culture centers and prizes, instructional manuals and films, and medical supervision to maximize the health benefit of exercise.[226] Educational initiatives at this time included extensive paramilitary training—riflery, parachuting, civil defense—and the founding of military academies for secondary education.[227] The Komsomol and Young Pioneer organizations also increasingly stressed discipline, courage, patriotism, and the ability to use weapons and gas masks.[228]

The Soviet government placed special emphasis on militaristic physical culture parades. Soviet journals heralded these parades as indicators of the importance of physical education and "the discipline of physical culture participants."[229] In the summer of 1937, the Politburo ordered that a physical culture parade be held on Red Square with more than forty thousand participants, including delegations from each republic and record holders in a number of sports.[230] An article about this event, entitled "The Parade of the Powerful Stalin Breed," stressed the unity of all the nationalities of the Soviet Union.

> The living poem created on Red Square by Russian, Ukrainian...[lists the nationalities of all republics] physical culture participants proclaims in a loud, sonorous voice, which echoes around the entire world, the blood brotherhood and indissoluble friendship of the peoples which populate the broad expanse of the country of Soviets;...and [declares] that the brave, strong Soviet youth are an inexhaustible reserve for our powerful Red Army.[231]

This quotation demonstrates that physical culture parades were more than just a display of discipline and potential military strength. Parades symbolized the unity of Soviet society. In them, all nationalities and social groups were symbolically united as they marched and performed synchronized exercises in perfect unison. Of course, Nazi marches also symbolized unity,

226. RGASPI f. 17, op. 3, d. 1016, ll. 37, 79–80.
227. GARF f. 7709, op. 7, d. 2, ll. 6–7; RGASPI f. 17, op. 3, d. 998, ll. 78–79.
228. TsKhDMO f. 1, op. 23, d. 1361, l. 24; RGASPI f. 17, op. 120, d. 326, ll. 15–18.
229. *Gimnastika* 1 (1937); *Partiinoe stroitel'stvo* 15 (1939): 28. A report on a physical culture parade in 1938 indicated, "if war breaks out tomorrow," athletes will quickly become "tankists, pilots, snipers, and sailors." *Izvestiia*, July 26, 1938, as cited in Edelman, *Serious Fun*, 44.
230. RGASPI f. 17, op. 3, d. 987, l. 91. See also GARF f. 3316 s.ch., op. 64, d. 1651, ll. 5–7, for the detailed plans behind a 1935 physical culture parade.
231. *Fizkul'tura i sport* 13 (1937): 4–5.

Fig. 6. Soviet physical culture poster, 1930s. "Work, build, and don't whine! The path to a new life has been shown to us." Poster identification number RU/SU 2317.21, Poster Collection, Hoover Institution Archives.

Fig. 7. Soviet poster of a physical culture parade, 1939. "An ardent greeting to the glorious sportsmen and sportswomen of the Soviet country." Poster identification number RU/SU 1827, Poster Collection, Hoover Institution Archives.

but a unity of the Aryan race, achieved via the exclusion of racial and ethnic minorities. With the Soviet order, all nationalities were to be united under socialism.

In some ways, then, Soviet public health and physical cultural programs resembled those in other countries. In an age of industrial labor and mass warfare, the physical well-being of the population represented an important resource, one that could be maintained through new forms of knowledge (epidemiology, social hygiene, anthropometry) and new practices (vaccinations, home inspections, group gymnastics). Soviet authorities borrowed some ideas from initiatives in other countries. But Soviet public health and physical culture had important differences as well. Even after the field of social hygiene fell into disfavor, Soviet health specialists continued to privilege social explanations of disease over biological ones. Soviet physical culture sought to unite all nationalities, in stark contrast to the racially exclusionary and ultimately genocidal policies of the Nazis. Soviet health care also had an important structural difference in that doctors remained entirely dependent on the state. In contrast to medical specialists in liberal democratic countries (who were also somewhat dependent on state patronage), Soviet physicians had no independent organizations or private practice possibilities, leaving the state as the sole patron and arbiter of public health.[232] This situation meant both greater uniformity in health care policy and more interventionist health measures. Of course, governments throughout the world vastly increased their roles as the guardians of public health at this time. But the absence of any legal checks on state intervention in the Soviet Union meant that Soviet health officials were more intrusive than their counterparts in most other countries.

Despite the Soviet government's commitment to social medicine and physical fitness, public health conditions in the Soviet Union remained deficient. Though vastly improved over the tsarist period, health services continued to be understaffed and underfunded throughout the interwar period. Particularly in far-flung regions, where transportation and communication were still limited, the peasant population lacked basic hygiene and medical care.[233] While Party leaders valued public health, they devoted

232. Solomon, "The Expert and the State," 209.
233. A government report in 1940 criticized the Commissariat of Health for not even being able to locate hundreds of doctors it had assigned to rural areas; GARF f. 7511, op. 1, d. 232, l. 3. And the State Sanitary Inspectorate found that cities and towns of Central Asian republics lacked adequate water supply and sewage systems; GARF f. 9226, op. 1, d. 47, ll. 1–2.

far greater resources to industrialization. Nonetheless, it is clear that fostering a healthy population was central to their vision of a new social order. In fact, Party leaders and Soviet specialists frequently conflated their society's ideological and physical health, and viewed both as essential to Soviet socialism.

3 Reproductive Policies

Whereas previous measures had only meant a scratching at the surface, and the removal of a few weeds to be transformed into plants, the Children Act will mean going down to the very roots and dealing with the soil and the conditions which produce the weeds.
—Report of the British Central Council on Child Welfare, 1909

The decline of the birthrate began in 1876, and since the opening of the twentieth century has revealed a menacing acceleration....If a stop is not speedily put to this evil Germany's world position will be in danger before long....The basis of the State is the family; it depends on the number and fertility of marriage. The main purpose of marriage is procreation.
—Memorandum of the German General Staff, 1917

In our life there must not be a gap between the personal and the social. We even have seemingly personal matters, such as the family and the birth of children, where the personal coincides with the social....The Soviet woman is not free from the great and honorable duty that nature has given her: she is a mother, she gives birth. And this is undoubtedly not only her personal affair but one of enormous social importance.
—AARON SOL'TS, "Abortion and Alimony," 1936

Modern state intervention went beyond measures to enhance the health and fitness of the existing population. Backed by scientific and medical expertise, and in the name of protecting the society, nation, or race, authorities in many countries intervened in reproduction to increase birthrates and "improve" their populations biologically. Previously reproduction had been considered a natural phenomenon—something that lay beyond state control or scientific management. Even seventeenth-century cameralist thinkers who viewed a large population as a source of cheap labor and national wealth had no ambition or even conception of managing reproduction to control the quantity and quality of children born. But when social scientists and government officials began to think of society as an object to be studied, sculpted, and improved, reproduction emerged as an important realm for intervention. Throughout the eighteenth century, demography and associated fields emerged as disciplines, and their practitioners began to study birthrates. In the nineteenth century officials began to compile regular censuses that made it possible to study long-term population trends and to aspire to influence them. In addition, the spread of Darwinist thought and the rediscovery of Mendelian genetics at the beginning of the twentieth century spurred new ideas about controlling the quality as well as the quantity of human beings. And in the wake of the First World War, when mass warfare made clear the necessity of a large population for national defense, political leaders across Europe and around the world sought to manage and increase their populations as never before.

While leaders in many countries shared pronatalist goals, the policies they adopted varied considerably from one country to another. In some countries authorities enacted antinatalist as well as pronatalist measures to control the "quality" as well as quantity of children born. Other countries, including the Soviet Union, promoted reproduction among all citizens, without regard to race, nationality, or mental and physical abilities. The particular reproductive policies adopted by the Soviet government were a result not only of socialist ideology, but also of the nurturist orientation of Russian disciplinary culture. Although Soviet policies, then, were part of an international trend toward state management of reproduction, they reflected a particular disciplinary and ideological orientation, as well as a distinct conception of the population. By placing in comparative context Soviet reproductive policies, from abortion legislation and the promotion of motherhood to eugenic policies and childraising programs, it is possible to demonstrate how the broader shift toward state interventionism assumed a particular form in the Soviet Union. Soviet reproductive policies also provide an important counterexample to the policies of other countries in the interwar period. Even as the Soviet government sought to shape its population, it rejected eugenics; and even as it embraced an essentialist view of women as mothers, it continued to emphasize women's roles in the workforce. The Soviet case thus helps illustrate the range of forms taken by increased state efforts to manage reproduction.

Birthrates and National Power

One founder of the new science of demography, Thomas Malthus, had warned of overpopulation in his 1803 *Essay on the Principle of Population*. Declines in mortality rates had indeed allowed populations to rise rapidly in the eighteenth century, as Britain's population jumped from

5.6 to 8.7 million between 1741 and 1801.[1] Moreover, rapid urbanization had contributed to the perception that the population overall, and the number of urban poor in particular, was expanding at an uncontrolled rate. By the late nineteenth century, however, fertility in Western European countries had declined, and warnings about overpopulation shifted to fears of underpopulation. In France, the first country to experience a decline in fertility, a census in 1854–55 revealed that the total number of deaths exceeded the total number of births. Worries about depopulation proliferated following defeat in the Franco-Prussian War, when French leaders began to fear that their population was too small to compete militarily with Germany. By 1900 an extraparliamentary commission on depopulation was created; it reported that the "development, prosperity and grandeur of France" depended on raising the birthrate. In other European countries falling fertility by the end of the nineteenth century also prompted warnings of national decline and demographic extinction. In Germany, the annual birthrate of 42.6 per thousand in 1876 had dropped to 28.2 by 1912, and the 1912 census provoked national alarm about "race suicide."[2] Even in non-European countries, where birthrates remained higher, political leaders sought to boost the size of their populations. Beginning in the 1910s, Iranian elites expressed concern that their country's population of 10–12 million was insufficient for the country to evolve into a modern society and maintain its economic independence.[3]

The First World War had an enormous impact on thinking about population, particularly in combatant countries. Mass warfare required huge numbers of troops, and made clear the link between population size and military power. Moreover, the horrendous casualties of the war triggered fears in many countries about their populations' capacities to sustain military action in the future. Political leaders came to see the size of the population as a critical resource for national defense, and they focused on reproduction as central to sustaining the population. As a member of the British government declared in 1915:

> In the competition and conflict of civilizations it is the mass of the nations that tells.... The ideals for which Britain stands can only prevail as long as they are

1. Maria Sophia Quine, *Population Politics in Twentieth-Century Europe: Fascist Dictatorships and Liberal Democracies* (New York, 1996), 1–2.

2. Ibid., 52–65,100–101.

3. Cyrus Schayegh, "Hygiene, Eugenics, Genetics, and the Perception of Demographic Crisis in Iran, 1910s–1940s," *Critique: Critical Middle Eastern Studies* 13:3 (fall 2004): 335, 353.

backed by sufficient numbers....Under existing conditions we waste before birth and in infancy a large part of our population.[4]

Similarly the German General Staff, in a 1917 memorandum on the German population and army, stated that the falling birthrate was "worse than the losses through the war" in causing population decrease.[5]

When fighting ceased, the major combatants were faced not only with the frightful human cost of the war, but with a demographic catastrophe. France lost 1,393,515 soldiers, Britain 765,400, and Italy 680,070. One German statistician calculated that in addition to its 2 million soldiers killed in action, Germany lost 750,000 civilian victims of the Allied blockade, 100,000 people to the 1918 influenza epidemic, up to 3.5 million never born because of the war, and 6.5 million people no longer in Germany due to territorial losses, for a total deficit of nearly 13 million.[6] Although World War I casualties cried out for more births to replenish the population, they actually accelerated the decline in fertility after the war. The loss of young men reduced the number of potential fathers so sharply that Britain's birthrate fell by roughly 40 percent between 1914 and 1930, leading one member of parliament to declare that population decline constituted "a danger to the maintenance of the British Empire."[7] One German demographer warned that Germany in 1924 had a birthrate of only 20.4 per thousand people, barely high enough to maintain the population at current levels, and he concluded, "We must...make possible to every married couple by means of economic insurance of parenthood that they shall fulfill their reproductive duties."[8]

4. As quoted in Pat Thane, "Visions of Gender in the Making of the British Welfare State: The Case of Women in the British Labour Party and Social Policy, 1906–1945," *Maternity and Gender Policies: Women and the Rise of the European Welfare States 1880s-1950s,* ed. Gisela Bock and Thane (London, 1991), 105.

5. Erich Ludendorff, *The General Staff and its Problems,* trans. F. A. Holt (London, 1920), vol. 1, 202.

6. Quine, *Population Politics,* 17–18; Cornelia Usborne, *The Politics of the Body in Weimar Germany: Women's Reproductive Rights and Duties* (London, 1992), 31.

7. Quine, *Population Politics,* 17–18; PRO MH 58/311. The number of births per thousand people in England and Wales fell from 25.5 in 1920 to 14.4 in 1933. See Thane, "Visions of Gender," 99–100.

8. A. Grotjahn, "Differential Birth Rate in Germany," *Proceedings of the World Population Conference,* ed. Margaret Sanger (London, 1927), 154. On Britain, see Richard A. Soloway, *Demography and Degeneration: Eugenics and the Declining Birthrate in Twentieth-century Britain* (Chapel Hill, 1990), 277. On Canada, see Cynthia R. Comacchio, "'The Infant Soldier': Early Child Welfare Efforts in Ontario," *Women and Children*

Fig. 8. British poster for National Baby Week, 1918. Britannia protects an infant and toddlers from the grim reaper. Poster identification number UK 1562, Poster Collection, Hoover Institution Archives.

In Russia, unlike in some other European countries, fertility remained high throughout the nineteenth century. But Russian casualties in the First World War proved as severe as those of other combatants, and when added to deaths during the Civil War and ensuing famine totaled 16 million.[9] This demographic cataclysm provoked concern among Soviet leaders and scholars, and prompted intensified attention to population statistics. The Central Statistical Administration compiled detailed monthly statistics on Civil War casualties for every province and district of the country.[10] It also established a commission to study the effect of First World War casualties and noted that these losses severely diminished the labor as well as the military capacity of the population. It called "the depreciation of the labor productivity of millions of the most able-bodied elements of the population" a matter in urgent need of statistical study.[11] One Soviet professor declared that the Russian Empire's prewar population of 172 million had fallen to 90 million as a result of wars, famine, and territorial losses. He equated a large population with national security and warned that some European countries, notably Germany, were threatening to overtake the population of the Soviet Union.[12]

The Commissariat of Health established its own commission in 1920 to account for wartime "physical-material losses of the population and state." In addition to tabulating the number of deaths, invalids, and refugees as a result of the First World War and Civil War, the commission studied the impact of epidemics, changes in fertility and mortality rates, the psychological and physical effects of war on children, and so forth. In the preface to the commission's published findings, Commissar Semashko wrote that this research was a first step in the "proper study of the social-biological legacies of the war," which he noted had a "destructive influence

First: *International Maternal and Infant Welfare, 1870–1945,* ed. Valerie Fildes et al. (New York, 1993), 106.

9. Ansley Coale, Barbara Anderson, and Erna Harm, *Human Fertility in Russia since the Nineteenth Century* (Princeton, 1979), 16; Frank Lorimer, *The Population of the Soviet Union* (Geneva, 1946), 40–41.

10. RGAE f. 1562, op. 21, d. 3552, ll. 1–20. See also Vl. Avaramov, "Zhervy imperialisticheskoi voiny v Rossii," *Izvestiia narodnogo komissariata zdravookhraneniia* 3, no. 1–2 (1920): 39–42; Serge Bagotzky, "Les pertes de la Russie pendant la guerre mondiale (1914–1917)," *Revue internationale de la Croix Rouge* 61 (1924): 16–21.

11. RGAE f. 1562, op. 21, d. 25, l. 17.

12. Prof. K. K. Skrobanskii, "Abort i protivozachatochnye sredstva," *Zhurnal akusherstva i zhenskikh boleznei* 35: 1 (1924), as cited in Janet Hyer, "Managing the Female Organism: Doctors and the Medicalization of Women's Paid Work in Soviet Russia during the 1920s," *Women in Russia and Ukraine,* ed. Rosalind Marsh (New York, 1996), 117.

on the health of the population."[13] Statistical study of wartime losses, while perhaps the only way to grasp the horrendous number of casualties, made human deaths abstract and promoted a mentality of seeing the population purely as a resource to be preserved and utilized. Indicative of this statistical-bureaucratic mentality were Central Statistical Administration reports that listed, alongside human casualty figures, the number of horses lost and the total number that remained to be mobilized.[14]

Despite wartime losses, the Soviet Union faced less of a decline in the postwar birthrate than did the countries of Western Europe. Because Soviet society was still largely a peasant population in the 1920s, its birthrate remained high even given the loss of young men during World War I and the Civil War. Nonetheless, Soviet officials and demographers continued to monitor population trends closely and were alarmed by the precipitous drop in fertility that accompanied industrialization, collectivization, and the 1932–33 famine. The Central Statistical Administration tabulated annual fertility and mortality rates for every administrative district in the country, so Soviet officials knew, for example, that there were nearly ten times as many deaths as births in Khar'kov oblast in 1933, due to the famine in Ukraine.[15] An extensive demographic study in 1934 revealed that the Soviet birthrate overall had fallen from 42.2 births per thousand people in 1928 to 31.0 in 1932. Moreover, S. G. Strumilin, the author of the study and one of the country's leading statisticians, demonstrated that the drop in fertility correlated with urbanization and the entrance of women into the industrial workforce— trends that had to continue if industrialization were to move ahead.[16]

Strumilin's other major finding was that among groups in the population, those with higher wages had lower fertility. Not only did workers have lower fertility than peasants but urbanized workers had lower fertility than peasant in-migrants to the city, and white-collar employees had the lowest fertility of all. This discovery contradicted previous research that had identified economic hardship as the primary cause of low fertility.[17]

13. *Trudy komissii po obsledivaniiu sanitarnykh posledstvii voiny 1914–1920* (Moscow, 1923), 5–6. Semashko was not alone in these concerns; see also Pitrim Sorokin's 1922 article, "Veruiu, Gospodi!" *Otechestvennye arkhivy* 2 (1992): 47–53; Ts.S.U., *Rossiia v mirovoi voine 1914–1918 goda (v tsifrakh)* (Moscow, 1925), 5, 10.

14. RGAE f. 1562, op. 21, d. 25, ll. 77–78.

15. RGAE f. 1562 s. ch., op. 329, d. 21, ll. 125–27. The totals for all Ukraine in 1933 were 449,877 births and 1,908,907 deaths; l. 109.

16. S. G. Strumilin, "K probleme rozhdaemosti v rabochei srede," in *Problemy ekonomiki truda* (Moscow, 1957), 194–98.

17. Strumilin, 201–4; V. Z. Drobizhev, *U istokov sovetskoi demografii* (Moscow, 1987), 22.

Soviet officials now had to revise their assumption that the birthrate would rise as material conditions improved. Increasingly they saw low fertility as the result of women's choices to have abortions—choices made by women who, in their view, could afford to have children but chose not to out of personal preference. One other factor that exacerbated the decline in fertility was the abnormally small population cohort that entered its child-bearing years in the mid-1930s. In addition to decimating a generation of young men, the First World War had greatly reduced the number of children born between 1915 and 1920. It was this reduced cohort that reached childbearing age in the mid-1930s, even further depressing the birthrate.[18] Consequently Soviet officials became as obsessed with declining birthrates as did their counterparts in Western Europe.

In addition to its demographic repercussions, the First World War also reinforced, among some world leaders, social Darwinist ideas about the competition of nations and the struggle of races to survive and propagate. Mussolini articulated these ideas most explicitly when he declared, "Fertile people have a right to an Empire, those with the will to propagate their race on the face of the earth."[19] Japanese leaders similarly maintained that overseas expansion and colonization helped the "regeneration" of a nation's people, and that nations that did not expand were doomed to decline.[20] United States exclusionists in the 1920s employed analogous logic to argue for limits on Asian and Mediterranean immigration to prevent "inferior stocks...from both diluting and supplanting good stocks."[21] Leaders throughout Europe linked falling birthrates in the 1930s to a decline in national power. One Spanish demographer warned that without more children, "Spain will be reduced, she will shrink, the national economy

18. E. A. Sadvokasova, *Sotsial'no-gigienicheskie aspekty regulirovaniia razmerov sem'i* (Moscow, 1969), 28–29.

19. David Horn, *Social Bodies: Science, Reproduction, and Italian Modernity* (Princeton, 1994), 59. See also Quine, *Population Politics*, 34; Carl Ipsen, *Dictating Demography: The Problem of Population in Fascist Italy* (New York, 1996), 65–68.

20. John Dower, *War without Mercy: Race and Power in the Pacific War* (New York, 1986), 271.

21. Prescott Hall used the following biological analogy to reinforce his point: "Just as we isolate bacterial invasions, and starve out the bacteria by limiting the area and amount of their food supply, so we can compel an inferior race to remain in its native habitat, where its own multiplication in a limited area will, as with all organisms, eventually limit its numbers and therefore its influence." Prescott F. Hall, "Immigration Restriction and World Eugenics," *Journal of Heredity* 10:3 (March 1919), 126–27, as cited in Sumiko Otsubo, "Eugenics in Imperial Japan: Some Ironies of Modernity, 1883–1945" (Ph.D. diss., Ohio State University, 1998), chapter 5.

will be without producers and consumers; the State, without soldiers; the Nation, without blood." Franco had the goal of increasing the Spanish population to 40 million within a few decades, and saw this as a means to recapture Spain's faded glory and world prominence.[22] The Swedish government appointed a population commission in 1935 following the publication of a best-selling book by Alva and Gunner Myrdal that described the falling birthrate as a slow, national suicide.[23] And a range of political leaders and scholars in interwar Romania also believed that the country's strength and survival rested on its birthrate and "human capital."[24]

Soviet leaders also envisioned reproductive competition between countries, but not in biological or racial terms. The Central Statistical Administration compiled annual charts on fertility, which showed in 1935, for example, that Soviet fertility was higher than that of all "the capitalist countries" (listing all the other countries of Europe).[25] I. A. Kraval', the head of the statistics division of Gosplan, argued that the Soviet Union's higher fertility proved the superiority of socialism over capitalism.[26] And in 1935 Stalin boasted that due to workers' improved material conditions, "the population has begun to multiply much more quickly than in previous times. . . . Now each year our population increases by around three million people. This means that each year we receive an increase equivalent to the whole of Finland."[27]

Party leaders, then, also had a sense of reproductive competition vis-à-vis other countries, but they conceived of this competition in ideological rather than racial terms. They never used phrases such as "national superiority" or "race suicide." Instead they claimed the Soviet Union's higher birthrate demonstrated that the population was thriving thanks to socialist economic and social conditions, not because of biological ascendancy. Given that the Soviet Union was a multinational federation in which all ethnic groups were supposed to be equal partners, Darwinian competition between nationalities made no sense. According to Marxist ideology,

22. Mary Nash, "Pronatalism and Motherhood in Franco's Spain," *Maternity and Gender Policies*, 163; Quine, *Population Politics*, 88.

23. Karin Johannisson, "The People's Health: Public Health Policies in Sweden," *The History of Public Health and the Modern State*, ed. Dorothy Porter (Amsterdam, 1994), 178.

24. Maria Bucur, *Eugenics and Modernization in Interwar Romania* (Pittsburgh, 2002), 63–64.

25. RGAE f. 1562, s. ch., op. 329, d. 83, l. 1. The report also listed the fertility rates of republics within the Soviet Union. Armenia had the highest fertility, followed by the Russian Federation, Turkmenistan, Belorussia, Azerbaijan, Ukraine, and Tajikistan.

26. *Pravda*, January 1, 1936, 8.

27. Quoted in "Zabota o zdorov'e detei," *Gigiena i zdorov'e* 9 (1938): 1.

national differences both within the Soviet Union and between other countries were to disappear over time, as all national and ethnic groups became merged under socialism. Rather than a competition between nations to propagate and dominate, Party leaders perceived a contest between capitalism and socialism, and a high birthrate among all Soviet nationalities would prove the superiority of the socialist system.

Soviet pronatalism was also distinguished by its avowed purpose for increasing the birthrate. In May 1918, with memories of the First World War still fresh, Soviet delegates to a congress on social welfare resolved that infant mortality be reduced and children's lives preserved "not for a new slaughter, but as builders of a new, beautiful, working life, as spiritually and physically strong citizens, fighters for the ideals of socialism and humankind." The resolution went on to reiterate that children not be raised for wars caused by "the criminal negligence of a capitalist state," but rather to provide productive labor to build the new society.[28] Reproduction in the Soviet Union, then, was to produce laborers rather than soldiers. Of course, Party leaders also had military concerns, particularly with the rising international tensions of the late 1930s, and they saw the country's large population as crucial to its military might. But unlike fascist leaders, they did not seek to increase the birthrate for the purposes of military aggression and domination.

While the motivations behind pronatalism varied, the demographic techniques used in different countries were strikingly similar. As was true of public health, demography had acquired a truly international character already in the nineteenth century, and by the twentieth century scholars were reading and translating the work of foreign colleagues, and meeting regularly to discuss their work. Perhaps the best examples of this exchange were a number of international conferences on population held in Europe between the wars. The Soviet Union sent representatives to most of these conferences, including the 1927 World Population Conference in Geneva. Delegates there came from a wide range of countries and political leanings, and yet they all shared the common assumption that populations could be scientifically studied and that governments should manage their populations.[29] The 1931 International Population Congress in Rome was also attended by officials and scholars from Asia, North America, South America, and most countries of Europe including the Soviet Union. The

28. As cited in Drobizhev, *U istokov sovetskoi demografii*, 110.
29. *Proceedings of the World Population Conference.* For further discussion, see Horn, *Social Bodies*, 50.

presiding president, Professor Corrado Gini (the honorary president of the Congress was Mussolini himself), opened the meeting with a call for intensified research on population trends and further research in "general biology, genetics, eugenics, anthropometry and hygiene." Sessions at the congress focused on "The Future of Populations," and included studies on "The Demographic Laws of War," and the question of depopulation. One French scholar concluded that some countries of Europe were in a state of virtual depopulation, "a dangerous situation," and that "for European nations, there is no problem more vital than the struggle against falling fertility." Another scholar cautioned that falling mortality rates of the "primitive races" meant that they would increase their populations much faster than would the "modern civilized countries," and that this fact should be considered by "every statesman and worker concerned with the future of mankind."[30]

International conferences and exchanges, then, spread not only demographic techniques but also population concerns. In countries around the world, including the Soviet Union, official demographers gathered population statistics as never before during the interwar period. Study and concern with population issues in turn spurred government efforts to manage reproduction. Although Soviet officials and social scientists shared in these concerns, they were distinguished by their rejection of social Darwinist thought and racial approaches to population questions. And the fact that they conceived of the population in nonracial terms and sought the reproduction of all groups within society determined the types of reproductive policies they adopted.

Contraception, Abortion, and Reproductive Health

Political leaders' consternation with population trends led them to contemplate ways to elevate their countries' birthrates. Once populations could be represented statistically, and fertility trends explained based on demographic studies, it became possible to conceive of state control of fertility. Aside from pronatalist propaganda, the primary means by which government officials sought to increase birthrates were restrictions on contraception and abortion. The Soviet Union, like other countries, discouraged contraception, outlawed abortion, and sought to regulate sexuality and reproductive health.

30. Fernand Bovenat, "L'avenir de la population européene," *Atti* 7: 88. See also *Atti* 1: xxxviii–xxxix; 6: 232–34.

In the early twentieth century, political leaders in many countries criticized contraception and abortion. In Germany abortion had been in the penal code since 1872, and during the First World War the advertisement of contraceptives was banned and antiabortion legislation was tightened.[31] The French government also took steps against contraception and abortion. It outlawed the advertisement and sale of contraceptives in 1920, stating, "In the aftermath of the war where almost one and a half million Frenchmen sacrificed their lives so that France could have the right to live in independence and honor, it cannot be tolerated that other French have the right to make a livelihood from the spread of abortion and Malthusian propaganda." And in 1923 the French government increased penalties for abortion to imprisonment for abortionists and their clients.[32] The Italian penal code of 1931 mandated prison terms of two to five years for anyone procuring or performing an abortion, and the Romanian 1936 penal code criminalized abortion.[33] Many non-European countries also banned abortion in the interwar period, including Turkey, Australia, and Japan.[34]

Soviet leaders were also extremely concerned about the effect of contraception and abortion on their country's birthrate. The Soviet government had legalized abortion in November 1920. The decree noted the growing number of illegal abortions (due to extreme economic hardship in the wake of the Civil War), and in the interest of women's health allowed free abortions in hospitals provided that they were performed by doctors. The decree, however, never recognized abortion as a woman's right. Indeed Semashko explicitly stated at the time that abortion was not an individual

31. Elisabeth Domansky, "Militarization and Reproduction in World War I Germany," *Society, Culture, and the State in Germany, 1870–1930,* ed. Geoff Eley (Ann Arbor, 1996), 450–51; Lisa Pine, *Nazi Family Policy, 1933–1945* (New York, 1997), 19–20. While the Weimar government relaxed penalties for abortion, the Nazi government in 1933 enacted even harsher laws against abortion and contraception, and during the Second World War decreed the death penalty for those who repeatedly carried out abortions; Claudia Koonz, *Mothers in the Fatherland: Women, the Family and Nazi Politics* (New York, 1987), 185–87.

32. William H. Schneider, *Quality and Quantity: The Quest for Biological Regeneration in Twentieth-Century France* (New York, 1990), 120; Karen Offen, "Body Politics: Women, Work, and the Politics of Motherhood in France, 1900–1950," *Maternity and Gender Policies,* 138.

33. Victoria de Grazia, *How Fascism Ruled Women: Italy, 1922–1945* (Berkeley, 1992), 58; Bucur, *Eugenics and Modernization,* 206.

34. Ayca Alemdaroglu, "Politics of the Body and Eugenic Discourse in Early Republican Turkey," *Body and Society* 11:3 (2005): 69; Milton Lewis, "Maternity Care and the Threat of Puerperal Fever in Sydney, 1870–1939," *Women and Children First,* 36–37; Otsubo, "Eugenics in Imperial Japan," chapter 6.

right, that it could depress the birthrate and hurt the interests of the state, and that it should be practiced only in extreme cases.[35]

The Soviet government legalized birth control in 1923, and two years later it established the Central Scientific Commission for the Study of Contraceptives. Debates at the time divided physicians between those who supported contraception as a means to reduce the number of abortions and prevent the spread of venereal disease, and those who argued that it would depress the birthrate and threaten the country's strength, and perhaps even its survival.[36] Soviet leaders resolved the matter in the 1930s when they did not allocate resources for the manufacture of contraceptives, ordering the withdrawal from sale of any remaining contraceptive devices in 1936.[37] Official concern about abortion, however, grew ever more intense. Even before the sharp drop in fertility during the 1930s, some doctors called abortion "a great antisocial factor" and "a threat to the steady growth of the population."[38] In an agitational mock trial published in 1925, the prosecutor asks a young woman who had an abortion, "Do you understand...that you have killed a future person, a citizen who might have been useful for society?"[39] Antiabortion propaganda, however, failed to have much effect. By the mid-1930s, the number of abortions in the Russian Federation almost equaled the number of births (1,319,700 abortions in hospitals versus 1,392,800 births in 1935). In large cities abortions far outnumbered births; there were 57,000 births and 154,600 abortions recorded in Moscow in 1934.[40]

The legislative centerpiece of the Soviet government's campaign to raise the birthrate was the decree of June 27, 1936, that outlawed abortion, except for medical reasons. Politburo discussion of the decree prior to its

35. See Wendy Z. Goldman, *Women, the State and Revolution: Soviet Family Policy and Social Life, 1917–1936* (New York, 1993), 255–56.

36. Susan Gross Solomon, "The Demographic Argument in Soviet Debates over the Legalization of Abortion in the 1920s," *Cahiers du monde russe et soviétique* 33 (1992), 66–67; Frances Lee Bernstein, *The Dictatorship of Sex: Lifestyle Advice for the Soviet Masses* (DeKalb, 2007), 167–68.

37. Peter Solomon, Jr., *Soviet Criminal Justice under Stalin* (New York, 1996), 212.

38. Goldman, *Women, the State and Revolution*, 288. See also N. B. Lebina, "Abortnaia politika kak zerkalo sovetskoi sotsial'noi zaboty," *Sovetskaia sotsial'naia politika 1920–1930-kh godov: Ideologiia i povsednevnost': Sbornik statei*, ed. P. V. Romanov and B. P. Iarskaia-Smirnova (Moscow, 2007).

39. A. E. Kanevskii, *Sud nad Annoi Gorbovoi, po obvineniiu v proizvodstve sebe vykidysha (aborta)* (Odessa, 1925), 7–8, as cited in Eric Naiman, *Sex in Public: The Incarnation of Early Soviet Ideology* (Princeton, 1997), 109.

40. RGAE f. 1562 s. ch., op. 329, d. 407, l. 67; *Izvestiia*, July 12, 1936, as cited in Lorimer, *The Population*, 127.

promulgation emphasized the importance of achieving the maximum possible birthrate.[41] The Politburo subsequently decided "to limit as much as
possible the list of medical reasons" for permitting an abortion, and this
decision was promulgated later in a November 1936 decree that limited
permission for abortions to cases in which hereditary diseases were likely
or in which a woman's life was endangered. The decree stated, "Abortion is not only harmful for a woman's health, but is also a serious social
evil, the battle with which is the duty of every conscious citizen, especially
medical personnel."[42]

The ban on abortion was preceded by a huge publicity campaign and
public discussion of a draft of the decree, and it was followed by further
propaganda on the new law's validity and importance. Numerous articles
emphasized the harm that abortions did to women's physical and mental
health.[43] (No mention was made of the extreme danger posed to the health
of women who subsequently had illegal abortions.) One article asserted
that the "single goal" of the decree was "the protection of the health of the
Soviet mother."[44] Semashko, now the former commissar of health, warned
that abortion not only could cause infertility, but that it could have an
adverse effect on a woman's other organs and nervous system. But he also
justified the ban on abortion as crucial to "the state task of increasing
the population of the Soviet Union." He went on to compare the fertility
rate of the Soviet Union with those of other industrialized countries and
argued that the abortion ban would allow the country to maintain or even
increase its superior birthrate.[45]

The abortion ban was but the most visible example of Soviet efforts to
control women's bodies. Soviet medical researchers sought more generally to maximize reproduction through a range of studies and measures
to safeguard women's reproductive capacities. Soviet medical specialists
in the 1920s used the language of industrial production to characterize
reproduction, including the term *productive capacity* to describe women's
ability to become pregnant and bear healthy babies.[46] A. S. Gofshtein,

41. *Sobranie zakonov i rasporiazhenii* 34 (July 21, 1936): 510–11; RGASPI f. 17, op. 3,
d. 976, l. 4.

42. RGASPI f. 17, op. 3, d. 980, l. 1; d. 982, ll. 126–30.

43. *Rabotnitsa i krest'ianka* 11 (1936): 6; 12: 1. See also *Izvestiia*, June 5, 1935.

44. *Pravda*, September 5, 1936, 4.

45. N. A. Semashko, "Zamechatel'nyi zakon (o zapreshchenii aborta)," *Front nauki i
tekhniki* 7 (1936): 38.

46. Hyer, "Managing the Female Organism," 113. Sex reform experts in Weimar
Germany were also influenced by industrial rationalization and sought, in the words of

in his article, "The Rationalization of Maternity," called mothers "producers" and wrote that pregnancy could be "productive" or "unproductive," depending on whether it ended with the birth of a healthy child or with miscarriage, abortion, or infant mortality. Gofshtein studied the histories of pregnant women and calculated that women would optimize their productivity by having three children, each four years apart. He noted that more frequent pregnancies weakened "the female organism," produced sickly children, and diminished women's value in the workforce.[47] Other Soviet doctors studied reproductive capacity by combining obstetrics and gynecology with anthropometry (for example, measuring women's pelvises). One researcher warned that women who worked in factories had more narrow (and hence inferior) pelvises than women who did not.[48]

Because women in the Soviet system were expected to serve as both mothers and workers, specialists showed particular concern with the effects of industrial labor on women's reproductive abilities. They conducted studies on the effect of heavy lifting and concluded that it could damage pelvic organs and cause problems with pregnancy. In 1921 and again in 1927 the Soviet government established employment guidelines to ensure that women were not in jobs that required heavy lifting, for fear that such work would harm their reproductive organs.[49] Health officials also promoted physical examinations and education as means to protect women's reproductive capacities. Delegates to the Third All-Union Conference on the Protection of Maternity and Infancy in 1926 stressed that young women from the beginning of their sexual maturity should have regular medical consultations, initially arranged through schools. They also noted that these consultations would give doctors the opportunity to educate women about the dangers of abortion and diseases. Throughout the 1920s sexologists carried out studies and educational efforts, most of

---

one scholar, "the extension of assembly line techniques into housework and the bedroom." Atina Grossmann, "The New Woman and the Rationalization of Sexuality in Weimar Germany," *Powers of Desire: The Politics of Sexuality*, ed. Ann Snitow, Christine Stansell, and Sharon Thompson (New York, 1983), 163.

47. A. S. Gofshtein, "Ratsionalizatsiia materinstva," *Vrachebnoe delo* 19 (1927), as cited in Hyer, "Managing the Female Organism," 113–18.

48. Hyer, "Managing the Female Organism," 115.

49. Ibid., 116–17; Thomas Schrand, "Industrialization and the Stalinist Gender System: Women Workers in the Soviet Economy, 1928–1941" (Ph.D. diss., University of Michigan, 1994), 159–60. See also GARF f. 5528, op. 5, d. 44, ll. 4–5.

which emphasized the social importance of women's reproductive health and childbearing.[50]

Soviet health officials devoted special attention to the battle with venereal disease. Fueling their concerns was the perception of a venereal disease epidemic in the wake of the First World War. Already prior to the October Revolution, in June 1917, the Pirogov Society had sponsored the All-Russian Meeting for the Fight against Venereal Disease. This conference created a national coordinating committee that was subsequently absorbed into the Central Commission for the Fight against Venereal Disease within the Commissariat of Health.[51] The commission was to centralize the efforts of government and nongovernment organizations (including the Commissariat of Internal Affairs, the International Red Cross, the Moscow University Medical Department, and the Pirogov Society), and in late 1918, it issued an alarmist report:

> With the end of the war, hundreds of thousands and even millions of those with venereal disease have returned to Russian cities and villages and (intentionally and unintentionally) have tirelessly spread a grave disaster for the country. They spread death and the extinction of the people. It is necessary to take quickly the most energetic, broad, and active measures in the battle with this grave disaster.... [It is necessary] to save, as much as possible, the population of the Russian Republic from extinction.[52]

Health officials' early focus on venereal disease created a link in Soviet medical discourse between sexuality and sickness. This implicit connection meant that sex, in the eyes of Soviet physicians, was something potentially deleterious that had to be controlled. In addition, perceptions of rampant venereal disease reinforced Soviet health officials' conviction that sex was a public rather than a private matter, as they argued that the new society could not be achieved until the masses were sexually healthy.[53]

50. *Resoliutsii III Vsesoiuznogo soveshchaniia po okhane materinstva i mladenchestva* (Moscow, 1926), 17–18; M. S. Malinovskii and E. M. Shvartsman, *Gigiena zhenshchiny*, 3rd ed. (Moscow-Leningrad, 1935), 5.

51. Bernstein, *Dictatorship of Sex*, 18–19. On British government efforts to prevent venereal disease, see the report of the 1923 British Committee of Inquiry on VD that called for more rigorous medical intervention and instruction; PRO MH 55, 191. See also Magnus Hirschfield, *The Sexual History of the World War* (New York, 1941).

52. GARF f. A-482, op. 1, d. 27, ll. 1–4.

53. Bernstein, *Dictatorship of Sex*, 19, 100–101. See also Dan Healey, *Bolshevik Sexual Forensics: Diagnosing Disorder in the Clinic and the Courtroom, 1917–1939* (DeKalb, 2009).

Even after the immediate crisis had passed, venereal disease remained a widespread problem and a principal focus of Soviet sexual enlightenment work. In an article entitled, "The Social Significance of Syphilis," one Soviet specialist cited the opinion of a British doctor who claimed that syphilis threatened the child, the family, and the state. He went on to warn that syphilitics often became infertile and that if they did have children, their offspring would be mentally deficient, causing "the state to suffer significant losses, not only losing able-bodied citizens, but also having to expend enormous resources on homes for the disabled."[54] Several organizations under the Commissariat of Health, including the State Institute of Social Hygiene and the State Venereological Institute, paid particular attention to venereal disease and patterns of sexual behavior. The Sexology Office of the State Institute of Social Hygiene conducted surveys on sex, while the Division of Social Venereology of the State Venereological Institute organized lectures and exhibits on venereal disease.[55]

The Commissariat of Health conducted extensive propaganda against the spread of venereal disease. Already in 1918 the venereal disease commission had issued a plan for lectures, discussions, and "tens of millions of brochures and posters" to educate the public about the dangers of venereal disease.[56] Moreover, an extensive network of venereal disease clinics conducted "sexual enlightenment work" as well as treating patients.[57] One strategy employed by health officials to teach people about the dangers of venereal disease were "sanitation trials"—mock trials held to condemn sexual licentiousness and raise awareness about the spread of venereal disease. A series of such trials was published in the mid-1920s and reached a wide audience through performances held around the country.[58]

Alongside educational work, Soviet authorities applied police measures to prevent the spread of venereal disease. The Soviet Criminal Code mandated up to six months imprisonment for anyone who knowingly infected another person with venereal disease.[59] The campaign against venereal disease focused particularly on prostitution. The Soviet Interdepartmental

54. *Gigiena i zdorov'e rabochei i krest'ianskoi sem'i* 8 (1926): 15.

55. Bernstein, *Dictatorship of Sex,* 21–22.

56. GARF f. A-482, op. 1, d. 27, l. 8. For an analysis of Soviet posters against venereal disease and prostitution, see Bernstein, *Dictatorship of Sex,* 114–23.

57. TsAGM f. 552, op. 1, d. 50, ll. 57–58. On the French National Social Hygiene Office's plays, films, and pamphlets about venereal disease, see Schneider, *Quality and Quantity,* 143.

58. Elizabeth A. Wood, *Performing Justice: Agitation Trials in Early Soviet Russia* (Ithaca, 2005), 114–27.

59. *Gigiena i zdorov'e rabochei i krest'ianskoi sem'i* 18 (1926): 14.

Commission on the Battle against Prostitution reported in 1921 that "in the interests of the physical and moral health of the entire population," measures had to be taken against prostitution. It blamed poverty, homelessness, and unemployment among women as the sources of prostitution. However, it also noted the existence of "professional prostitutes" who should be seen as "social parasites and labor deserters" and brought to justice.[60] Throughout the 1920s, Soviet officials relied on prophylactories where prostitutes could receive housing, medical attention, and job training in order to change their way of life. But by the 1930s, the Soviet government adopted the more coercive approach of incarcerating prostitutes in labor camps.[61]

Venereologists also focused on chance sexual encounters as a major cause of the spread of venereal disease. One doctor noted that during the summer, parks in Moscow, particularly Sokol'niki, were "hot-spots" of sexual activity and transmission of venereal diseases. He advocated not only the policing of parks, but also the distribution of prophylactics, in case chance sexual encounters could not be prevented. Another specialist cited the residences of migratory workers as sites where venereal diseases were commonly spread and recommended that doctors conduct medical checks and educational work there.[62] Indeed, interventions in people's residences and homes increasingly became a part of the government campaign against venereal disease. The director of a Moscow venereal disease clinic, noting that patients did not always tell their families of their illness, sent medical personnel to the homes of venereal disease patients to check whether other family members were infected and to educate them about the dangers of venereal disease.[63]

The fight against prostitution and venereal disease was part of a broader Soviet effort to control sexuality. In contrast to the prerevolutionary period when questions of marriage, sex, and morality fell under the authority of the Orthodox Church, sex during the 1920s came under the purview of Soviet medical specialists who viewed it primarily as a health issue to be managed through education and treatment. But these specialists employed a highly normative approach to sex that emphasized heterosexual sex in marriage with the object of procreation as the only legitimate form of sexual behavior. Sexologists such as G. N. Sorokhtin linked masturbation to "a pathological

60. GARF f. 4085, op. 12, d. 37, l. 32. On prostitution as the cause of venereal disease, see also *Voprosy zdravookhraneniia: Ofitsial'nyi otdel* 35 (1929): 430.

61. Bernstein, *Dictatorship of Sex,* 21; N. B. Lebina, *Povsednevnaia zhizn' sovetskogo goroda: Normy i anomalii, 1920–1930 gody* (St. Petersburg, 1999), 93–97.

62. TsAGM f. 552, op. 1, d. 50, ll. 74, 87.

63. TsAGM f. 552, op. 1, d. 26, ll. 3–6.

increase in egocentrism" and social deviance.[64] Aron Zalkind, a leading Soviet psychologist, denounced the "disorganization of sexual life," and described sexual energy as a working-class resource that should be preserved
for the sake of production.[65] Party leaders expressed similar concerns, as
Lenin himself labeled promiscuity "a sign of degeneration" and sought to
redirect sexual energy toward the tasks of socialist construction.[66]

Such stances by Party leaders and specialists paved the way for more repressive sexual policies in the 1930s. During the Great Break, the discipline
of social venereology suffered the same fate as the field of social hygiene,
and open discussion of sex and sexual behavior ceased. The journal of the
State Venereological Institute began instead to publish articles on medical
statistics, diagnoses, and medication. The lively theoretical debates of the
mid-1920s thus gave way to a more practical and coercive approach to
sexual problems. With the First Five-Year Plan, health officials focused
their efforts to combat venereal disease on factory construction sites, while
workers were exhorted to channel all their energies, sexual and otherwise,
to industrialization.[67] But it would be wrong to see this shift as the end
of attempts to rationalize sexuality and reproduction. As Frances Bernstein points out, the 1930s in a sense saw the realization of sexologists'
vision of sexual normalcy—abstinence except in the case of procreation,
the elimination of deviance, and an emphasis on reproductive needs of the
collective at the expense of the individual.[68] The Soviet government no longer permitted scholarly debate or discussion about sex in the 1930s, but
it imposed norms of sexual behavior and reproductive health all the more
vigorously, using police measures rather than education.

Promoting Motherhood and Family

Once reproduction came to be seen as a state concern, government leaders
around the world began to provide material support for mothers. A wide
range of people, from state officials and health experts, to members of

64. As quoted in Naiman, *Sex in Public*, 121. For a full discussion of Soviet sexologists'
condemnations of masturbation, see Bernstein, *Dictatorship of Sex*, 138–45.

65. A. B. Zalkind, *Polovoi vopros v usloviiakh sovetskoi obshchestvennosti: Sbornik statei*
(Leningrad, 1926), 6–14, 47–59. Other Soviet specialists made similar pronouncements about
the need to preserve and redirect sexual energy; see Bernstein, *Dictatorship of Sex*, 133–34.

66. K. Tsetkin, "Lenin o morale i voprosakh pola," *Komsomol'skii byt: Sbornik*, ed.
O. Razin (Moscow/Leningrad, 1927), 18–21.

67. Bernstein, *Dictatorship of Sex*, 185–87.

68. Ibid., 5–8, 190–92.

women's organizations and religious groups, agitated for increased government aid to mothers. Although the politics of maternalist welfare and the policies adopted varied from one country to another, the overall trend was toward extensive state aid and propaganda to promote motherhood. Soviet policies fit within this international trend, although they also had distinctive features, including a construction of gender that emphasized women's roles as workers as well as mothers.

State support and collective responsibility for mothers and children entailed a considerable departure from liberal principles in Britain and France. Already in the late nineteenth century, a number of social reformers began to question the adequacy of the capitalist wage system in providing for maternal and child welfare. They argued that free market determination of wages did not take account of the number of children families were raising and the collective interests of society in providing for children. Such ideas grew even stronger in the twentieth century. A leading British feminist, Eleanor Rathbone, pointed out that wages took no account of varying families' needs and advocated family allowance systems to balance the cost of reproduction. She also noted that paying benefits to mothers would compensate them for their unpaid domestic and reproductive work. From a nonfeminist perspective the French social commentator Fernand Boverat came to very similar conclusions, arguing that children were a collective resource. He stated that redistribution of income from the childless to those with children was fair and necessary, because children born to any couple would sustain France's economic and military capacity.[69]

World War I provided an additional impetus for maternal welfare assistance. Although the German League for the Protection of Mothers agitated for maternity insurance and childcare facilities prior to the war, the German government finally decreed substantial benefits for mothers in 1916.[70] By the early 1920s, extensive family allowance schemes had been established by state decree or employer initiatives in France and Belgium, and through collective bargaining in Austria.[71] Governments in the interwar

---

69. Susan Pedersen, *Family, Dependence, and the Origins of the Welfare State: Britain and France, 1914–1945* (New York, 1993), 2–4.

70. Paul Weindling, "German-Soviet Cooperation in Science: The Case of the Laboratory for Racial Research," *Nuncius* 1 (1986): 252–53; Quine, *Population Politics*, 105–6; Usborne, *The Politics of the Body*, 20–21.

71. Pedersen, *Family, Dependence, and the Origins of the Welfare State*, 4. The Japanese government enacted a Maternal and Child Protection Law in 1937, which provided assistance to needy mothers; Otsubo, "Eugenics in Imperial Japan," chapter 6; Dower, *War without Mercy*, 271

period also adjusted their tax codes to reward families with children and punish people with none. Beginning in 1920 the French government added a 25 percent surcharge on the income tax of male and female celibates over thirty years old and a 10 percent surcharge on couples who remained childless after ten years of marriage, and in 1927 Mussolini instituted a bachelor tax on unmarried Italian men between the ages of twenty-five and sixty-five.[72] Italy and France also awarded birth bonuses to encourage people to have children. In 1935, the Italian government decreed aid to large families in Italy and bonuses to soldiers and civil servants for the birth of each new child, while the 1939 French Family Code introduced a birth premium of several thousand francs for the first child born within two years of marriage.[73] The Nazi government also awarded grants to large families beginning in 1935, but it gave them only to "hereditarily healthy" German families. It thereby practiced a selective type of pronatalism that encouraged reproduction only among people it deemed physically and racially fit.[74]

The Soviet government offered financial inducements similar to those in Italy and France. The same decree that outlawed abortion granted women a two thousand ruble annual bonus for each child they had over six children, and a five thousand ruble bonus for each child over ten children. These bonuses drew an immediate response from women with seven or more children. Local officials were deluged by requests from (primarily peasant) women who qualified for these bonuses.[75] Significantly, the Soviet government encouraged reproduction among all members of the population, without distinction by class or ethnicity. A government report in November 1936 clarified that mothers with seven or more children should receive bonuses regardless of their social origins, and even regardless of whether their husbands had been arrested for counterrevolutionary activity.[76] Thus the Soviet government promoted reproduction even among those it considered class enemies.

The Soviet government also sought to increase the birthrate among national minorities. Officials in Kazakhstan, for example, sought to raise the

---

72. Quine, *Population Politics*, 71; Ipsen, *Dictating Demography*, 73.

73. Quine, *Population Politics*, 79; Offen, "Body Politics," 138, 150; Horn, *Social Bodies*, 89–90.

74. Pine, *Nazi Family Policy*, 109. On Nazi antinatalism, see below the section on eugenics.

75. *Sobranie zakonov i rasporiazhenii* no. 34 (July 21, 1936), 511; GARF f. 5446, op. 18a, d. 2753, l. 4. The Soviet government had to allot 35 million rubles in 1936 alone to pay such bonuses; GARF f. 5446, op. 18a, d. 2753, l. 31.

76. GARF f. 5446, op. 18a, d. 2754, l. 32.

birthrate among Kazakh women. Even prior to the abortion ban, very few Kazakh women had abortions, so antiabortion propaganda in Kazakhstan was directed primarily at Slavic women living there. But Soviet authorities did target pronatalist propaganda and incentives at Kazakh women, substantial numbers of whom received bonuses for having seven or more children.[77] Already in the 1920s, Soviet health officials had stressed the need to increase postnatal care among national minorities in order to reduce infant mortality, and beginning in 1936 the Soviet government expanded maternity wards and nurseries in Central Asian republics.[78]

In addition to bonuses paid to individuals, the Soviet government encouraged motherhood through maternity facilities and pronatalist propaganda. Within months of coming to power, the Soviet government founded a large number of maternity homes, nurseries, milk kitchens, and pediatric clinics. With the pronatalist push of the mid-1930s, funding for maternity wards and nurseries increased even more, though not enough to meet the needs of the millions of women in the workforce. In principle, however, the Soviet government committed itself to complete care for mothers and children.[79] The Soviet government also sought to ensure that women did not avoid pregnancy for fear of losing their jobs or wages. As early as 1921 the government decreed that pregnant women who were unable to work were entitled to receive their full salary from workers' insurance funds. By 1927 Soviet law guaranteed women eight weeks of paid leave both before and after giving birth.[80]

The Soviet government also celebrated motherhood and portrayed having children as a natural and fulfilling part of a woman's life. Articles in the Soviet press stressed the happiness that children brought to women. One testimonial from a woman with five children described how much her children loved her, while another article claimed that children took care

77. Paula Michaels, "Motherhood, Patriotism, and Ethnicity: Soviet Kazakhstan and the 1936 Abortion Ban," *Feminist Studies* 27:2 (2001): 312–16, 322–23.

78. *Resoliutsii III Vses. soveshchaniia po okhrane materinstva i mladenchestva*, 2, 10; Michaels, "Motherhood, Patriotism, and Ethnicity," 320–21. See also Cassandra Cavanaugh, "Backwardness and Biology: Medicine and Power in Russian and Soviet Central Asia, 1868–1934" (Ph.D. diss., Columbia University, 2001), chapter 5.

79. Drobizhev, *U istokov sovetskoi demografii*, 109, 122; GARF f. 5446, op. 18a, d. 2754, l. 45. See, for example, the draft of a pamphlet by Elena Stasova, "For Women in the USSR All Paths Are Open," in which she emphasizes the material aid provided by the Soviet government to mothers. RGASPI f. 17, op. 120, d. 202, l. 11.

80. GARF f. 4085, op. 12, d. 320, l. 16; A. V. Mol'kov and N. A. Semashko, eds., *Sotsial'naia gigiena: Rukovodstvo dlia studentov-medikov* (Moscow-Leningrad, 1927), 318.

of each other, so that having many children was an advantage rather than a burden.[81] Governments around the world launched similar propaganda campaigns to promote motherhood. Many countries began to celebrate Mother's Day, including the United States, which declared it a national holiday in 1914. The French government bestowed bronze, silver, or gold medals on women with five, eight, or ten children, respectively. The Nazi government gave mothers of many children the Cross of Honor of the German Mother and allowed women who bore their fifth child to name a national leader as the godfather of their baby (though when Hindenburg proved more popular than Hitler in this category, the program was suspended).[82]

Although the Soviet effort to glorify motherhood resembled pronatalist propaganda in other countries, it was distinguished in one crucial way. The Soviet government encouraged and expected women to continue working while pregnant and after giving birth. To ensure that pregnant women could find or maintain jobs outside the home, the Politburo approved a decree in October 1936 that made it a criminal offense to refuse to hire or to lower the pay of women during pregnancy.[83] The Soviet construction of gender emphasized women's roles as both workers and mothers and denied there was any contradiction between the two. By contrast, many officials and social commentators in Western Europe blamed feminism and women's employment outside the home for the decline in the birthrate. In the early 1920s, General Maitrot in France stated, "There are too many women typists and civil servants here and not enough *mères de famille*. With respect to natality, the German mothers have beaten the French mothers; this is Germany's first revenge against France."[84] Nazi leaders also stressed traditional gender roles, and some of their financial incentives for childbearing required women to give up paid employment.[85]

---

81. *Martenovka* May 1, 1936, 5; *Rabotnitsa i krest'ianka* 15 (1936): 5. See also *Gigiena i zdorov'e* 4 (1938): 6.

82. Offen, "Body Politics," 138, 150; Pine, *Nazi Family Policy,* 96; Koonz, *Mothers in the Fatherland,* 185–86.

83. RGASPI f. 17, op. 3, d. 981, l. 69.

84. Offen, "Body Politics," 138.

85. David L. Hoffmann and Annette F. Timm, "Utopian Biopolitics: Reproductive Policies, Gender Roles, and Sexuality in Nazi Germany and the Soviet Union," *Beyond Totalitarianism: Stalinism and Nazism Compared,* ed. Michael Geyer and Sheila Fitzpatrick (New York, 2009), 117. With the increasing shortage of labor after 1936, Nazi leaders actually eliminated this requirement in an effort to mobilize women's labor.

In their efforts to raise the birthrate, policymakers in many countries glorified not only motherhood but also the family. Already in the nineteenth century, some social commentators expressed alarm over the disintegration of traditional families. The influential French sociologist Frédéric Le Play warned that urbanization had undermined the family and had fostered the corrupting influences of individualism, socialism, and feminism. He held up the patriarchal family of rural societies as his ideal, noting that peasant families had very high fertility, and he proposed legal measures to strengthen the family. Given French concerns about the birthrate and pro-family activism by Catholic organizations, his ideas resonated with many political leaders and social thinkers.[86] During the interwar period, political leaders throughout Europe began to emphasize the importance of the family to social stability and national strength. Both the Salazar dictatorship in Portugal and the Franco regime in Spain sought to restore the family as the pillar of society.[87] Nazi leaders heralded the traditional peasant family as a bulwark against the fragmentation and alienation of modernity. They promoted an essentialized vision of women as mothers and, in contrast to other countries, paid family allowances to fathers rather than mothers, stating, "a man will no longer be materially or morally worse off in competition with the so-called clever bachelor, merely because he has done his duty to the nation."[88]

Soviet attempts to strengthen the family paralleled those of other countries in content and (pronatalist) objectives. But unique to the Soviet Union was the fact that the family there had been denounced as a bourgeois institution. It was by no means predetermined that Soviet leaders would choose the family as the institution through which to pursue pronatalist ambitions. There was a clearly articulated alternative model for the sexual and social organization of Soviet society: childbirth outside of wedlock and collective responsibility for childraising. The leading Soviet feminist, Aleksandra Kollontai, had advanced a vision of love freed from the confines of marriage and women spared the burden of childraising through collective responsibility and state-funded childcare. Other Soviet thinkers in the 1920s supported this view, such as sociologist S. Ia. Vol'fson, who

86. Quine, *Population Politics*, 55–58. Beginning in the nineteenth century and continuing through the interwar period, commentators contrasted the sterilizing effect of the city with the "natural" fertility of the countryside. See Horn, *Social Bodies*, 98–99.

87. Quine, *Population Politics*, 86; Nash, "Pronatalism and Motherhood," 160–66.

88. Koonz, *Mothers in the Fatherland*, 178; Gisela Bock, "Antinatalism, Maternity, and Paternity in National Socialist Racism," *Maternity and Gender Policies*, 243.

Fig. 9. Nazi pronatalist poster, 1938. "Support the relief organization Mother and Child."
Poster identification number GE 3869, Poster Collection, Hoover Institution Archives.

looked forward to the day when the family "will be sent to a museum of antiquities."[89]

Many Party leaders including Lenin, however, believed in the importance of marriage. They regarded sexual liberation and the elimination of the family as distractions from (if not perversions of) socialism.[90] Medical specialists too sought to maintain the institution of marriage. Dr. A. O. Uspenskii stated, "Normal sex only takes place in marriage; without it one can't talk about normal sex."[91] Soviet jurists also blamed family disintegration for the thousands of homeless or neglected children who represented an enormous social problem.[92] Ultimately Party leaders chose to maintain and even bolster the family. Not only did the family serve instrumentalist functions of increasing the birthrate and obligating parents to raise their children, it also corresponded to leaders' sense of propriety and notions of how socialist society should be organized (feminist voices notwithstanding).

In the mid-1930s, the Soviet government took steps to buttress the family. The 1936 decree that outlawed abortion also made divorce much more difficult. It largely reversed a 1918 decree that had deliberately weakened the institution of marriage by facilitating a quick and easy divorce at the demand of either spouse.[93] The new law required that both spouses appear in court to file for divorce. It also raised the fee for divorce from 3 to 50 rubles (with a fee of 150 rubles for a person's second divorce and 300 rubles for their third).[94] The Soviet government also sought to enhance the prestige and significance of marriage in the eyes of the population. Marriage registration offices were made more dignified, officials were instructed to treat marrying couples with politeness and respect, marriage certificates were beautified, and wedding rings began to be sold in shops. A propaganda campaign stressed the sanctity of marriage and family.[95]

89. S. Ia. Vol'fson, *Sotsiologiia braka i sem'i* (Minsk, 1929), 450, as cited in Goldman, *Women, the State, and Revolution,* 1.

90. Tsetkin, "Lenin o morale," 18–21.

91. As quoted in Bernstein, *Dictatorship of Sex,* 163. See also K. N. Kovalev, *Voprosy pola, polovogo vospitaniia, braka i sem'i* (Moscow, 1931), 2.

92. *O rassledovanii i rassmotrenii del o nesovershennoletnikh* (Moscow, 1937), 25–32; Goldman, *Women, the State, and Revolution,* 324.

93. *Pervyi kodeks zakonov ob aktakh grazdanskogo sostoianiia, brachnom, semeinom i opekunskom prave* (Moscow, 1918), as cited in Goldman, *Women, the State, and Revolution,* 49.

94. *Sobranie zakonov i rasporiazhenii raboche-krest'ianskogo pravitel'stva Soiuza Sovetskikh Sotsialisticheskikh Respublik* 34 (July 21, 1936): 515.

95. Nicholas S. Timasheff, *The Great Retreat: The Growth and Decline of Communism in Russia* (Russia, 1946), 200; *Pravda,* June 26, 1935, 1; *Rabotnitsa i krest'ianka* 12 (1936): 2; *Komsomol'skii rabotnik* 8 (1940): 3.

In tandem with its drive to strengthen the family, the Soviet government sought to enforce paternal obligations. A 1933 decree that required all births to be registered within one month included provisions for a mother to name the father of her child regardless of whether they were married or even whether he was present. Men who did not acknowledge paternity of a child would still be registered as the father if a mother named him as such and provided any evidence of cohabitation.[96] In 1936 the same law that outlawed abortion and made divorce more difficult also tightened regulations on child support. It set minimum levels of child support as one fourth of the unmarried or divorced father's salary for one child, one third for two children, and one half for three or more children. It also increased the penalty for nonpayment of child support to two years in prison.[97] In subsequent years the Soviet government proved serious about paternal responsibility and took numerous steps to track down delinquent fathers. Soviet propaganda also emphasized the importance of paternity; a lead article in *Pravda* entitled "Father" stated that "a father who does not want to accept his paternal obligations is the destroyer of the family."[98]

The Soviet government did not champion the family as a private commitment or as a means to personal fulfillment.[99] Instead it explicitly promoted the maintenance of one's family as an obligation to society and to the state. Komsomol chief Aleksandr Kosarev stated in 1934, "The stronger and more harmonious a family is, the better it serves the common cause.... We are for serious, stable marriages and large families. In short, we need a new generation that is healthy both physically and morally." A Soviet jurist added that "marriage receives its full value for the state only if there is progeny."[100] Soviet propaganda also stressed that parents were to raise their children for the sake of the Soviet state. As one commentator wrote in 1936, "Hand in hand with the state's establishments, the parents must rear children into conscious and active workers for socialist society.... Parents must instill in their children ... readiness to lay down their life at any moment for their socialist country."[101]

96. *Gosudarstvennoe upravlenie: Kodifitsirovannyi sbornik zakonodatel'stva RSFSR na 1 ianvaria 1934 goda* (Moscow, 1934), 49.

97. *Sobranie zakonov i rasporiazhenii* 34 (July 21, 1936): 515–16.

98. GARF f. 9492 s.ch., op. 1, d. 2, l. 183; *Pravda*, June 9, 1936, 1.

99. Frances Bernstein notes that, unlike sex reformers in interwar Western Europe who advocated the companionate marriage and sexual fulfillment for both spouses, Soviet sexual enlightenment workers made no reference to sexual pleasure in marriage; Bernstein, *Dictatorship of Sex*, 161.

100. TsKhDMO f. 1, op. 23, d. 1074, ll. 98–99, 108; *Sotsialisticheskaia zakonnost'* 2 (1939).

101. V. Svetlov, "Socialist Society and the Family," *Changing Attitudes in Soviet Russia: Documents and Readings*, ed. Rudolf Schlesinger (London, 1949), 334.

Other countries also promoted the family not as an independent entity but as an instrument of the state or, in the Nazi case, of the race. For all the Nazis' rhetoric about restoring traditional families, the model that they promoted directly violated the conservative ideal of limited state intrusion into private life. Nazi policy strove to create a family unit that facilitated rather than guarded against state intervention, and one that served state goals of population growth and racial purity, rather than individual liberties concerning reproduction and childrearing. As Hitler had written in *Mein Kampf,* "Marriage cannot be an end in itself, but must serve the one higher goal, the increase and preservation of the species and the race."[102] The 1935 Marriage Health Law required people to obtain a certificate of fitness to marry, and Nazi eugenic policies intervened directly in the reproductive choices of married couples. Moreover, despite its incessant profamily propaganda, the Nazi government enacted a 1938 law that sanctioned divorce in cases of "premature infertility" and "refusal to procreate," and once the war began it even encouraged extramarital sex if it produced more "Aryan" babies.[103] As Jacques Donzelot writes regarding French family policy in the modern era, the family was made "a sphere of direct intervention," and there occurred a "transition from a government of families to a government through families."[104]

State intervention in family matters necessitates one qualification to the characterization of Soviet policies as "strengthening" the family. While the Soviet government encouraged marriage, discouraged divorce, and emphasized familial responsibility, it did not fortify the family's control or autonomy. On the contrary, it reaffirmed the social and civic role of the family, and weakened the family as a bulwark against state intervention in private life. The Soviet family, as did families in many societies, acted as the key institution that mediated between individual desire and state interests.[105] Soviet officials utilized the institution of the family to create norms of sexual behavior and social organization, because they believed that stable marriages and large families would promote population growth.

102. Pine, *Nazi Family Policy,* 15. See also Koonz, *Mothers in the Fatherland,* 14, 180.

103. Pine, *Nazi Family Policy,* 16–18; Hoffmann and Timm, "Utopian Biopolitics," 108.

104. Jacques Donzelot, *The Policing of Families,* trans. Robert Hurley (New York, 1979), 89, 92.

105. On the establishment of marriage in European culture as the only kind of sexual expression that befit civilization, see Isabel Hull, *Sexuality, State, and Civil Society in Germany, 1700–1815* (Ithaca, 1996), 294–96.

Party leaders also chose the family because it corresponded to their own sense of propriety. Most Party leaders refused to embrace Kollontai's model of non-legally-binding romantic unions and collective responsibility for childraising, and by the 1930s they had firmly rejected it.[106] The family comprised a normative model of monogamous heterosexual relationships that fit their notions of how society was to be organized. It was just prior to the campaign to strengthen the family that the Soviet government recriminalized homosexuality.[107] Dan Healey notes that the recriminalization of sodomy coincided with Soviet authorities' drive to cleanse cities of "social anomalies" and to promote the (heterosexual) family.[108] In 1936, Commissar of Justice Nikolai Krylenko called homosexuals "declassed rabble from the dregs of society" and declared that they had no place "in the environment of workers taking the point of view of normal relations between the sexes, who are building their society on healthy principles."[109] Emphasis on the family should thus be seen as part of a larger effort by the Soviet government to make heterosexuality and procreation compulsory in the interests of the state and the social whole.

Contrary to the expectations of leaders in the Soviet Union and elsewhere, abortion bans, pronatalist incentives, and profamily legislation failed to raise the birthrate markedly in any country. The birthrate in Spain remained low throughout the 1930s and 1940s, and rose (and then very slightly) only when the economy improved in the 1950s and 1960s. There is no evidence that Spanish women ever subscribed to government propaganda about their biological destiny as mothers.[110] In Nazi Germany, where the harshest repressive measures against abortion were implemented, fertility

106. The elimination of small-scale capitalism at the end of the 1920s was also significant, because it meant that Party leaders were no longer fearful of bourgeois influences within the family; David Hoffmann, *Stalinist Values: The Cultural Norms of Soviet Modernity, 1917–1941* (Ithaca, 2003), 106.

107. Laura Engelstein, "Soviet Policy toward Male Homosexuality: Its Origins and Historical Roots," *Journal of Homosexuality* 25: 3/4 (1994): 155–78. The decree recriminalizing male homosexuality was drawn up in 1933 and issued in March 1934; see *Istochnik* 5/6 (1993): 164–65.

108. Dan Healey, *Homosexual Desire in Revolutionary Russia: The Regulation of Sexual and Gender Dissent* (Chicago, 2001), 182–90. Healey also discusses here the virulent propaganda war between fascism and communism that included mutual accusations of homosexuality, and through which homosexuality became associated with fascism in the eyes of Soviet officials.

109. *Sovetskaia iustitsiia* 7 (1936), as cited in James Riordan, "Sexual Minorities: The Status of Gays and Lesbians in Russian-Soviet-Russian Society," in *Women in Russia and Ukraine*, 160.

110. Nash, "Pronatalism and Motherhood," 174.

rose somewhat from 1933 to 1936, but then remained stagnant, never even reaching levels of the late 1920s. Even this slight increase in fertility was probably due more to the improved economy than to pronatalist policies. Despite Nazi glorification of and monetary rewards for large families, the number of families with four or more children actually decreased during the Nazi era. Moreover, draconian laws against abortion did not prevent a large number of illegal abortions, up to 1 million annually.[111]

The popular response to the Soviet pronatalist campaign was similarly lackluster. Government reports claimed that the population received the decree banning abortion "enthusiastically," and some women who received birth bonuses did write letters thanking Stalin and promising to have more children.[112] Yet in practice the response of most Soviet women was far from enthusiastic. The ban on abortion led to a huge number of illegal abortions. Commissariat of Health reports in October and November 1936 cited thousands of cases of women hospitalized after poorly performed illegal abortions. Of the 356,200 abortions performed in hospitals in 1937, and 417,600 in 1938, only 10 percent had been authorized, and the rest were incomplete illegal abortions.[113] In response the Soviet government stepped up efforts to identify those who performed illegal abortions, and in 1937 arrested and convicted 4,133 abortionists. As the law dictated, those found guilty of performing abortions were sentenced to a minimum of two years in prison.[114] But despite considerable efforts, Soviet authorities found it difficult to catch underground abortionists, because women who entered hospitals after botched abortions rarely cooperated with police.[115] In oral history interviews, David Ransel found that virtually

111. Bock, "Antinatalism," 245; Pine, *Nazi Family Policy,* 181; Koonz, *Mothers in the Fatherland,* 187.

112. GARF f. 5446, op. 18a, d. 2753, ll. 15, 22, 26, 35. Evidence gathered during discussions of the 1936 constitution indicates that even prior to the allocation of increased resources for mothers, peasants in particular were requesting monetary support for large families; GARF f. 3316, op. 40, d. 18, l. 117.

113. GARF f. 5446, op. 18a, d. 2753, l. 85; RGAE f. 1562 s.ch., op. 329, d. 407, ll. 22–25. Another 1937 report noted that the figure of 323,438 cases of incomplete abortions that had to be completed in hospitals in the RSFSR was clear evidence of a mass of underground abortions; GARF f. A-482, op. 29, d. 5, l. 9.

114. *Sovetskaia iustitsiia* 34 (1936): 16; RGAE f. 1562 s.ch., op. 329, d. 407, l. 25; TsAGM f. 819, op. 2, d. 27, ll. 12–15. Those who had performed multiple abortions often received four years imprisonment or more.

115. From 1938 to 1940, prosecutions for abortion declined, and despite a rise in convictions in 1941, the criminalization of abortion overall proved to be, in the words of one leading scholar, "a particularly ineffective extension of the criminal law." Solomon, *Soviet Criminal Justice,* 220–21.

every Russian village had one person who performed illegal abortions and that self-performed abortions were also common.[116]

The ban on abortion did result in a rise in the birthrate, but this rise was limited and temporary. The birthrate per thousand people rose from 30.1 in 1935, to 33.6 in 1936, to 39.6 in 1937. But in 1938 the birthrate began to decline again, and by 1940, marital fertility for European Russia was below the 1936 level.[117] The enormous social disruption of the purges and mobilization for war in part accounted for the decline of the birthrate beginning in 1938. But even before these disruptions the birthrate had not even approached preindustrialization levels, and evidence on illegal abortions indicates that Soviet women as a whole did not abide by the government's abortion ban. As Soviet authorities had noted in 1920, but then chose to ignore in 1936, the outlawing of abortion only drove women to seek illegal abortions. Repression proved ineffective at raising the birthrate.

The glorification of motherhood and birth bonuses also failed to have much effect. The women who received the bonuses were primarily peasant women who already had many children prior to the introduction of monetary incentives.[118] The resources allotted to expand maternity wards and child care were insufficient to improve markedly the lives of mothers. Government priorities continued to focus on heavy industry, while childcare and communal dining facilities remained woefully underfunded.[119] And given the equally underfunded consumer sector, women had enormous difficulty simply obtaining basic necessities for their children. Commissariat of Education reports in 1937, for example, stated that some children did not attend school because their mothers could not obtain shoes and clothing for them.[120] Such severe shortages of food, clothing, and housing throughout the 1930s deterred women from having more children despite government exhortations.

116. David L. Ransel, *Village Mothers: Three Generations of Change in Russia and Tatariia* (Bloomington, 2000), 71–72.

117. Lorimer, *The Population*, 134; Coale, Anderson, and Harm, *Human Fertility*, 16. Fertility in the first quarter of 1938 was substantially below the 1937 level; RGAE f. 1562 s.ch., op. 329, d. 186, l. 5. For further discussion, see Goldman, *Women, the State and Revolution*, 294–95.

118. GARF f. 5446, op. 18a, d. 2753, l. 8.

119. GARF f. 5446, op. 17, d. 315, ll. 71–72; TsAGM f. 1289, op. 1, d. 174, ll. 3–4.

120. TsKhDMO f. 1, op. 23, d. 1264, ll. 6, 29. See also Elizabeth Waters, "The Modernization of Russian Motherhood, 1917–1937," *Soviet Studies* 44: 1 (1992): 123–35; Elena Osokina, *Za fasadom "Stalinskogo izobilia": Raspredelenie i rynok v snabzhenii naseleniia v gody industrializatsii, 1927–1941* (Moscow, 1998).

One other crucial consideration is women's place in the workforce. Women were recruited in large numbers into industry during the 1930s, and the official emphasis on motherhood was not intended to free women from their obligation to perform "socially useful labor" outside the home. The Soviet gender order assigned a dual societal role to women as both workers and mothers. At no time during the campaign to bolster the family did Soviet officials suggest that a woman's place was in the home. On the contrary, the Soviet government stressed women's obligation to make an economic contribution in the workplace as well as to produce and raise children. Soviet propaganda in the 1930s depicted female heroines as both valiant workers and devoted mothers.[121] Soviet law did allow women paid maternity leave—a fact Stalin took care to stress publicly—but this was only another small inducement for women to have children.[122] The realities of Soviet life saddled women with the double burden of full-time work and uncompensated domestic chores.

Eugenics

State control over reproduction reached its apogee in the eugenics movement, which originated in the nineteenth century and led to government sterilization programs in a number of countries during the twentieth century. In eugenics we find the most extreme example of state and expert attempts to effect a biosocial transformation of the population. In retrospect, particularly in light of the Nazi's extensive eugenic policies, the dangers of eugenics are acknowledged and condemned. But in the early twentieth century, a wide range of government officials and health experts, from many different countries and political affiliations, heralded eugenics as a science that would improve humankind.[123]

121. Karen Petrone, *Life Has Become More Joyous, Comrades: Celebrations in the Time of Stalin* (Bloomington, 2000), 59; Gail Warshofsky Lapidus, *Women in Soviet Society* (Berkeley, 1978), 103–15. See also Melanie Ilic, *Women Workers in the Soviet Interwar Economy: From "Protection" to "Equality"* (New York, 1999).

122. See Stalin's statement for the resolutions of the 1935 Congress of Collective Farm Shock Workers, RGASPI f. 17, op. 120, d. 138, l. 85.

123. As one scholar writes, eugenics was "embraced by social reformers, established intellectuals, and medical authorities from one end of the political spectrum to the other, including British conservatives and Spanish anarchists." Frank Dikötter, "Race Culture: Recent Perspectives on the History of Eugenics," *American Historical Review* 103: 2 (April 1998): 467.

In the eyes of many social reformers, eugenics offered a chance to raise the physical and mental capacity of the population, and to eliminate hereditary diseases and handicaps. For them it represented an application of science to human reproduction that would better society as a whole. Some social scientists believed that criminal behavior and indigence were the consequences of heredity, and for them eugenics held out the possibility of eliminating previously intractable social problems by the means of a simple medical procedure. Moreover, eugenicists argued that while social reforms would enhance only a single generation, biological improvements engineered by eugenics would enrich the gene pool of all future generations. This type of hereditarian thinking greatly raised the stakes in debates and policies about reproduction, for it indicated that current reproductive policies would shape the population for generations to come.

Eugenics was a term coined by Francis Galton, the cousin of Charles Darwin. Galton had been promoting the idea that human stock could be improved by selective breeding since the 1860s, but first used the term *eugenics,* meaning "well-born," in 1883. Both Galton and his disciple Karl Pearson used statistics extensively in their efforts to explain human heredity. Pearson and W. F. R. Weldon, a zoology professor, also developed the new science of biometrics that made possible the statistical measure of large populations. Galton saw eugenics primarily as a means to increase the "better stocks," but he and subsequent British eugenicists also sought to limit reproduction of the "unfit." Galton moreover believed the Anglo-Saxon race to be superior to other races and thought that superior races were destined to supplant the inferior ones.[124] Eugenics from its inception, therefore, combined racism and social Darwinism with scientism—the belief that human society could be improved through scientific study and management.

One important concept behind the development of eugenics was Quetelet's idea of using statistics to show the characteristics of the average citizen. Previously a national or ethnic group was described in terms of its culture, geography, religion, or language; now it was possible to describe a group using its average physical measurements.[125] The compilation of statistical averages over time permitted demographers to identify positive and negative changes in the population. When eugenicists combined these data with Darwin's ideas about the evolution of species, they began to conceive of reproductive policies that would improve the average qualities of

124. Mark H. Haller, *Eugenics: Hereditarian Attitudes in American Thought* (Brunswick, N.J., 1963), 8–17.
125. Ian Hacking, *The Taming of Chance* (New York, 1990), 107–8.

a population. Eugenics reflected the shift away from individual medicine and toward social medicine. Some social Darwinists expressed alarm that modern medicine might be preserving genetically inferior humans, who according to "the survival of the fittest" would previously not have survived. In this view, care of the individual actually harmed society as a whole by allowing the weak to survive and reproduce. Some thinkers saw society as an organism (to be protected from diseased cells), and they embraced eugenics as a means for medicine to strengthen society as a whole.[126]

Eugenicist thought developed differently in different countries, according to varying ideologies, religions, and population concerns. It is possible to divide eugenicist thought into the categories of negative (or hard) and positive (or soft) eugenics: the former stressed selective breeding and measures to prevent reproduction among individuals deemed defective, and the latter advocated healthier conditions of reproduction to produce healthier offspring. Whereas negative eugenics predominated in the Protestant countries of northern Europe and in the United States, positive eugenics was more prevalent in the Catholic countries of southern Europe and in developing countries, including the Soviet Union.

Corresponding to the division between negative and positive eugenics were two different theories of genetics—Mendelian and Lamarckian. The former, named after the nineteenth-century Austrian monk Gregor Mendel whose studies of plant genetics were rediscovered at the beginning of the twentieth century, posited that acquired characteristics could not be inherited.[127] Mendelian genetics was bolstered by the work of August Weismann, whose research indicated that human reproductive cells (or "germ plasm") were unaffected by changes in other bodily cells. In other words, people's physical or mental improvement would not improve the capabilities of children they subsequently had. Lamarckian genetics, on the other hand, followed the ideas of the French evolutionist Jean Baptist de Lamarck, who believed that characteristics acquired by living organisms would be passed on to their offspring. Throughout most of the nineteenth century, Lamarckism was accepted by scientists, including Charles Darwin, and even throughout the first half of the twentieth century debates continued over the inheritability of acquired characteristics.[128] The Mendelian-

126. See Gisela Bock, "Sterilization and 'Medical' Massacres in National Socialist Germany: Ethics, Politics, and the Law," *Medicine and Modernity: Public Health and Medical Care in Nineteenth and Twentieth Century Germany* (Cambridge, 1997), 155.

127. The word *genetics* was actually not used until 1906.

128. See Diane Paul, *Controlling Human Heredity 1865 to the Present* (Atlantic Highlands, N.J., 1995), 40–42.

Lamarckian controversy therefore figured prominently in the thinking of eugenicists and the policies they proposed.

Negative eugenicists saw restriction of "defective" individuals' reproduction as a means to solve social problems. At the 1927 World Population Conference, a member of the Eugenics Society of London argued that pauperism, insanity, and imbecility were all hereditary conditions, and that "a few thousand family stocks probably provide the great burden of inherent defectiveness which the community has to bear."[129] The director of the Genetics Department of the Carnegie Institution in Washington agreed with this idea, noting that the members of some "defective families" all became vagrants while those of other families all became thieves. In other words, he argued that genetic defects determine not only deviance but the precise type of deviance. He concluded that "the cutting-off of reproduction of certain defective individuals would reduce...the proportion of defectives in the population."[130]

The U.S. population was already large, and immigration more than made up for the decline in the birthrate, so eugenicists there focused on "race betterment," meaning the physical and mental health of the population, as well as the ethnic composition. Ideologically, progressivism in the early twentieth century made it easier for some psychiatrists and other professionals to promote eugenics, because it created, as one scholar writes, "a political culture that authorized scientifically inspired state intervention as a solution to social problems."[131] The eugenics movement in the United States was already strong in the first decade of the twentieth century, and a number of states passed laws providing for the sterilization of the mentally unfit. The constitutionality of these laws was upheld by the Supreme Court in a 1927 case on the forced sterilization of a mentally handicapped woman. Chief Justice Oliver Wendell Holmes, writing for the majority, sanctioned the sterilization of "those who already sap the strength of the State," and asserted that "it is better for all the world, if instead of waiting for their imbecility, society can prevent those who are

---

129. *Proceedings of the World Population Conference*, 326–32.

130. Ibid., 343–44.

131. Ian Robert Dowbiggin, *Keeping America Sane: Psychiatry and Eugenics in the United States and Canada, 1880–1940* (Ithaca, 1997), 236. The ideas of women's organizations about moral reform and scientific motherhood also influenced the U.S. eugenics movement; see Alisa Klaus, "Depopulation and Race Suicide: Maternalism and Pronatalist Ideologies in France and the United States," *Mothers of a New World: Maternalist Politics and the Origins of Welfare States*, ed. Seth Koven and Sonya Michel (New York, 1993), 189–90.

manifestly unfit from continuing their kind." In reference to the mentally handicapped woman and her ancestors, he added, "Three generations of imbeciles are enough."[132]

Nazi eugenicists greatly admired the forced sterilizations carried out in the United States, and shortly after coming to power they enacted the Law for the Prevention of Hereditarily Diseased Offspring. As early as the 1912 international eugenics conference in London, German eugenicists had advocated negative eugenic measures as a means to wipe out hereditary defects, and the sterilization bill drafted by the Prussian Health Council in 1932 focused primarily on hereditary defects as well.[133] Nazi eugenics targeted the racially as well as physically and mentally "inferior." During the years of Nazi rule, 400,000 people, half of them women, were forcibly sterilized in Germany.[134] The Nazi version of race hygiene of course ultimately went beyond eugenics to include the mass murder of Jews, the Roma, and up to 200,000 mentally ill or physically disabled people in the most extreme version of eliminating "the unfit" from the body social.[135]

Eugenics also became part of emerging welfare programs in Scandinavia during the 1920s and 1930s. In 1929, Denmark became the first Scandinavian country to pass a sterilization law, and Sweden followed in 1934. Swedish reformers argued that sterilization of the mentally handicapped would save substantially on the cost of institutional care and poor relief, and that it was a state interest "to keep the human race in good order, and to improve it."[136] In 1941 the Swedish parliament extended the Sterilization Act to cover the severely physically as well as mentally handicapped. One parliament member called the law "an important step in the direction of a purification of the Swedish stock, freeing it from the transmission of

132. Haller, *Eugenics,* 130–41.

133. Quine, *Population Politics,* 104; Pine, *Nazi Family Policy,* 12. On continuities between the Weimar and Nazi periods, see Atina Grossmann, *Reforming Sex: The German Movement for Birth Control and Abortion Reform, 1920–1950* (Oxford, 1995), chapter 6.

134. Bock, "Antinatalism," 234–40.

135. Dikötter, "Race Culture," 470. See also Michael Burleigh and Wolfgang Wippermann, *The Racial State: Germany 1933–1945* (New York, 1991).

136. Dikötter, "Race Culture," 468; Gunnar Broberg and Mattias Tydén, "Eugenics in Sweden: Efficient Care," *Eugenics and the Welfare State: Sterilization Policy in Denmark, Sweden, Norway, and Finland,* ed. Broberg and Nils Roll-Hansen (East Lansing, 1996), 100–103. See also Ann-Sofie Kälvemark, *More Children of Better Quality? Aspects of Swedish Population Policy in the 1930s* (Uppsala, 1980), 56–59, 108–12; Ida Blom, "Voluntary Motherhood 1900–1930: Theories and Policies of a Norwegian Feminist in International Perspective," *Maternity and Gender Policies,* 34; Anne-Lise Seip and Hilde Ibsen, "Family Welfare, Which Policy? Norway's Road to Child Allowances," *Maternity and Gender Policies,* 50–51.

genetic material which produces, in future generations, such individuals as are undesirable among a sound and healthy people."[137]

Eugenics in France, Italy, and Latin America assumed a much different character. In these countries, positive eugenics (encouraging "healthy" reproduction) predominated over negative eugenic measures (sterilization of the genetically "unfit"). At the 1912 International Eugenics Congress in London, French and Italian delegates rejected the Mendelian views of their German and British colleagues, and instead focused on environmentalist ideas about creating a healthier population through public health.[138] When French delegates returned home they founded the French Eugenics Society, but they adhered to their Lamarckian roots and focused on educating people about healthy conditions of procreation.[139] It is not surprising that many officials and experts working in public health were drawn to Lamarckian over Mendelian eugenics. Mendelian eugenics actually undercut traditional public health, because (as noted above) medical care for the sick and poor could be construed as interfering with natural selection and the elimination of the unfit. Neo-Lamarckian ideas, on the other hand, indicated that social problems were not only the symptom but also a cause of hereditary ills. By improving the hygiene, living standards, and moral behavior of the population, one could also better the genetic material that would be passed on to future generations. This thinking gave additional impetus to public health and welfare programs, and additional urgency for state intervention to prevent the genetic degeneration that might ensue from poverty, alcoholism, and other social problems.[140]

Also significant in France, Italy, and other Catholic countries was the opposition of the Catholic Church to sterilization. In 1930, Pope Pius XI issued his encyclical "On Christian Marriage," that condemned eugenics in no uncertain terms: "Public authorities have no direct power over the bodies of their subjects.... Where no crime has taken place and there is no cause present for grave punishment they can never, under any circumstance, damage or interfere with the integrity of the body, either for reasons of eugenics or any other reason." The Catholic Church also

137. Broberg and Tyden, "Eugenics in Sweden," 107. By 1960, well over 50,000 people in Sweden had been sterilized in accordance with eugenic laws, and only in 1975 were these laws revoked. See Dikötter, "Race Culture," 468; Johannisson, "The People's Health," 176–77.

138. Quine, *Population Politics*, 104.

139. Nancy Leys Stepan, *'The Hour of Eugenics': Race, Gender, and Nation in Latin America* (Ithaca, 1991), 80.

140. Stepan, *'The Hour of Eugenics,'* 74–91.

denounced negative eugenics as "zootechnics applied to the human species," and thereby created a significant religious and moral obstacle to the practice of sterilization in Catholic countries.[141] Population concerns in France and Italy also meant that most eugenicists there maintained a coalition with pronatalist organizations that opposed negative eugenics.[142]

Italian eugenicists explicitly used the term *positive eugenics* (also referred to as "euthenics") to distinguish their programs from the "negative eugenics" of Nazi Germany. Italian fascists also made much less of race than did the Nazis, and thus did not need negative eugenics to enforce racial purity. Mussolini, in a 1932 interview, rejected the idea of a pure race and argued that "it is often precisely from happy mixtures that a nation derives strength and beauty." Some Italian eugenicists accordingly saw genetic mixing as a source of racial strength.[143] Latin American doctors largely followed the lead of Italian and French eugenicists. Rather than pursuing negative eugenic policies such as sterilization, they sought to extend the principles of public health into the sphere of reproduction. They linked eugenics with obstetrics and infant welfare, as well as with campaigns against alcoholism, tuberculosis, and venereal disease. As Nancy Leys Stepan argues, Latin American physicians' neo-Lamarckian approach justified their efforts to improve people's health and well-being, because it meant "that improvements acquired in an individual's lifetime could be handed on genetically, that progress could occur."[144]

Eugenics in the Soviet Union much more closely resembled the Latin model than the Anglo-Saxon model. As in every country, there was a variety of medical opinion in the Soviet Union, but overall a Lamarckian orientation predominated, in keeping with the environmental emphasis in Marxism and Russian disciplinary culture. Particularly given Soviet officials' goal of revolutionary transformation, it is not difficult to see the appeal of eugenics. Here was a supposedly scientific method to improve

141. De Grazia, *How Fascism Ruled Women,* 54; Horn, *Social Bodies,* 61.

142. Schneider, *Quality and Quantity,* 8, 119; Horn, *Social Bodies,* 61. By the 1930s, however, some French eugenicists broke with natalist groups and advocated negative eugenic practices including sterilization. See Schneider, *Quality and Quantity,* 9.

143. Horn, *Social Bodies,* 59–62; De Grazia, *How Fascism Ruled Women,* 53.

144. Stepan, '*The Hour of Eugenics,*' 74, 80. Eugenic thought did vary from one Latin American country to another depending on political and social conditions. The left-wing government in Mexico favored improved reproductive health for all segments of the population, while in Argentina, with its conservative government and a population of European descent concerned with maintaining its racial purity, eugenicists showed more interest in biotypology—the cataloguing of the population by biological and racial type. See Stepan, '*The Hour of Eugenics,*' 55–60, 119.

and transform the population.[145] But ultimately eugenics was not only rejected, but vehemently denounced by the Soviet government.

Eugenic ideas were imported to Russia from Western Europe prior to the Revolution. Between 1890 and 1910 a number of young Russian scientists were trained in Western Europe, and in this same period many works on experimental biology, genetics, and evolution were translated and published in Russia. Partly as a result of these connections, between 1900 and 1930 there was a profusion of interest in Russia in the newly emerging fields of eugenics, biogeochemistry, and biological physics—all of which signaled a concern with the scientific management of reproductive issues. The first eugenic research was conducted in Russia in 1914 when the Institute of Experimental Biology was formed, and during the First World War, the Russian Academy of Sciences created the Commission on the Study of Natural Productive Forces.[146]

After the Revolution, the Soviet government embraced eugenics and in 1920 created the Russian Eugenics Society under the Commissariat of Health. The following year the Soviet Academy of Sciences founded its Bureau of Eugenics. These official organizations helped Russian eugenicists keep up their contacts with eugenicists abroad, as the Russian Eugenics Society selected a representative to the International Commission of Eugenics; established contacts with eugenic societies in the United States, Britain, and Germany; and sent its president to the 1924 International Congress of Eugenics in Milan.[147] The society's journal, *Russian Eugenics Journal,* reviewed a large number of foreign books on eugenics and published the programs of foreign eugenic societies. It also published articles analyzing the impact of the war on the populations of Europe, and advocating registration and control of marriage for eugenic reasons.[148]

145. An American socialist, Hermann Muller, who worked at the Moscow Institute of Genetics, wrote to Stalin in 1936 to laud eugenics as control over human biological evolution "in the service of social evolution." On Muller's letter and Stalin's (highly negative) reaction to it, see Elof Axel Carlson, *Genes, Radiation, and Society: The Life and Work of H. J.* Muller (Ithaca, 1981), 233.

146. Mark Adams, "Eugenics in Russia, 1900–1940," *The Wellborn Science: Eugenics in Germany, France, Brazil, and Russia,* ed. Adams (New York, 1989), 157–60; Mark Adams, "Eugenics as Social Medicine in Revolutionary Russia: Prophets, Patrons, and the Dialectics of Discipline-Building," *Health and Society in Revolutionary Russia,* eds. Susan Gross Solomon and John F. Hutchinson (Bloomington, 1990), 206.

147. Adams, "Eugenics as Social Medicine," 204–7; Loren Graham, *Between Science and Values* (New York, 1981), 232–35.

148. A. V. Gorbunov, "Vliianie mirovoi voiny na dvizhenie naseleniia Evropy," *Russkii evgenicheskii zhurnal* 1: 1 (1922): 39–63; Prof. I. Liublinskii, "Brak i evgenika," *Russkii evgenicheskii zhurnal* 5: 2 (1927): 49–89. The Commissariat of Health's Department of

Soviet thinkers in the 1920s advocated both negative and positive eugenic policies. Geneticist Nikolai Kol'tsov, at the 1921 All-Russian Conference on the Protection of Maternity and Infancy, heralded eugenics as a new science that had much in common with animal and plant breeding. With apparent regret he conceded that governments should not breed people the way animal owners breed horses, but he endorsed government assistance for mothers as a eugenic responsibility of the state.[149] In 1928, Aleksandr Serebrovskii proposed artificial insemination using the sperm of a "talented and valuable producer." He claimed that "in these conditions, human selection would make gigantic leaps forward."[150] The same year Z. O. Michnik argued that the hereditarily ill should not reproduce while "the gifted, healthy and strong are obliged to pass their natural resources along to the next generation." She asserted that to ensure the quality of future generations "the business of reproduction should be rationalized, orderly, and regulated."[151]

Eugenics was initially accepted in the Soviet Union without much controversy, but in 1925 a debate between Mendelian and Lamarckian geneticists erupted. Because Russian disciplinary traditions clashed with the genetic determinism of Mendelian eugenics, most Soviet eugenicists maintained a Lamarckian orientation. Iurii Filipchenko, however, argued that acceptance of Lamarckism meant acknowledging that the poor living conditions suffered by workers for generations left them genetically degraded. He advocated instead for Mendelism, which denied that years of oppression and poverty would have any effect on proletarian genes.[152] In addition to illustrating the complexity of eugenic debates in the Soviet Union, Filipchenko's argument points to a more general complication in Mendelian-Lamarckian debates. Whereas Mendelian genetics is generally associated with negative eugenics and Lamarckism is associated with positive eugenics, it was possible to advocate sterilization policies from a Lamarckian perspective. One prominent neo-Lamarckian in France, Frédéric

---

Foreign Information also reported on eugenic ideas promoted in other countries; GARF f. A-482, op. 35, d. 144, ll. 306–12.

149. N. K. Kol'tsov, "Evgenika, kak nauchnaia baza v rabote Otdela okhrany materinstva i mladenchestva," *Materialy pervogo Vserossiiskogo soveshchaniia po okhrane materinstva i mladenchestva* (Moscow, 1921), 41–49. He also warned that women's refusal to have enough children had caused the extinction of "many races" and "entire cultured nations" in the past.

150. Adams, "Eugenics as Social Medicine," 216.

151. Z. O. Michnik, "Soznatel'noe materinstvo i regulirovanie detorozhdeniia," *Zhurnal po izucheniiu rannego detskogo vozrasta* 1 (1928): 72.

152. Graham, *Between Science and Values*, 239.

Hoursay, maintained that the cumulative negative effects of damaging environments could create a heredity so tainted that social reforms could not rescue it, and that sterilization of unfit individuals (such as chronic alcoholics) would be necessary.[153]

Filipchenko's arguments notwithstanding, most Soviet eugenicists continued to espouse Lamarckism and positive rather than negative eugenic policies. N. M. Volotskoi, who in 1923 had endorsed a sterilization program, subsequently strove to develop a Marxist eugenics that emphasized environmental factors.[154] Even more common were sexual enlightenment workers who, without using the term *eugenics*, concentrated on ways to boost the population's reproductive health. Many of these specialists considered both hereditarian and environmentalist factors as important, but focused on the latter because of their dedication to improving people's health and well-being.[155] Doctor B. A. Ivanovskii, for example, stated that "changes in the social sphere and upbringing are just as important as hereditary factors in the improvement of the race."[156]

Despite the strong appeal of eugenics in the Soviet Union, and Lamarckian ideas that seemed compatible with Marxism, the Soviet eugenics movement eventually ran afoul of official ideology. In 1930, at the time when a Marxist orthodoxy was imposed on all social sciences, the Soviet government disbanded the Russian Eugenics Society. And in keeping with the fervor of the industrialization drive, Russian eugenicists were forced to concede that the development of natural resources was more important and practical than the eugenic development of the population.[157] The formal termination of the eugenics movement, however, did not mean the end of eugenic thinking among Soviet scientists. Many eugenicists moved to the Gorky Research Institute of Medical Genetics where they continued to discuss human genetics without using the term *eugenics*. Publications of the institute endorsed findings published in the British journal *Annals of Eugenics* and contained many articles on eugenic topics, from the genetic origins of human diseases to the effects of intraethnic marriages and

153. Stepan, *'The Hour of Eugenics,'* 111.

154. Adams, "Eugenics as Social Medicine," 210; Graham, *Between Science and Values*, 243.

155. Bernstein, *Dictatorship of Sex*, 173.

156. As quoted in Frances Lee Bernstein, "'What Everyone Should Know about Sex': Gender, Sexual Enlightenment, and the Politics of Health in Revolutionary Russia, 1918–1931" (Ph.D. diss., Columbia University, 1998), 334.

157. Adams, "Eugenics as Social Medicine," 219.

inbreeding on the population of Moscow.[158] The Soviet government also permitted the establishment in Moscow of the German-Soviet Laboratory for Racial Biological Research that, despite a precarious existence, operated from 1931 to 1938.[159]

The final demise of Soviet eugenics came in 1936–37, when the work of geneticists at the Gorky Institute became associated with fascist eugenics. Trofim D. Lysenko and his followers attacked hereditary genetics in order to buttress their own Lamarckian genetics, and they denounced a number of leading medical geneticists who were subsequently arrested and shot during the purges.[160] The fact that eugenics was ultimately condemned as a fascist science demonstrates not only the influence of Marxist ideology but also Party leaders' desire to differentiate socialist from fascist reproductive policies. Contrary to their claim, eugenics was not exclusively a fascist science, because it was practiced widely in nonfascist countries such as the United States. But with the rising ideological and international tensions of the 1930s, Soviet authorities rejected eugenics more firmly than ever, not only because it contradicted Soviet nurturist and universalist thought, but because they associated it with fascism.

Eugenics is perhaps the clearest example of state and expert attempts to effect a biosocial transformation through control of reproduction. The appeal of eugenics lay in its promise to improve the human species through technocratic means. In an age when population management seemed not only possible but necessary, it is not surprising that so many political leaders and social reformers turned to eugenics. But equally interesting is the way that eugenics assumed such different forms depending on political ideologies, social conditions, religion, and the ethnic mix of populations. As discussed above, the principal divide in Western Europe was between the Protestant countries of northern Europe that pursued negative eugenic policies and the Catholic countries of southern Europe that favored positive eugenics. The same divide seems apparent in North and South America where negative eugenics prevailed in the United States, while positive eugenics held sway in Latin America.

---

158. Adams, *The Wellborn Science*, 188–89; *Trudy Mediko-geneticheskogo nauchno-issledovatel'skogo instituta im. M. Gor'kogo* (Moscow, 1936), 15–16, 201ff.

159. Weindling, "German-Soviet Cooperation in Science," 105–7. The Politburo's 1936 antiabortion decree itself reflected eugenic thought, as it permitted abortion when hereditary diseases or disabilities were possible; RGASPI f. 17, op. 3, d. 982, ll. 126–30. A 1938 conference on abortion commissions reiterated the permissibility of abortion when the mother or father had a hereditary illness; GARF f. A-482, op. 29, d. 20, ll. 5–10.

160. Adams, *The Wellborn Science*, 196.

Expanding the comparison, however, makes clear that nonreligious factors also played a significant role in the reception of eugenic thought. In the Soviet Union and Romania—two predominantly Orthodox Christian countries of Eastern Europe—Russian physicians dabbled in positive eugenics (before the movement was outlawed completely by the Soviet government), whereas Romanian eugenicists gravitated toward negative eugenics, largely due to the influence of German and American medical science. Though Romanian public health legislation did not go as far as sterilization, Romanian eugenicists, many of whom had studied in Germany or in the United States (under the auspices of the Rockefeller Foundation) argued strongly for Mendelism over Lamarckism. Although they sought environmental improvements to public health, they insisted that environmental factors could not modify hereditary traits.[161]

Positive eugenics held sway in most other developing countries. In Republican Turkey, despite the influence of German medical thought, negative eugenics was rejected and sterilization was outlawed in 1936. Turkish eugenicists instead emphasized improvements in hygiene, reproductive health, and child care as the means to better the population.[162] As in Russia, physicians and social scientists in Turkey blamed the downtrodden condition of the masses on living conditions rather than any inherent deficiencies. Moreover, their reluctance to adopt negative eugenics reflected their opposition to the racist hierarchies in some European eugenic studies that marked Turks as an inferior racial group.[163] Japanese eugenicists similarly questioned Mendelian genetics which, in combination with European racial hierarchies, would have permanently assigned the Japanese a low status. Instead they maintained a Lamarckian orientation that emphasized education and physical fitness for women as the means to improve the biological quality of the population.[164] In Republican China too, apart from a passing interest in Mendelian genetics in the 1930s, medical researchers and physicians were drawn to positive eugenics and programs of sex education and social hygiene.[165] Even in countries such as Egypt, where

161. Bucur, *Eugenics and Modernization*, 59–61, 67. Bucur notes that Romanian eugenicists differed from their German counterparts in their emphasis on voluntary rather than coercive measures, and in their less persistent interest in racial purity (79).

162. Alemdaroglu, "Politics of the Body," 70–71.

163. Ibid., 71–72. Alemdaroglu notes that Turkish eugenicists did not label even their country's ethnic minorities as inferior, in keeping with Kemalist discourse on national unity.

164. Otsubo, "Eugenics in Imperial Japan," chapter 7.

165. Frank Dikötter, *Imperfect Conceptions: Medical Knowledge, Birth Defects, and Eugenics in China* (New York, 1998), 5, 71–74.

the principal concern was overpopulation, discussions of sterilization won little support among specialists who instead proposed state services to improve peasant women's hygiene, health, and living standards.[166]

In the Soviet Union, the final demise of eugenics occurred for explicitly ideological reasons—the rejection of eugenics as a fascist science. Even apart from ideological pronouncements, however, negative eugenics never generated much support among Soviet intellectuals. Like their counterparts in European Catholic countries and in many developing countries, Soviet social scientists and health professionals campaigned for improvements in people's living environment and reproductive health rather than for sterilizations as the means to enhance the quality of the population. With its sense of moral obligation to uplift peasants and workers, the Soviet intelligentsia did not blame the masses for their downtrodden condition nor accept their inferiority as immutable. Reproductive policies focused on hygiene and maternal welfare dovetailed far better with their agenda of social amelioration than did negative eugenics. As committed as they were to social transformation, Soviet specialists rejected a science of biological manipulation based on genetic determinism.

Infant Care and Childraising

The final step in state efforts to transform the population through control of reproduction was intervention in the realm of infant care and childraising. Once children came to be seen as belonging not only or even primarily to their parents, but rather to the society, nation, or race, governments initiated programs and legislation to ensure infant health and the proper upbringing of children. Health experts and government officials increasingly set norms for care of children and enforced these norms through a range of educational and interventionist programs—maternity care centers, home medical visits, removal of children from parents deemed unsuitable, and extrafamilial youth organizations. Soviet officials shared this more general state concern with infant care and childraising, and adopted similar methods of state intervention, even as the content of their programs diverged somewhat from those in other countries.

Doctors in Western Europe first began to publish works on the medical care and rearing of children in the late eighteenth and early nineteenth

---

166. Omnia El Shakry, "Barren Land and Fecund Bodies: The Emergence of Population Discourse in Interwar Egypt," *International Journal of Middle East Studies* 37 (2005): 360–61. On similar ideas in Iran, see Schayegh, "Hygiene, Eugenics, Genetics," 337–39.

centuries, initially as part of the cult of domesticity that sought to insulate the bourgeois family from the lower classes.[167] By the late nineteenth century, concern for infant and child welfare was extended to the entire population, as the health of lower-class children came to be seen as essential to the overall well-being of society. The Parisian physician Alfred Caron coined the term *puericulture* to refer to the scientific cultivation of infants and children, which he claimed was crucial "from the point of view of improving the species." One of the leading physicians in France, Adolphe Pinard, subsequently championed puericulture in the 1890s, and made the mother-child diad a crucial sphere of medical care. Pinard's ideas spread quickly throughout Europe and beyond, and puericulture's component fields of obstetrics, gynecology, and pediatrics all burgeoned as a result.[168] The means by which ideas circulated were once again publications and international meetings. Concerns about infant health and child care received great attention at the International Congress on the Protection of Children, convened in Paris in 1883, in Bordeaux in 1895, and in Brussels in 1913. Pinard addressed the tenth International Congress on Health and Demography in Paris in 1900, and touted his ideas about the importance of prenatal and postnatal care as a means to prevent degeneration.[169] One reason that puericulture developed so quickly as a field was that it addressed widespread concerns about degeneration. Although similar in its aims to negative eugenic policies, puericulture offered a benevolent way to ensure the biological fitness of succeeding generations.

The ideas of puericulture subsequently exerted considerable influence among physicians and state officials in Latin America. As one scholar writes, puericulture made the mother-child unit a special site of medical attention and focused on teaching women to raise healthy children for the good of the country. Children were thus presented "as biological-political resources of the nation, and the state was regarded as having an obligation to regulate their health."[170] Also promoting this line of thinking were Pan-American Child congresses, held regularly from 1916 on, that emphasized the need for governments to ensure the welfare of children.[171]

167. Donzelot, *The Policing of Families*, 17.
168. Schneider, *Quality and Quantity*, 63, 74; Stepan, '*The Hour of Eugenics*,' 78.
169. Sylvia Schafer, *Children in Moral Danger and the Problem of Government in Third Republic France* (Princeton, 1997), 6–7; Schneider, *Quality and Quantity*, 69.
170. Stepan, '*The Hour of Eugenics*,' 78.
171. Donna J. Guy, *Women Build the Welfare State: Performing Charity and Creating Rights in Argentina, 1880–1955* (Durham, 2009), 34–35.

In the early twentieth century, military considerations became a more explicit motivation for infant and child care programs, as policymakers sought to guarantee a healthy pool of future soldiers. The French publicist Paul Strauss wrote in 1900 that puericulture "insures the child against the dangers and risks of its uncertain life. In the state of armed peace and the economic rivalry of nations, it constitutes the strongest and surest work for national defense."[172] Military preparedness was also a principal concern of British reformers worried about child nutrition and care. Following the poor performance of the British army in the Boer War, the government sponsored several studies on the physical condition of schoolchildren, which revealed that poor housing and nutrition correlated directly with smaller and less healthy children. The 1905–6 British Commission on the Physical Deterioration and Feeding of Schoolchildren concluded "that it is essential for the State to intervene at the earliest possible moment and secure, if possible, at least some sort of minimum nourishment for the children whom it obliges to come to school." The British government also funded programs to reduce infant mortality, including visits by medical personnel to the homes of new mothers.[173]

Throughout the world, the First World War intensified concern with child welfare. Alan Brown, known as the father of Canadian pediatrics, wrote in 1919, "The Great War has impressed upon us as never before the grave necessity not only of conserving the children, but of affording them every opportunity to develop normally. It has become a patriotic duty as well as a professional one for the physicians...to thoroughly inform themselves of the best method of preventing infant mortality and of conserving child life."[174] State assistance focused particularly on infant health and included both direct medical supervision and educational programs for mothers. To highlight the importance of infant health, Britain celebrated "Baby Week" in June 1917, when the Bishop of London declared that "while nine soldiers died every hour in 1915, twelve babies died every hour, so that it was more dangerous to be a baby than a soldier.

172. Schneider, *Quality and Quantity*, 69. As Nancy Stepan writes, children came to be "thought of as biological-political resources of the nation." Stepan, *'The Hour of Eugenics,'* 78.

173. PRO Parliamentary Papers 1903 vol. XXX Microfiche 109.257, 22; 1907 vol. LXV Microfiche 113.608, 273–77; PRO ED 24/106; PRO RG 41/3. The commission noted that several other European countries already provided meals to needy children. It also recommended mandatory courses for "elder children (especially girls) in schools" to teach them about infant hygiene and nutrition.

174. Comacchio, "'The Infant Soldier,'" 105.

The loss of life in this war has made every baby's life doubly precious."[175] The following year the British government passed the Maternity and Child Welfare Act that authorized large-scale expenditures for infant welfare clinics and home visits by infant care specialists. While humanitarian concerns about child poverty provided some impetus for these programs, the Eugenics Society also endorsed these programs as a means to improve the population.[176]

Concern with infant and child care in Russia followed a similar trajectory. Eighteenth-century efforts to create foundling homes and reduce infanticide and infant mortality were followed by a nineteenth-century emphasis on pediatric medicine and improved health care for children.[177] While Russia lacked a large bourgeoisie and did not develop a cult of domesticity as did Western Europe, Russian physicians devoted considerable effort to studying and improving children's health. Much of this work was done by zemstvo doctors and philanthropic societies, and as such reflected local, nonstate initiatives.[178] By the eve of the First World War, however, programs to improve infant health assumed a far more centralized character. In May 1913, a tsarist decree founded the All-Russian Guardianship for Maternal and Infant Welfare. This body was under the patronage of Empress Aleksandra Fedorovna, and as such it enjoyed the status of a quasi-state organization. Preexisting philanthropic societies, such as the Moscow Society against Infant Mortality, became affiliated with the All-Russian Guardianship, which proceeded to fund and coordinate programs around the country.[179]

With the outbreak of the First World War, the All-Russian Guardianship and its affiliates expanded their efforts with an emphasis on aid "to children of those called to take part in the defense of the motherland." To

175. J. M. Winter, *The Great War and the British People* (Cambridge, Mass., 1986), 192–93.

176. PRO MH 48/160; Lara Marks, "Mothers, Babies, and Hospitals: 'The London' and the Provision of Maternity Care in East London," *Women and Children First*, 49; Jane Lewis, "Models of Equality for Women: The Case of State Support for Children in Twentieth-Century Britain," *Maternity and Gender Policies*, 85. The British government eventually extended such efforts to its colonies as well. In 1937 it sent a memorandum to colonial administrators calling for the training of midwives and infant care specialists to reduce infant mortality. Lenore Manderson, "Women and the State: Maternal and Child Welfare in Colonial Malaya, 1900–1940," *Women and Children First*, 172.

177. Ransel, *Village Mothers*, 8, 31, 291.

178. For further discussion of prerevolutionary initiatives to improve childraising and children's health, see Catriona Kelly, *Children's World: Growing Up in Russia, 1890–1991* (New Haven, 2007), chapter 1.

179. GARF f. 1795, op. 1, d. 10, l. 2; d. 7, ll. 26–27.

this end, they opened nurseries, milk kitchens, and consultation points where doctors not only checked infants but instructed mothers in infant care. In 1916 the All-Russian Guardianship procured money (6,000 rubles for the Moscow Society against Infant Mortality alone) to administer these programs and to provide food for orphans and children of refugees.[180] At the 1916 Congress of the All-Russian Guardianship, one speaker warned of the sharp rise in infant mortality during wartime and called for aid to mothers and children, citing the assistance provided to refugee families in Austria and Germany. Another speaker called on the state and civic organizations to open more nurseries and milk kitchens for infants. He stressed that "each young life…may be of much benefit to the motherland."[181] Under the Provisional Government, the All-Russian Guardianship continued and expanded its work. In the summer of 1917 it took steps to reduce infant mortality, including an appeal to the Ministry of Labor to ensure that women factory workers with infants were given time to nurse their babies. The guardianship and its affiliated organizations also assumed an increasingly centralized character. They strove to coordinate their efforts according to a national plan of action, and even expressed their intention of becoming a "unified state institution" under the Ministry of State Care.[182] These aspirations were realized under the Soviet government when the Department for the Protection of Maternity and Infancy was formed.

The Soviet Commissariat of Social Security set up the Department for the Protection of Maternity and Infancy in 1918. Its guiding principles included the following: "1) Childbirth is the social function of women, and it is the obligation of the state to place the working woman in conditions which facilitate her fulfillment of this function; 2) The education of the mother-citizen is the duty of the state;…4) Children, as future citizens of the Soviet Socialist Republic, are from the very first days of life an object of concern for the Socialist State."[183] Much of the expertise for this new branch of the bureaucracy came from prerevolutionary specialists who had long advocated for children's well-being and who got the chance to promote it under the Soviet government.[184] The immediate task

180. GARF f. 1795, op. 1, d. 7, ll. 1, 12, 26. The Tula Department of the Committee of the Grand Duchess Elizaveta Fedorovna spent 6,000 rubles on the construction of nurseries in 1915 alone; RGIA f. 1253, op. 1, d. 69, ll. 7–9.

181. A. A. Redlikh, *Voina i okhrana materinstva i mladenchestva* (Petrograd, 1916), 29–30.

182. GARF f. 4100, op. 1, d. 69, ll. 4–6; f. 1795, op. 1, d. 7, ll. 26–27.

183. GARF f. A-413, op. 2, d. 1, l. 16.

184. Kelly, *Children's World*, 61–62.

of the Department for the Protection of Maternity and Infancy was the reduction of infant mortality during the Civil War. Vera Lebedeva, the first head of the department, wrote in a 1918 report of the "colossal loss of population and the battle for the lives of infants." She added that, unlike Germany, which sought population increase to augment military power, the Soviet state sought to preserve young lives for the sake of future productive labor.[185]

After the Civil War had ended, Lebedeva reported that the department (now under the Commissariat of Health) would expand its efforts beyond mothers in need to promote infant health among all parts of the population. During the 1920s, the department opened hundreds of clinics for mothers and their babies, and by the late 1930s, Soviet officials put even greater emphasis on maternity wards and infant clinics.[186] The Soviet government also founded the State Scientific Institute for the Protection of Maternity and Infancy in 1922. Scientific study entailed a process of normalization whereby charts were compiled on the average height and weight of babies, and infants were subsequently compared with these charts to determine if they were of normal size.[187] This process of examination and classification was extended to children as well. The Soviet government developed three classifications of "defective" children: physically defective, mentally defective, and morally defective. Based on their diagnoses, doctors prescribed appropriate treatments, for example sending "morally defective children" to reform schools.[188]

Both in the Soviet Union and in other countries around the world, the principle and institutions of state interference in infant and child care had become firmly established by the interwar period. These institutions in turn inculcated norms of infant care, hygiene, and nutrition through educational programs for new mothers and potential mothers. Government officials from France to Argentina to Japan all promoted scientific mothering and mandated the teaching of puericulture for schoolgirls.[189] The U.S. government's 1921 Sheppard-Towner Maternity and Infancy Protection Act provided federal grants for child health clinics, and for nurses to

185. *Pervyi Vserossiiskii s"ezd komissarov sotsial'nogo obespecheniia* (Moscow, 1918), 36.

186. RGASPI f. 17, op. 120, d. 305, ll. 63–64.

187. Drobizhev, *U istokov sovetskoi demografii*, 143; *Gigiena i zdorov'e rabochei i krest'ianskoi sem'i* 20 (1926): 7.

188. GARF f. A-482, op. 11, d. 19, l. 64; d. 79, l. 36.

189. Sheldon Garon, *Molding Japanese Minds: The State in Everyday Life* (Princeton, 1997), 359; Schneider, *Quality and Quantity*, 122; Stepan, 'The Hour of Eugenics,' 121.

Fig. 10. Soviet poster comparing infant mortality rates, 1923. "For every hundred children born in these different states, this number dies in the first year of life." Of the countries shown here (all of them European), the Soviet Union has the highest rate (20). Poster identification number RU/SU 907, Poster Collection, Hoover Institution Archives.

visit pregnant women and new mothers.[190] Egypt's Public Health Administration in 1927 founded its Child Welfare Section that offered education
for mothers regarding child care.[191] In the Soviet Union, educational efforts took the form of posters and journals that instructed mothers on the
importance of breast-feeding, the correct way to bathe infants, and the
dangers of sharp-edged or dirty toys. Books on parenting listed foods that
contained vitamins, stressed the value of fresh air, and noted that laziness
in children is often the result of disorder and uncleanliness in people's
homes.[192] Soviet authorities also inculcated habits of infant care through
healthy baby contests, modeled on North American competitions (held
in conjunction with livestock exhibitions) that awarded ribbons to the
healthiest babies.[193]

Beyond assistance and advice for new mothers, governments intervened
directly in families to guarantee the "proper" care of children. State intervention, and the concomitant erosion of parental authority, had begun
already in the nineteenth century. An 1889 French law stated that "fathers
and mothers who, through their habitual drunkenness, their notorious and
scandalous misconduct, or through ill treatment, compromise the safety,
health or morality of their children" would lose parental custody. Some
critics argued that this law gave the state too much power to intervene in
the family, but others countered that the state, as the guardian of social and
national collectivities, should act to protect children, "who will one day become soldiers and citizens," and to ensure "that the race not degenerate."[194]
The British Inter-Departmental Commission on Physical Deterioration also

190. Molly Ladd-Taylor, "'My Work Came Out of Agony and Grief': Mothers and the
Making of the Sheppard-Towner Act," *Mothers of a New World,* 321–22; Theda Skocpol,
Protecting Soldiers and Mothers: The Political Origins of Social Policy in the United States
(Cambridge, Mass., 1992), 511. On infant care bureaus in the Netherlands, see Hilary
Marland, "The Medicalization of Motherhood: Doctors and Infant Welfare in the Netherlands, 1901–1930," *Women and Children First,* 89; and on home visits for new mothers in
Germany see Pine, *Nazi Family Policy,* 23–24.

191. El Shakry, "Barren Land and Fecund Bodies," 361.

192. V. P. Lebedeva, ed., *Kniga materi: Kak vyrastit' zdorovogo i krepkogo rebenka i sokhranit' svoe zdorov'e* (Moscow, 1926), 19–53; *Gigiena i zdorov'e rabochei i
krest'ianskoi sem'i* 19 (1926): 8–9; R. O. Lunts and Ia. F. Zhorno, *Uchebnik anatomii,
fiziologii, dietetiki i gigieny rebenka rannego vozrasta* (Moscow/Leningrad, 1938), 102–4;
E. A. Arkin, *Pis'ma o vospitanii detei* (Moscow, 1936), 43, 78. See also A. Makarenko,
A Book for Parents, trans. Robert Daglish (Moscow, n.d.), 118, which said that proper
upbringing, not heredity, would determine whether the child became a valuable person.

193. *Gigiena i zdorov'e rabochei i krest'ianskoi sem'i* 17 (1926): 9; 18 (1926): 16.

194. Schafer, *Children in Moral Danger,* 19–21, 80; Donzelot, *The Policing of Families,*
83–84.

recommended greater intervention in homes to protect children's health, and the British parliament in 1909 passed the Children Act, which empowered the government to remove children from parents "found begging, or wandering, or destitute," or from drunken or criminal parents.[195] The German state began to interfere directly in families during the First World War. At this time, it ordered that all children receive regular checkups from physicians in schools, and that unhealthy children be removed from their parents and sent to the countryside to improve their health.[196]

Soviet state intrusion similarly entailed compulsory medical examinations of children. The school, as an institution where the state exercised control over children's upbringing, became a site where medical personnel could monitor children's health. Already in 1918 the Commissariat of Health issued instructions telling school doctors not only to improve sanitation and treat illnesses, but to oversee the health and physical development of all children.[197] During the Civil War, when concern with epidemics was at its height, school doctors received broad authority to inspect each child on a daily basis, and to send them to public baths if they were unclean. While a shortage of medical personnel sometimes prevented the "systematic, detailed examination of students" to which Soviet health officials aspired, health inspectorates were established in virtually every school by 1920.[198] Soviet health officials also intervened in people's homes to supervise the care of infants and children. Citing the examples of Belgium and Germany, Lebedeva established in the 1920s a system of home visits by nurses to check on the health of new-born babies. She explained that "the nurse-visitor is a bearer of the idea of rational infant care" and noted that the Moscow Institute for the Protection of Maternity and Infancy would train nurse-visitors in scientific childcare techniques. The Soviet government also operated some "homes of the mother and infant," where new mothers would stay for several months with their babies under the supervision of medical experts.[199]

195. PRO Parliamentary Papers 1904 Microfiche 110.279, 55–63, 91; PRO HO 45/20115.

196. Domansky, "Militarization and Reproduction," 451. The Weimar constitution also empowered the state to institute "the necessary arrangements" to protect children from neglect; H. W. V. Temperley, ed., *A History of the Peace Conference of Paris*, vol. 3 (London, 1920), 368.

197. GARF f. A-482, op. 1, d. 37, l. 18.

198. GARF f. A-482, op. 11, d. 40, l. 3, 20, 76.

199. V. Lebedeva, "Okhrana materinstva i mladenchestva," *Sotsial'naia gigiena: Rukovodstvo*, 348–53; *Materialy pervogo Vserossiiskogo soveshchaniia po okhrane materinstva*

The Soviet state claimed the power to remove infants and children from their parents, either temporarily or permanently, in order to improve the child's health or to safeguard their upbringing. Sick and malnourished children were sent to special sanatoria until their health improved and they could be returned to their families.[200] Soviet law provided for the permanent removal of children from their families "in cases of parents' failure to fulfill their responsibilities," and in the late 1930s, Soviet courts invoked this law regularly to take children away from "negligent" parents.[201] Infants and children removed from their parents were placed in state orphanages. The Soviet government established a large number of orphanages to house not only children removed from their parents' custody but the millions of children left orphaned and homeless by the First World War and Civil War, and by collectivization and famine in the 1930s. Although these institutions remained overcrowded and underfunded, Soviet officials nonetheless viewed them as places where children could be shaped into productive citizens. Soviet law and government directives stated that children in orphanages should be inculcated with "labor discipline," and "habits of discipline and collective work."[202]

Parallel with state intervention and the decline of parental authority was the growth of extrafamilial youth organizations. As discussed in the previous chapter, such organizations in other countries included the Boy Scouts and the Girl Scouts. In the Soviet Union these organizations were disbanded after the Revolution, but in a different guise they were reconstituted with the formation of the Komsomol and the Young Pioneers in 1922. Both organizations borrowed mottoes and laws (to be prepared, honest, clean, and courageous) directly from those of the scouts, but they

---

i mladenchestva, 9. See also *Sotsial'noe obespechenie za piat' let: 30 apr. 1918 g.–30 apr. 1923 g.* (Moscow, 1923), 16; *Gigiena i zdorov'e rabochei i krest'ianskoi sem'i* 18 (1926): 1.

200. GARF f. A-482, op. 11, d. 40, l. 6; d. 79, l. 33; f. 5528, op. 5, d. 39, l. 2.

201. A. I. Aliakrinskii, *Brak, sem'ia i opeka: Prakticheskoe rukovodstvo dlia organov ZAGS* (Moscow, 1930), 124; TsAGM f. 528, op. 1, d. 465, ll. 25–26. The Russian 1882 family code, which was drafted but never implemented, also stressed parents' obligation to prepare children for productive citizenship and stipulated that abusive or neglectful parents could be deprived of custody. See William G. Wagner, *Marriage, Property, and Law in Late Imperial Russia* (New York, 1994), 166–67.

202. Aliakrinskii, *Brak*, 109; GARF f. A-482, op. 1, d. 27, l. 26. On Soviet orphanages, see Alan M. Ball, *And Now my Soul Is Hardened: Abandoned Children in Soviet Russia, 1918–1930* (Berkeley, 1994); Dorena Caroli, *L'enfance abandonée et délinquante dans la Russie soviétique (1917–1937)* (Paris, 2004); T. M. Smirnova, "Children's Welfare in Soviet Russia: Society and the State, 1917–1930s," *Soviet and Post-Soviet Review* 36: 2 (2009): 169–81. On harsh measures against juvenile crime, see Solomon, *Soviet Criminal Justice*, 197–209.

Fig. 11. Soviet poster promoting medical checkups for infants, 1930s. "The clinics are full—the children's graveyard is empty. Children must not die!" Poster identification number RU/SU 1630, Poster Collection, Hoover Institution Archives.

omitted religious adages to honor God and be reverent. While similar in form, Soviet youth groups stressed different values—collectivism and atheism rather than rugged individualism and religion.[203] Soviet organizations were also distinguished both by the degree to which they put the state above the family, and by their exclusively state-run character. The hero and role model for the Young Pioneers was Pavlik Morozov, a boy who allegedly denounced his own father to Soviet authorities.[204] Whereas youth organizations in other countries taught patriotism, they did not sanction the denunciation of ones parents. And although extrafamilial organizations in other countries were often run by nonstate entities—political parties, trade unions, and churches—the Soviet Union only permitted organizations run by the state.[205] Forms of Soviet intervention in childraising had much in common with those in other countries. What distinguished Soviet extrafamilial organizations was their scope, their exclusive state basis, and the values that they taught.

At every stage of reproduction and childraising, then, modern states encroached on the authority of individuals and families. Reproduction became a state concern, something that was no longer regarded as a natural phenomenon but rather as something to be monitored, regulated, and controlled. Particularly for industrialized countries with falling birthrates, pronatalism and various means to increase the population intensified in the wake of the First World War. Reproductive policies that resulted from this new orientation included abortion bans, campaigns against venereal disease, efforts to control sexuality, the promotion of the family as a vehicle of state interests, and a new emphasis on children's health and upbringing. Perhaps more than in any other sphere, government efforts to influence reproduction reveal social reformers' and state officials' transformational ambitions—ambitions to refashion society that were not exclusive to the Soviet Union.

Within this broader rubric of state and expert control of reproduction, Soviet reproductive policies may be characterized in several ways. The Soviet government sought to increase the birthrate, but unlike governments

203. For the Young Pioneers' Rules of Behavior, see RGASPI f. 17, op. 120, d. 326, ll. 15–16. Young Pioneer membership grew from 6.7 million in 1934 to 11 million in 1939; TsKhDMO f. 1, op. 23, d. 1361, l. 1.

204. Some versions of the story in the mid-1930s did not mention that the traitor denounced by Pavlik Morozov was his father. See Robert W. Thurston, "The Soviet Family during the Great Terror, 1935–1941," *Soviet Studies* 43: 3 (1991): 559–60. See also Kelly, *Children's World*, 103.

205. Domansky, "Militarization and Reproduction," 460.

of northern Europe and the United States it did not seek to limit the reproduction of those deemed unfit. Soviet specialists spurned negative eugenics even prior to the government's denunciation of eugenics as a fascist science, and in this sense they resembled their counterparts in the Catholic countries of Europe and in most developing countries around the world. The Soviet government also sought to regulate sexuality, improve reproductive health, and introduce modern methods of childraising, and by the 1930s it utilized increasingly coercive means to do so. Soviet reproductive policies and strictures on childraising reflected the more general modern ethos of social intervention based on scientific norms and state needs. This ethos was born of European social science and modern medicine, and was shaped fundamentally by the demands of mass warfare and large-scale industrial production. In the Soviet case, this ethos was further reinforced by the Revolution, which seemed to mandate the creation of an entirely new society, complete with new people. And the simultaneous creation of a new political system meant that the Soviet state was forged at a historical moment when social concerns and state security far outweighed family autonomy and individual liberties.

4 Surveillance and Propaganda

The most important task of state information is to illuminate the moods of all groups of the population and the factors that influence changes in these moods.
—Cheka Order No. 85, February 23, 1922

[Nadezhda Krupskaia] summed up the task of the present regime: Its purpose is, she said, to enable every human being to obtain personal cultivation. The economic and political revolution that had taken place was not the end, it was the means and basis of a cultural development still to be realized.... The economic change was for the sake of enabling every human being to share to the full in all the things that gave value to human life.
—JOHN DEWEY, "The Great Experiment and the Future," 1928

Surveillance and propaganda were central features of the Soviet system. The Soviet government established an extensive surveillance network that included an enormous security police apparatus, widespread use of informants, perlustration of letters, and regular government reports on the "political moods of the population." Alongside efforts to monitor the thoughts of its citizens, the Soviet government sought to shape people's thinking via educational programs and propaganda campaigns. For Party leaders, instilling "class consciousness" was crucial to ensuring political support for their regime. Viewed in isolation, the Soviet government's widespread use of surveillance and propaganda might appear to be purely the product of its ideologically inspired drive to reshape society. Indeed Soviet leaders saw propaganda and other forms of political education as essential tools to build socialism and create the New Soviet Person.

When placed in international context, however, the extensive use of surveillance and propaganda appear to be more general phenomena—tools employed by all modern states to monitor and influence the thinking of their citizens. The ideal of popular sovereignty required the involvement of the population in the affairs of governance, no longer as passive subjects, but as enlightened citizens. And with the rise of mass warfare, governments throughout Europe and around the world became concerned with the morale and political reliability of their populations, and they deployed new technologies of surveillance and propaganda accordingly.

The Bolsheviks had experience conducting revolutionary propaganda even before taking power. Following the October Revolution they adopted new governmental practices of surveillance and erected an enormous propaganda apparatus to build political support for the new order. Surveillance and propaganda, then, should be understood as technologies of rule that became widespread during the First World War, a moment of mobilization for total war. The fact that this was also the founding moment of the Soviet state meant that practices of surveillance and propaganda became fundamental components of the Soviet system. Indeed Soviet officials quickly emerged as international leaders in the use of propaganda, and politicians in other countries even began to imitate Soviet propaganda techniques. The Soviet case thus dramatically illustrates the changing nature of politics in the twentieth century. Even in states that were not democratic, mass politics required that political leaders know and influence the thinking of their populations.

Monitoring Popular Moods

The First World War marked a watershed in the realm of surveillance. Governments had engaged in domestic intelligence gathering long before the war, but these operations had been limited in both their scope and purpose. The primary function of domestic intelligence in the nineteenth century had been to contain concrete political threats, in particular those of revolutionaries who sought to overthrow existing regimes. In Russia, the tsarist government had a sizeable security police—one that was larger than those of other European countries.[1] Indeed some historians have argued for the "unmistakable affinities" between the tsarist police state and the Soviet state.[2] It is true that the tsarist security police exercised extensive powers that, when combined with the lack of individual rights and freedoms under the tsarist autocracy, led to widespread abuse of police powers and provided little

---

1. See Jonathan Daly, *Autocracy under Siege: Security Police and Opposition in Russia, 1866–1905* (DeKalb, 1998).
2. Richard Pipes, *A Concise History of the Russian Revolution* (New York, 1996), 397–99.

basis for future protection of civil liberties or democratic government. But the types and degree of state surveillance under the prewar tsarist government were not comparable to those of the Soviet regime. The tsarist police concentrated on a relatively small number of people—suspected revolutionaries and opponents of the regime. Prior to the First World War it did not monitor the population as a whole, nor was it concerned with the thoughts and sentiments of those it did observe, only with their activities.

The shift toward comprehensive government efforts to monitor and shape "popular moods" occurred during the First World War. It was then, under conditions of total wartime mobilization, that governments undertook vastly expanded operations to measure the ideas, attitudes, and loyalty of their populations. Surveillance in this sense involved much more than keeping tabs on subversive individuals in society. It entailed a new ambition to map and then transform people's thinking. Moreover, the goal of these efforts was not simply to protect the government from subversion or revolutionary overthrow. Instead it was to fashion an enlightened and loyal public that would contribute wholeheartedly to the war effort. The Soviet state was heir to these forms of surveillance, which sought to know people's thoughts in order to transform them and create self-motivated, conscious citizens.

The principal combatant countries in the First World War all developed elaborate surveillance systems for monitoring popular opinion. One form of intelligence gathering was perlustration—the clandestine opening of selected letters passing through the mail. Perlustration had been practiced on a small scale for some time, beginning with the seventeenth-century French government's "black offices" and spreading to Russia in the late eighteenth century.[3] It was only during the First World War, however, that the scale of perlustration vastly increased. Initially governments used perlustration as a security measure to prevent soldiers writing home from inadvertently revealing sensitive information that might fall into enemy hands. As the war continued, and as concern over the morale of troops increased, perlustration of letters became a means for authorities to gauge popular attitudes among both soldiers and civilians.

The French government, for example, introduced military postal censorship in 1915 as a means of counterespionage, but by 1916 it ordered censors to report on the content of soldiers' letters as well. Censors began systematic analysis of popular moods within the French Army and included in their reports both statistical data and long quotations to illustrate soldiers'

3. Daly, *Autocracy under Siege*, 41–42.

opinions.[4] In Britain, the postal censorship staff grew from 170 employees at the end of 1914 to 1,453 one year later. In 1917 it stopped delivery of 356,000 letters suspected of revealing information useful to the enemy.[5] By the end of 1917, British postal censors expanded their function from guarding military secrets to gathering information on soldiers' and civilians' morale, and the British Army began to use the information collected by postal censors to write weekly intelligence summaries on public opinion concerning the war.[6]

A similar pattern of expansion in the perlustration of letters occurred in Russia. Prewar tsarist "black offices" did not attempt to filter the entire population's mail and instead focused on a list of suspected revolutionaries whose letters they read in order to collect information on subversive activity. After the Revolution of 1905, the security police widened its purview somewhat to include Duma deputies and oppositionist politicians, but it still made no attempt to monitor the population as a whole. Prior to the First World War, the St. Petersburg postal system had only twelve employees in its black office, while the Moscow system had only seven.[7]

When the war began, the tsarist government issued its Temporary Statute on Military Censorship that pertained to both press and postal controls. The statute authorized the perlustration of all correspondence to and from the front, as well as all letters sent to newspapers, all outgoing letters of enemy prisoners of war, all incoming letters from Russian prisoners of war, and soon thereafter, the correspondence of entire minority groups within the empire deemed to be unreliable, such as Jews, Balts, Germans, and Poles. As Peter Holquist has noted, these measures marked both a quantitative and qualitative expansion of the prewar practice of perlustration. No longer did tsarist officials limit themselves to the scrutiny of individual suspects' letters. They now intercepted entire categories of mail and engaged in surveillance of whole groups of the

4. David Englander, "The French Soldier, 1914–1918," *French History* 1:1 (1987): 50.

5. Nicholas Hiley, "Counter-Espionage and Security in Great Britain during the First World War," *English Historical Review* 101:400 (July 1986): 640, 647.

6. David Englander, "Discipline and Morale in the British Army, 1917–1918," *State, Society and Mobilization in Europe during the First World War*, ed. John Horne (New York, 1997), 137.

7. V. S. Izmozik, *Glaza i ushi rezhima: Gosudarstvennyi politicheskoi kontrol' za naseleniem Sovetskoi Rossii v 1918–1928 godakh* (St. Petersburg, 1995), 19. See also Peter Holquist, *Making War, Forging Revolution: Russia's Continuum of Crisis, 1914–1921* (Cambridge, Mass., 2002), 207.

population. Military censorship offices opened hundreds of thousands of letters every week.[8]

As elsewhere, the immediate job of military postal censors in Russia was to prevent the spread of sensitive information. But there too they were soon called on to monitor popular attitudes toward the war. In fact, already early in the war Russian military censors wrote weekly summaries of the mail's content, including quotations from particular letters and statistics on the number of patriotic, apathetic, and discontented letters. By the end of 1915, when the Russian Army had suffered crushing defeats and retreated hundreds of miles into its own territory, military censors were instructed to report not only on soldiers' morale but on questions of a general political nature.[9]

Beyond perlustration, European governments developed other means of surveillance during the war. In November 1915, the German War Ministry ordered commanders in rear military districts to report on conditions in their districts, and a few months later it explicitly asked for reports on "the mood of the civilian population."[10] From the summer of 1917 on, prefects in every French department sent reports on popular moods to the Ministry of the Interior, and soon thereafter the French military ordered its generals in rear districts to compile monthly reports on local morale, which were based on information collected by military officers, government prefects, and the local police.[11] In Britain the military, the police, the Ministry of Munitions, and the Ministry of Labor all developed intelligence apparatuses. The Intelligence Branch of the army's General Staff monitored the moods not just of soldiers but of the entire population from the end of 1917 until 1920. It issued weekly intelligence summaries based on a range of sources—postal surveillance, newspaper correspondence columns, graffiti, and eavesdropping. Plainclothes police officers stationed at town halls, railway stations, military depots, dance halls, and pubs recounted

8. Holquist, *Making War,* 208. See also Jonathan W. Daly, *The Watchful State: Security Police and Opposition in Russia, 1906–1917* (DeKalb, 2004), 160.

9. Holquist, *Making War,* 209.

10. Peter Holquist, "Information Is the Alpha and Omega of Our Work," *Journal of Modern History* 69 (1997): 442. In the United States, domestic political surveillance greatly expanded during the war; see Jörg Nagler, "Victims of the Home Front: Enemy Aliens in the United States during the First World War," *Minorities in Wartime: National and Racial Groupings in Europe, North America, and Australia during the Two World Wars,* ed. Panikos Panayi (Oxford, 1993), 203.

11. Jean-Jacques Becker, *The Great War and the French People* (Dover, N. H., 1985), 228–32; J. Flood, *France, 1914–1918: Public Opinion and the War Effort* (New York, 1990), 147.

overheard conversations and unpatriotic talk, and their information was supplemented by reports from a network of volunteer informants.[12]

In Russia, reporting on popular moods began two years earlier than in other combatant countries with the exception of Germany. And in contrast to Germany, where the military introduced such a system, in Russia it was the government that concerned itself with knowing the sentiments of the population. Beginning in October 1915, the Russian Ministry of Internal Affairs required provincial and district police offices to compile monthly reports on the population's "moods" and circulated a set of questions to be answered in each report.[13] By that time, opposition to the government was growing rapidly—by the summer of 1915 the Progressive Bloc in the Russian Duma had emerged as a powerful coalition that criticized the tsarist autocracy and its handling of the war. The tsarist security police also gathered information through a network of informants, the total number of which was just over fifteen hundred at the time of the autocracy's collapse in 1917.[14]

The February Revolution marked a political turning point in Russian history, though not in the realm of surveillance. Following the overthrow of the tsarist autocracy, the Provisional Government took power and, in a symbolic break with the repressive policies of the old regime, dissolved the tsarist police network. But military postal-censorship departments continued to operate, reporting on the mood of troops and their civilian correspondents. Moreover, the Provisional Government ordered the provincial commissars of its new Ministry of Internal Affairs to report on events in the localities, and by mid-April it circulated specific directives on the gathering of information. The ministry used sixteen thematic categories to organize this information, including, for example, "the peasant movement" on unrest in the countryside, and it subsequently instructed provincial commissars to focus not just on events but on "trends in sociopolitical life."[15] The Provisional Government's Central Committee for Sociopolitical Enlightenment compiled information on levels of political support for the government and even drew weekly maps shaded with color pencils to identify locales of political support or opposition, as well as the location of "agrarian unrest," "food supply crisis," and so forth.[16]

12. David Englander, "Military Intelligence and the Defence of the Realm," *Bulletin— Society for the Study of Labour History* 52:1 (1987): 27–29.

13. Holquist, *Making War*, 209.

14. Daly, *Watchful State*, 213.

15. Holquist, *Making War*, 218–19

16. GARF f. 9505, op. 2, dd. 7–10, 13, 16.

Of particular concern were the ideas and morale of Russia's soldiers. The Provisional Government expanded efforts begun under the tsar to monitor popular moods within the army and introduced explicitly political organs to do so. At the end of April 1917, the Provisional Government appointed commissars to the major fronts both to ensure the compliance of officers, some of whom were hostile to the new order, and to safeguard the loyalty of troops.[17] Aleksandr Kerensky, the future leader of the Provisional Government and minister of war in May 1917, created a cabinet of the war minister with a political department, a surveillance department, and a department for liaison with troops. The political department issued regulations for commissars, and in late summer 1917 the head of the War Ministry Commissariat ordered commissars attached to military units to provide "detailed weekly summaries" on troops' attitudes toward the government, and it even distributed standardized forms for these summaries.[18]

Under the Provisional Government, then, surveillance became more developed, more routinized, and more political. The goals of surveillance were no longer limited to preventing espionage, and the apparatus to collect information grew larger and more sophisticated. But the basic tools of surveillance—perlustration of letters, use of informants, and regular reporting on popular moods—predated the February Revolution and were common to countries throughout Europe during the First World War. Knowledge of the population's sentiments in turn guided government efforts to bolster patriotism. Surveillance under the Provisional Government thus became linked with adult education and political propaganda campaigns—efforts to ensure that soldiers in the new, democratic Russia were no longer subservient subjects of the tsar but active citizens, ready to fight for their country and its cause.

Wartime Propaganda

In conjunction with their surveillance efforts, wartime governments launched massive propaganda campaigns to shape people's thinking and secure their

17. Allan K. Wildman, *The End of the Russian Imperial Army*, vol. 2, *The Road to Soviet Power and Peace* (Princeton, 1987), 23–24; Mark von Hagen, *Soldiers in the Proletarian Dictatorship: The Red Army and the Soviet Socialist State, 1917–1930* (Ithaca, 1990), 27. See also John Erickson, *The Soviet High Command: A Military-Political History, 1918–1941* (New York, 1962), 41–45.

18. Wildman, *End of the Russian Imperial Army*, 24; Holquist, *Making War*, 215–18.

loyalty. The use of propaganda to rally populations of course did not begin with the First World War. From the time of the French Revolution and Napoleonic Wars the character of warfare shifted from that of professional soldiers fighting for their sovereigns to mass, conscripted armies fighting for their nations. Mass warfare required the mobilization of the entire population behind the cause, and wartime propaganda served this purpose. In Russia, universal military conscription was decreed by Aleksandr II in 1874, following the advice of War Minister Dmitrii Miliutin and others who drew lessons from the Prussian national army's crushing defeats of Austria in 1866 and France in 1871. Aleksandr II's decree cited Bismarck's Germany as proof that "the strength of a state is not in the number of troops alone, but is primarily in the moral and intellectual qualities of those troops. Those qualities only reach the highest stage of development when the business of defending the fatherland becomes the general affair of the people (*narod*), when all, without distinction of title or status, unite for that holy cause."[19]

During the First World War, governments both quantitatively and qualitatively increased their efforts to influence the thinking of their populations. It was in the context of total war, and in particular the remobilization in the second half of the war, that political and military leaders came to see the national will as crucial to military victory. Accordingly, propaganda took on dramatically new forms and dimensions, as for the first time it was directed toward every member of society.[20] By the end of the war, not only had political and military leaders expanded and centralized propaganda efforts, they broadened their goals to include the education and "enlightenment" of their soldiers. More than any other event, the Russian Revolution itself made clear to observers around the world that the continuation of the war effort and the very survival of existing political regimes depended on the minds of the masses.

From the beginning of the First World War, the governments of belligerent countries engaged in rigorous censorship of the press and sought to control information about the war.[21] But initially official propaganda

19. As quoted in Joshua Sanborn, *Drafting the Russian Nation: Military Conscription, Total War, and Mass Politics, 1905–1925* (DeKalb, 2003), 3–4.

20. Leonard V. Smith, Stéphane Audoin-Rouzeau, and Annette Becker, *France and the Great War, 1914–1918* (New York, 2003), 53. As the authors write, the First World War marked the birth of modern propaganda.

21. In France, for example, a series of government decrees at the beginning of the war sought to control all publications, and the Bureau de la Presse oversaw censorship throughout the war. Moreover, journalists were forbidden access to the front, so government

was primarily directed at foreign, neutral countries, while home front propaganda remained limited to specific goals of recruitment (in Britain), war loans, and industrial mobilization. More general propaganda in support of the war effort was conducted unofficially by newspapers and churches, not by governments.[22] By 1917, however, a crisis in civilian morale prompted the French and British governments to launch large-scale propaganda campaigns through parastatal organizations—nominally independent organizations connected to the state. In France the Union of Large Associations against Enemy Propaganda (Union des Grandes Associations contre la Propagande Ennemie), formed in March 1917, was led by government officials and spread its message of patriotism through the League of Education (La Ligue de l'Enseignement) and the republican school system. The British War Cabinet, in response to industrial strikes in May 1917, founded the National War Aims Committee—nominally an autonomous organization led by members of parliament. The committee relied on the structure and personnel of political parties (the Conservative and Liberal, but not the Labour, parties) to spread propaganda in support of the war effort.[23] In Italy a similar parastatal organization (nominally private but headed by a government minister) formed to merge the propaganda efforts of various patriotic associations. Following the rout of the Italian Army at Caporetto in October 1917, the Italian government began to propagandize the population directly with public lectures, posters, and leaflets. In February 1918 it formed the Commissariat for Civilian Assistance and Propaganda to oversee both welfare and propaganda efforts.[24]

For most of the war, British generals relied on army chaplains to maintain morale among soldiers, but by the spring of 1918 they assumed direct

---

reports provided the only official source on military developments. See Flood, *France, 1914–1918,* 25–26.

22. John Horne, "Remobilizing for 'Total War': France and Britain, 1917–1918," *State, Society, and Mobilization,* 198. Russian newspapers similarly engaged in unofficial war propaganda; Richard Stites, "Days and Nights in Wartime Russia: Cultural Life, 1914–1917," *European Culture in the Great War: The Arts, Entertainment, and Propaganda, 1914–1918,* ed. Avriel Roshwald and Stites (New York, 1999), 10–12.

23. Horne, "Remobilizing for 'Total War,'" 199–201. In March 1918, the British government created its Ministry of Information, which was in charge of all foreign and domestic propaganda. The National War Aims Committee continued to operate separately, but with Ministry of Information oversight. See M. L. Sanders and Philip M. Taylor, *British Propaganda during the First World War* (London, 1982), 78–79.

24. Paul Corner and Giovanna Procacci, "The Italian Experience of 'Total' Mobilization, 1915–1920," *State, Society and Mobilization,* 228–29.

responsibility for political education of troops and began to develop a comprehensive program of civic instruction.[25] German generals similarly took control of education and propaganda within the army. In July 1917 they established a central organization subordinated to the General Staff to coordinate all patriotic instruction. Their plan stressed that "propaganda work...should not bluntly deny what is generally believed...but should rather bring enlightenment." It went on to state that "the army and the public at home are in close touch, and thus education at home and in the army must proceed side by side."[26] The Austro-Hungarian High Command also bolstered its propaganda and educational work among troops. In early 1918 the minister of war wrote to all commanders stating that the Russian Army had disintegrated because its "educational organs" had been too weak to withstand revolutionary agitation. In March military leaders established the Enemy Propaganda Defense Agency within the army to train officers and oversee patriotic instruction. Themes it promoted included the following: love of the Habsburg dynasty, mutual respect for all nationalities, and the viability and advantages of the Austro-Hungarian state. Generals were concerned not only with the example of the Russian Revolution but with Italian propaganda aimed at fomenting nationalist unrest in the Austro-Hungarian Army.[27]

Russian wartime propaganda was also conducted by a parastatal organization—the Skobelev Committee, named for the popular nineteenth-century military leader and self-declared Russian nationalist General Mikhail Skobelev. Nominally a private organization, the Skobelev Committee had close ties to the tsarist government and sought to teach patriotism and subservience to the tsar and the Orthodox Church. The tsar granted the Skobelev Committee the exclusive right to film footage at the front, which it used to produce patriotic feature films and documentaries, such as *The Storming and Capture of Erzurum* (on the Caucasian front). Given the committee's limited resources and personnel—it had only five cameramen to cover all fronts—it did not fully

25. Englander, "Discipline and Morale," 140–43.

26. Erich Ludendorff, *The General Staff and its Problems*, trans. F. A. Holt (London, 1920), vol. II, 385–38. In contrast to the militaries in other countries, the German military during the First World War assumed much greater control over all internal affairs, including in the realm of propaganda; see David Welch, "Mobilizing the Masses: The Organization of German Propaganda during World War I," *War and Media: Reportage and Propaganda, 1900–2003*, ed. Mark Connelly and David Welch (New York, 2005), 19–20, 35–37.

27. Mark Cornwall, "Morale and Patriotism in the Austro-Hungarian Army," *State, Society, and Mobilization*, 83–85.

realize film's potential as a propaganda tool, but nonetheless its use of new technologies proved innovative and extremely popular. Skobelev Committee films were shown throughout the country and, beginning in 1916, at the front using cars equipped with generators, projectors, and roll-out screens.[28]

Patriotic posters represented another new medium to convey a propaganda message. Russia's first World War I posters were produced by private organizations and were limited in their objectives, calling for donations of money and warm clothing for soldiers. In 1916 the tsarist government issued posters to promote its war loan drive, and it modeled these on British patriotic posters. In fact an exhibition of British patriotic posters was held in Petrograd that year, followed by Russian war loan poster exhibitions in London and New York in 1917.[29] One Russian commentator noted that an entirely new type of poster had emerged during the war, the function of which was not to promote products but to act as "the agitator and organizer of the masses."[30]

In contrast to Britain and France, Russia lacked well-developed political party networks and a republican school system through which to spread propaganda and political education. The tsarist autocracy's opposition to private initiative meant that few vehicles existed for the self-mobilization of Russian society. As institutions of limited local self-government, the zemstvos represented the only widespread nonstate organizations that offered the intelligentsia such a role. As in other spheres, the war forced the autocracy to allow greater involvement of the intelligentsia in educational efforts. In fact, Pavel N. Ignat'ev, the new minister of education in 1914, heralded the war as opportunity to teach patriotism and said that zemstvos should lead a campaign of public lectures on Russian history, geography, and the war. He was certainly correct to view the

---

28. Hubertus Jahn, *Patriotic Culture in Russia during World War I* (Ithaca, 1995), 40, 155–57; Denise J. Youngblood, "A War Forgotten: The Great War in Russian and Soviet Cinema," *The First World War and Popular Cinema*, ed. Michael Paris (New Brunswick, 2000), 173. The Skobelev Committee's use of mobile cinema foreshadowed the Bolsheviks' reliance on film propaganda and paralleled the French and British deployment of cinema vans during the First World War; Horne, "Remobilizing for 'Total War,'" 206. See also Pierre Sorbin, "France: The Silent Memory," *First World War and Popular Cinema*, 115–37.

29. Jahn, *Patriotic Culture*, 63, 68. Jahn also discusses the World War I publishing boom in patriotic prints and postcards (see 13–16).

30. Vera Slavenson, "Sovremennyi plakat'," *Russkaia mysl'* 3–4 (1917): 81–94.

war as an opportunity to engage the peasantry, as peasants' demand for wartime newspapers and maps increased dramatically.[31]

Zemstvo activists responded enthusiastically to what they saw as an opportunity to accelerate the cultural and civic transformation of the villages. They expanded a program of adult education with the aim of enlightening peasants and making them into citizens. They also organized lectures, increased the number of libraries, and established "reading huts" (*izby chital'nye*)—village houses containing books and newspapers, an institution the Soviet government subsequently championed as a means to enlighten peasants. On postal days, peasants packed local libraries and reading huts to get the latest news on the war. Given the large percentage of peasants who remained illiterate, librarians and teachers read aloud from newspapers and entertained questions and comments from the audience. What ultimately undermined wartime educational efforts was a severe shortage of resources and qualified personnel. Even as peasants petitioned for more schools and libraries, by 1916 zemstvo officials lacked the money to maintain their current infrastructure. Moreover, the Russian Army conscripted more than half of all male teachers, leaving a severe shortage of educators in villages at the very moment they were needed the most.[32]

It is significant that the Russian intelligentsia's longstanding dream of enlightening the downtrodden masses was given a wider opportunity only in the context of war. Although the intelligentsia had hoped to educate and uplift Russia's peasants and workers, its wartime educational programs had the additional burden of teaching patriotism and rallying support for the war effort. The purpose of such programs, then, included not just literacy but a particular political goal—the preparation of citizen-soldiers ready to fight for their country. And whereas other European countries faced the same combined challenge of mass warfare, mass politics, and the need for political education, Russia's population lagged far behind in terms of basic education, so that literacy and other skills had to be taught in conjunction with wartime propaganda. These conditions, in combination with an underdeveloped educational system and the overall scarcity of resources and personnel, severely hampered enlightenment efforts during the First World War.

---

31. Scott Seregny, "Zemstvos, Peasants, and Citizenship: The Russian Adult Education Movement and World War I," *Slavic Review* 59:2 (summer 2000): 294–97.

32. Ibid., 305–11. Seregny contrasts this situation with that in France and Germany, where not only were school systems far more established but where a smaller percentage of teachers were drafted.

The collapse of the tsarist autocracy in February 1917 presented a chance to build popular support on a democratic basis. No longer fettered by a repressive autocratic government, members of the intelligentsia greatly expanded efforts to enlighten peasants and workers and to integrate them into the polity. But the Provisional Government also operated under the enormous strain of war, and in the end had only eight chaotic months in which to school millions of soldiers, workers, and peasants in the responsibilities of liberal democratic citizenship. As Sergei Chakhotin, a Kadet Party member heading the Provisional Government's Central Committee for Sociopolitical Enlightenment, would later recall, the intelligentsia in early 1917 possessed enormous faith that the masses would gain political consciousness and support the newly democratic Russian state, but in the course of that year "these unfounded expectations were replaced by disappointment, mixed often with animosity toward that very same people in whom they had up until then believed."[33]

The Provisional Government did develop an extensive apparatus for propaganda and political enlightenment. It absorbed the Skobelev Committee and made it an official government branch charged with patriotic propaganda.[34] Provisional Government leaders also incorporated and transformed another semiautonomous organization, the Bureau for Organizing Morale. Following the outbreak of the First World War, engineering societies had formed the Committee for Military-Technical Assistance, and after the February Revolution this committee formed its Bureau for Organizing Morale. Bureau members set as their task the overcoming of "the popular masses' sociopolitical illiteracy," which they claimed derived from "the tsarist regime's criminal unwillingness to grant the people light and knowledge."[35] As minister of war, Kerensky incorporated the bureau into the War Ministry and renamed it the Committee for Sociopolitical Enlightenment. Committee members saw the military as the place both of greatest need and greatest opportunity to raise the population's civic consciousness. They stated that "the fastest way to implant knowledge in the country is through the army," and they noted that the army's organizational resources made it easier "to introduce and disseminate those principles

33. Sergei Chakhotin, "V Kanossu!" *Smena vekh*, 2nd ed. (Prague, 1922), 151–52, as quoted in Holquist, *Making War*, 105. See also Daniel T. Orlovsky, "The Provisional Government and its Cultural Work," *Bolshevik Culture: Experiment and Order in the Russian Revolution*, ed. A. Gleason et al. (Bloomington, 1985), 39–56.

34. Peter Kenez, *The Birth of the Propaganda State: Soviet Methods of Mass Mobilization, 1917–1929* (New York, 1985), 105–6.

35. GARF f. 9505, op. 1, d. 1, l. 1.

of political knowledge without which we will be unable to handle the immense tasks standing before Russia."[36]

Most military officers did not resist these efforts to educate and politicize their soldiers. Although they deeply resented the Petrograd Soviet's "Order No. 1," which established soldiers' committees and Soviet authority within the army, many officers saw a need for some sort of political education to transform passive troops into conscious citizen-soldiers. In September 1917 the War Ministry's Political Directorate introduced compulsory adult education for all soldiers and established a department to distribute pamphlets and books to troops.[37] The Central Committee for Sociopolitical Enlightenment organized courses to train lecturers and sent out speakers to address both military and civilian audiences in an effort to raise consciousness and win political support.[38]

Ultimately, of course, the Provisional Government failed to build support among Russian soldiers and the population as a whole.[39] But its failure did not reflect a lack of political engagement on the part of the population. Rather, in the course of the First World War and Russian Revolution the country's soldiers and peasants had become highly politicized, while worker radicalism, well established before the war, became even more intense. The real problem faced by leaders of the Provisional Government was that the lower classes had their own revolutionary aspirations. Soldiers, peasants, and workers wanted an end to the war, immediate land redistribution, and workers' control of the factories. Moreover, the Provisional Government was not alone in 1917 in its efforts to indoctrinate the masses. Revolutionary parties, foremost among them the Bolsheviks, were able to expand greatly their agitation and propaganda campaigns following the collapse of the autocracy and the introduction of freedoms of assembly and the press. Bolshevik slogans such as "Peace, Land, and Bread" resonated with peasants' and workers' notions of social justice and further eroded support for the Provisional Government.

36. GARF f. 9505, op. 1, d. 1, ll. 1–3.

37. Holquist, *Making War,* 216–17.

38. GARF f. 9505, op. 1, d. 4, ll. 9–10; op. 2, d. 5, ll. 1–16.

39. For a discussion of politics in the localities in 1917, see Aaron B. Retish, *Russia's Peasants in Revolution and Civil War: Citizenship, Identity, and the Creation of the Soviet State, 1914–1922* (New York, 2008); Michael C. Hickey, "The Rise and Fall of Smolensk's Moderate Socialists: The Politics of Class and the Rhetoric of Crisis in 1917," *Provincial Landscapes: Local Dimensions of Soviet Power, 1917–1953,* ed. Donald J. Raleigh (Pittsburgh, 2001).

Soviet Surveillance

At the time they took power in October 1917, Bolshevik Party leaders had no formal plan to conduct surveillance, let alone establish an all-pervasive surveillance apparatus. Why, then, did they not only perpetuate but vastly expand the perlustration of letters, the use of informants, and the systematic reporting on popular moods, all carried out by a newly formed security police for which they also lacked any preexisting plan? Certainly the Bolsheviks' choices were determined in part by the political exigencies of their situation—a situation they helped create when they seized power as a minority party in a country riven by social strife and political fragmentation. As they struggled to maintain power in the face of armed opposition and growing anarchy, Lenin and his fellow leaders did not hesitate to employ surveillance and coercion. Knowledge of the population, and of its various segments' political allegiances, was essential information as they sought to build support and quell opposition. Such knowledge would also prove vital to their ideological goal of social transformation.

The forms of surveillance Party leaders employed, however, did not stem from any political or ideological plan, but rather were drawn from preexisting practices. Surveillance technologies developed during the First World War offered them a means to gather the information they desperately needed on their opponents and on the political opinions of the population as a whole. In some cases they received reports they did not even request from former Provisional Government officials who continued to monitor popular moods after the October Revolution—an extreme example of bureaucratic continuity over a revolutionary divide. Equally significant for understanding the continuation of surveillance is the fact that even after the Soviet government ended Russia's involvement in the First World War, the country remained at war. And it was in the course of a bloody civil war, when the very survival of the new regime depended on the mobilization of popular support and the rooting out of political opponents, that all-encompassing surveillance became institutionalized within the Soviet system. At a moment of total war, Party leaders perpetuated and expanded surveillance practices that had been deployed on a mass scale during the First World War.

Perlustration of mail continued to hold a central place in the exercise of surveillance. A Soviet government decree on censorship and perlustration in July 1919 created a new structure to monitor the mail, telegraph, radio, and telephone. The government designated a substantial number of bureaucrats to perform each task, with a total of more than ten thousand officials involved in all forms of perlustration. In terms of personnel, there was significant carryover from the Provisional Government; at the end of 1918 roughly half of the employees of the Moscow military postal-telegraph control bureau had begun work there before the October Revolution.[40]

While the practices and even the personnel involved in perlustration remained somewhat constant, the Soviet government began to use this form of surveillance for new purposes. Information gathered in perlustrated letters continued to provide one of the principal sources for reports on "political moods" of the population. But this information also began to be used by the Soviet security police to identify and arrest people engaged in "speculation"—buying and selling items, especially food, outside the state system of rationed goods and controlled prices. Petrograd security police reports in 1918 stated that perlustration was playing a large role in the battle against this form of (now illegal) petty capitalism.[41] Throughout the Civil War, postal control boards continued to have responsibility for perlustration, but they submitted their intelligence to Communist Party and security police authorities, and in August 1920, they became a part of the Special Department of the security police.[42]

As was true with perlustration, the system developed during the First World War for reporting on popular moods in the military continued under the Soviet government. In December 1917, Red Army leaders complained that political commissars appointed by the Provisional Government were sending them reports on troops' moods, using forms printed by the Provisional Government. But rather than dismissing these commissars, they directed them to continue conveying reports, and to go beyond the items listed on the old forms. In January 1918, the Red Army's political administration issued new guidelines for these reports, with categories such as "the removal of counter-revolutionary elements."[43] During the Civil War, the Red Army's political administration formed its "information branch" that compiled data on military units throughout the country. Officials of this branch designed charts that categorized soldiers' "mood," "discipline," "level of consciousness," "relationship to Soviet power," and "relationship to Communists." In cases of defeatist moods, they also provided explanations ranging from "insufficient food supply" to "weakness of political work."[44] As with perlustration, then, Soviet reports on popu-

40. Izmozik, *Glaza i ushi rezhima*, 49–50, 54.
41. RGASPI f. 5, op. 1, d. 2484, ll. 11–13.
42. Izmozik, *Glaza i ushi rezhima*, 66.
43. Holquist, *Making War*, 218
44. GARF f. 130, op. 4, d. 261, ll. 4–11.

lar moods took similar practices and personnel and applied them to new political goals.

The Communist Party soon developed its own surveillance apparatus as well. By 1919 the information department of the Party's Central Committee was compiling regular reports by province on relations between the population and local Party organizations.[45] In addition to Party organs, branches of the government wrote reports on the population's ideas and attitudes. The Commissariat of Internal Affairs, the Russian Telegraph Agency, and the security police all submitted regular reports to Party leaders.[46] While the flood of reports generated by the burgeoning Soviet bureaucracy seems redundant, it reflected officials' fixation with understanding the ideas and political loyalties of the population. Lenin himself, in August 1918, requested that he receive reports on the moods of workers and peasants in the localities, and throughout the Civil War, Party leaders were sent information on popular moods.[47] Soviet leaders did not seek to discern popular sentiment in order to accommodate it—those people who opposed their authority and policies they labeled "backward," "lacking political consciousness," or "counterrevolutionary." Rather Soviet officials sought to know the population in order "to enlighten" and transform it. In a time of Civil War, the survival of the Soviet state, as well as the broader project of integrating people into a new, socialist polity, depended on this mission.

That the Soviet government's use of surveillance reflected a broader shift in the nature of politics is best conveyed by the fact that its enemies in the Civil War also engaged in surveillance. The White armies established extensive surveillance networks for the purpose of knowing and shaping the sentiments of the population. The Whites in the South—General Anton Denikin's Armed Forces of South Russia and its nascent government— formed a surveillance and agitation branch that was both to report on the population's attitudes and to disseminate propaganda to build popular support. This branch established information offices throughout the territory controlled by Denikin and his army, and White officials working at these offices submitted increasingly standardized summaries on the "mood of the population." In addition, the Don Cossack government (the All-Great Don Host), first allied with and later subordinated to Denikin's army, formed its own surveillance department with branch offices

---

45. RGASPI f. 17, op. 65, d. 5, ll. 98–101.
46. Izmozik, *Glaza i ushi rezhima*, 31–32, 67.
47. Ibid., 27.

and agents who traveled throughout the territory. Some of these agents worked openly as agitators and lecturers on behalf of the Whites. Others masqueraded as students, doctors, or railway workers while they gathered information on popular moods. These surveillance agents submitted reports that the central Don Cossack administration incorporated into its daily summaries on the population's attitudes.[48] While the Whites may have proven less successful than the Communists at winning popular support during the Civil War, the fact that this rather disparate group of political and military leaders (which included both monarchists and constitutional democrats) saw the need to monitor and influence the population's thinking showed that they understood the new political terrain of the era.

Soviet reports on popular moods helped to guide political work. A September 1919 Red Army report on soldiers' "political and cultural-enlightenment condition," for example, characterized both the "political consciousness" and the "popular mood" of each brigade. It attributed the "revolutionary mood" of one brigade to regular political enlightenment work, and it blamed the lack of political consciousness in another brigade on the absence of experienced propagandists. It also reported on the resources and methods of political work—most brigades had a small library and regular lectures, while some had literacy classes and theater performances as well.[49] Security police reports on popular moods often attributed opposition to both economic hardship and a lack of political enlightenment. One 1919 security police report stated that "anti-Soviet moods of the population [persist] in areas of food supply crisis." Another such report noted that Uglich had become a center for "bands of White guards," given the town's remote location and the fact that "the town's population is utterly undeveloped politically."[50] A third report noted that the population of Iaroslavl' Province, "as a legacy of its backwardness," easily fell under the influence of counterrevolutionaries, and that peasants there had developed "a reactionary mood" following grain requisitions.[51]

Already during the Civil War, the security police assumed the leading role in carrying out surveillance. Whereas prior to the Revolution, Bolshevik leaders had not envisioned a security police force, on December 7, 1917, they established the All-Russian Extraordinary Commission for Combating Counterrevolution and Sabotage, known by its acronym Ch.K.,

48. Holquist, *Making War*, 227–29.
49. RGASPI f. 17, op. 66, d. 84, ll. 51–54.
50. Izmozik, *Glaza i ushi rezhima*, 68.
51. GARF f. 130, op. 3, d. 415, l. 88ob.

or "Cheka." Intended as a temporary commission to deal with a specific political threat (a general strike of state employees), this body became a permanent security police organization that conducted surveillance for a range of purposes.[52] In addition to reporting on popular moods, the security police collected data on those it suspected of political opposition, and based on this data it carried out widespread arrests, incarcerations, and executions. In an April 1919 circular, Martin Ia. Latsis, one of the founders and leaders of the Soviet security police, stated that the security police needed to monitor every former tsarist official, military officer, police officer, landowner, banker, and cleric. The following year he wrote that "entire classes are counterrevolutionaries," and he advocated rigorous observation of "all members of the large and petty bourgeoisie."[53] Security police operations to keep tabs on those it deemed subversive resembled the tsarist police's monitoring of political oppositionists and revolutionaries. What distinguished the Soviet security police was not only the vastly expanded scale of its operations—watching thousands and eventually millions of people—but that it scrutinized entire social groups rather than just individuals.

The security police even categorized segments within the bourgeoisie and assessed the political danger they posed. A security police report from June 1919 judged that "a majority of specialists are opponents of Soviet power," and directed security police operatives to question workers on the "political views" of specialists at their factories. The report went on to delineate five subcategories of specialists, from those who were "overt or secret counterrevolutionaries" to those whose political allegiance remained to be "decoded." The report called for agents to monitor specialists' activities closely and maintain card files on them, and stated that counterrevolutionaries should be "arrested and incarcerated in a concentration camp."[54]

To sustain this extensive system of surveillance, the security police expanded exponentially in size. In December 1917 its central apparatus had only 25 members; that number grew to 219 in March, 481 in June, and 779 in September. Even more rapid was the growth of the security police organization at the local level, as it sought to extend its control to every part of the country. By the summer of 1921 the total number of security police employees was about 60,000, and in addition to employees, the

---

52. For more on the founding of the Soviet security police, see George Leggett, *The Cheka: Lenin's Political Police* (New York, 1986), 16–18.

53. Izmozik, *Glaza i ushi rezhima*, 60, 62.

54. RGASPI f. 17, op. 66, d. 65, ll. 51–55.

security police enlisted an extensive network of informants.[55] A security police conference resolved that all Party members in the Red Army were to act as informants, gathering information both on suspicious individuals and on the mood of soldiers.[56] "Special Departments" of the security police were established in every military unit and in other institutions as well. As Vladlen Izmozik concludes, by the end of the Civil War the security police structure reached into every sphere of political and economic life.[57] Created as a temporary body to deal with the threat of counterrevolution, the Cheka and its methods of surveillance had been institutionalized as permanent features of the Soviet system.

The conclusion of the Civil War presented the opportunity for Communist Party leaders to scale back the level of surveillance in Soviet society. With the defeat of the White armies, the immediate threat of counterrevolution receded and wartime surveillance practices seemed less necessary. Lenin's introduction of the New Economic Policy (NEP) at the Tenth Party Congress in 1921 provided a model of how, at least in the economic realm, Party leaders could step back from the policies of War Communism. But the overwhelming majority of Party members did not embrace the NEP. At best they saw it as a strategic retreat, necessitated by economic collapse and peasant opposition to grain requisitions. At worst Party members viewed the NEP as a sell-out to the very "bourgeois elements" they had shed their blood to defeat during the Civil War. Far from signaling a political liberalization of the Soviet system, the introduction of the NEP prompted Party leaders to pursue even greater vigilance to defend their Revolution, whose future remained uncertain.

One danger that consumed Party leaders was the possibility of NEP contagion. Under a socioeconomic system that permitted small-scale capitalism, that rewarded those who exploited the labor of others, people might be drawn away from the ideals of socialism and instead embrace bourgeois values. As economic determinists, Party leaders saw the petty bourgeois milieu created by the New Economic Policy as shaping people's mentality and behavior. Some Party moralists feared that rank-and-file Party members themselves might be corrupted. The Party's Central Control Commission, established in 1920, oversaw a hierarchy of control commissions charged with maintaining the highest standards of ideological and ethical purity among Party members. At the Eleventh Party Congress in 1922, the

55. Izmozik, *Glaza i ushi rezhima*, 60, 65.
56. RGASPI f. 17, op. 84, d. 114, l. 10.
57. Izmozik, *Glaza i ushi rezhima*, 74

chair of the Central Control Commission, Aaron Sol'ts, warned of "degeneration" within the Party and pointed out that the NEP increased the likelihood that the Party's weak members would fall into petty bourgeois ways.[58] The Eleventh Party Congress resolved that control commissions must purge "all those who disgrace the Party" including "alien, harmful, and degenerate elements" and those who adopt an "uncommunist way of life" through "private trade, drunkenness, or moral dissoluteness."[59]

Beyond its potential ill effects on members of the Party, the New Economic Policy increased the ranks and visibility of the bourgeoisie itself. NEPmen opened businesses, shops, and factories. Some even began to flaunt their wealth, wearing expensive clothing and dining at newly opened restaurants and nightclubs. Soviet officials not only bitterly resented NEPmen's conspicuous consumption, they worried that the NEP had emboldened these class enemies, who might seek not only greater economic influence but greater political control as well. A 1922 security police decree called for monitoring "the growth of the petty bourgeois element" within society.[60] The continued use of surveillance represented a means to keep tabs on NEPmen as well as to monitor the possible spread of petty bourgeois sentiments throughout society.

In addition to general fears of bourgeois contamination, there were in 1921 a series of rebellions that induced Party leaders to maintain or increase surveillance. The Kronstadt Rebellion, which coincided with the Tenth Party Congress in March 1921, left Party members deeply shaken regarding their lack of social support within the country. Although bloodily suppressed, the rebellion prompted the Party's Central Committee to issue a circular calling for a comprehensive system of state surveillance "for the purposes of timely and comprehensive information gathering [*osvedomlenie*] and the taking of corresponding measures."[61] Widespread revolts among the peasantry, including a large-scale rebellion in Tambov Province, also occurred at the end of the Civil War. This unrest coupled

58. A. A. Sol'ts, "Iz otcheta tsentral'noi kontrol'noi komissii na XI s"ezde RKP(b)," *Partiinaia etika: Dokumenty i materialy diskussii 20-kh godov*, ed. M. A. Makarevich (Moscow, 1989), 141–42.

59. Makarevich, ed., *Partiinaia etika*, 147–48. On measures at the Eleventh Party Congress to strengthen the Central Control Commission, see Leonard Schapiro, *The Communist Party of the Soviet Union*, 2nd ed. (New York, 1971), 261.

60. Izmozik, *Glaza i ushi rezhima*, 107–8.

61. Ibid., 80. See also V. K. Vinogradov, "Ob osobennostiakh informatsionnykh materialov OGPU kak istochnika po istorii sovetskogo obshchestva," *"Sovershenno sekretno": Lubianka—Stalinu o polozhenii v strane (1922–1934 gg.)*, ed. G. N. Sevost'ianov et al., 10 vols., vol. 1, pt. 1 (Moscow, 2001), 31–73.

with the presence of anti-Communist conspiracies—for example the Petrograd Combat Organization whose members were arrested in June 1921 for plotting an armed uprising—further contributed to Party leaders' siege mentality.[62]

While the New Economic Policy served to placate economic unrest, particularly among the peasantry, Party leaders were left with a reinforced sense of minority rule. At the time they took power in the name of the working class, less than 5 percent of Russia's population were workers, while the overwhelming majority (roughly 85 percent) were peasants. And with Civil War casualties, economic collapse, and urban depopulation, the proletariat grew even smaller. The vanguard party that was to lead Russia and eventually the entire world to socialism found itself surrounded by peasants and bourgeois enemies with little popular support. Nor could the Communists expect help from abroad, given the failure of proletarian revolution to spread. Instead they perceived "capitalist encirclement," a sense of siege exacerbated by Allied military intervention during the Civil War, which although limited and ineffectual, symbolically communicated capitalist leaders' eagerness to crush the Soviet state in its infancy. In this context, Party leaders clung to existing surveillance practices, both to forestall anti-Soviet conspiracies and to monitor the thinking of an overwhelmingly peasant population that they desperately hoped to transform.

In early 1922 the Soviet security police did undergo reorganization and renaming. Speaking at the Ninth All-Russian Congress of Soviets in December 1921, Lenin praised the Cheka and its role defeating anti-Soviet opposition during the Civil War, but noted that under the New Economic Policy there was a need for "more revolutionary legality." Delegates to the congress passed a resolution restricting the Cheka's authority in favor of a greater role for judicial organs. On February 6, 1922, the Soviet government abolished the Cheka and transferred its powers to the newly constituted State Political Administration (Gosudarstvennoe politicheskoe upravlenie), or GPU, which the following year would be renamed the Unified State Political Administration, or OGPU. Despite these superficial changes, however, the Soviet security police continued to function much as it had before. Felix Dzerzhinsky, who had been head of the Cheka,

---

62. At this time, the Cheka's deputy head, Iosif Unshlikht, sent a memo to the Politburo outlining a plan for "an organized and systematic struggle with counterrevolutionary movements." See Stuart Finkel, "An Intensification of Vigilance: Recent Perspectives on the Institutional History of the Soviet Security Apparatus in the 1920s," *Kritika* 5:2 (spring 2004): 303. On anti-Bolshevik conspiracies in this period, including those organized by émigrés such as Boris Savinkov, see Leggett, *The Cheka*, 288–96.

continued to head the security police under its new name, and in late February 1922 Lenin warned that NEPmen must be watched and punished mercilessly. On August 22, 1922 the Soviet government once again granted the security police extrajudicial powers, and the new security police organization continued to engage in surveillance much as it had done in its previous incarnation.[63]

With the decrease in government-controlled resources under the New Economic Policy, the security police did initially suffer budget cuts and some reduction in personnel, though these were soon reversed. When Commissar of Finances G. Ia. Sokol'nikov argued in 1924 for further reductions in the security police budget, Dzerzhinsky vehemently opposed these cuts. He claimed that prior cuts meant that the security police already were "not in a condition to carry out the task assigned to us," and he argued successfully to the Politburo that "now the internal situation is very tense due to an onslaught of various anti-Soviet, espionage, and bandit forces. We already carried out reductions to their limit."[64] Other security police officials at this time called for an increase in personnel. The head of the counterintelligence department, A. Kh. Artuzov, reported that "given the weakness of Soviet power in the countryside, a fundamental task of the OGPU—the prevention of uprisings in the village—will be impossible to fulfill without a sufficient number of agents in the most dangerous localities."[65] The head of the secret operations department, T. D. Deribas, meanwhile complained of insufficient personnel to monitor all those who posed a threat—anarchists, Mensheviks, Socialist Revolutionaries, monarchists, sectarians, and former tsarist police officers, bureaucrats, and landowners.[66]

Of course, the security police had a financial interest in exaggerating the threat of counterrevolution, but it seems clear that Party leaders and security police officials alike shared a genuine fear of internal enemies. And whether or not those listed by Deribas posed any real danger, a large number of tsarist-era elites and former members of oppositionist political parties still resided in the Soviet Union in the 1920s. One factor, then, that fueled the continuation of Soviet surveillance was the postrevolutionary landscape in which the security police operated. Following a period of

63. Leggett, *The Cheka,* 343–52. See also S. V. Leonov, "Reorganizatsiia VChK v GPU," *Istoricheskie chteniia na Lubianke, 1999 god: Otechestvennye spetssluzhby v 1920–1930-kh godakh* (Moscow, 2000); A. L. Litvin, "'Na kazhdogo intelligenta dolzhno byt' delo': Kak VChK peredelyvali v GPU i chto iz etogo vyshlo," *Rodina* 6 (1995): 31–34.

64. RGASPI f. 76, op. 3, d. 305, l. 50.

65. RGASPI f. 76, op. 3, d. 306, l. 6.

66. RGASPI f. 76, op. 3, d. 306, l. 141.

radical political change, there were many people whose loyalty could be questioned simply because of their prior allegiances. And given their Civil War experiences, Soviet officials perceived alternative allegiances to be the basis of violent opposition.

Surveillance during the 1920s and 1930s gradually became more elaborate. The security police established a "Special Department" in every large institution, including factories, universities, hospitals, and so forth. It employed a large number of undercover operatives (*sekretnye sotrudniki*)—according to one source more than ten thousand in Moscow alone by the end of the 1920s.[67] In addition the security police recruited thousands of informants who, either voluntarily or under pressure, carried out surveillance. At one high school in the Donbass region, thirteen out of twenty staff members acted as security police informants. In addition to reporting on general attitudes among students and teachers, these informants recounted to the security police virtually every conversation they had with one teacher who was under suspicion.[68] A 1935 Central Committee report stated that the security police employed 27,650 resident agents and 270,777 informants.[69] Based on the material provided by informants and agents, the security police created files on hundreds of thousands of Soviet citizens.[70] These dossiers in turn were used by the security police to make arrests and conduct interrogations. Thus surveillance served not only to monitor popular moods but to identify and eliminate those deemed to be "anti-Soviet elements."[71]

Communist Party members also carried out surveillance. The Party had a cell in every Soviet institution, and beginning in the early 1920s its members were obligated to provide the security police with information on

67. Izmozik, *Glaza i ushi rezhima*, 117, citing the estimate of a Soviet security police officer who fled to the West in 1930—G. Agabekov, *GPU: Zapiski chekista* (Berlin, 1930), 18.

68. Volodymyr Semystiaha, "The Role and Place of Secret Collaborators in the Informational Activity of the GPU-NKVD in the 1920s and 1930s (on the basis of materials in the Donbass region)," *Cahiers du monde russe* 42:2–4 (2001): 235–36, 240.

69. RGASPI f. 671, op. 1, d. 118, l. 4, as cited in David Shearer, "Elements Near and Alien: Passportization, Policing, and Identity in the Stalinist State, 1933–1952," *Journal of Modern History* 76 (December 2004): 846. See also David R. Shearer, *Policing Stalin's Socialism: Repressions and Social Order in the Soviet Union, 1924–1953* (New Haven, 2009), 134–40.

70. Already in 1922, Dzerzhinskii had ordered the establishment of a classificatory system to organize surveillance materials; Finkel, "An Intensification of Vigilance," 314.

71. For further discussion, see Cynthia V. Hooper, "Terror from Within: Participation and Coercion in Soviet Power, 1924–1964" (Ph.D. diss., Princeton University, 2003), 60.

the political moods of fellow workers.[72] In addition, a Central Committee circular in September 1921 instructed each Party cell to submit daily, weekly, and monthly reports on the mood of various social and occupational groups—workers, peasants, soldiers, white-collar workers, and so forth. In cases of anti-Soviet moods, strikes, rebellions, and banditism, reports were to detail the political and economic conditions pertaining to these phenomena, as well as the population's attitudes toward the Communist Party and Soviet decrees. Party officials were also to report on "cultural enlightenment work" and its effectiveness in influencing popular moods.[73] The Central Committee's Information-Instructional Department then compiled all of the data from local Party cells and issued monthly reports on the "general political and economic conditions" of each province. This information in turn was used to guide the political enlightenment work of local Party organizations.[74]

Another important source of data for the Information-Instructional Department were letters that peasants and workers sent to newspapers. While clearly less candid than private correspondence, these letters were nonetheless regarded as a source of information. Department officials referred to unpublished letters as "materials that characterize the moods of the masses." In accordance with Party directives, editorial offices of major newspapers submitted weekly summaries of all the letters they received not only to the Information-Instructional Department but directly to Lenin, and later to Stalin and Molotov. For example, the editors of the two leading newspapers for Soviet peasants, *Krest'ianskaia gazeta* and *Bednota,* sent Stalin reports (including sample letters) summarizing the views peasants expressed on specific themes.[75] Party leaders also gathered information from letters written to them directly. Throughout the 1920s and 1930s people sent letters and petitions to Soviet authorities, often complaining of injustices or pleading for assistance.[76] During collectivization, for example, thousands of peasants wrote to Party leaders. Mikhail Kalinin, as head of the Soviet government's Central Executive Committee,

72. Semystiaha, "Role and Place of Secret Collaborators," 233.

73. RGASPI f. 17, op. 11, d. 108, ll. 88–92ob.

74. RGASPI f. 17, op. 11, d. 44, ll. 3–4.

75. Izmozik, *Glaza i ushi rezhima,* 87–88. Beginning in 1924, the Commissariat of Internal Affairs also began to receive samples of letters sent to *Krest'ianskaia gazeta;* see Hooper, "Terror from Within," 123.

76. See Sheila Fitzpatrick, *Stalin's Peasants: Resistance and Survival in the Russian Village after Collectivization* (New York, 1994); Golfo Alexopoulos, *Stalin's Outcasts: Aliens, Citizens, and the Soviet State, 1926–1936* (Ithaca, 2003).

received an enormous quantity—3,847 letters in the span of just four days in April 1930. Officials in the Central Executive Committee Information Department wrote reports summarizing peasant letters and including excerpts to provide examples of peasants' thinking.[77]

What these various forms of surveillance revealed was widespread discontent among the population. Although my focus here is on the mechanisms of surveillance, a brief discussion of the content of surveillance reports helps to explain the continued insecurity of Party leaders and their insistence on maintaining surveillance practices. Perlustrated letters frequently contained condemnations of Soviet rule. One 1924 letter stated, "Nonparty people claim that it would have been better to perish in the yoke under the old regime than to live under Soviet freedom which is like living in prison." The author of another 1924 letter wrote, "The October Revolution...was not a social revolution but rather an artificial, pernicious result of the political demagoguery of the Bolsheviks."[78] Even more common were indications of economic hardship and discontent. In 1925 a perlustrated letter from Tambov Province claimed that "for a hundred versts all around there is great hunger," while another letter pronounced that "there are a lot of starving people from the countryside here in Leningrad."[79] Surveillance reports from the 1930s indicated not only economic discontent but political opposition, including direct denunciations of Stalin and the Party leadership.[80] In a sense the elaborate Soviet surveillance system was self-perpetuating, because it produced a constant stream of information indicating the presence of anti-Soviet sentiments and economic discontent, which in turn further heightened Party leaders' insecurity and their determination to continue surveillance.

The insecurity of Party leaders became even more manifest at moments of crisis. When Lenin died in January 1924, Dzerzhinsky sent a telegram to all security police offices ordering close observation of "the mood of the masses," and special attention to the behavior of monarchists, White guardists, and other counterrevolutionaries.[81] During the 1927 War Scare,

77. Nicolas Werth and Gaël Moullec, eds., *Rapports Secrets Soviétiques 1921–1991: La Société Russe dans les Documents Confidentiels* (Paris, 1994), 132–34.

78. Vladlen S. Izmozik, "Voices from the Twenties: Private Correspondence Intercepted by the OGPU," *The Russian Review* 55: 2 (April 1996): 289–90.

79. Ibid., 292.

80. TsAOPIM f. 635, op. 1, d. 41, ll. 16–17; TsKhDMO f. 1, op. 23, d. 1072, ll. 108–9. See also Sarah Davies, *Popular Opinion in Stalin's Russia: Terror, Propaganda and Dissent, 1934–1941* (New York, 1997), chapter 8.

81. RGASPI f. 76, op. 3, d. 287, l. 19

the security police issued a special report "On the Reaction of Various Strata of the Population of the USSR to the Danger of War." Among other things the report named a number of "anti-Soviet" groups that might take advantage of an impending war, and it warned that kulaks were conducting "anti-Soviet agitation" and even preparing for "armed action."[82] The connection between a heightened external threat and greater surveillance of internal enemies reveals Party and security police leaders' fear of simultaneous attack from capitalist countries and internal enemies—a fear that would subsequently fuel their use of state violence.

Party leaders' "socialist offensive" in the early 1930s prompted a further expansion of surveillance. During collectivization the security police vastly increased its reporting on the countryside. Using its standard surveillance techniques—perlustrated letters, statements by informants, and observations of agents—the security police issued special reports on "Collectivization and Political Moods in the Village," "Kulak Terror," and so forth. The reports included extracts from peasants' private letters, including letters written by those deported as kulaks, and also analyzed the linkages between difficult material conditions and poor morale on newly formed collective farms.[83] One report described "kulak" agitation against collective farms, poor peasants' eagerness to confiscate kulaks' belongings, and the unease of middle peasants who feared they might be the next targets of dekulakization.[84]

The severe shortages and famine that resulted from collectivization and grain requisitions precipitated another crisis in 1932–33. At that time Party officials sent emergency communications reporting on starvation in famine regions of Ukraine, the North Caucasus, and the Volga.[85] Simultaneous food shortages and ration reductions in cities provoked widespread unrest, including workers' strikes. Because they ruled in the name of the working class, Party officials were particularly alarmed by workers' protests. They produced special surveillance reports on unrest—for example, on the wave of strikes among textile workers in the Ivanovo region.[86]

82. RGASPI f. 17, op. 85, d. 289, ll. 2–19.

83. Viktor Danilov and Alexis Berelowitch, "Les Documents de la VCK-OGPU-NKVD sur la Campagne Soviétique 1918–1937," *Cahiers du monde russe* 35:3 (1994): 633–82, here at 636–46.

84. Werth and Moullec, eds., *Rapports Secrets Soviétiques 1921–1991*, 116–17.

85. Ibid., 147–59.

86. See Jeffrey J. Rossman, *Worker Resistance under Stalin: Class and Revolution on the Shop Floor* (Cambridge, Mass., 2005). For more on strike activity, see Donald Filtzer, *Soviet Workers and Stalinist Industrialization: The Formation of Modern Soviet Industrial*

While economic crises and political discontent were themselves cause for surveillance of the population, Party leaders had more general reasons for continuing to monitor people's thinking. Their goal was to transform a rural, undeveloped country with a semiliterate, peasant population into a modern, industrialized socialist state with a large, politically conscious proletariat. The elimination of capitalism and private farming in favor of a state-run economy and collectivized agriculture in itself meant the expansion of state control over every aspect of economic life. Party leaders' attempt to mobilize human resources for the industrialization drive required even greater knowledge of the population. Perhaps most important, Party leaders' goal of instilling a new type of consciousness—of fundamentally changing the way that people thought and acted—necessitated a thorough understanding of people's thinking, and in conjunction with that, renewed efforts at political enlightenment. As one Party official stated, Soviet citizens were to be taught "to shoulder all the burdens of organizing socialism."[87]

Official reports throughout the 1930s noted the persistence of petty bourgeois behavior, and called for redoubled efforts to instill in workers and peasants the proper political consciousness. With regard to religion, for example, officials decried the ongoing religious belief and worship among large segments of the population, and they devoted considerable resources to atheist propaganda.[88] Party and government reports also deplored widespread drunkenness and workers' preference for drinking and card playing over officially prescribed forms of leisure.[89] Given the priority of the industrialization drive, Party reports focused particularly on raising workers' productivity and emphasized instilling political consciousness as the means to do so. One report called for enlightenment work among "politically undeveloped youth who just arrived" at the factory, while another declared the greatest task facing the Party to be "the reeducation of newly arrived workers in the spirit of those who will fulfill the tasks of the proletariat."[90] While Party and security police surveillance reports often blamed anti-Soviet agitators for negative popular moods, they also

Relations, 1928–1941 (New York, 1986), 81–85; GARF f. 5475, op. 13, d. 276, l. 9; d. 426, l. 76.

87. TsAOPIM f. 634, op. 1, d. 221, l. 53.

88. GARF f. 5451, op. 13, d. 76, l. 51; f. 7952, op. 3, d. 522, ll. 1–4; TsAOPIM f. 432, op. 1, d. 220, ll. 25–26. See also William B. Husband, *"Godless Communists": Atheism and Society in Soviet Russia, 1917–1932* (DeKalb, 2000); Daniel Peris, *Storming the Heavens: The Soviet League of the Militant Godless* (Ithaca, 1998).

89. RGASPI f. 17, op. 114, d. 255, l. 66; TsAGM f. 1289, op. 1, d. 173, l. 1.

90. TsAOPIM f. 635, op. 1, d. 69, l. 16; f. 432, op. 1, d. 50, l. 169.

attributed these to inadequate education and propaganda.[91] Surveillance therefore provided an impetus for additional political enlightenment work and even indicated which social groups were in need of such work.

One other dimension of Soviet surveillance that fed its proliferation was the government's encouragement of popular denunciation.[92] While the security police and the Party directed most surveillance, Soviet officials also promoted a range of popular surveillance practices that allowed workers and peasants to report on their bosses, as well as on one another.[93] From the time of the Revolution, Party leaders sought to involve the masses in the policing of the new socialist society. Shortly after taking power, Lenin called for "the collaboration of the masses of workers and peasants in the stock-taking and monitoring of the rich, swindlers, parasites, hooligans." He explained that "the land, the banks, and the factories" were now "the property of the people," and he championed popular oversight to guard against "the enemies of socialism."[94] Party leaders also saw popular input as a means to break down the barriers between the state and the masses, and to guard against bureaucratism.[95] Institutions such as the Worker-Peasant Inspectorate (Rabkrin) and the Komsomol's Light Cavalry gave voice to employees who wished to criticize the corruption or incompetence of their bosses.[96] Soviet newspapers, with the help of "worker correspondents" and "rural correspondents," frequently published exposés of factory and collective farm mismanagement.[97] These practices, which began

91. Davies, *Popular Opinion in Stalin's Russia,* 14.

92. For an overview of this phenomenon, see Sheila Fitzpatrick, "Signals from Below: Soviet Letters of Denunciation during the 1930s," *Accusatory Practices: Denunciation in Modern European History, 1789–1989,* ed. Fitzpatrick and Robert Gellately (Chicago, 1997), 85–120.

93. For a thorough analysis of these practices, see Hooper, "Terror from Within," chapter 2.

94. V. I. Lenin, "Kak organizovat' sorevnovanie?" *Polnoe sobranie sochinenii* (Moscow, 1958–65), vol. 35, 200. This article was reprinted in *Pravda* (January 20, 1929) during a renewed push for popular involvement at the beginning of the First Five-Year Plan.

95. Ironically, the mobilization of workers and peasants to oversee the bureaucracy required the creation of additional layers of bureaucracy; Hooper, "Terror from Within," 80.

96. See E. A. Rees, *State Control in Soviet Russia: The Rise and Fall of the Workers' and Peasants' Inspectorate, 1920–1934* (Basingstoke, 1987).

97. On Soviet newspapers, see Jeffrey Brooks, *Thank You Comrade Stalin!: Soviet Public Culture from Revolution to Cold War* (Princeton, 2000); Matthew Lenoe, *Closer to the Masses: Stalinist Culture, Social Revolution, and Soviet Newspapers* (Cambridge, Mass., 2004); Julie Kay Mueller, "A New Kind of Newspaper: The Origins and Development of a Soviet Institution" (Ph.D. diss., University of California, Berkeley, 1992); Steven Coe, "Peasants, the State, and the Languages of NEP: The Rural Correspondents' Movement in the Soviet Union, 1924–1928" (Ph.D. diss., University of Michigan, 1993).

in the 1920s and expanded dramatically in the early 1930s, are crucial to understanding the popular denunciation of elites.[98]

Practices of popular surveillance also permitted common people to critique the behavior of one another. Although whistle-blowing in the national and local press focused on managers, a profusion of smaller newspapers (often "wall newspapers"—typewritten sheets posted on the wall of a factory or collective farm office) collected and published denunciations of individual workers' or peasants' absenteeism, negligence, or drunkenness.[99] "Comradely courts" empowered workers to pass judgment on co-workers accused of absenteeism or lax discipline.[100] "Societies for police collaboration" represented another means for common people to monitor and report on the behavior of others. In the Russian republic alone, these organizations had forty-five thousand volunteer members by 1930.[101]

Popular involvement in policing and surveillance came increasingly under government control during the 1930s. Soviet leaders retained a fundamental distrust of grassroots initiative, so even as they promoted these forms of popular participation, they sought to manage them as well. Every instrument of popular involvement was eventually incorporated into a Union-wide bureaucratic hierarchy. Bureaucrats then began to provide questionnaires and procedures that volunteers were required to follow. Moreover, the security police established links with Rabkrin and newspaper editorial offices in order to gather the information they received from letters and complaints. Komsomol Light Cavalry volunteers, who had operated largely on their own initiative during the First Five-Year Plan, found their activities increasingly restricted by the mid-1930s, while Rabkrin was abolished in 1934 and its volunteers came under the supervision of the security police.[102] Nonetheless, popular involvement in policing contributed to the pervasiveness of surveillance in the Soviet system. Practices of reporting and denunciation led Soviet citizens to monitor others' behavior. Not only did the Soviet system lack any legal protections for individual

98. By 1934, Rabkrin had roughly 750,000 active volunteers and had mobilized another 4.74 million people for mass raids during the preceding year, while a quarter of a million Komsomol members had participated in Light Cavalry investigations. See Hooper, "Terror from Within," 94–95.

99. O. Rubtsov, *Stengazetu kazhdyi den'* (Moscow, 1931). See also RGASPI f. 17, op. 114, d. 558, l. 5; GARF f. 5469, op. 15, d. 10, l. 144.

100. GARF f. 5469, op. 15, d. 10, l. 155. See also I. S. Dvornikov, *Tovarishcheskie sudy i ikh rol' v bor'be za ukreplenie trudovoi distsipliny* (Moscow, 1956).

101. Hooper, "Terror from Within," 85–86. On popular involvement in the judicial system, see ibid., 87–92.

102. Ibid., 118–125, 145, 162.

rights and privacy, it encouraged Soviet citizens to scrutinize and denounce one another.

To return to the origins of the Soviet surveillance system and the relative role of Marxist-Leninist ideology in its formation, we should note that both the Bolsheviks' seizure of power and their agenda of social transformation intensified the need for surveillance. Violent political and social change sparked widespread opposition, which in turn heightened Party leaders' insecurity and their surveillance efforts. But the techniques of mass surveillance were developed and practiced in all the major combatant countries during the First World War, and Soviet authorities inherited these techniques from their predecessors in the tsarist and Provisional governments. What occurred was not the genesis of surveillance from Bolshevik ideology but rather the ideologizing of preexisting surveillance practices. Surveillance was attached to the Bolsheviks' ideological agenda and institutionalized within the new Soviet state.

The creation of multiple surveillance bureaucracies and the encouragement of popular denunciation served to perpetuate and expand surveillance. The very nature of the Soviet security police was to uncover political opposition and conspiracies, which in turn generated a need for even greater surveillance. But more fundamentally, Soviet surveillance reflected Party leaders' fervent desire to know and shape the thinking of the population. The Soviet state was born at a moment of total war, when monitoring people's political attitudes and loyalties were crucial determinants of a government's ability to mobilize human resources and to eliminate opposition. And after victory in the Civil War, Party leaders attached surveillance practices to their ideological agenda of eliminating class enemies and building socialism.

Political Enlightenment

The Bolsheviks had regarded propaganda and political enlightenment to be essential tools of the revolutionary movement since well before 1917. As early as the 1890s, the Russian Social Democrats had printed leaflets and conducted propaganda among industrial workers. In his landmark work, *What Is to Be Done?* (1902), Lenin had distinguished between agitation, which was to be conducted orally and was to arouse workers' indignation, and propaganda, which was to be communicated primarily in printed form and was to instill a broader political awareness. Lenin stated that the working class "is first and foremost in need of all-round and live political knowledge, and is most capable of converting this knowledge into active struggle."[103] He and other Bolshevik leaders viewed propaganda not as an emotional appeal to rile up the masses but rather as a form of political education or enlightenment.[104] As Marxist revolutionaries, the Bolsheviks therefore recognized propaganda's importance even before the explosion of government propaganda during the First World War.

On taking power in 1917, the Bolsheviks turned their efforts from overthrowing the existing regime to maintaining power themselves, and their use of propaganda proved to be extremely innovative. Fascist leaders in Italy and Germany subsequently admired and imitated Soviet propaganda techniques.[105] In a number of ways the Soviet program of "political enlightenment" resembled the wartime propaganda of other countries, and it also shared the objectives of political education under the Provisional Government. Like their predecessors, Party leaders utilized new media (films, leaflets, propaganda posters) and existing institutional structures (in particular the military) to reach as broad an audience as possible. They emphasized broad enlightenment objectives such as literacy and political consciousness, that is, an awareness of the larger political situation and ones place in it. They even relied on many of the same personnel as had the Provisional Government, including members of the non-Party intelligentsia, to conduct political education. But the type of political consciousness they sought to instill was class consciousness—a self-awareness among peasants and workers of their role in the struggle against the bourgeoisie. As Red Army political workers resolved, the foundation of political enlightenment was "revolutionary Marxism, which will awaken and organize the class consciousness and creative initiative of the armed toiling masses."[106] And the type of citizen they aimed to create was the New Soviet Person, an entirely new kind of human being whose mentality and personal qualities were fundamentally different from those who lived under capitalism.

Central to the Communists' political enlightenment program was their ability to communicate with the population. Before examining the institutions and media that allowed them to accomplish this goal, I will pause to

103. Robert C. Tucker, ed., *The Lenin Anthology* (New York, 1975), 40, 55.

104. I use the term *political enlightenment* to capture this broader meaning of propaganda. In his study of Soviet propaganda, Peter Kenez defines propaganda as "the attempt to transmit social and political values in the hope of affecting people's thinking, emotions, and thereby behavior." Kenez, *Birth of the Propaganda State*, 4.

105. Ibid., 10.

106. *Politrabotnik* vol. 1 (1920), 15, as quoted in von Hagen, *Soldiers in the Proletarian Dictatorship*, 96.

consider briefly the flip side of these efforts, namely censorship. To shape people's thinking, Soviet officials sought not only to convey their message but to limit the ability of others to circulate a different version of events. Unlike the Provisional Government, the Soviet government moved quickly to limit freedom of expression. Party leaders closed opposition newspapers, arrested those who spoke out against them, and outlawed other political parties. Eventually Soviet authorities established an elaborate and far-reaching censorship apparatus that controlled all media within the country.[107] Of course, they did not invent censorship, and their use of it should be placed in broader context. As noted above, the governments of all combatant countries in the First World War practiced censorship and sought to control information that would influence popular opinion. Whereas other countries relaxed or abolished censorship at the end of the war, the Soviet state institutionalized and continued it.

The more daunting goal facing Party leaders was "to enlighten" an overwhelmingly peasant population. At the height of the Civil War in March 1919, Lenin introduced a resolution to the Eighth Party Congress that called for improved propaganda work in villages throughout the country. The resolution directed local Party organizations to set up village reading huts—copying the approach of zemstvo activists—to provide newspapers and lectures that would raise peasants' political consciousness. The Congress also repeated a call, first issued by the Soviet government in 1918, for literate citizens to read aloud newspaper articles and decrees to illiterates. Finally the Congress recommended the establishment of regional propaganda committees to train and supervise activists, and in this way it vastly expanded the existing Party propaganda network.[108]

While the Party already had considerable propaganda experience dating from before the Revolution, its prior campaigns had been directed primarily at workers and soldiers, and to win support of the peasantry it had to extend its network to the countryside. It was also during the Civil War that propaganda structures became institutionalized within the Party itself. In August 1920, the Communist Party's Central Committee established its Agitation and Propaganda (Agitprop) Section. Agitprop subsections included political education, publishing, and distribution of propaganda

107. See A. Blium, *Za kulisami 'Ministerstva pravdy': Tainaia istoriia sovetskoi tsenzury, 1917–1929* (St. Petersburg, 1994); I. Davidian, "Voennaia tsenzura v Rossii, 1918–1920," *Cahiers du monde russe* 38: 1–2 (1997): 117–25.

108. Kenez, *Birth of the Propaganda State,* 57.

Fig. 12. Soviet literacy poster, 1923. "Eliminate illiteracy! Illiteracy harms the country's economy and increases the mortality of the population. The lower a country's illiteracy rate, the larger its harvest." Shows illiteracy and mortality as worse in Russia than in Belgium. Poster identification number RU/SU 2340, Poster Collection, Hoover Institution Archives.

in the provinces.[109] The Central Committee's Agitprop Section gradually grew to be an enormous bureaucracy itself and directed all Party propaganda campaigns.

Peasant illiteracy continued to pose an obstacle to propagandists. Partly for this reason, Soviet authorities relied on nonliterary forms of propaganda (films, posters, and theater) as I will discuss below. But equally significant is the degree to which the Soviet government, as the Provisional Government before it, made the teaching of literacy a top priority. In addition to desiring a literate citizenry in order to spread its political message, Soviet authorities shared the Russian intelligentsia's commitment to educating and uplifting the masses. They believed that peasants had to become literate to reach their full potential as human beings and to participate fully in civic life. They also assumed that a literate peasantry would understand and share their political values. As the Red Army's director of agitation and enlightenment, Valentina Suzdal'tseva, proclaimed, "An illiterate and benighted person is incapable of apprehending with any depth, processing, or consciously mastering the high ideals of Communist morality." She added that an illiterate person "cannot understand the complicated tasks of socialist construction."[110]

In December 1919 the Soviet government issued a decree on illiteracy that obliged all illiterates between the ages of eight and fifty to study and learn to read. The decree began, "For the purpose of allowing the entire population of the Republic to participate consciously in the political life of the country..." It assigned primary responsibility for the teaching of literacy to the Commissariat of Enlightenment (except within the army where political departments were in charge) and gave the commissariat the right to draft literate citizens as teachers. To give illiterate adults time to study, the decree freed them from work for two hours per day without reduction of pay.[111] Already in 1918, Nadezhda Krupskaia called for a network of literacy posts or centers (*likpunkty*) that could reach peasants in every village across the country. Although limited resources hampered the creation of these literacy centers during the Civil War, by the 1920s thousands of them were in operation.[112]

109. Ibid., 123.
110. "Iz otcheta Politupravleniia pri Revvoensovete Respubliki o partiino-politicheskoi rabote v Krasnoi Armii s nachala ee organizatsii do 1 oktiabria 1920 g.," October 8, 1920, in *Partiino-politicheskaia rabota v Krasnoi Armii (aprel' 1918–fevral' 1919): Dokumenty*, vol. 1 (Moscow, 1961), 70, as quoted in von Hagen, *Soldiers in the Proletarian Dictatorship*, 96–97.
111. Kenez, *Birth of the Propaganda State*, 76–77.
112. Ibid., 75.

The Soviet government, again like its predecessor, focused much of its political enlightenment work on the army, both because of the need to win troops' loyalty and because of the enormous opportunity the army represented as a means to reach a crucial segment of the population. Red Army commanders, including Trotsky, Mikhail Frunze, and Mikhail Tukhachevsky, shared the ideal of soldiers as enlightened citizens, and in 1918 Trotsky told Red Army officers theirs was not just a combat mission but "a great cultural and moral mission."[113] Immediately prior to the outbreak of the Civil War in 1918, the Soviet government created the Universal Military Training Administration (Vsevobuch) to prepare workers and peasants for military service. The director of this civilian organization, Nikolai Podvoiskii, was an ardent promoter of comprehensive general education for all soldiers. He hired hundreds of non-Party intelligentsia to teach literacy, art, literature, natural history, and physical culture.[114]

The Red Army had its own political administration that oversaw the work of political departments in military districts. Each department had sections for agitation, information, culture, and so forth. The responsibilities of political departments grew enormously during the Civil War and included all propaganda and enlightenment work within the army. Political departments published pamphlets and newspapers, held meetings and lectures, and put on political theater performances. Commissions under political departments compiled lists of all illiterate soldiers and taught them to read and write. In the second half of 1919, the budget for Red Army political departments was 450 million rubles, an enormous sum, particularly considering the desperate shortage of resources at the time.[115]

During the Civil War, the Communist Party created a hierarchy of educational institutions to educate Party members and train propagandists. At the top of the hierarchy were the Socialist (later Communist) Academy, founded in 1918, and Communist universities, which numbered ten by 1922. Below these were Party schools to train propagandists in short-term courses. By 1921 there existed 255 Party schools with a total of 50,000

113. L. D. Trotskii, *Kak vooruzhalas' revoliutsiia*, vol. 1 (Moscow, 1923), 327, as quoted in von Hagen, *Soldiers in the Proletarian Dictatorship*, 93.

114. von Hagen, *Soldiers in the Proletarian Dictatorship*, 93–94. The ambitions of Podvoiskii and his employees clashed somewhat with those of Party and Red Army leaders who saw cultural education as secondary until after the Civil War had been won. Soldiers themselves had even another agenda as they were often more interested in acquiring practical skills than in high culture or Soviet patriotism. See ibid., 94.

115. Ibid., 91–95. To put this sum in perspective, given the runaway inflation of the era, von Hagen compares it with R. W. Davies's calculation of total Soviet defense expenditures of 10.74 billion rubles for the same period; R. W. Davies, *The Development of the Soviet Budgetary System* (New York, 1958), 42–43.

students. The lowest rungs of Party education were schools of political literacy (*politgramotshkoly*) that offered evening classes to provide rank-and-file Party members with a basic understanding of Marxism-Leninism and of the political tasks confronting the Soviet government.[116] At the close of the Civil War in November 1920, these institutions were subordinated to the Chief Committee for Political Enlightenment (Glavpolitprosvet)—a newly formed board of the Commissariat of Enlightenment that was headed by Krupskaia and answered directly to the Party's Central Committee. The Chief Committee for Political Enlightenment took charge of all political education, from adult literacy classes to Party schools, and strengthened government and Party control at the expense of the Red Army.[117]

Soviet propaganda during the Civil War took a variety of forms. Books, pamphlets, and newspapers were deemed particularly important by Soviet leaders. In May 1919 the Soviet government created the State Publishing House (Gosizdat) and its largest division was the agitation-propaganda department.[118] In addition to reading huts (which numbered 24,413 nationwide by 1920), workers' and soldiers' clubs played an important role distributing printed propaganda and holding lectures.[119] Trade unions, Red Army units, and Komsomol organizations all formed clubs, which in addition to providing a venue for political education were to offer an alternative to more decadent pastimes such as drinking and card playing. Emel'ian Iaroslavskii, a leading Party member, emphasized the need for orderly and attractive workers' clubs, implying that such an environment would encourage among workers decorous and edifying leisure.[120]

Soviet reading huts and workers' clubs had counterparts in other countries. Government-run workers' clubs in Fascist Italy, for example, very much resembled Soviet clubs in that they sought to instill political values and guide workers' leisure in accordance with state interests.[121] In Republican Turkey, the Kemalist government established "people's houses,"

116. Kenez, *Birth of the Propaganda State,* 129–31.

117. Sheila Fitzpatrick, *The Commissariat of Enlightenment: Soviet Organization of Education and the Arts under Lunacharsky, October 1917–1921* (New York, 1970), 243; von Hagen, *Soldiers in the Proletarian Dictatorship,* 132.

118. Kenez, *Birth of the Propaganda State,* 100–101

119. Ibid., 135–37. The number of soldiers' clubs in the Red Army increased to over a thousand by October 1919; Elizabeth A. Wood, *Performing Justice: Agitation Trials in Early Soviet Russia* (Ithaca, 2005), 42.

120. RGASPI f. 89, op. 9, d. 75, ll. 1–4. Ayca Alemdaroglu, "Politics of the Body and Eugenic Discourse in Early Republican Turkey," *Body and Society* 11:3: 65.

121. Lewis Siegelbaum, "The Shaping of Soviet Workers' Leisure: Workers' Clubs and Palaces of Culture in the 1930s," *International Labor and Working Class History* 56 (October 1999): 89.

modeled in part on clubs in Fascist Italy. These institutions, like Soviet clubs and reading huts, introduced peasants to literature, sports, science, and modern agriculture, as well as to Turkish nationalism and other elements of Kemalist ideology.[122] The parallel between the Soviet and Turkish governments' efforts was especially strong, given that both regimes strove to modernize largely peasant populations and even pursued many similar goals, such as full literacy, secularization, and women's emancipation.[123] Soviet officials, then, were not alone either in their ambitions to acculturate and indoctrinate the masses, or in the types of institutions they established to pursue these goals.

Soviet leaders recognized the importance of film as a powerful new propaganda medium, and in fact Lenin stated, "Of all the arts, for us the cinema is the most important."[124] The Commissariat of Enlightenment formed a film division in January 1918, and in May of that year the Soviet government created a state film organization. The Skobelev Committee, made up mostly of Socialist Revolutionaries and Mensheviks in 1917, detached itself from the government following the October Revolution and continued to produce newsreels, anti-Bolshevik in spirit. Following the dispersal of the Constituent Assembly, Party officials closed down the Skobelev Committee and confiscated its property. In August 1919, the Soviet government nationalized the entire film industry (though in reality most private studios by that time were already defunct) and transferred formerly private buildings and equipment to the state film organization. In the course of the Civil War, this organization and its studios made about sixty films, mostly short propaganda films (*agitki*) promoting causes such as Red Army service and epidemic disease prevention.[125]

Other media used by the Soviet government included propaganda posters, political theater, and agitational vehicles. Borrowing from and expanding on the widespread use of political posters during the First World War, Soviet officials produced hundreds of Civil War posters to

122. Alemdaroglu, "Politics of the Body," 65.

123. Adeeb Khalid, "Backwardness and the Quest for Civilization: Early Soviet Central Asia in Comparative Perspective," *Slavic Review* 65:2 (summer 2006): 234.

124. As quoted in Richard Taylor, "Agitation, Propaganda and the Cinema: The Search for New Solutions, 1917–1921," *Art, Society, Revolution: Russia, 1917–1921,* ed. N. A. Nilsson (Stockholm, 1979), 237.

125. Kenez, *Birth of the Propaganda State,* 106–10. On the distribution of films to Soviet villages during the 1920s, see the documentary film, "Oblast' poteriannogo kino," dir. A. Gershtein, T. Lahusen, T. McDonald, A. Nikitin (Chemodan Films, 2008).

impart information and rally the population.[126] Political theater represented a powerful means of communication, particularly with less literate segments of the population. Political enlightenment workers in the army recognized that lectures were too dry and saw theater as a means to educate and entertain soldiers simultaneously. Theater also had the potential to reach soldiers at an emotional as well as intellectual level, and thus to galvanize them to fight for the Soviet government.[127] Given the challenges of spreading propaganda in a vast country with an underdeveloped communication network, agitational trains and ships provided a powerful means to reach peasants in villages across the country. These vehicles brought books, newspapers, films, lecturers, and theaters to the countryside and allowed propagandists to reach a much wider audience than before.[128]

The Communists' propaganda skills should not be understated, and indeed it was not just their program of "Peace, Land, and Bread," but their effectiveness at communicating with soldiers and workers that helped them build support. At the same time, we should remember that all political parties and movements conducted propaganda during 1917 and throughout the ensuing Civil War. The First World War and mass mobilization had brought a tectonic shift in the nature of politics, and leaders of all ideological stripes could no longer neglect the need to convey a political message.

Commanders of the White armies created very similar propaganda instruments to those of the Red Army. In June 1918, the White Army in the South formed a "military-political department" that issued appeals to the civilian population and published pamphlets and periodicals for its soldiers.[129] The nascent White government in the South formed its Informational-Agitational Department whose propaganda bureaus organized lectures and published pamphlets and posters. The department even organized an agitational school to train propagandists.[130] Continuing a practice of First World War zemstvo activists, and paralleling efforts of the Soviet government, the Whites' Informational-Agitational Department established a network of reading huts to distribute pamphlets and newspapers to the

126. Kenez, *Birth of the Propaganda State*, 111–12.

127. Wood, *Performing Justice*, 42–43. On the use of one particular type of political theater, agitation trials, during the Civil War, see Wood, *Performing Justice*, 44–56.

128. Robert Argenbright, "Soviet Agitational Vehicles: Bolsheviks in Strange Places," *Space, Place, and Power in Modern Russia: Essays in the New Spatial History*, ed. Mark Bassin, Christopher Ely, and Melissa K. Stockdale (DeKalb, 2010).

129. Holquist, *Making War*, 222.

130. Kenez, *Birth of the Propaganda State*, 63–64, 113.

population. It also used agitational trains and steamships to disseminate printed materials, as well as propaganda plays and films. As Peter Holquist concludes, the Whites too sought "to elevate citizens to the proper level of consciousness," and they "engaged in many of the same 'cultural-enlightenment measures' practiced by the Soviet side."[131]

The Communists' victory in the Civil War reflected not the fact that they used propaganda, but the fact that their propaganda message and their efforts to impart it won more support. The Soviet state as it emerged during the Civil War, and as it continued throughout the 1920s, 1930s, and Second World War, was a mobilizational state par excellence. Through a combination of propaganda, incentives, and coercion, Communist leaders mobilized key segments of the population behind their state and its programs. They proved adept both at utilizing new media and at constructing institutions to conduct propaganda. These institutions, formed at a moment of total war, became integral parts of the Soviet state.

The end of the Civil War in some ways seemed to lessen the urgency of political education. With the immediate military threat of the White Armies eliminated, Soviet leaders no longer needed to galvanize large numbers of soldiers to defend the Revolution. At the same time, given their agenda of social transformation, they were eager to enlighten the peasantry and instill a new consciousness. As was true in the realm of surveillance, the introduction of the New Economic Policy was reason to redouble rather than relax political work. To overcome the "petty bourgeois" influences of small-scale capitalism, Soviet officials intensified their political enlightenment campaigns.

Some of these efforts had concrete political goals such as instilling loyalty to the Soviet government. Throughout the 1920s, for example, Red Army political workers used the Lenin cult and history lessons to teach soldiers allegiance to the Soviet state.[132] As indicated above, however, many Party leaders never conceived of political enlightenment as a narrow patriotic education project. Like other members of the intelligentsia, they sought to uplift the masses culturally and believed that all peasants and workers should not only become literate but should develop an appreciation of literature.[133] In his 1921 speech to the Second Congress of Politi-

---

131. Holquist, *Making War*, 227.

132. Von Hagen, *Soldiers in the Proletarian Dictatorship*, 289–94. See also Nina Tumarkin, *Lenin Lives: The Lenin Cult in Soviet Russia* (Cambridge, Mass., 1983).

133. This "cult of literature" became even more pronounced in the 1930s; see Katerina Clark and Karl Schlögel, "Mutual Perceptions and Projections: Stalin's Russia in Nazi

cal Enlightenment (Glavpolitprosvet) Workers, Lenin defined the tasks of political enlightenment very broadly—the fight against illiteracy, efforts to raise cultural standards, and the inculcation of a Communist attitude toward work.[134] Commissar of Education Anatoly Lunacharsky told readers that the greatest goal of self-education should not be to acquire specialized skills but rather "to turn oneself into a conscious citizen."[135] Political enlightenment workers continued to use the same media discussed above (newspapers, posters, films, and political theater) to address a range of issues, from hygiene and work discipline to the struggle against alcoholism and foul language.[136] Soviet officials also created the Society for the Elimination of Illiteracy that set up thousands of adult literacy centers attended by more than 8 million people during the 1920s.[137] The number of students enrolled in adult literacy classes rose to more than 14 million by 1932, and illiteracy declined dramatically as a result.[138]

Equally important to the creation of a fully literate society was primary schooling. Since before the Revolution, Russian progressive educators had seen a modern educational system as a vehicle to enlighten the peasantry and create a more rational and egalitarian society. Their ideas paralleled those of progressive pedagogues and radical pedagogical theorists abroad who saw education as a means of social change.[139] Indeed,

---

Germany—Nazi Germany in the Soviet Union," *Beyond Totalitarianism: Stalinism and Nazism Compared,* ed. Michael Geyer and Sheila Fitzpatrick (Cambridge, 2009), 436–37.

134. Lenin, "Novaia ekonomicheskaia politika i zadachi politprosvetov," *Polnoe sobranie* 33: 165–67.

135. *Pomoshch' samoobrazovaniiu* no. 1 (1923), 4, as quoted in Catriona Kelly, *Refining Russia: Advice Literature, Polite Culture, and Gender from Catherine to Yeltsin* (New York, 2001), 268.

136. Wood, *Performing Justice,* 70–71; Steve Smith, "The Social Meaning of Swearing: Workers and Bad Language in Late Imperial and Early Soviet Russia," *Past and Present* 160 (August 1998): 192–98. On efforts to promote "disciplined" and "cultured" language in the 1930s, see GARF f. 3316, op. 41, d. 85, ll. 41–42; F. Kulikov, "Za novogo cheloveka: Iz dnevnika kul'tarmeitsa," *Na rubezhe* 10 (1935): 101.

137. Similar to quasi-governmental organizations to counter religion and alcoholism, the Society for the Elimination of Illiteracy had chapters organized by Party and state officials; Kenez, *Birth of the Propaganda State,* 153–57.

138. *Izmeneniia sotsial'noi struktury sovetskogo obshchestva, 1921-seredina '30-kh godov* (Moscow, 1979), 206; TsAGM f. 1289, op. 1, d. 185, l. 2. Of course, literacy itself did not guarantee "political consciousness." See V. Vasilevskaia, "Kak chitaiut knigu malogramotnye," *Krasnyi bibliotekar'* 5/6 (1931): 90–96; GARF f. A-2306, op. 39, d. 78, l. 3.

139. Mark Johnson, "Russian Educators, the Stalinist Party-State and the Politics of Soviet Education, 1929–1939" (Ph.D. diss., Columbia University, 1995), 29. See also Randall David Law, "Humanity's Workshops: Progressive Education in Russia and the Soviet Union, 1856–1927" (Ph.D. diss., Georgetown University, 2001). For the views of a leading

Soviet pedagogues in the 1920s sought to emulate the progressive pedagogy of John Dewey, and on his visit to Moscow in 1928, Dewey highly
praised Soviet education.[140] For its part, the Soviet government decreed
universal primary education and sought to establish state-run schools in
every village throughout the country. Despite a shortage of resources and
qualified teachers, over time it increased the number of children in schools
dramatically.[141]

Not all Party leaders shared the expansive understanding of education
articulated by Lenin. Certainly those who led the Commissariat of Enlightenment, Lunacharsky and Krupskaia, did conceive of enlightenment in
very broad terms. But economic planners and Komsomol militants focused
more narrowly on vocational training and political indoctrination. They
pushed for educational programs that would serve the immediate needs of
industrialization, collectivization, and the development of class consciousness. During the Great Break period, 1928–31, this militant approach to
enlightenment displaced more gradualist and humanistic notions of education.[142]

At the same time, it would be wrong to conclude that the Soviet government abandoned its aims of human and social transformation. On the contrary, the Great Break marked a new drive to transform Soviet society as
rapidly as possible. While economic change was to be at the center of this
transformation, Party leaders and Komsomol militants alike continued to
place a great deal of emphasis on political enlightenment. In fact, they de-
manded that teachers become agents of revolutionary change. During the
First Five-Year Plan, thousands of Komsomol members were mobilized to
teach, so that the number of rural school teachers more than doubled, and

---

American renovationist, see George Counts, *Dare the School Build a New Social Order?*
(Carbondale, 1978).

140. E. Thomas Ewing, "The 'Virtues of Planning': American Educators Look at Soviet
Schools," *Education and the Great Depression: Lessons from a Global History,* ed. Ewing
and David Hicks (New York, 2006); David C. Engerman, *Modernization from the Other
Shore: American Intellectuals and the Romance of Russian Development* (Cambridge,
Mass., 2003), 176–77.

141. Larry E. Holmes, *The Kremlin and the Schoolhouse: Reforming Education in
Soviet Russia, 1917–1931* (Bloomington, 1991), 148. See also Larry Gringlas, "Shkraby
ne Kraby: Rural Teachers and Bolshevik Power in the Russian Countryside, 1921–1928"
(M.A. thesis, Columbia University, 1987).

142. Fitzpatrick, *Education and Social Mobility,* 123, 144–45; Holmes, *The Kremlin
and the Schoolhouse,* 109–19.

Fig. 13. Soviet education and literacy poster, 1920. "Children! It is terrible to be illiterate! One lives as if one is in a dark forest. . . . But when an illiterate person goes to school, it is as if a blind person begins to see!" Poster identification number RU/SU 1271, Poster Collection, Hoover Institution Archives.

the number of students in all primary schools increased from 11 million to 23 million.[143]

The new Commissar of Enlightenment in 1929, A. S. Bubnov, called on schools to participate in the "class struggle" against kulaks, religion, and illiteracy.[144] He and other new leaders of the commissariat envisioned a merging of the community and the classroom, whereby education would have a direct role in building socialism. Accordingly, they emphasized

143. Fitzpatrick, *Education and Social Mobility*, 174–75. See also E. Thomas Ewing, *The Teachers of Stalinism: Policy, Practices, and Power in Soviet Schools of the 1930s* (New York, 2002).

144. Holmes, *The Kremlin and the Schoolhouse*, 119–20.

technical training for collective farm peasants and industrial workers, and the number of students in technical institutes tripled between 1928 and 1932.[145] Alongside the greater emphasis on technical training, Soviet educational programs continued to stress literacy, antireligious propaganda, and Marxism-Leninism. In education, then, the Great Break represented an end to a gradualist, humanistic approach. Instead Soviet officials adopted a more blunt and dogmatic approach that corresponded to the militancy of the collectivization and industrialization drives, but that nonetheless continued to prioritize political enlightenment.

For Soviet authorities, the expansion of education and the spread of literacy would allow peasants and workers to participate fully in cultural affairs and public life. In this sense, Soviet literacy programs resembled those in other countries where teachers and professionals similarly sought to uplift the masses through the rapid expansion of educational opportunities. But the Soviet project involved more than literacy and civic awareness. Party leaders and theorists aspired to create a new type of humanity—the New Soviet Person, whose values and ways of thinking would be qualitatively different from those who lived under capitalism. Throughout the NEP era, when small-scale capitalism and private farming continued, the creation of the New Person remained out of reach. But with the establishment of an entirely noncapitalist, state-run economy in the 1930s, Party authorities believed that they had entered a new stage in history, and that the New Soviet Person could become a reality.

The New Soviet Person

The conceptual origins of the New Person ideal can be traced to the Enlightenment and French Revolution. The fundamental premise of Enlightenment thought—that the social world was neither preordained by God nor fixed by tradition, but rather of humankind's own making—suggested that human behavior itself might be altered. The French Revolution gave force to this notion in two ways. First, it overturned the existing order and ushered in a period of intense social ferment. Second, the new principle of popular sovereignty required all people to play an active part in politics and hence to think and act in new ways. Inspired by the revolutionary ideal of remaking men and women into virtuous citizens,

145. Fitzpatrick, *Education and Social Mobility*, 188. See also Holmes, *The Kremlin and the Schoolhouse*, 126–33.

radical thinkers began to imagine the New Person—a qualitatively different type of human being who was not limited by the petty instincts of the past.

Nineteenth-century Russian intellectuals drew on these ideas as they struggled to overcome the oppressive tsarist autocracy. Nikolai Chernyshevsky, in his novel *What Is to Be Done?* depicted a circle of new people characterized by rationality, selflessness, and moral purity. Chernyshevsky's prototypical new man, Rakhmetov, prepares himself for the revolution with daily gymnastics, heavy physical labor, and complete celibacy and sobriety.[146] Lenin was profoundly influenced by Chernyshevsky's novel, and took it as a model for how revolutionaries should live their lives. At the same time, he and other Marxists distanced themselves from the "utopian" socialism of Chernyshevsky in favor of "scientific" Marxism. They saw the New Person as emerging not among intelligentsia circles but among the proletariat, and only after proletarian revolution had overthrown the capitalist order.[147]

While the ideal of the New Person held particular currency among Russian radicals, it reflected more general intellectual currents both in Russia and abroad. In early twentieth-century Russia, Marxists, futurists, symbolists, neo-Slavophiles, and Orthodox philosophers, despite their extreme ideological differences, all were displeased with the current state of human relations and wished to refashion both society and the psycho-physical features of its members. Some blamed bourgeois individualism and advocated a collectivist reorientation, whereas others saw human existence as debased by science and prescribed a "vitalist" revolution of the spirit. But all saw a revolutionary transformation of human relations as necessary. Russian professionals, while less radical in the solutions they proposed, were also deeply concerned with the social antagonisms and disorder of the modern era. Particularly following the turmoil of the 1905 Revolution, they sought not only political reform but the refurbishing of society and its members.[148]

146. Nikolai Chernyshevsky, *What Is to Be Done?* trans. Michael R. Katz (Ithaca, 1989), 278–83.

147. Peter Fritzsche and Jochen Hellbeck, "The New Man in Stalinist Russia and Nazi Germany," *Beyond Totalitarianism*, 307–8.

148. Daniel Beer, *Renovating Russia: The Human Sciences and the Fate of Liberal Modernity, 1880–1930* (Ithaca, 2008), 8–11. On Anton Pavlov's desire to create psychological-physiological science capable of reshaping and rationalizing human behavior, see Torsten Rüting, *Pavlov und der neue Mensch: Diskurse über Disziplinierung in Sowjetrussland* (Munich, 2002).

In other countries as well, a range of social thinkers in the early twentieth century contemplated the need to refashion human beings given the
demands of modern, industrial civilization. Proponents of solidarism in
France, for example, advocated the scientific deployment of social forces
and an end to exploitation as a means to return society to its natural state
of harmony.[149] American intellectuals in the 1920s also leaned away from
individualism in favor of collectivism. John Dewey argued that the rugged
individualism of America's pioneering days was irrelevant in the "collective age," and he called for an "integrated individuality" connected to others through social networks.[150] One of Dewey's followers, George Counts,
after a visit to the Soviet Union, heralded efforts to create a new human
psychology, one suited to industrial life, and he advocated the Soviet approach of "directing the course of social evolution through control of educational agencies."[151] Even Herbert Hoover called for a "better, brighter,
broader" individualism that "invites responsibility and service to our fel-
lows." Hoover explained that large economic enterprises rendered discon-
nected individuals useless in modern society and said that only through
the collective work of associations and organizations could individuals
accomplish their goals.[152]

Following the October Revolution, Party leaders made collectivism a
central value of the Soviet order. While their emphasis on collectivism was
not unique, Party leaders established a particular type of modern industrial civilization—one based on a noncapitalist, state-run economy. In their
minds, collectivization and the First Five-Year Plan paved the way for a
true socialist society and the New Person who would inhabit it. As previously envisioned by Russian Marxists, the creation of the New Person thus
became closely tied with industrialization and the state-run economy. In

149. Paul Rabinow, *French Modern: Norms and Forms of the Social Environment*
(Cambridge, Mass., 1989), 169–70, 185–86; Sanford Elwitt, *The Third Republic Defended: Bourgeois Reform in France, 1880–1914* (Baton Rouge, 1986), 23. French urban
planners such as Le Corbusier also sought to inculcate in people a collectivist consciousness
via city planning, model communities, and communal housing. Le Corbusier in fact worked
on projects in the Soviet Union and became a mentor for Soviet Constructivist architects.
See Katerina Clark, *Petersburg, Crucible of Cultural Revolution* (Cambridge, Mass., 1995),
51; S. Frederick Starr, "Visionary Town Planning during the Cultural Revolution," *Cultural
Revolution in Russia, 1928–1931*, ed. Sheila Fitzpatrick (Bloomington, 1978), 207–40.
    150. Engerman, *Modernization from the Other Shore*, 181.
    151. Counts visited the Soviet Union as part of Stuart Chase's expert delegation in
1927, and he applauded both the Soviet education system and Soviet social and economic
planning. See Engerman, *Modernization from the Other Shore*, 175–81.
    152. As quoted in Engerman, *Modernization from the Other Shore*, 180–81.

this period, when the country was being transformed from a backward peasant society into an advanced industrial power, people too were being transformed. As one Soviet psychologist wrote in 1931, "The creation of a new type of human being has become our first priority."[153]

The collectivization drive represented Party leaders' attempt to establish a new order in the countryside. By forcing peasants to join collective farms, Soviet authorities changed peasants' relationship to the means of production and, in theory, their mentalities as well. No longer small property holders, peasants could now outgrow their petty bourgeois ways and adopt a socialist lifestyle. According to Semashko, peasants who joined collective farms lived "a collectivist life" that altered their individualist way of thinking.[154] Another Soviet official hailed the "reeducation of collectivized peasants," millions of whom were learning to place "social interests above personal ones."[155] Stalin himself described collectivization as a means to educate peasants "in the spirit of collectivism," and help their progress toward communism.[156]

For Party leaders, the industrialization drive was even more central to the creation of the New Soviet Person. During the First Five-Year Plan alone, the number of industrial workers doubled as millions of peasants migrated to cities and took jobs in factories.[157] Soviet theorists expected proletarianization to transform former peasants' worldview and consciousness. Maksim Gorky, for example, described how a peasant lad arriving at a factory "falls into a world of phenomena that strike at his imagination and arouse his mind, freeing it from ancient, savage superstitions and prejudices. He sees the work of reason, embodied in complex machinery.... Very soon he is convinced that the factory for him is a school that opens the possibility of freely developing his abilities." Gorky concluded that the "New Per-

---

153. M. Gelmont, "Pedologo-pedagogicheskoe izuchenie kollektivizirovannogo truda i byta," *Pedologiia* 13 (1931): 17, as cited in Igal Halfin, *Terror in My Soul: Communist Autobiographies on Trial* (Cambridge, Mass., 2003), 231. It was during the First Five-Year Plan that pedology became the leading Soviet pedagogical and psychological science. Combining pedagogy, developmental psychology, and physiology, pedology was seen as a means to educate and transform workers and peasants into the New Soviet Person. On the rise and fall of pedology, see Halfin, *Terror in My Soul*, 233–43; Johnson, "Russian Educators," 47, 291–304.

154. S. Garshtein, *Za zdorovyi kul'turnyi byt* (Moscow, 1932), 5.

155. RGASPI f. 17, op. 120, d. 138, ll. 36–37.

156. *XVII s"ezd VKP(b), 26 ianv.–10 fevr. 1934 g. Sten. otchet* (Moscow, 1934), 29–30.

157. More than 23 million peasants moved to Soviet cities during the 1930s; David L. Hoffmann, *Peasant Metropolis: Social Identities in Moscow, 1929–1941* (Ithaca, 1994), 1–2.

son" developing in the Soviet Union "feels himself to be the creator of a new world."[158]

Officials soon discovered, however, that newly proletarianized workers (and cadre workers as well) did not automatically adopt officially prescribed thinking and behavior. Most continued to place their own self-interests ahead of "building socialism," as labor turnover skyrocketed and productivity declined.[159] Politburo member Lazar Kaganovich blamed labor turnover on "the mass of new workers entering the ranks of the proletariat who frequently bring petty-bourgeois attitudes to enterprises," and Party authorities declared the greatest task facing them to be "the reeducation of newly arrived workers in the spirit of those who will fulfill the tasks of the proletariat."[160] As factory foremen struggled to train new recruits for industrial labor, Party directives reminded them that they must also raise workers' cultural level and create the New Person on whom the socialist system could be based.[161] Political instructors took up this challenge by organizing new lectures, reading circles, and newspapers. Political instruction was so time-consuming that industrial managers began to complain that daily meetings were interfering with factory work.[162] The fact that political work was expanded at the expense of industrial production underscores Party officials' commitment to political enlightenment.

Party propagandists sought to teach peasants and workers to sacrifice personal interests for the sake of the collective. According to Soviet ideology, individuals could find fulfillment only by joining the collective, and the New Soviet Person was to be free of egotism and selfishness. In contrast to liberal democratic systems that constituted a liberal subjectivity through private property and individual rights, the Soviet system promoted an illiberal subjectivity, where private life was eradicated and individuals were to discover their better selves by contributing to the social whole. As one of his moral principles, Soviet educator Anton Makarenko stated, "The interests of the collective are superior to the interests of the individual." He argued that members of a collective have a duty to one another that

158. M. Gor'kii, "O starom i o novom cheloveke," (1932) *Sobranie sochinenii* 26 (Moscow, 1953): 288–89.

159. RGASPI f. 17, op. 116, d. 30, l. 82; *Ekonomicheskoe stroitel'stvo* 9/10 (1930): 45; Ia. Kats, "Tekuchest' rabochei sily v krupnoi promyshlennosti," *Plan* 9 (1937): 21.

160. *Voprosy profdvizheniia* 1/2 (1933): 26–27; TsAOPIM f. 432, op. 1, d. 50, l. 169.

161. *Sputnik kommunista* 2 (1930): 38–39.

162. *Komsomol'skaia pravda*, May 20, 1932, 3; *Istoriia Moskovskogo avtozavoda im. I. A. Likhacheva* (Moscow, 1966), 197; *Govoriat stroiteli sotsializma: Vospominaniia uchastnikov sotsialisticheskogo stroitel'stva v SSSR* (Moscow, 1959), 280.

goes beyond friendship and that requires joint participation in the work of the collective.[163] A number of other values and qualities followed from the principle of collectivism. Makarenko emphasized "the real solidarity of the working people," "the abolition of greed," and "respect for the interests and life of [one's] comrades."[164] Addressing a Young Pioneer leader in 1933, Kaganovich said, "I am asking how much our children have progressed in truly human terms with respect to how they relate to one another, with respect to getting rid of the mentality of the past, egotism, vanity, selfishness, with respect to getting rid of all the bad elements that have lingered from the past."[165]

The First Five-Year Plan was a transitional period—a time for building the socialist economy and forging the New Soviet Person. Once the First Five-Year Plan and the collectivization drive had been completed, Stalin and his fellow leaders felt they had eliminated capitalism and its petty bourgeois milieu.[166] Now the New Soviet Person could become a reality. Unfettered by capitalist exploitation and free to benefit from the fruits of their own labor, Soviet workers could finally realize their full potential, both in industry and in life. Here was a promethean leap forward not only in terms of industrial progress but in terms of human development.

For the remainder of the decade, Soviet leaders, theorists, and writers alike heralded the emergence of the New Person. A special congress on children's literature in 1936 encouraged writers "to help form the consciousness and character of the future citizens of a classless socialist society." One speaker at the congress, V. Bubenkin, proclaimed that Soviet society "is giving birth to a New Person with healthy ideas, tastes, and habits," and he concluded that writers should produce literature to imbue children with "new, noble communist qualities."[167] A Komsomol journal boasted that the Soviet Union was creating "a generation of new people, for whom lying, deviousness, chauvinism, hypocrisy...and other abominations of bourgeois society are foreign."[168] The New Soviet Person, then,

---

163. A. Makarenko, *Problems of Soviet School Education*, trans. O. Shartse (Moscow, 1965), 62, 139. For further discussion, see Oleg Kharkhordin, *The Collective and Individual in Russia: A Study of Practices* (Berkeley, 1999), 204.

164. A. S. Makarenko, *A Book for Parents*, trans. Robert Daglish (Moscow, n.d.), 410.

165. Lewis Siegelbaum and Andrei Sokolov, *Stalinism as a Way of Life: A Narrative in Documents* (New Haven, 2000), 384.

166. I. V. Stalin, "Otchetnyi doklad XVII s"ezdu partii o rabote TsK VKP(b)," (January 26, 1934) *Sochineniia* vol. 13 (Moscow, 1952), 308–9.

167. *Komsomol'skaia pravda*, January 29, 1936, 1; January 30, 1936, 3.

168. *Komsomol'skii rabotnik* 8 (1940): 1–2.

was supposed to be free of the selfish egotism and hypocrisy of capitalist society. Devotion to the collective would bring out in people the highest human qualities—selflessness, modesty, honesty, and sincerity.

Heroism was a trait that Gorky added to the qualities of the New Person. He argued that individuals possessed an inner strength and beauty, but that these could not be realized if confined to selfish pursuits. Workers could fulfill their heroic potential only if they mobilized their willpower and energy to serve the higher cause of socialism.[169] Although Gorky's ideas clearly had Nietzschean overtones, he did not see superhuman abilities as the exclusive preserve of the *übermensch*. On the contrary, he claimed that every individual who set aside his or her own selfish interests could become a hero and help propel humanity forward toward communism. In his words, the New Person would "create a universal brotherly society, each member of which works according to his ability and receives according to his need."[170]

Beginning in 1935, the Stakhanovite movement produced hero-workers who served as the incarnation of the New Soviet Person. When a Donbass miner named Aleksei Stakhanov reportedly mined more than one hundred tons of coal in a single shift, Commissar of Heavy Industry Ordzhonikidze ordered widespread publicity to make Stakhanov a hero.[171] Soon Stakhanovites began to set production records in other branches of industry, often by experimenting with their machinery and violating established work routines.[172] While Stakhanovite record-setting frustrated industrial managers' efforts to routinize production, this unleashing of worker creativity corresponded to Party leaders' belief that in the socialist era workers' productive capacity would no longer be limited. As Gorky wrote, "The Stakhanovite movement is a fiery eruption of mass energy, an eruption evoked by the colossal successes achieved by labour, by the realization...of its power to emancipate toiling humanity from the yoke of the past."[173] As the collective owners of the means of production, workers could use their own ingenuity to dramatically increase industrial output. The New Soviet Person, then, was characterized by labor creativity and

169. Fritzsche and Hellbeck, "The New Man in Stalinist Russia," 308.

170. Gor'kii, "O starom i o novom cheloveke," 290.

171. RGASPI f. 85, op. 29, d. 640, ll. 3–7. For a full discussion of Stakhanov's record, see Lewis Siegelbaum, *Stakhanovism and the Politics of Productivity in the USSR, 1935–41* (New York, 1988), 67–74.

172. TsAGM f. 415, op. 2, d. 448, ll. 10–13.

173. *Labour in the Land of Socialism: Stakhanovites in Conference* (Moscow, 1936), 5.

purposefulness and, in contrast to workers under capitalism, found labor personally enriching and fulfilling.

At the First All-Union Conference of Stakhanovites, Stalin called them "new people, people of a special type."[174] One Stakhanovite after another described the personal transformation they had undergone. Many emphasized their humble roots and the exploitation and poverty their families had previously suffered. Stakhanov himself stated that he came from a poor village where as a boy he worked from dawn to dusk hauling sacks of grain for a kulak mill owner. His "real life" began only after he became a Soviet coalminer and heroic worker.[175] A. V. Dushenkov said that previously he had been "an inactive and unenlightened worker," but that as a Stakhanovite he was "astonished by the unexpected change that took place in me."[176] A propagandist addressing the conference declared that the Stakhanovite movement had turned recalcitrant workers and drunkards into labor heroes, and he expressed pride at having contributed to "the great process of remaking people which is going on in our country."[177]

Soviet authorities highlighted the material and cultural advances of Stakhanovites. At a conference for Stakhanovite combine drivers, speakers boasted about their acquisition of bicycles, gramophones, and books.[178] In Soviet journals, fine clothing received special attention as an indication of cultural maturity, particularly for female Stakhanovites.[179] Stakhanovites were also shown to have new, spacious accommodations that they kept meticulously clean and tastefully decorated.[180] As cultural models, Stakhanovites were shown to frequent lectures, films, and the theater.[181] Stakhanovites' fine clothing and cultural activities symbolized their emergence as the New Soviet Person. They acted as living examples of the Soviet Union's progress toward a modern, prosperous, socialist society. Not coincidentally the first industrial Stakhanovites were of peasant origin, and their Stakhanovite autobiographies stressed their transformation from backward peasants into conscious workers, from uncouth country bumpkins into cultured

174. Ibid., 15.

175. Ibid., 126–27.

176. Ibid., 220.

177. Ibid., 216–17.

178. RGASPI f. 17, op. 120, d. 146, ll. 11, 43.

179. *Rabotnitsa i krest'ianka* 6 (1936): 12–13; *Gigiena i zdorov'e* 21 (1936): 7. See also Siegelbaum, *Stakhanovism*, 231.

180. *Rabotnitsa i krest'ianka* 8 (1936): 10–11.

181. *Kul'turnaia rabota profsoiuzov* 5 (1938): 48. See also GARF f. 5451, op. 20, d. 21, l. 18.

urbanites.[182] As an iconic representation of the New Soviet Person, then, Stakhanovites were more than just hero workers. They had reached their full potential in all spheres, and their productive and cultured lives were to serve as an example of what people were becoming under socialism.[183]

By providing an example, Stakhanovites were supposedly elevating the material level of all workers and peasants. In 1935, Stalin said that model collective farm workers helped to raise "all collective farm members, both former middle peasants and former poor peasants, to the level of prosperous peasants, to the level of people who enjoy the abundance of products and who lead a fully cultured life."[184] Iaroslavskii referred to the "leading role" of both Party members and Stakhanovites, and said that their "personal example...can attract the backward workers, can convert them into leading workers, and can reeducate them."[185] Unlike in capitalist society, material gains were not made through the exploitation of others, and the improved standard of living was something that would ultimately be shared by all. In championing Komsomol members' desire for material goods, Komsomol chief Aleksandr Kosarev said, "Our young people do not want to arrogate things...by exploiting someone else. They know they can achieve for themselves only by raising the living standards of the whole collective in which they live and work."[186]

From a practical perspective, Party leaders used Stakhanovite records to raise production norms and publicized Stakhanovites' material well-being to induce workers to produce more.[187] But to understand Stakhanovism simply as a cynical attempt to raise labor productivity would be to miss its broader meaning.[188] The purported attainment of socialism in 1934 meant that for the first time in history workers were to enjoy fully the fruits of their own labor. Speaking at the Seventeenth Party Congress, Stalin proclaimed that "socialism means not poverty and deprivation, but the elimination of poverty and deprivation, and the organization of a rich and cultured life for all members of society." He concluded that "Marx-

182. Aleksandr Kh. Busygin, *Moia zhizn' i moia rabota* (Leningrad, 1935); Ivan Gudov, *Sud'ba rabochego* (Moscow, 1974).

183. For further discussion, see Jochen Hellbeck, *Revolution on My Mind: Writing a Diary under Stalin* (Cambridge, Mass., 2006), 255.

184. RGASPI f. 17, op. 120, d. 139, l. 6.

185. RGASPI f. 89, op. 9, d. 91, l. 8.

186. TsKhDMO f. 1, op. 23, d. 1074, ll. 107–8.

187. RGAE f. 7995, op. 1, d. 344, ll. 116–20; TsAGM f. 176, op. 4, d. 4, l. 181; *Profsoiuznyi rabotnik* 1 (1937): 3.

188. As Lewis Siegelbaum points out, Stakhanovites held a central place in "the cultural mythology of the 1930s" in the Soviet Union; Siegelbaum, *Stakhanovism*, 210.

ist socialism means not the reduction of personal needs…but the comprehensive fulfillment of all the needs of culturally developing, laboring people."[189]

Even under socialism, Party leaders did not expect people's transformation to proceed automatically. Stalin himself, in a 1935 speech, admitted that it would take a long time "to reshape human psychology."[190] While Soviet authorities placed their faith in the power of economic factors to change individuals' thinking and behavior, they also relied on cultural and educational means to create the New Person. Stalinist art and literature communicated collectivist values, while fictional heroes embodied qualities of the New Person—selfless service and sacrifice for the good of the collective.[191] Soviet authorities also developed new bases of self-identification, designed to attach peasants' and workers' identities to larger, collective units connected to the building of socialism. The factory history project, for example, called on workers to describe their past and present roles in the factory. This ritual encouraged them to identify with a laboring collective and to achieve validation through contributions to Soviet industrialization.[192]

Jochen Hellbeck has persuasively argued that Soviet authorities purposefully set out to make people into revolutionary subjects.[193] Rather than seeking to repress or obliterate people's sense of self, Soviet institutions and propaganda were intended to foster conscious citizens, who would voluntarily participate in the building of socialism and derive their sense of self from doing so. In this way, state power was productive, for it offered people a coherent sense of self and purpose. The process of creating the New Person required of people intense self-reflection and work to transform themselves. Soviet publications urged people to test their knowledge, to become more cultured, and "to work on yourself."[194] To induce people to reflect on their lives and understand their role in building socialism, Soviet authorities encouraged and even required people to engage in autobiographical writing and speaking. Requir-

189. *XVII s"ezd VKP(b)*, 26, 30–31.

190. RGASPI f. 17, op. 120, d. 138, ll. 78–80.

191. RGASPI f. 477, op. 1, d. 20, ll. 161–62; Regine Robin, "Stalinism and Popular Culture," *The Culture of the Stalin Period*, ed. Hans Gunther (New York, 1990), 33; Christel Lane, *The Rites of Rulers* (New York, 1981), 207.

192. *Gor'kii i sozdanie istorii fabrik i zavodov: Sbornik dokumentov*, ed. L. M. Zak and S. S. Zimina (Moscow, 1959).

193. Jochen Hellbeck, "Working, Struggling, Becoming: Stalin-Era Autobiographical Texts," *The Russian Review* 60:3 (July 2001): 340–59. See also, Hellbeck, *Revolution on My Mind*.

194. See, for example, the last page of *Ogonek* 1–3 (1936): 10.

ing such autobiographical reflection represented an important subjectivizing practice in that it sought to shape people's sense of self. Communist Party members in particular, but many other Soviet citizens as well, were obliged to tell their life stories as part of the larger revolutionary narrative of building socialism.[195] Autobiographical reflection also encouraged self-improvement, by getting people to recognize selfish habits and to refocus their attention on the heroic, collective task of socialist construction.[196]

While Party leaders clearly stood to gain social support by inducing people to understand their lives in these terms, they also believed that such an understanding was necessary for people's own personal growth. They wanted all Soviet citizens to become more educated and cultured. The Soviet system was enormously repressive, imprisoning and even executing those who did not conform, but its power was also productive. For those citizens who chose to embrace official values, the Soviet system offered a means of self-fulfillment—a way of escaping the competition and alienation of the capitalist system, of participating in the world-historical task of building socialism, and of cultivating the best qualities within themselves.[197] Although seldom realized in practice, the ideal of the New Person represented a political alternative to liberal individualism.

The concept of the New Person, then, can be traced to the French Revolution when popular sovereignty required the making of virtuous citizens who, no longer subjects, would on their own initiative govern and defend the nation. The rise of social science disciplines produced new forms of authority, including that of social scientists who sought to reform human behavior. By the late nineteenth and early twentieth centuries, a range of social thinkers and political leaders sought to fashion a new type of humanity that corresponded to modern industrial civilization. Common to many of their ideas was the sense that individuals must merge with the collective in order to prosper and contribute to society as a whole. Soviet authorities' efforts to create the New Person thus corresponded to a more general modern ethos that sought not only a rational social order but collectivist individuals who could function in the mass industrial age.

195. Igal Halfin, "From Darkness to Light: Student Communist Autobiography during NEP," *Jahrbücher für Geschichte Osteuropas* 45:2 (1997): 210–36.

196. Hellbeck, "Working," 351.

197. Stephen Kotkin, *Magnetic Mountain: Stalinism as a Civilization* (Berkeley, 1995), 21–23; Jochen Hellbeck, "Self-Realization in the Stalinist System: Two Soviet Diaries of the 1930s," *Russian Modernity: Politics, Knowledge, Practices*, ed. David L. Hoffmann and Yanni Kotsonis (New York, 2000), 234–35.

The New Soviet Person, however, had distinctive characteristics as well. Crucial to his/her formation was a completely state-run economy centered on heavy industry, with no private property or free market. The Soviet emphasis on collectivism represented not a modified version of liberalism but a caustic rejection of petty bourgeois individualism—one that saw individuals as fulfilling their human potential only by joining the collective. The ideal of the New Soviet Person applied to women as well as men, and the Soviet government (at least in theory) espoused a gender order that assigned women an equal role in economic and social life. And in contrast to the Nazi New Person—a male soldier whose exclusive purpose was the defense of Germany against a degenerate Europe—the New Soviet Person was intended as a universal ideal for all humanity.[198]

The universality of this model was further exemplified by Soviet nationality policy. Party leaders upheld the New Soviet Person as a model for all citizens, including national minorities, and in contrast to European colonial rulers, they sought to homogenize the population rather than perpetuate differences between the rulers and the ruled.[199] Adeeb Khalid notes that while Soviet (and also Republican Turkish) authorities drew on European orientalist thought regarding the ethnic classification of peoples, they did so not to assert inequalities but to force political participation and revolutionary change on all peoples.[200] Adrienne Edgar similarly points out that Soviet initiatives to emancipate women in Central Asia had little in common with French and British colonial policies, but had much in common with the modernizing regimes of interwar Turkey, Iran, and Afghanistan, where officials also promoted women's emancipation as part of their attempt to create a modern, homogeneous population.[201] Soviet nationality policy was characterized by "state-sponsored

198. Fritzsche and Hellbeck, "The New Man in Stalinist Russia," 314. In addition, the New Nazi Person was conceived primarily in physical terms, while the New Soviet Person was supposed to transform his/her mind and personality, through reading, self-criticism, and conscious efforts to unlearn bourgeois habits; Fritzsche and Hellbeck, "The New Man in Stalinist Russia," 340.

199. For a comparison of Soviet nationality policy with European colonial policies, see Peter Blitstein, "Cultural Diversity and the Interwar Conjuncture: Soviet Nationality Policy in its Comparative Context," *Slavic Review* 65:2 (summer 2006): 273–93.

200. Khalid, "Backwardness and the Quest for Civilization," 250–51. Khalid notes that the transformational ambitions of Soviet and Kemalist authorities in some ways meant their social intervention and destruction of traditions was far greater than that of European colonialists, particularly in the Soviet case; 232–33.

201. Adrienne Edgar, "Bolshevisms, Patriarchy, and the Nation: The Soviet 'Emancipation' of Muslim Women in Pan-Islamic Perspective," *Slavic Review* 65:2 (summer 2006):

evolutionism"—an approach, informed both by Marxist conceptions of historical stages and European anthropological theories of cultural evolution, that saw all ethnic groups progressing toward a common endpoint. Soviet officials saw the "backwardness" of certain national minorities as stemming from socioeconomic conditions, not racial or biological inferiority, and they believed that they could push these peoples along a common path of historical development that would lead to socialism and ultimately communism.[202]

More generally Soviet authorities' efforts to know and shape the thinking of the population reflected both international trends and Soviet particularities. During the First World War the governments of all belligerent countries sought to know and influence people's ideas, attitudes, and "political moods." Mass politics and mass warfare required the mobilization of the population and people's involvement as conscious, active political participants. As Joshua Sanborn has argued, the tsarist government discovered the danger of mass politics combined with minority rule when it engaged in mass mobilization during the First World War and was overthrown, and the Provisional Government soon suffered the same fate. The Communists solved the problem of mass politics and its centrifugal forces by establishing a monopoly over mobilizational resources, through political propaganda and censorship.[203] In other words, they successfully combined minority rule and mass mobilization by deploying and institutionalizing wartime practices effectively.

In the most basic sense, Soviet surveillance and propaganda derived from the changed nature of politics in an era of popular sovereignty and mass warfare. Under autocracies of the old regime, the population was expected simply to obey the monarch, while under modern political systems, even non-democratic ones, citizens were to play an active role in politics based on an understanding of the national interest and their role in attaining it. In the modern era, political power became internal rather than ex-

252–72. Edgar explains that, in contrast to regimes in Turkey and Iran that had a certain national legitimacy, Soviet rule in Central Asia was perceived by indigenous populations as alien and imperial even if not intended that way (271–72). On Soviet policy toward women in Central Asia, see also Douglas Northrop, *Veiled Empire: Gender and Power in Stalinist Central Asia* (Ithaca, 2004).

202. My characterization of Soviet nationality policy, including the term *state-sponsored evolutionism*, is drawn from Francine Hirsch, *Empire of Nations: Ethnographic Knowledge and the Making of the Soviet Union* (Ithaca, 2005), 6–9.

203. Sanborn, *Drafting the Russian Nation*, 97.

ternal, subjectivizing rather than subjecting.[204] For political leaders it was essential to know and influence people's thoughts. The First World War infused these tasks with great urgency, and it prompted new practices of surveillance and political education. These practices were perpetuated and institutionalized by the Soviet government which, despite its authoritarian character, sought to create revolutionary citizens who would construct a new, socialist society.

It was no accident that a self-consciously ideological government came to power in Russia at this moment of total war. The mobilizational demands of mass warfare explain the increasing emphasis on ideology that became widespread by the Second World War.[205] British and French domestic propaganda campaigns late in the First World War already included Wilsonian rhetoric heralding a new democratic world order. Also, a new type of democratic war leader emerged during the First World War. As seen in Clemenceau, Lloyd George, and Wilson, this new leader, through his persona and oratory, appealed directly to the populace, a style later perfected by Churchill and Roosevelt.[206] Mass appeals based on the intellectual and emotional pull of ideologies characterized the mobilizational politics not only of the Soviet regime but of governments throughout interwar Europe. Despite their vastly different appeals—democracy and national self-determination (liberalism), defense of the race (fascism), proletarian revolution (socialism)—all political leaders relied on ideological messages and new media to marshal popular support.

204. Keith Michael Baker, "A Foucauldian French Revolution?" *Foucault and the Writing of History*, ed. Jan Goldstein (Cambridge, Mass., 1994), 194.

205. Horne, "Remobilizing for 'Total War,'" 17. Horne cites Raymond Aron's idea that the First World War was over hegemony while the Second World War was over ideology.

206. Ibid., 14–15.

5 State Violence

> One must not forget that the [rebel]...is a plant which grows only
> on certain ground, and the most certain method is to make the
> ground unsuitable for him....If one wishes to cultivate a plot of
> ground upon which wild plants have encroached, it is not enough
> to uproot them...once one has ploughed, one must isolate the con-
> quered soil, enclose it, and then sow it with good grain, which alone
> will render it unsuitable to weeds.
> —GENERAL DUCHEMINON on the suppression of colonial rebellions in Indo-
> china, 1895

> The organs of state security are faced with the task of mercilessly
> crushing this entire gang of anti-Soviet elements...and, finally, of
> putting an end, once and for all, to their base undermining of the
> foundations of the Soviet state.
> —NKVD Operational Order 00447, 1937

No discussion of Soviet social intervention would be complete without
an examination of state violence. Indeed state violence, and the Gulag in
particular, is frequently regarded as emblematic of the Soviet system as a
whole. In 1937–38 alone, according to official figures, the Soviet security
police arrested 1,575,000 people, of whom it executed 681,692 and incarcerated another 663,308. By the end of 1940, the Soviet government
had imprisoned more than 1,930,000 people in Gulag labor camps, and
these figures do not even include deportations of over one and a half million "kulaks" to special settlements during the collectivization drive of the
early 1930s.[1] Soviet repression during this period amounted to an unprecedented scale of violence perpetrated by a state against its population.

---

1. Nicolas Werth, "A State against its People: Violence, Repression, and Terror in the
Soviet Union," *The Black Book of Communism: Crime, Terror, Repression,* trans. Jonathan Murphy and Mark Kramer (Cambridge, Mass., 1999), 190–91, 213. This execution
figure does not include those who died from torture during interrogations or who died in

Reflecting a popularly held view, *The Black Book of Communism* attributes Soviet state violence to communist ideology. Estimating the total number of deaths caused by Communist regimes to be around 100 million, the book's editor, Stéphane Courtois, claims that the "crimes" of these regimes fit a recognizable pattern including "execution by various means, such as firing squads, hanging, drowning, battering, and, in certain cases, gassing, poisoning, or 'car accidents'; destruction of the population by starvation, through man-made famine, the withholding of food, or both; deportation, through which death can occur."[2] Writing about the Soviet regime in particular, Courtois concludes that its use of terror "stemmed from Leninist ideology," and in the foreword to this volume, Martin Malia applauds this "emphasis on ideology as the wellspring of Communist mass murder."[3]

It is true that Marxism's emphasis on class conflict and violent proletarian revolution provided an ideological justification for violence. Moreover, Soviet leaders envisioned violence as one means of creating a new society. In 1920, Nikolai Bukharin wrote, "Proletarian compulsion in all its forms, beginning with execution by shooting and ending with the compulsory labor obligation, is—however paradoxical this may sound—*the means for producing a communist humanity from the human material of the capitalist epoch.*"[4] In a general sense, then, both Marxist doctrine and Soviet leaders espoused violence as part of the revolutionary process.

As argued earlier, however, ideology does not provide a blueprint for policy, nor does it dictate a single course of action. Marxism's emphasis on class war does not explain Soviet leaders' decisions to use state violence in particular situations, or the forms of state violence they deployed.[5] Although the Bolsheviks used exemplary violence during the Civil War, the primary form of Soviet state violence throughout the interwar period was excisionary violence—the forcible removal of specific segments of the population and the isolation or elimination of these groups. Through de-

---

prison camps. On deportations during collectivization, see Lynne Viola, *The Unknown Gulag: The Lost World of Stalin's Special Settlements* (New York, 2007).

2. Stéphane Courtois, "Introduction," *Black Book of Communism*, 4.

3. Stéphane Courtois, "Conclusion: Why?" *Black Book of Communism*, 737; Martin Malia, "Foreword," *Black Book of Communism*, xix.

4. N. I. Bukharin, *Problemy teorii i praktiki sotsializma* (Moscow, 1989), 168, 454. The italicized portion of the quotation was underlined by Lenin who noted in the margin, "Precisely!"

5. Immediately after the October Revolution, the Bolsheviks did not engage in systematic state violence, and it was only in the summer of 1918, at a moment of crisis during the Civil War, that Lenin ordered the "Red Terror."

cossackization Soviet commissars pursued the "total extirpation" of the Cossack elite; with dekulakization Stalin declared "the liquidation of the kulaks as a class"; via the passport regime officials expelled socially marginal groups from urban areas; and during the mass operations of 1937–38 the security police sought "once and for all" to eliminate "anti-Soviet elements." The purpose of excisionary violence, whether in the form of deportations, incarcerations, or executions, was to extract from society those deemed socially harmful or politically dangerous.

Excisionary violence did not originate in Russia, and it was not unique to Marxist regimes. We therefore need to explore the conceptual and practical origins of such violence. How did political leaders come to categorize their populations and presume to solve political problems through social excision? Where and when did technologies of social isolation, such as concentration camps, develop?[6] Here I will take an approach to understanding Soviet state violence focused on how it was conceived and implemented. I will explore both the conceptual and practical prerequisites for the forms of state violence employed by Soviet leaders. As in other types of state intervention discussed in this book, large-scale deportations, incarcerations, and executions were predicated on a conception of society as an artifact to be refashioned. They were made possible by statistical representations of the social field and social cataloguing of the population. They were legitimated by professionals' discourse on deviance and renovation that, however well intended, sanctioned the removal of individuals who allegedly posed a danger to the social whole.

In addition I will discuss how Soviet leaders carried out such massive programs of state violence, including the bureaucratic, judicial, and police structures that allowed them to deport, incarcerate, and execute large numbers of people. I will also highlight the technologies of social excision they employed. Some of these technologies, such as concentration camps, first developed in a colonial context and then were deployed throughout Europe itself during the First World War. During the Russian Civil War, the Soviet government (as well as the White armies) perpetuated the use of

6. Similar questions can be raised regarding other monocausal explanations of Soviet state violence, such as the idea that it is attributable solely to Stalin's psychological penchant for brutality. Opposed to this idea, David Priestland, *Stalinism and the Politics of Mobilization: Ideas, Power, and Terror in Inter-war Russia* (New York, 2007), shows that Stalin operated within the same political and ideological framework as did other Bolshevik leaders; and Erik van Ree, *The Political Thought of Joseph Stalin: A Study in Twentieth-Century Revolutionary Patriotism* (London, 2002), argues that Marxist ideology was central to Stalin's thinking and policies.

deportations and internments, and these practices became institutionalized within the Soviet system in the form of the Gulag. Also during the Civil War, the Soviet government founded the security police, which subsequently carried out most Stalinist state violence.

Finally I will discuss how the practices and instruments of state violence became attached to Soviet leaders' goals of refashioning society. In the case of dekulakization, the Soviet government categorized several million peasants as kulaks and, according to assigned subcategories, dispossessed, deported, or executed them. This massive enactment of state violence provoked resistance and social upheaval, which in turn prompted further measures of social control, including the internal passport system.[7] Believing they had created a socialist order and facing a rising international threat, Soviet leaders in the late 1930s sought to deal definitively with continued internal opposition and potential "fifth columnists" through another massive wave of state violence.[8] Historical contingency and international developments, then, also played a central role in Stalinist state violence.

I do not argue that techniques of social categorization and social excision in themselves caused Soviet state violence. Deportations, incarcerations, and executions carried out by the Soviet government were the result of decisions by Party leaders, who acknowledged no limits on their authority and wielded unchecked, dictatorial power. Social cataloguing, technologies of social excision, and highly centralized bureaucratic and police apparatuses were all conditions of possibility for the forms of state violence enacted by Party leaders. I thus present techniques of social categorization and social excision as conceptual and practical preconditions of

7. David R. Shearer, *Policing Stalin's Socialism: Repressions and Social Order in the Soviet Union, 1924–1953* (New Haven, 2009), 5–6.

8. On the political and social dynamics behind "The Great Terror," see Gabor Tamas Rittersporn, *Stalinist Simplifications and Soviet Complications: Social Tensions and Political Conflicts in the USSR* (Philadelphia, 1991); J. Arch Getty, *Origins of the Great Purges: The Soviet Communist Party Reconsidered, 1933–1938* (New York, 1985); Wendy Z. Goldman, *Terror and Democracy in the Age of Stalin: The Social Dynamics of Repression* (New York, 2007). On the foreign threat as a motive for Stalinist repressions, see Oleg Khlevniuk, "The Objectives of the Great Terror, 1937–1938," *Soviet History, 1917–1953: Essays in Honour of R. W. Davies* (Basingstoke, 1995), 158–76; and "The Reasons for the 'Great Terror': The Foreign Policy Aspect," *Russia in the Age of Wars, 1914–1945,* ed. Silvio Pons and A. Romano (Milan, 2000), 159–69; E. A. Rees, "The Great Purges and the XVIII Party Congress of 1939," *Centre-Local Relations in the Stalinist State, 1928–1941,* ed. Rees (Basingstoke, 2002), 191–211; Silvio Pons, *Stalin and the Inevitable War, 1936–1941* (London, 2002). For additional citations and a review of debates about Stalinist violence, see Kevin McDermott, *Stalin: Revolutionary in an Era of War* (New York, 2006), 104–9.

Soviet state violence, not as direct causes. These conceptual and practical preconditions occurred in other countries as well but, with certain exceptions such as Nazi Germany, did not result in massive state violence. The direct cause of Soviet state violence was the Stalinist leadership's ruthless determination to remove "kulaks" during collectivization and eliminate potential fifth columnists prior to the Second World War. Stalin and his fellow leaders used preexisting techniques of state violence to pursue their goals of revolutionary transformation and state security.

Origins of Modern State Violence

To illuminate the conceptual and technical origins of social categorization and social excision, I will pursue two lines of inquiry. First I will look at developments within social science to show how nineteenth-century sociologists, psychologists, and criminologists came to conceive of malignant segments within the body social and the practical steps they took to remove them. Second, I will look at the influence of colonialism—the ways that colonial rule promoted the categorization of indigenous peoples and spawned new technologies to isolate groups deemed socially or politically dangerous. These practices of social cataloguing and removal represented important antecedents to Soviet state violence in the forms it would later take.

Political leaders' use of coercion against their own populations was of course not new to the modern era. Throughout history rulers have killed, displaced, or enslaved their subjects, particularly in the aftermath of military conquest, but also in response to real or perceived threats to their domination. Only in the modern era, however, did governments draw on social scientific studies that sought to resolve social problems through categorization of the population. Nineteenth-century disciplinary developments, including those in economics, demography, psychology, and criminology, made it possible to identify groups and type individuals who allegedly posed a peril to the political or social order. These disciplines also replaced the traditional metaphorical relationship between the individual and society with a conception of individuals as component parts of the overall social body—a concept that implied that an individual's illness or deviance might infect society as a whole.[9]

9. See Catherine Gallagher, "The Body versus the Social Body in the Works of Thomas Malthus and Henry Mayhew," *Representations* 14 (1986): 83–106.

In Western Europe, social reformers and government officials focused in particular on the urban poor as a group that posed a health risk and political threat. Some even engaged in the physical typing of the lower classes, and described urban workers in the same terms they used for criminals—ugly, repulsive, and ignorant. These efforts reflected a more general sense that the working class, criminals, and immigrants were part of an urban morass where epidemics and crime festered, and where a riotous mob could form.[10] Both to counter political unrest and to quell a range of social problems—crime, poverty, and infectious disease—authorities increasingly conducted inspections and compiled social statistics, which in turn prompted interventions to regulate or remove "malignant" segments of the population.

Nineteenth-century developments in criminology led to a new conception of crime and a new approach to policing. So-called moral statisticians Adolphe Quetelet and André-Michel Guerry published analyses of crime statistics in the early 1830s that showed that crime rates remained virtually constant from year to year, an indication that crime was not the result of economic downturns and poverty as previously assumed. While both Quetelet and Guerry regarded crime as the product of social organization, subsequent criminologists came to focus on individual-biological explanations of crime, notably Cesare Lombroso whose 1876 book *Criminal Man* argued that the criminal was a distinct anthropological type with distinguishing physical features.[11] Also in the course of the nineteenth century, authorities in a number of countries developed a "scientific" approach to policing that included surveillance and documentation to label and remove criminals from society. In Germany, for example, a consensus developed among both government officials and the educated public that violent policing, rather than self-help or self-restraint, was necessary to stem the rising tide of criminality and political unrest.[12]

---

10. Louis Chevalier, *Laboring Classes and Dangerous Classes in Paris during the First Half of the Nineteenth Century,* trans. Frank Jellinek (New York, 1973), 369, 413. See also Gareth Stedman Jones, *Outcast London: A Study in the Relationship between Classes in Victorian Society* (Oxford, 1971).

11. The reception of Lombroso's work varied from one country to another, depending on disciplinary developments in psychiatry and criminal jurisprudence within those respective countries. See Richard Wetzell, *Inventing the Criminal: A History of German Criminology, 1880–1945* (Chapel Hill, 2000), 21–31. On Lombroso, see also David Horn, *The Criminal Body: Lombroso and the Anatomy of Deviance* (New York, 2003).

12. Alf Lüdtke, "The Permanence of Internal War: The Prussian State and its Opponents, 1870–1871," *On the Road to Total War: The American Civil War and the German Wars of Unification, 1861–1871,* ed. Stig Förster and Jörg Nagler (New York, 1997), 388–90.

While removal of individuals from society long predated the nineteenth century, an important step in the development of modern excisionary violence occurred with the concept of a criminal class. Already in the early nineteenth century, many British sociologists and social thinkers had come to accept the idea that there was a "criminal class," understood to be a distinct group within society. They thus attributed crime not to socioeconomic conditions but rather to this social stratum that could be documented and quantified through crime statistics. The delineation of a criminal class in turn contributed to the idea of removing this social stratum, not as a form of retribution but rather as a means of prophylaxis. The British government founded penal colonies in Australia and deported ("transported") roughly 150,000 convicts there in the course of the nineteenth century. As one scholar concludes, the aim of the transportation system was less to punish or deter crimes than to extract permanently the "criminal class" from British society.[13] In France also, criminologists came increasingly to see criminals as particular types who could not be reformed and instead had to be removed from society. In the mid-nineteenth century, Benedict Augustin Morel proposed that humans when exposed to a pathological environment, such as the urban criminal underworld, would develop antisocial behaviors that could be passed on to their children. While French criminologists stopped short of the anatomical determinism of Lombroso, they nonetheless saw urban space as a criminal breeding ground and recidivist criminals as a particular stratum that needed to be physically removed from society.[14] In 1852, the French government began to deport political prisoners to a penal colony in French Guiana, and two years later it began to deport common criminals as well.[15]

The aftermath of the Paris Commune in 1871 marked another important step in the development of excisionary violence. Following the suppression of the commune, French military tribunals carried out quick trials of the communards. They then drew up lists of the guilty and placed

---

13. Robert Hughes, *The Fatal Shore* (New York, 1987), 40–41, 66, 161–68. The deportation of convicts from Britain actually dated from the early seventeenth century, when small numbers of felons with commuted deaths sentences were sent to labor on plantations in the North American colonies. On Britain's 1869 Habitual Criminals Bill, see Daniel Pick, *Faces of Degeneration: A European Disorder, c. 1848—c. 1918* (New York, 1989), 182–83.

14. Stephen A. Toth, *Beyond Papillon: The French Overseas Penal Colonies, 1854–1952* (Lincoln, 2006), 4–5, 31–33. See also Pick, *Faces of Degeneration*, 39.

15. Robert Nye, *Crime, Madness, and Politics in Modern France: The Medical Concept of National Decline* (Princeton, 1984), chapter 3; Toth, *Beyond Papillon*, 10–11.

the worst offenders—revolutionary leaders, foreigners, criminals, and deserters—in the first category for execution or deportation. The French military executed roughly twenty thousand communards and deported another five thousand to penal colonies in New Caledonia. As General G. A. A. Galliffet declared, "We have more than enough foreigners and scum here, we have to get rid of them."[16] Military officials thus carried out executions not in the midst battle but in its aftermath when the immediate revolutionary threat had passed. They were motivated perhaps partly by a desire for retribution but more fundamentally by a determination to excise from French society those they deemed incorrigible.

French government leaders refused to recognize the Commune as a political event and instead portrayed the communards as immoral criminals, even referring to them as vermin. The execution and deportation of communards, in the words of one scholar, "amounted to a social cleansing of Paris."[17] Viscount Othenin d'Haussonville, who headed a parliamentary commission on crime, believed that most communards were recidivist criminals. He and others linked concerns about national decline (following the humiliating defeat in the Franco-Prussian War) with the problem of recidivism, and recommended the deportation of not only dangerous criminals but repeat petty offenders as well.[18] French penal legislation in the mid-1880s allowed for the mass deportation of repeat offenders, vagrants, beggars, and other social marginals.[19]

The Paris Commune—both its short-lived existence and its bloody demise—became an important reference point for Marxist revolutionaries. Karl Marx himself heralded the Commune as "the bold champion of the emancipation of labor," and "the glorious harbinger of a new society."[20] But he and Frederick Engels also drew lessons from the Paris Commune that reinforced their concept of the dictatorship of the proletariat. Reflecting on the Commune, Engels concluded that "the state is nothing but a machine for the oppression of one class by another," and he declared that following a victorious proletarian revolution, the state would continue as "an evil inherited by the proletariat" to be used against its enemies until "such time as a generation reared in new, free social conditions is

---

16. Robert Tombs, *The War against Paris 1871* (New York, 1981), 179–80, 191.

17. Alice Bullard, *Exile to Paradise: Savagery and Civilization in Paris and the South Pacific, 1790–1900* (Stanford, 2000), 67, 81.

18. Toth, *Beyond Papillon*, 31–33.

19. For further discussion, see Nye, *Crime, Madness, and Politics*, 59–95.

20. Karl Marx, *The Civil War in France* (Moscow, 1952), 102, 130.

able to throw the entire lumber of the state on the scrap heap."[21] Later Marxists, including Trotsky, also drew lessons from the repression of the communards, and stressed that revolutionaries needed a centralized apparatus to wage war against the capitalists in the same way that capitalists used their state apparatus to suppress revolutionaries.[22]

In Russia the tsarist government had a long tradition of exiling criminals and revolutionaries. Beginning in the late seventeenth century, tsarist authorities deported small numbers of convicts and political prisoners to remote regions and in some cases consigned these prisoners to forced labor. In 1827, governor-general of Siberia, Mikhail Speranskii, instituted regulations for transporting convicts and utilizing their labor. His objective was to settle exiles as agricultural colonists, with the long-term goal of integrating Siberia into the Russian Empire.[23] As was true with authorities in Western Europe, nineteenth-century tsarist officials also had concerns with the working class as a potential revolutionary force. Throughout the second half of the nineteenth century, they sought to regulate factory work and mediate labor disputes.[24] From a very different perspective, the liberal intelligentsia in Russia was similarly concerned with the lower classes. Eager to ameliorate the downtrodden condition of the masses, liberal professionals also harbored fears that Russia's politically oppressive and economically underdeveloped conditions had spawned deviance and disorder among workers and peasants. These liberals, then, blamed the autocracy for poverty, alcoholism, and crime among the lower classes, but they also suffered a mixture of unease and guilt in relation to the masses.[25]

By the late nineteenth and early twentieth centuries, Russian social thinkers began to embrace the idea of "social defense"—a new principle of penal policy developed by Franz von Liszt and other German legal reformers during the 1880s. In contrast to classical deterrence theory, this approach sought punishments based not on the crime but on the future dan-

21. Frederick Engels, "Introduction," *The Civil War in France* by Karl Marx (Moscow, 1952), 28–29.

22. Leon Trotsky, *Terrorism and Communism: A Reply to Karl Kautsky* (Ann Arbor, 1961, original 1920), 88–89.

23. Abby M. Schrader, *Languages of the Lash: Corporeal Punishment and Identity in Imperial Russia* (DeKalb, 2002), 79–83. See also Andrew Gentes, "Roads to Oblivion: Siberian Exile and the Struggle between State and Society in Tsarist Russia, 1593–1917" (Ph.D. diss., Brown University, 2002).

24. Reginald E. Zelnik, *Labor and Society in Tsarist Russia: The Factory Workers of St. Petersburg, 1855–1870* (Stanford, 1971), 92–96.

25. See Laura Engelstein, *The Keys to Happiness: Sex and the Search for Modernity in Fin-de-siècle Russia* (Ithaca, 1992), 24.

ger posed by the criminal. In cases of incorrigible repeat offenders it called for indefinite incarceration to protect society against crime.[26] The concept of social defense was influential across Europe, including in countries such as France where social thinkers had largely rejected biologically determinist theories of criminality. These ideas were also enthusiastically discussed by Russian criminologists and psychologists who endorsed the prolonged isolation of certain criminals to protect society. The context in which ideas of social defense took hold in Russia included the upsurge in social disorder at the turn of the century, particularly with the Revolution of 1905.[27]

One Russian criminologist argued that "criminals with morally corrupted natures...should not be terrorized with severe penalties but simply isolated, as it were, removed from everyday life with a view to protecting society from their harmful influence."[28] Others concurred, and in paternalistic terms maintained that such isolation was for criminals' own good, because it sheltered them from the pernicious influences of the modern world.[29] The criminologist A. A. Zhizhilenko advocated labor colonies where "dangerous recidivists could be accommodated" and ultimately "restored to an honest way of life."[30] The principle of social excision—physical isolation of those who posed a threat to society—was therefore well established among Russian psychologists and criminal anthropologists in the late imperial period. Some of these specialists would continue to play a prominent role formulating penal policy under the Soviet government. Although it would be wrong to blame these liberal professionals for Soviet state violence, their prescriptions for eliminating deviance indicate that ideas of social renovation, by coercive removal of tainted individuals, extended far beyond the Bolsheviks.

By the early twentieth century, then, the idea of removing and isolating criminals from society had become well established among Western

26. Wetzell, *Inventing the Criminal*, 33–34.
27. Daniel Beer, *Renovating Russia: The Human Sciences and the Fate of Liberal Modernity, 1880–1930* (Ithaca, 2008), 125. On fears of a rising tide of lower-class crime and disorder, see Joan Neuberger, *Hooliganism: Crime, Culture, and Power in St. Petersburg, 1900–1914* (Berkeley, 1993).
28. B. I. Vorotynskii, "Psikho-fizicheskie osobennosti prestupnika-degenerata," *Uchenye zapiski Kazanskogo Universiteta* 3 (1900): 101, as quoted in Beer, *Renovating Russia*, 126.
29. Beer, *Renovating Russia*, 127.
30. A. A. Zhizhilenko, "Mery sotsial'noi zashchity v otnoshenii opasnykh prestupnikov," *Pravo* 35 (1910): 2078–91; 36 (1910): 2136–43; 37 (1910): 2167–77, here at 2171, as quoted in Beer, *Renovating Russia*, 128.

European and Russian psychologists and criminologists. Moreover, this principle of social excision was increasingly seen as applicable not just to individuals but to entire strata deemed a threat to society. The delineation of deviant groups depended on social statistics and categorization, techniques that in turn served to legitimize the very idea of social excision. These principles and techniques of social cataloguing would later inform the thinking of criminologists in the Soviet era and become one of the bases of Soviet excisionary violence.

Prior to the First World War, government practices of excisionary violence within European countries themselves remained limited, but such was not the case in European colonies. Though modern state interventionism did not originate in a colonial setting, methods of excisionary violence did evolve and expand in the colonies, as colonial administrators developed new technologies of social control.[31] Not only did the experience of imperialism feed European theories of cultural and racial superiority, it also spawned practices of excisionary violence, including forced population transfers and protogenocidal massacres.[32]

Concentration camps were invented in a colonial setting. In 1896 the Spanish military governor of Cuba, Valeriano Weyler y Nicolau, sought to suppress a revolt there during the Spanish-American War by imprisoning part of the civilian population, with the aim of preventing guerillas from hiding amongst and receiving aid from civilians. Four years later, British generals Frederick Sleigh Lord Roberts and Hubert Horatio Kitchener established concentration camps for the same purpose during the Boer War.[33] These first uses of concentration camps received widespread attention among military theorists (and in the case of the Boer War, among the general public as well). In particular, two future Russian military commanders studied the Spanish and British use of concentration camps.

31. C. A. Bayly notes that efforts to categorize and civilize society originated not in the colonies but within Europe itself; C. A. Bayly, *Empire and Information: Intelligence Gathering and Social Communication in India, 1780–1870* (Cambridge, 1996), 179. See also James Scott, *Seeing Like a State: How Certain Schemes to Improve the Human Condition Have Failed* (New Haven, 1998), 378.

32. On the continuing value of Hannah Arendt's "boomerang thesis," the idea that racist thought and violent practices of colonialism were reimported into Europe and contributed to twentieth-century totalitarianism, see Richard H. King and Dan Stone, "Introduction," *Hannah Arendt and the Uses of History*, ed. King and Stone (New York, 2007).

33. Isabel Hull, *Absolute Destruction: Military Culture and the Practices of War in Imperial Germany* (Ithaca, 2005), 73. See also S. B. Spies, *Methods of Barbarism: Roberts and Kitchener and Civilians in the Boer Republics, January 1900–May 1902* (Cape Town, 1977).

General Staff Colonel Iadov Grigor'evich Zhilinskii, a Russian military observer in Cuba who later became commander of the northwest front in World War I, reported in great detail on the imprisonment of civilians in concentration camps. Vasilii Iosifovich Gurko, who went on to become Russian commander-in-chief in 1916, similarly observed and reported on British anti-insurgency measures and concentration camps during the Boer War.[34]

Military observation and international interchange between military specialists had already become well established in the second half of the nineteenth century. Aleksei Nikolaevich Kuropatkin, who played a leading role in the Russian conquest and administration of Central Asia, spent an extensive period in Algeria in 1875 and wrote on French methods of subjugating the native population. Nor was this flow of ideas unidirectional, as Hubert Lyautey, the leading theorist and practitioner of French colonial warfare in Algeria, Indochina, Madagascar, and Morocco, carefully studied the Russian conquest of both the Caucasus and Central Asia. In his writings, Lyautey emphasized that combating rebel bands was not enough. He stressed the need to remove rebels and transform the social milieu in order to eradicate insurgencies.[35]

As was the case with other forms of state intervention, social categorization and enumeration provided a statistical representation of the population on which administrators could act. Censuses were originally developed and utilized by officials in colonial settings.[36] Through its censuses and categorizations, the British administration in India consolidated, rather than discovered, the caste system, as well as an entire hierarchy of "martial races."[37] British administrators in East Africa similarly cata-

34. Iadov Grigor'evich Zhilinskii, *Ispano-Amerikanskaia voina: Otchet komandirovannogo po vysochaishemu poveleniiuk ispanskim voiskam na ostrove Kuby* (St. Petersburg, 1899); Vasilii Iosifovich Gurko, *Voina Anglii s iuzhno-afrikanskimi respublikami, 1899–1901 gg.: Otchet komandirovannogo po vysochaishimu poveleniiuk voiskam iuzhno-afrikanskikh respublik V. I. Gurko* (St. Petersburg, 1901), as cited in Peter Holquist, "To Count, to Extract, and to Exterminate: Population Statistics and Population Politics in Late Imperial and Soviet Russia," *A State of Nations: Empire and Nation-Making in the Age of Lenin and Stalin,* ed. Ronald Grigor Suny and Terry Martin (New York, 2001), 123.

35. Holquist, "To Count," 119–20, 132.

36. Ian Hacking, *The Taming of Chance* (New York, 1990), 17.

37. Nicholas Dirks, "Castes of Mind," *Representations* 37 (1992): 56–78; Pradeep Barua, "Inventing Race: The British and India's Martial Races," *Historian* 58:1 (1995): 107–16. See also Benedict Anderson, *Imagined Communities,* expanded ed. (New York, 1991); and Bernard Cohn, "The Census, Social Stratification, and Objectification in South Asia," *An Anthropologist among the Historians* (New Delhi, 1987).

logued tribes according to their military strength and political loyalty.[38] This process of differentiating and cataloguing colonial populations in turn guided colonialists who would rely on some groups and target others during colonial revolts.[39]

The Russian Empire differed fundamentally from the overseas empires of Western European countries in that it was a contiguous land empire. The ideology of empire espoused by Russian elites tended to differ accordingly, as many of them saw their empire as based on Russian peasant migration and cultural cross-borrowing and assimilation—in their view a more natural and humane enterprise than the overseas imperialism of Britain and France.[40] It was also a multiethnic, multiconfessional empire with a far more diverse population than that of Western European countries. Russian officials undertook measures similar to those of European colonialists to catalogue the peoples they conquered, but their concerns with ethnic categorization extended to the entire population, including nationalities living in areas such as the western borderlands, that had been part of the Russian Empire for centuries.

Ethnic cataloguing in imperial Russia illustrates the ways that statistics profoundly influenced the thinking of tsarist bureaucrats and Russian intellectuals. Several government ministries, including the Ministry of Internal Affairs and the Ministry of Finance, as well as the zemstvos compiled population statistics, each institution relying on its own agendas and

38. See the British War Office report on Somaliland, PRO WO 106/18. On the British use of censuses as a means of colonial conquest in South Africa, see Clifton Crais, *The Politics of Evil: Magic, State Power, and the Political Imagination in South Africa* (New York, 2002), 79–82.

39. On the British suppression of the Mau Mau uprising during the postwar period, see Catherine Elkins, *Imperial Reckoning: The Untold Story of the British Gulag in Kenya* (New York, 2005).

40. Robert Geraci, "Genocidal Impulses and Fantasies in Imperial Russia," *Empire, Colony, Genocide: Conquest, Occupation, and Subaltern Resistance in World History*, ed. A. Dirk Moses (New York, 2008), 361–62. Geraci notes that those espousing this view did not deny that Russian colonists would acquire from native peoples elements of culture and even blood (miscegenation was generally not proscribed), though they believed that russification would be the dominant trend. See also Nathaniel Knight, "Grigor'ev in Orenburg, 1851–1862: Russian Orientalism in the Service of Empire?" *Slavic Review* 59:1 (spring 2000): 74–100; Adeeb Khalid, "Russian History and the Debate over Orientalism," *Kritika* 1:4 (fall 2000): 691–99; Nathaniel Knight, "On Russian Orientalism: A Response to Adeeb Khalid," *Kritika* 1:4 (fall 2000): 701–15, for differences in imperial ideology among Russian administrators.

categories.[41] The Russian military, beginning in the mid-nineteenth century, also tabulated and conceptualized the empire's population through
the new discipline of military statistics. Dmitrii Alekseevich Miliutin, who
would later become minister of war, founded the discipline of military
statistics at the General Staff Academy following an 1845 tour of Europe,
where he had studied the Prussian military in particular. The publications
on military statistics by Miliutin and other General Staff officers disaggre-
gated the population into ethnic categories and provided not only numbers
but extensive ethnographic descriptions of different peoples of the empire.
Although supposedly an objective undertaking, the categorization and de-
scription of ethnic groups invariably entailed normative judgments and
hierarchies. Military statistical studies offered qualitative assessments of
each "element" of the population and concluded that the ethnic Russian
core of the empire was politically reliable, in contrast to ethnic minorities
who were undesirable. While military theorists characterized Russians as
patriotic and loyal, they described Jews as unpatriotic and selfish, and
Poles and Muslims as alien and unreliable.[42]

As I will discuss below, these conclusions contributed directly to the
tsarist government's massive deportations of Germans, Jews, and Muslims
from the western borderlands and the Caucasus during the First World
War. Even prior to these deportations, however, the Russian military engaged in population resettlement in the Caucasus and Central Asia, some
of these efforts dating from the early nineteenth century in the case of the
Caucasus.[43] Following the Crimean War, population transfers in the Caucasus assumed a far great scale when tsarist administrators there, including Dmitrii Miliutin, sought to consolidate control of the region along the
Black Sea coast. In 1858 Tsar Aleksandr II approved the deportation of
hostile mountain tribes, and during subsequent campaigns in the western
Caucasus, the Russian military sought to "cleanse" the region of undesir-

41. See David W. Darrow, "The Politics of Numbers: Zemstvo Land Assessment and
the Conceptualization of Russia's Rural Economy," *The Russian Review* 59:1 (January
2000): 52–75.

42. Holquist, "To Count," 113–15. See also D. A. Miliutin, *Pervye opyty voennoi
statistiki*, 2 vols. (St. Petersburg, 1847–1848); A. M. Zolotarev, *Zapiski voennoi statistiki*,
2 vols. (St. Petersburg, 1885). For further discussion of tsarist military leaders' understanding of ethnicity, see Joshua Sanborn, *Drafting the Russian Nation: Military Conscription,
Total War, and Mass Politics, 1905–1925* (DeKalb, 2003), 65–74.

43. On the tsarist military's resettlement of Ossetians and Kabardians, as well as the
settlement of Cossacks, in the North Caucasus, see Thomas Barrett, *At the Edge of Empire:
The Terek Cossacks and the North Caucasus Frontier, 1700–1860* (Boulder, 1999), 41–42.

able groups using excisionary violence—burning villages and deporting or killing people.

Statistical knowledge and ethnic categorization did not necessarily dictate state violence in the Caucasus. Much of the ethnographic and statistical data on indigenous peoples was produced by the Caucasian Division of the Imperial Geographical Society, and tsarist administrators believed that this data would allow them to utilize ethnic groups more effectively by assigning each of them roles in the economic order. As part of the pacification campaign in the coastal mountain region of the western Caucasus, some administrators foresaw the relocation of "highland Circassians" to lowlands where they could work as agricultural laborers and be integrated into society under Russian governance. The vast majority of indigenous peoples, however, resisted resettlement, and in 1864 some 370,000 chose to emigrate to the Ottoman Empire rather than live under Russian rule.[44]

Altogether roughly 450,000 people were expelled from the Caucasus between 1858 and 1864, including not only Circassians (the Adygei, the Cherkess, and Kabardians), but Nogais and others as well. Inhabitants of the coastal mountain region who refused resettlement or emigration were forcibly driven out by Russian military expeditions that destroyed villages and hunted down refugees in mountain gorges. Viceroy Grand Duke Mikhail proclaimed the "complete cleansing of the Black Sea shoreline and the resettlement of the mountaineers to Turkey." Officials of the Main Staff of the Caucasus Army reported that "not one of the mountaineer inhabitants remains on their former places of residence, and measures are being taken to cleanse the region in order to prepare it for the new Russian population."[45] Imperial conquest and control of Central Asia proceeded along similar lines. Military theorists from the 1870s on emphasized the need to replace to native inhabitants with the "Russian element" in order "to influence strongly the transformation of the physiognomy of the entire country."[46]

Nineteenth-century administrators, both within Europe and in its colonies, came increasingly to rely on social statistics in their quest to exercise

44. Dana Lyn Sherry, "Imperial Alchemy: Resettlement, Ethnicity, and Governance in the Russian Caucasus, 1828–1865" (Ph.D. diss., University of California, Davis, 2007), 5, 9–12.

45. Austin Jersild, *Orientalism and Empire: North Caucasus Mountain Peoples and the Georgian Frontier, 1845–1917* (Montreal, 2002), 23–25.

46. Holquist, "To Count," 116–20, quoting M. I. Veniukov, "Ocherk politicheskoi etnografii stran lezhashchikh mezhdu Rossieiu i Indeiu," *Sbornik gosudarstvennykh znanii* 3 (1877): 61–65.

control and counter perceived political threats. Statistics did not cause state violence, but they provided a representation of the population that officials could rely on in their efforts to identify and excise groups deemed a danger to society as a whole. Although the thinking behind excisionary violence did not originate with colonialism, Europeans' conquest and rule of non-European peoples involved social and ethnic categorizations and new technologies of violence, including concentration camps. Through colonialism and colonial warfare, the application of violence became part of the lived experience of a large number of military officers and colonial administrators, many of whom would play a leading role during the First World War. With the war, excisionary violence would be practiced on a large scale within Europe itself.

Internments, Deportations, and Genocide during the First World War

The First World War marked a new stage not only in the scale of warfare but in the merging of the military and civilian spheres. The blurring of distinctions between soldiers and civilians was apparent in occupation policies, for example in the Germans' use of forced civilian labor, but it was also evident in governments' policies toward civilians within their own countries. Many governments in the war established internment camps for "enemy aliens"—nonnaturalized foreigners from combatant countries. And the Austro-Hungarian Empire, the Russian Empire, and the Ottoman Empire all engaged in deportations or internments of national minorities who were their own subjects. The Ottoman government went as far as genocide against its Armenian subjects. The First World War, then, saw state violence toward civilians on a scale and in forms previously employed only in a colonial context.

German occupation policies in northern France and Belgium illustrate the ways in which the civilian population was subjected to state violence. Without any handbook, plan, or ideological scheme, German military commanders in northern France completely instrumentalized the civilian population. In pursuit of resources for the war effort, they issued identity cards to every person and, beginning in the fall of 1914, compelled civilians to perform forced labor. As the war continued, they established a network of labor camps. By 1916, with severe labor shortages in Germany, the German government began the deportation of Belgian workers, roughly sixty thousand of whom were sent for forced labor in Germany. And in preparation for the 1918 offensive, the German military also deported civilians from northern France. None of these measures had been planned prior to the war, nor were they intended as any form of ethnic cleansing. Instead this use of state violence against civilians resulted from decisions by German commanders based on military-operational imperatives.[47]

The German military similarly instrumentalized the civilian population on the eastern front. It issued identity documents to all inhabitants over age ten, and it also inventoried all material resources—factories, houses, buildings, and livestock. Beginning in 1915, German authorities employed forced labor, and in November 1916 they ordered all adult men between seventeen and sixty to report to labor camps. Most forced laborers worked in the occupation zone, but at least thirty-four thousand were forcibly transported to Germany for labor there.[48] In its attempt to guarantee the health and utility of human resources in occupied territory, German officials mandated the compulsory cleaning of local populations in military baths and disinfecting stations. This objectification of civilians, as instruments to be documented, cleaned, and utilized, was part of what one historian has termed "a severe grid of control over the territory and its native populations, directing all activity in the area and turning it to the uses of the military state."[49]

Equally important were government policies toward populations within their own countries. Shortly after the outbreak of the First World War, the British government created internment camps for all German reservists residing in Britain, and then in May 1915 it ordered the internment of all adult German males residing in Britain who were not naturalized British citizens.[50] Germany, France, Canada, and Australia also created internment camps, which held, respectively, 110,000, 60,000, 8,000, and 4,500 "enemy aliens."[51] On its entry into the war, the United States government detained 6,300 enemy aliens in four major internment camps run by the war department.[52] In Russia, the tsarist government interned roughly half of the 600,000 "enemy aliens"—German, Austrian, and Ottoman subjects—

47. Hull, *Absolute Destruction*, 234–40, 248–57.

48. Ibid., 244–47.

49. Vejas Gabriel Liulevicius, *War Land on the Eastern Front: Culture, National Identity, and German Occupation in World War I* (New York, 2000), 8, 106.

50. PRO HO 45/10729/255193, 45/10946/266047. See also Panikos Panayi, *The Enemy in Our Midst: Germans in Britain during World War One* (New York, 1991).

51. Eric Lohr, *Nationalizing the Russian Empire: The Campaign against Enemy Aliens during World War I* (Cambridge, Mass., 2003), 178. See also Jean-Claude Farcy, *Les Camps Concentration Français de la Première Guerre Mondiale* (Paris, 1995).

52. Jörg Nagler, "Victims of the Home Front: Enemy Aliens in the United States during the First World War," *Minorities in Wartime: National and Racial Groupings in Europe,*

residing there at the outbreak of the war.[53] Fearing espionage and sabotage, governments dealt with the perceived threat of "enemy aliens" by removing them from society and isolating them in concentration camps.

In multinational empires, rulers engaged in similar practices toward their own subjects who were members of national minorities they did not trust. Since 1912 the Austro-Hungarian police had maintained a secret list of possible enemies of the state, mainly Serbs, Croats, and Romanians living near the borders. On the day of mobilization in July 1914, the police force undertook mass arrests. The Austro-Hungarian government also created internment camps for suspect national minorities, in which it interned a large number of Ruthenians and, after Italy entered the war, at least seventy-five thousand of its ethnic Italian subjects.[54]

The Russian government carried out massive deportations of its own subjects from both the western borderlands and the Caucasus. These deportations directly reflected the thinking promoted by tsarist military statistics—namely that segments of the population, identifiable and enumerated by ethnicity, were politically unreliable and posed a security threat during wartime. In December 1914 Russian commanders ordered the deportation of all adult male ethnic Germans from the Polish provinces of the Russian Empire to interior provinces. Chief of Staff Nikolai Ianushkevich claimed that ethnic Germans were spying for the German Army, and he ordered that entire families be encouraged to leave. Other Russian military leaders called for the "full cleansing of the element harmful to the war from the region of military activity."[55]

In January 1915 Ianushkevich ordered the expulsion of "all Jews and suspect individuals" from the region of military activity, again under the assumption that Jews were politically unreliable and engaged in spying for Germany and Austria-Hungary. By that spring the Russian Army began mass deportations of Jews intended to clear not only the front area but entire provinces. As a result, hundreds of thousands of Jews were deported

North America, and Australia during the Two World Wars, ed. Panikos Panayi (Oxford, 1993), 211.

53. Lohr, *Nationalizing the Russian Empire,* 122–27.

54. Holger H. Herwig, *The First World War: Germany and Austria-Hungary, 1914–1918* (New York, 1997), 127, 160; Mark Cornwall, "Morale and Patriotism in the Austro-Hungarian Army, 1914–1918," *State, Society, and Mobilization in Europe during the First World War,* ed. John Horne (New York, 1997), 175–76.

55. Lohr, *Nationalizing the Russian Empire,* 130–31. Lohr notes that Russian commanders saw ethnic Germans as unassimilated aliens, and he quotes a letter in which Ianushkevich stated that "German colonists" who had taken Russian subjecthood nonetheless harbored a "criminal attraction toward their German fatherland" (133).

by train to locations east of the Volga, and some groups of Jews were even driven west across no-man's land into German and Austrian controlled territory.[56] Also in January 1915 the Russian viceroy of the Caucasus ordered the deportation of Russian-subject Muslims, accusing them of spying for or aiding Ottoman troops. A total of over ten thousand Muslims were deported, including over five thousand to an internment camp established on an uninhabited island in the Caspian Sea, and the rest to interior Russian provinces.[57]

Large-scale deportations by the tsarist government during the First World War lowered barriers to subsequent use of this form of excisionary violence. Not only were such actions legitimated as security measures, but they became part of the lived experience of both their victims and their perpetrators. Once established as a government practice, and more specifically as a form of social prophylaxis, deportations and internments could more readily be deployed by subsequent military and political leaders, either to protect national security or to promote an ideological agenda. The deportation of minority groups also reinforced, however unfairly, the assumption of military statisticians that the population could be categorized by ethnicity as a measure of political loyalty and social worth. In fact some Russian leaders worried about the effect deportees would have on the interior provinces to which they were deported. In 1915, commander of the Petrograd Military District, M. D. Bonch-Bruevich, subsequently a leader of the Red Army, warned that "purely Russian provinces are being completely defiled by elements hostile to us," and he went on to suggest that deportees be registered "in order to liquidate without a trace this entire alien element at the end of the war."[58]

The most extreme case of excisionary violence during the First World War took place in the Ottoman Empire. On the eve of the war, the Ottoman government deported 200,000 Greek subjects from coastal areas as a security measure. Then in the spring of 1915 it began to deport Armenian subjects from eastern Anatolia as the beginning of what was to become the Armenian genocide.[59] There had been discussion of ethnic deportations prior to the war by the Committee of Union and Progress, which had come to dominate the Ottoman government. Since 1909, the radical

56. Sanborn, *Drafting the Russian Nation,* 119–21; Lohr, *Nationalizing the Russian Empire,* 137–39.

57. Lohr, *Nationalizing the Russian Empire,* 151–52.

58. As quoted in ibid., 155.

59. Norman M. Naimark, *Fires of Hatred: Ethnic Cleansing in Twentieth-Century Europe* (Cambridge, Mass., 2001), 27.

wing of the committee had discussed the "final solution to the Armenian problem," including deportations and the achievement of ethnic homogeneity. In February 1914 the committee had convened secret meetings to plan the removal of "non-Turkish population centers." Following the Russian repulse of the Turkish offensive in the early months of the war, the Ottoman government issued a provisional law in May 1915 that granted military commanders the power "in case of military necessity, or when spying or treason are suspected, to remove inhabitants individually or en masse from villages or cities and settle them in other areas." Using this law, Turkish officers began the deportation of Armenians to concentration camps in the Syrian desert. Along the way, army units and Kurdish bands slaughtered Armenians, and of those who arrived at their destination a high percentage died in concentration camps.[60]

Deportations themselves were not new to the Ottoman Empire, which had practiced them since the sixteenth century, but previous deportations had as their intention the more effective enslavement of a segment of the population, not its annihilation. The deportation of Armenians during the First World War, a massive military and bureaucratic operation, was conceived as part of a total war strategy. Turkish leaders followed an annihilationist ethic they borrowed from Prussian military doctrine, and they understood deportation as a means to more effectively exterminate the Armenians.[61]

Genocide and mass exterminatory violence are generally believed to be the product of ideology, and in particular of utopian ideologies such as Nazism or Soviet communism that included claims of history making. But as Isabel Hull points out, whole peoples have been destroyed in the absence of any grand ideological designs. Genocide can occur as a "byproduct of institutional routines and organizational dynamics as they operate during wartime and generate 'final solutions' to all sorts of perceived problems." She concludes that "the ends, the 'final solutions,' were in fact expectations and habits that resulted from the means itself, violence, and from the institutional measures taken to wield or control it."[62] Ideological goals, of course, could be attached to practices of state violence, as I will discuss below. But rather than seeing state violence as emanating from

60. Hull, *Absolute Destruction*, 263, 271–77.

61. James J. Reid, "Total War, the Annihilation Ethic, and the Armenian Genocide, 1870–1918," *The Armenian Genocide: History, Politics, Ethics*, ed. Richard G. Hovannisian (New York, 1992), 41–44.

62. Hull, *Absolute Destruction*, 2. Hull's study focuses not only on the Armenian genocide, but on German occupation policies during the First World War and on the German suppression of the Herero uprising in Southwest Africa in 1904.

ideology, it is more accurate to see practices of state violence established prior to and during the First World War, and subsequently ideologized and wielded to aims of social transformation.

The Russian Civil War and the 1920s

If the First World War saw the blurring of boundaries between soldiers and civilians, then this merging of the military and civilian spheres became even more pronounced during the Russian Civil War. In many cases, the distinction between combatants and civilians vanished entirely, as both Red and White commanders applied extensive coercion against whomever they saw as enemies. Indeed the battle lines themselves were often far from clear, and beyond the military struggle with the Whites, the Bolsheviks faced the enormous task of quelling peasant revolts and anarchist uprisings throughout the country. In this context, political and military leaders resorted to social categorization and technologies of excisionary violence with greater intensity than ever.

Population politics during the First World War, including the use of social statistics and ethnic cataloguing, deportations, and internment camps, provided an important template for the state violence of the Civil War. Chronologically, one conflict virtually blended into the next, as Russian society was continuously at war from 1914 to 1921. Practices and experiences during the First World War therefore informed the actions of authorities on both sides of the Civil War. More concretely, the tsarist officer corps provided much of the leadership for both the Red and White armies. Tukhachevsky was only the most salient example of a Red Army commander who had trained at the General Staff academy and served in the imperial Russian Army. Of all tsarist officers who had fought in the First World War, 70 percent went on to fight in the Civil War—40 percent with the White armies and 30 percent with the Red Army.[63]

The ferocity of the Civil War and the sense of a life-or-death struggle that pervaded the thinking of leaders on both sides also contributed to the continuation and intensification of state violence. In the months after the October Revolution, the Bolsheviks faced a desperate fight to maintain power, and as discussed in the previous chapter, they formed the security police (Cheka) at a moment of crisis in December 1917. Initially

---

63. A. G. Kavtaradze, *Voennye spetsialisty na sluzhbe Respubliki sovetov, 1917–1920 gg.* (Moscow, 1988), 176–77.

a purely investigative force, the security police soon began to carry out arrests and summary executions.[64] While Bolshevik moderates opposed the broadening of police authority, Lenin pushed for an expansion of state violence. On August 9, 1918, he warned Nizhnii Novgorod officials that "a Whiteguardist rising is brewing," and he ordered them to execute those found possessing weapons and to carry out "mass deportations of Mensheviks and unreliable elements." The same day he telegrammed Penza officials calling for "merciless mass terror against the kulaks, priests and White Guards," and ordering that "unreliable elements [are] to be locked up in a concentration camp outside the town."[65]

M. S. Uritsky, the head of the Petrograd security police, resisted calls for state terror, but on August 30, 1918, he was assassinated.[66] This event combined with an assassination attempt against Lenin the same day convinced Bolshevik leaders that a counterrevolutionary conspiracy threatened their existence. The Soviet government promptly created special security police tribunals (*troiki*) to deal with "counterrevolutionary elements." The Commissariat of Justice protested extrajudicial sentencing and executions, but Lenin and other Bolshevik leaders overrode these concerns.[67] Dzerzhinsky, the head of the security police, drafted an "Appeal to the Working Classes" calling for "massive terror" against counterrevolutionaries. On September 5, the Soviet government decreed that "it is essential to protect the Soviet Republic against its class enemies by isolating these in concentration camps."[68] The security police established a network of concentration camps that held sixteen thousand people by May 1919, and more than seventy thousand by September 1921.[69] Some of these concentration camps were located on the sites of First World War prisoner-of-war camps.[70]

Concentration camps operated as a form of excisionary violence that removed suspected enemies from society and sought to neutralize opposition in this way. But Soviet authorities also employed forms of exemplary

64. George Leggett, *The Cheka: Lenin's Political Police* (New York, 1986), 18, 32.

65. Leggett, *Cheka*, 103.

66. Alexander Rabinowitch, *The Bolsheviks in Power: The First Year of Soviet Rule in Petrograd* (Bloomington, 2007), 317.

67. Rabinowitch, *Bolsheviks in Power*, 331–32; Leggett, *Cheka*, 47, 59.

68. Leggett, *Cheka*, 109–10.

69. Werth, "A State against Its People," 80. The latter figure does not include the 50,000 inmates of the concentration camps in Tambov Province during the peasant revolt there in 1921.

70. Anne Applebaum, *Gulag: A History* (New York, 2003), xxxiii.

violence, such as the burning of villages, hostage taking, and public executions. In their own words these forms of exemplary violence constituted the "Red Terror," intended literally to terrify opponents and frighten them into submission. Martin Latsis, a leader of the security police, justified terror in the following terms: "One must not only destroy the active forces of the enemy, but also demonstrate that anyone who raises a hand in protest against class war will die by the sword. These are the laws the bourgeoisie itself drew up in civil wars to oppress the proletariat."[71]

Lest these instances of state violence be interpreted as manifestations of Bolshevik ideology or fanaticism, it is important to point out that the Whites used very similar methods during the Civil War. They too carried out summary executions, incarcerated suspected enemies, and burned down villages. Even the Greens—insurgent peasant groups who rejected both Red and White authority—established tribunals ("people's courts"), punitive detachments, and mandatory labor conscription.[72] The Russian Civil War thus witnessed an intensification of state practices of excisionary and exemplary violence, as well as social and ethnic cataloguing to determine the targets of such violence.

Although the forms of state violence practiced by all sides in the Civil War were remarkably similar, the targets of such violence were different. Writing in *Red Terror*, the official journal of the Soviet security police, Latsis declared in November 1918, "We are not waging a war against individual persons. We are exterminating the bourgeoisie as a class."[73] Lenin actually disagreed with this position. While he too distrusted "bourgeois specialists," he sought to protect them in the belief that their expertise was needed to build socialism. But even though this statement was too extreme for Lenin, it reflected the political-sociological template on which he and other Bolshevik leaders operated. They saw the Civil War as a class war, in which workers and poor peasants were their supporters while merchants and kulaks were their opponents. In the same way that tsarist military statisticians had categorized ethnic groups within the population according to their political loyalty, the Bolsheviks categorized sociological groups as friends or foes.

Bolshevik leaders also used other criteria for social-political typing, as did the White armies as well. Cossacks, who had held a privileged place in

71. As quoted in Werth, "A State against Its People," 74.
72. Peter Holquist, *Making War, Forging Revolution: Russia's Continuum of Crisis, 1914–1921* (Cambridge, Mass., 2002), 204–5.
73. As quoted in Leggett, *Cheka*, 114.

the tsarist social order, were seen during the Civil War as the enemies of the Bolsheviks and as the allies of the Whites. When the Red Army occupied the Don region in the spring of 1919, the Soviet government decreed a policy of "decossackization," which in its most virulent form included the "total extirpation" of the Cossack elite. Commissars in the region placed Cossacks in three categories—rich, middle, and poor—the first of which (more than 20 percent of the population in some regions) were to be exterminated on the orders of military tribunals. The Soviet government also planned a colonization program intended to dilute the Cossack "element" with "peasant elements from Central Russia" as a means to secure the Don region.[74]

Within a few months the Soviet government moderated its policies, and rather than targeting Cossacks as a group, it sought to punish only those who had fought with the Whites. In 1920 it ordered that Cossacks who had served as officers in anti-Soviet armies be sent to concentration camps. In practice, some local authorities incarcerated all Cossacks regardless of their actions in the Civil War, but officially the Soviet government had abandoned its policy of decossackization.[75] Soviet leaders continued to view Cossacks with suspicion nonetheless, and in October 1920 in the north Caucasus the Politburo ordered the expulsion of thousands of Cossack families and the settlement of "mountaineers" in their place. As Peter Holquist has pointed out, Soviet leaders in implementing this policy were using the same categories as had tsarist officials, only in reverse. Whereas tsarist officers had deported indigenous peoples and established Cossack settlements in order to secure the Caucasus, Soviet authorities did the opposite. Both assumed that political loyalty could be gauged by ethnic or social categories.[76]

At the close of the Civil War, the Soviet government and Red Army faced widespread peasant revolts, including a large scale uprising in Tambov Province led by Aleksandr Antonov. At its peak in late 1920, Antonov's army numbered more than fifty thousand and controlled the entire province with the exception of a few urban centers. General Tukhachevsky, in charge of crushing the revolt, adopted extreme measures, including the use of poison gas against "bandits" hiding in the forest and the deportation of families and in some cases entire villages suspected of aiding the insurgents. In suppressing the revolt, Soviet authorities carried

74. Peter Holquist, "'Conduct Merciless Mass Terror': Decossackization on the Don, 1919," *Cahiers du monde russe* 38: 1–2 (January–June 1997), 131–35.
75. Holquist, *Making War*, 201.
76. Holquist, "To Count," 129.

out summary executions of 15,000 people and imprisoned or deported an additional 100,000.[77]

Suppression of the Antonov revolt and similar peasant unrest elsewhere in 1920–21 marked an important step in the development of Soviet practices of state violence, and of a specific conception of the enemy not as political opponents but as "bandits." Given that the Civil War had been a conflict without clear battle lines, leaders on both sides had used violence to assert political control over territory and civilian populations. But prior to 1920, the Bolsheviks had normally labeled the foe "White Guards," "class enemies," or in the case of rival socialist parties, as "Mensheviks," "SRs," and so forth. The use of the term *bandits* reflected the Bolsheviks' new understanding of peasant insurgency not as political opposition but as criminal deviance and rebellious lawlessness, in turn justifying extraordinary measures.

In the mid-1920s, Tukhachevsky wrote a series of articles that summarized the lessons he learned suppressing peasant revolts. He argued that anti-insurgency operations should focus on the entire population rather than on individuals, and that segments of the population deemed unreliable should be physically removed from the region. In terms of the methods of removal, he recommended "the deportation of bandits' families who are hiding their members.... If deportation cannot be organized immediately, then one should establish a wide set of concentration camps." He concluded that if "the cleansing of the population" proceeded in tandem with military operations against insurgent bands, then "the bands will be exterminated either on the fields of battle, or will be extracted from their territorial regions during cleansing."[78] Thus for Tukhachevsky, the former tsarist officer and Civil War commander, the key to establishing Soviet control over a region was "to cleanse" the population, and the techniques for doing so were deportations and concentration camps.

Red Army commanders and Party leaders were not the only ones whose thinking and behavior were shaped by their experiences during the Civil War. An entire cadre of Party officials, military officers, government administrators, and security police agents carried out deportations, incarcerations, and summary executions during this period of total warfare.

77. Werth, "A State against Its People," 110–17; Holquist, "To Count," 131. See also V. P. Danilov, ed., *Antonovshchina: Dokumenty i materialy* (Tambov, 1994); Erik C. Landis, *Bandits and Partisans: The Antonov Movement in the Russian Civil War* (Pittsburgh, 2008).

78. M. Tukhachevskii, "Bor'ba s kontrrevoliutsionnymi vosstaniiami," *Voina i revoliutsiia* 6 (1926): 6, 9; 7 (1926): 11–13, as cited in Holquist, "To Count," 131.

These practices would continue to inform their behavior, including their readiness to employ state violence, in the years ahead.[79] In future periods of crisis and mobilization, and in particular during collectivization, Party leaders would enact similar policies that would be carried out by some of the same government administrators, security police officers, and Red Army veterans who had perpetrated state violence during the Civil War.[80]

The era of the New Economic Policy is often seen as a time of political moderation and limited state violence. Indeed the end of grain requisitioning and the introduction of a limited market economy did much to placate the peasantry and defuse popular unrest. But to characterize the 1920s in the Soviet Union as a period of relative tranquility would be to overlook events on the country's periphery. From 1923 to 1927, the Soviet government undertook large-scale military operations in the Caucasus and Central Asia in order to consolidate control over these regions. Both Red Army units and security police troops carried out pacification programs that included summary executions, incarcerations, and deportations. These campaigns in fact were modeled after the anti-insurgency operations carried out by Tukhachevsky in Tambov Province at the end of the Civil War. For example, a 1925 military operation in the North Caucasus employed more than seven thousand troops backed by artillery and aircraft to quash unrest in the Chechen Autonomous Republic. Soviet forces shelled more than a hundred villages in pursuit of their goal—"the extraction of the bandit element"—and the operational summary reported that "more than 300 persons of the bandit-element were extracted."[81] On a smaller scale Soviet authorities in Siberia conducted a campaign in 1926–27 against "bandits" and those who aided them. The "most incorrigible" of these were arrested and either shot or incarcerated in concentration camps.[82]

Despite the Red Army's conquest of Central Asia in 1920, rebellions against Soviet rule continued throughout much of the decade.[83] Mikhail

79. On the glorification of violence during the Civil War and its legacy, see Sanborn, *Drafting the Russian Nation*, 175–76.

80. See Stephen G. Wheatcroft, "Agency and Terror: Evdokimov and Mass Killing in Stalin's Great Terror," *Australian Journal of Politics and History* 53 1 (2007): 20–43.

81. Holquist, "To Count," 111. On the Soviet government's mass deportations in Azerbaijan amidst interethnic conflict in the 1920s, see Jörg Baberowski, *Der Feind ist überall: Stalinismus im Kaukasus* (Munich, 2003), 15–19.

82. PP OGPU Sibkraia Zakovskii, "Dokladnaia zapiska tov. Syrtsovy i Eikhe," Shishkin Collection, box 3, Hoover Archives.

83. Werth, "A State against Its People," 138–40. The drawing of borders in Central Asia sparked widespread ethnic conflict and expulsions; Terry Martin, *The Affirmative Action Empire: Nations and Nationalism in the Soviet Union, 1923–1939* (Ithaca, 2001),

Frunze, the commander who led the conquest, outlined tactics that Red Army officers would use to suppress rebel groups (the *Basmachi*). Aiming for the "complete annihilation" of the Basmachi, Frunze stressed the need to isolate them from the local population. He developed "flying columns" of cavalry and a network of forts to pursue the rebels and cut them off from supplies.[84] Frunze also emphasized political education to win over the local population and erode support for the Basmachi. Continued by Frunze's successors, these tactics proved successful over the next several years and by 1926, rebel groups had either been annihilated or had fled to Afghanistan.[85]

The continued deployment of these methods of state violence on the country's periphery also included the perpetuation of Civil War practices of extrajudicial sentencing and executions. The abolition of the Cheka in 1922 entailed a reorganization of the security police to refocus its work on investigating rather than sentencing, but the security police retained the authority to sentence and execute prisoners in regions on the periphery considered dangerous by Soviet leaders. In the North Caucasus, for example, specially appointed security police officials (Permanent Plenipotentiaries of the OGPU) were granted martial law authority. Security police leaders, including Efim Evdokimov and Mikhail Frinovskii, oversaw several thousand extrajudicial executions of North Caucasus "rebels" in the second half of the 1920s. Evdokimov went on to play central roles organizing the Shakhty trial, dekulakization tribunals, and the mass operations of 1937–38, and Frinovskii became Nikolai Ezhov's deputy in 1937 and was charged with overseeing the mass operations.[86] Thus there was significant continuity from the Civil War era to the 1930s both in terms of repressive practices and of security police personnel.

Also during the 1920s, the Soviet government institutionalized the labor camp system. As discussed above, Soviet leaders first created concentration camps in 1918 to isolate "White guards" and other enemies. By

---

59–74. Moreover, the 1927 unveiling campaign in Uzbekistan caused violent unrest, to which the Soviet government responded with arrests and military force; Douglas Northrop, *Veiled Empire: Gender and Power in Stalinist Central Asia* (Ithaca, 2004), 139–47.

84. Alexander Marshall, "Turkfront: Frunze and the Development of Soviet Counter-Insurgency in Central Asia," *Central Asia: Aspects of Transition*, ed. Tom Everett-Heath (London, 2003), 11. Marshall speculates that Frunze borrowed these techniques from British tactics in the Boer War. He also endorses Frunze's claim to be the true "Father of Modern Soviet Counter-Insurgency" over the more commonly named Tukhachevsky (see 20).

85. Marshall, "Turkfront," 11–20.

86. Wheatcroft, "Agency and Terror," 23, 27–28, 32.

April 1919 concentration camps assumed a new form and function as the Soviet government established forced labor camps under the administration of the Commissariat of Internal Affairs. Dzerzhinsky advocated the use of labor camps to coerce "those unable to work without compulsion" to perform socially useful labor.[87] Throughout the Civil War the primary function of concentration camps continued to be the incarceration of enemies, but their use for forced labor set an important precedent.

Related to the issue of forced labor in the camps was reeducation. By the end of the Civil War, Soviet officials had already begun to tout labor camps as a means to reeducate class enemies and social deviants. Labor was seen as transformative—a means to alter the bourgeoisie's relationship to the means of production and hence to instill in them a proletarian consciousness. To assist in this process, labor camp administrators created reading rooms and educational programs. In 1921 the head of the Tambov camp proclaimed,

> In the concentration camp, reeducation proceeds on a broad basis. The bandits themselves have come to recognize...what Soviet power means and what it will strive for. Political enlightenment work is carried out. Discussion circles have been organized....In the concentration camp we have over two thousand prisoners. Every day in the [camp] library there are up to one hundred of them reading.

The camp administrator went on to admit that some "bandits" might not respond to political enlightenment and would have to be executed, but he contended that most prisoners could be reeducated and released as "conscious" individuals.[88] Subsequent Soviet labor camps also maintained libraries and political enlightenment programs which, although chronically underfunded, had as their aim the reeducation of prisoners and their ultimate reintegration into society.[89] At the same time, a tension persisted between those authorities who approached labor camps as a tool for reeducation and those who were interested first and foremost in utilizing prisoners' labor. Already in the early 1920s, some Soviet officials, includ-

87. Leggett, *Cheka*, 176–79.

88. "'Sfotografirovannye rechi': Govoriat uchastniki likvidatsii antonovshchiny," *Otechestvennye arkhivy* 2 (1996): 65.

89. See Steven A. Barnes, *Death and Redemption: The Gulag and the Shaping of Soviet Society* (Princeton, 2011). The Solovetskii labor camp had a library with 30,000 books; Applebaum, *Gulag*, 26. See also Iurii Brodskii, *Solovki: 20 let osobogo naznachenii* (Moscow, 2002).

ing Dzerzhinsky, advocated using forced labor as a means to get workers for economic projects in remote areas.[90]

In 1922 the Soviet government decreed that the security police establish a large labor camp complex on the Solovetskii islands in the White Sea near Arkhangelsk. The first prisoners arrived the following summer, and by 1925 their number had grown to six thousand. The Solovetskii camp would become a model for the enormous Gulag prison camp system established in the 1930s. Prisoners were forced to perform hard labor, initially as a tool of reeducation, though beginning in 1926 as a source of revenue for the state. In that year, camp administrators set up contracts with state enterprises primarily for the production of timber. As a result the Solovetskii camp expanded geographically, as inmates were forced to log the forests of the region.[91]

The respective roles of labor camps as sites of reeducation and as means of exploiting prisoners' labor remained in tension throughout the remainder of the 1920s and into the 1930s. Despite their pronouncements about the reeducation of class enemies, labor camp administrators clearly prioritized meeting production quotas regardless of the suffering inflicted on their prisoners.[92] Ideologically, Soviet penal specialists reconciled the dual function of labor camps. In 1929 Evsei Shirvindt, chief of the prison agency of the security police, declared that labor camp inmates' participation in the First Five-Year Plan would help them recognize the importance of their labor to society and hence help them develop a new consciousness.[93] Theorist I. L. Averbakh subsequently elaborated on these ideas in his monograph, *From Crime to Labor*. He advocated the use of penal labor on high-profile socialist construction projects, such as the White Sea Canal, because work on these projects "gives each inmate the possibility to feel the full political resonance of his own personal labor as part of an enormous whole."[94] After completion of the White Sea Canal, roughly 12,500 of the best inmate workers were deemed fully reformed and re-

90. G. M. Ivanova, *Labor Camp Socialism: The Gulag in the Soviet Totalitarian System* (Armonk, N.Y., 2000), 186.

91. Werth, "A State against Its People," 136–38; Applebaum, *Gulag*, 20–22.

92. Nick Baron, "Conflict and Complicity: The Expansion of the Karelian Gulag, 1923–1933," *Cahiers du monde russe* 42/2-3-4, 639.

93. Michael Jakobson, *Origins of the Gulag: The Soviet Prison Camp System 1917–1934* (Lexington, 1993), 141.

94. I. L. Averbakh, *Ot prestupleniia k trudu* (Moscow, 1936), 24. See also Maxim Gorky et al., *Belomor: An Account of the Construction of the New Canal Between the White Sea and the Baltic Sea* (New York, 1935).

leased, because through their labor they had demonstrated their commitment to socialism.[95]

Here then we see concentration camps—a form of state violence from colonial warfare and the First World War—retaining a similar form but gaining a new meaning under the Soviet government. Soviet criminologists heralded the transformative effect of manual labor and the significance of forcing everyone to contribute to the building of socialism. The idea of labor as redemptive was itself not specifically Soviet or even Marxist—French penal reformers in the nineteenth century, for example, had promoted agricultural prison colonies in the interior of France as sites where convicts would make an economic contribution to society but would also attain spiritual redemption through labor.[96] In the Soviet context, forced labor acquired special significance for the "parasitic classes" who previously had allegedly exploited others' labor. For them, forced labor provided a means to transform their consciousness and to instill a sense of proletarian identity that would allow them to transcend their petty, selfish instincts and join the socialist collective.

To put it more broadly, concentration camps under the Soviet government acquired a new function. Whereas previously governments had used concentration camps during colonial conquest and wartime, Soviet authorities employed concentration camps during peacetime, and they did so not just to contain perceived threats but to reshape society. While the practice of isolating segments of the population in concentration camps had its roots in colonial warfare and the First World War, the idea of applying this technique to reeducate an entire social class was something new. Soviet leaders thus institutionalized wartime practices and applied them to a peacetime program of social transformation.

The Bolsheviks, invoking a revolutionary mandate, were fully prepared to use state violence to refashion society. But their agenda of social transformation should be placed in the wider context of ideas on social renovation circulating among intellectuals before and after the Revolution. As discussed above, liberal professionals in the late imperial period had prescribed the removal of habitual criminals and social deviants to protect the overall health of society. In the 1920s, psychologists and criminologists continued to delineate categories of social deviance and propose programs

95. Jakobson, *Origins of the Gulag*, 141. On libraries and political enlightenment departments for the White Sea Canal project, see *Gulag v Karelii, 1930–1941: Sbornik dokumentov i materialov* (Petrozavodsk, 1992).
96. Toth, *Beyond Papillon*, 4–7.

of social excision and coercive rehabilitation.[97] While Soviet leaders saw class struggle as central to the victory of socialism, they did not have a clear program for dealing with "bourgeois remnants" following the Revolution. As Daniel Beer has demonstrated, it was here that the disciplines of criminology and psychiatry provided a framework for designating "class aliens" as deviants who might infect the new social order if not removed and isolated. Beer calls the meshing of the biomedical sciences with Soviet Marxism "enabling in the sense that it articulated and sanctioned the excisionary means to combat [the remnants of the old order]."[98]

Among the specialists Beer cites is Vladimir Osipov, professor of psychiatry at Kazan University and subsequently at the Military Medical Academy in Leningrad. In the 1920s, Osipov applauded the Soviet legal system's "biosocial perspective" that entailed criminal punishment focused not on retribution but rather on "social defense [*sotsial'naia zashchita*] from harmful and dangerous antisocial elements."[99] Criminologist G. N. Udal'tsov similarly emphasized "social danger" and "social defense" in declaring that "people who manifest anti-social reactions and are therefore the enemies of society should be isolated with the aim of coercively healing or reeducating them."[100] Timofei Segalov, another criminologist, called for "prophylactic" measures to secure "the life and work of the healthy by means of isolating the sick, by means of filtering out those who have not adapted to particular labor processes."[101] While liberal professionals never advocated mass deportations or anything like it, their discourse on deviance and social renovation nonetheless legitimated the idea of removing certain individuals in order to purify society as a whole. This mode of thought could have resulted in far more benign policies, and hence should not be seen as a direct cause of state repression, but it nonetheless contributed to the intellectual climate that sanctioned Soviet leaders' use of excisionary violence.

97. On the origins and institutions of Soviet criminology, see Sharon A. Kowalsky, "Who's Responsible for Female Crime? Gender, Deviance, and the Development of Soviet Social Norms in Revolutionary Russia," *Russian Review* 62:3 (July 2003): 370–72.

98. Beer, *Renovating Russia,* 203.

99. Vladimir Osipov, "K voprosu o khuliganstve," *Khuliganstvo i prestuplenie: Sbornik statei,* ed. L. G. Orshanskii et al. (Moscow/Leningrad, 1927), 85, as quoted in Beer, *Renovating Russia,* 195.

100. G. N. Udal'tsov, "Pravonarusheniia v voiskakh s tochki zreniia patologicheskoi fiziologii," *Obozrenie psikhiatrii, nevrologii i refleksologii* 2 (1927): 132, as quoted in Beer, *Renovating Russia,* 195.

101. Timofei Segalov, "Prestupnoe khuliganstvo i khuliganskie prestupleniia," *Khuliganstvo i khuligany: Sbornik,* ed. V. N. Tolmachev (Moscow, 1929), 73–74, as quoted in Beer, *Renovating Russia,* 198.

By the end of the 1920s, Soviet authorities had repeatedly utilized excisionary violence, both during the Civil War and in consolidating control in the Caucasus and Central Asia. Practices of social excision were well-established and had been expounded on by leading Soviet military commanders such as Tukhachevsky. These practices were backed by an extensive incarceration network in the form of the corrective labor camp system. Moreover, a longstanding discourse on social renovation and the elimination of deviance legitimated the principle of physically removing those deemed harmful to the social whole. When merged with the Bolsheviks' agenda of social transformation, this excisionary impulse targeted those seen as unwilling or unable to adapt to the new order. All of these factors, while not direct causes, provided the necessary preconditions for Stalinist state violence of the 1930s.

Collectivization and Passportization

Collectivization represented the Party leadership's massive and violent attempt to transform the Soviet peasantry through the abolition of private agriculture and the establishment of state-controlled collective farms. That it coincided with the Soviet industrialization drive and the establishment of a planned economy demonstrates that it was part of an overall attempt to eliminate capitalism and move the country toward socialism. The process of collectivization was multifaceted and involved not only economic change but the destruction of rural elites, an assault on peasant religiosity and traditional culture, and an effort to transform not only the livelihood but the mentality of the peasantry. My focus here will be on how and why the Soviet government employed large-scale state violence, with particular attention to dekulakization—the dispossession and/or deportation of several million peasants labeled kulaks.

Collectivization suited both the ideological inclinations and practical needs of Party leaders. The elimination of private agriculture meant the abolition of capitalism in the countryside, and the establishment of state-run collective farms gave the government control over grain and other agricultural resources, which in turn would help pay for industrialization.[102] But Party leaders' decision to collectivize agriculture does not

---

102. On the decision to pursue wholesale collectivization, see R. W. Davies, *The Socialist Offensive: The Collectivization of Soviet Agriculture, 1929–1930* (Cambridge, Mass., 1980), 399–408.

explain how they proceeded with collectivization. Party officials could have collectivized agriculture gradually through a series of penalties and incentives to induce peasants to join collective farms. Instead they carried out collectivization extremely rapidly in the style of a military campaign that included massive coercion. Even more striking are the particular forms of coercion they used. Party leaders did not stop at forcing peasants to join collective farms. Instead they deployed specific forms of violence—dispossessions, deportations, and even executions—to physically eliminate "kulaks" from the village. Collectivization, then, was carried out via excisionary violence, the forcible removal of an entire social category of the population.

In a December 1929 speech, Stalin announced the policy of "liquidation of the kulaks as a class." He stated, "Dekulakization represents a component part of the formation and development of collective farms. Therefore it is absurd and frivolous to expatiate now about dekulakization. When a head has been cut off, no one cries over the hairs."[103] Already in the summer and fall of 1929 several regional Party committees had taken it on themselves to dispossess and exile groups of kulaks as part of their efforts to collectivize agriculture.[104] Following Stalin's speech, this policy became a central part of the collectivization drive. On January 11, 1930, Genrikh Iagoda as de facto head of the security police sent a memo to his subordinates ordering the removal of "kulak elements" from the countryside, and warning that if not dealt with decisively the kulaks would instigate a series of uprisings against collectivization.[105] Iagoda subsequently issued a directive to all regional security police chiefs instructing them to submit estimates of the number of kulaks liable to dekulakization in their areas. Based on the figures he received, Iagoda two weeks later issued dekulakization quotas for each region.[106] He also established, with the aid of Evdokimov, a network of extrajudicial tribunals (*troiki*) to handle the sentencing and exile or execution of kulaks.[107]

103. Iosif V. Stalin, *Sochineniia*, vol. 12 (Moscow, 1952), 170.

104. Viola, *Unknown Gulag*, 19.

105. V. Danilov, R. T. Manning, and L. Viola, eds., *Tragediia sovetskoi derevni: Kollektivizatsiia i raskulachivanie. Dokumenty i materialy, 1927–1939*, 5 vols. (Moscow, 1999–2006), vol. 2, 103–4.

106. N. Ivnitskii, *Kollektivizatsiia i raskulachivanie* (Moscow, 1994), 102–10; Nicolas Werth, "The Mechanism of a Mass Crime: The Great Terror in the Soviet Union 1937–1938," *The Specter of Genocide: Mass Murder in Historical Perspective*, ed. Robert Gellately and Ben Kiernan (New York, 2003), 225–26.

107. Wheatcroft, "Agency and Terror," 32.

Fig. 14. Soviet election poster, 1920s. "Elect poor and middle peasants to the rural soviets. Throw kulaks out on their ears!" Poster identification number RU/SU 1337, Poster Collection, Hoover Institution Archives.

On January 30, 1930, the Politburo approved a resolution, "On Measures for the Elimination of Kulak Households in Districts of Complete Collectivization." The resolution classified kulaks in the following three categories: (1) "counterrevolutionary activists," who were to be fully dispossessed and arrested by the security police; (2) "remaining elements of kulak activists," who were to be dispossessed of all but personal items and deported; (3) all remaining kulaks, who were to be dispossessed only of their means of production and resettled on new land beyond the boundary of the collective farm. The control figure for the first category was 60,000 people, all of whom were to be incarcerated in concentration camps or, in the case of particularly dangerous individuals, executed. The projected number for the second category was 150,000 families slated for deportation to the Northern Territory, Siberia, the Urals, and Kazakhstan.[108]

The actual process of collectivization and dekulakization was extremely violent and chaotic. While the security police handled the arrest of first-category kulaks and deportation of second-category kulaks, a range of plenipotentiaries—local activists, committees of poor peasants, brigades of urban workers—played a leading role in the labeling and dispossession of kulaks. In many cases, expropriations assumed the form of drunken looting as collectivizers consumed alcohol found in kulaks' homes and ripped shirts off their backs.[109] The designation of kulaks was itself quite arbitrary. While authorities in Moscow sought to define, categorize, and enumerate kulaks with great precision, local activists often had no clear idea which peasants were kulaks. Frequently any peasant who resisted collectivization was labeled a kulak, and even Party reports acknowledged that some middle peasants had been incorrectly labeled kulaks and dispossessed.[110] The security police themselves greatly exceeded Politburo quotas. From January through September 1930, they arrested 283,717 people, of whom 124,889 were kulaks (the remainder were clergy, former landlords, and so forth). They also executed around 30,000 people. The total number of kulaks deported in 1930 was more than half a million people, with the total for 1930 and 1931 reaching between 1.6 million and 1.8 million people.[111]

108. Davies, *Socialist Offensive*, 203–4; Viola, *Unknown Gulag*, 22–23.

109. GARF f. 5475, op. 13, d. 426, ll. 12–14; *Ob "edinennaia IV Moskovskaia oblastnaia i III gorodskaia konferentsiia VKP(b)* (Moscow, 1934), 51; "Kollektivizatsiia: Istoki, sushchnost', posledstviia: Beseda za 'kruglym stolom,'" *Istoriia SSSR* 3 (1989): 43.

110. RGASPI f. 17, op. 114, d. 314, l. 50.

111. R. W. Davies and S. G. Wheatcroft, *The Years of Hunger* (New York, 2004), 492; Viola, *Unknown Gulag*, 30–32.

Dekulakization, then, was not a carefully controlled police operation. At the same time, it was predicated on sociological classification and technologies of social excision. It reflected a conviction that peasants could be categorized by class, and it relied on preexisting practices of deportation and incarceration. Moreover, dekulakization corresponded to many of the assumptions and practices of Soviet excisionary violence as it had developed during the Civil War and 1920s. Party leaders, and Iagoda in particular, assumed that kulaks left in the villages would sabotage collective farms and instigate uprisings. Local Party officials shared this mentality, as shown by the fact that even before Stalin called for the liquidation of the kulaks as a class, they had begun to dispossess and exile kulaks. Party leaders and Party officials alike viewed the task of establishing a new order in the countryside as inextricably linked with the removal of "socially alien elements." As a 1931 security police memorandum stated, the goal of deportations was "to cleanse [the region] totally of kulaks."[112]

Collectivization coincided with a reorganization of the Soviet penal detention system. In June 1929 the Politburo had decided to create a network of self-supporting prison camps, now renamed corrective-labor camps. These camps were placed under the control of the Main Administration of Corrective-Labor Camps (Glavnoe upravlenie ispravitel'no-trudovykh lagerei, or GULag) of the security police. Similar to the preexisting Solovetskii Camp of Special Designation, which also came under the Gulag administration, these new labor camps were intended to hold a total of fifty thousand inmates and were to be located in remote regions "to develop mineral deposits using convict labor." Had it not been for collectivization, the creation of a network of labor camps might have become just another effort to reorganize the penal system, but with thousands of arrests during dekulakization, the Gulag mushroomed into an enormous complex of labor camps.[113]

In addition to the thousands of first-category kulaks arrested and sent to labor camps, more than 1.5 million second-category kulaks were deported from their native regions. Such massive deportations raised the problem of where to relocate these people. It was only in January 1930, with collectivization already underway, that Soviet leaders seriously contemplated the issue. Iagoda developed the idea of special settlements, what he ini-

---

112. N. Ia. Gushchin, *"Raskulachivanie" v Sibiri (1928–1934)* (Novosibirsk, 1996), 111–12.

113. Oleg Khlevniuk, *The History of the Gulag: From Collectivization to the Great Terror,* trans. Vadim A. Staklo (New Haven, 2004), 9.

tially termed "colonization villages," composed of two hundred to three hundred households and located in remote regions. He argued that kulaks deported to these settlements could support themselves through farming while simultaneously providing a permanent labor force in forestry, mining, and other industries.[114] Thus the process of physically removing kulaks from the countryside was also linked to the supply of (forced) labor for resource extraction in remote regions.

At the end of January the Soviet government established commissions to decide the precise locations in the far north, Siberia, the Urals, and Kazakhstan to which deported kulaks were to be sent. Subsequent government committees produced a huge number of plans, statistical reports, graphs, and budgets for the special settlements. Some even drew up detailed blueprints, with layouts and housing designed to instill a collectivist consciousness. In the minds of Moscow bureaucrats the special settlements seemed to offer the opportunity to create a new environment where petty bourgeois classes could be refashioned into model proletarians. But as Lynne Viola writes, this was "planning grafted onto chaos, a projection of communist visions of order onto the disorder of a reality of the regime's own making." The lack of preparation combined with the massive scale of deportations meant that hundreds of thousands of kulaks were being sent to places without adequate food or shelter. The remoteness of the settlements made shortages even more severe. Those deported suffered from exposure, starvation, outbreaks of infectious diseases, and extremely high mortality. Viola concludes that poor administration and coordination compounded "what was intrinsically a disaster in the making."[115]

As was the case with labor camps, a tension existed over the role of special settlements. Were they primarily a means to reeducate kulaks, or were they first and foremost a mechanism to supply labor for the economic development of remote regions? While most Soviet officials seemed to regard the special settlements principally as a source of labor, there were others who focused on the importance of removing "petty bourgeois elements" from society and reeducating them through hard labor. Commissar of Internal Affairs Vladimir N. Tolmachev, for example, argued that the utilization of special settlers' labor was secondary to the tasks of isolating and reeducating them.[116] The Soviet government did mandate the building of schools in special settlements with the idea that kulak youth in particu-

114. Viola, *Unknown Gulag*, 4.
115. Ibid., 57–61, 75–92 (quotations from 57, 92).
116. GARF f. 393, op. 43a, d. 1797, ll. 120–21 ob.

lar could be taught the value of socialism and reintegrated into society. In reality authorities once again lacked the personnel and resources to realize their visions. The shortage of teachers was so severe that deportees had to be hired to reeducate their own children. In theory, though, the Soviet government sought the reeducation and reintegration of former kulaks, and in 1938 it decreed that the children of special settlers on reaching the age of sixteen could leave the settlements for work or study.[117]

Collectivization and rapid industrialization created enormous social upheaval in the Soviet Union during the early 1930s. Exacerbating this upheaval was a severe famine, itself caused by collectivization and grain requisitioning, in 1932–33. With famine looming in the countryside, urban food supplies threatened, and industrial projects falling behind schedule, Party leaders in late 1932 took a series of measures in response to this economic crisis. Among the decrees they issued was one establishing an internal passport system, a system that became a means to identify and remove social aliens, and as such a central component of Soviet excisionary violence. The Politburo formulated the decree on November 15, and issued it December 27, 1932.[118]

Contrary to longstanding conventional wisdom, the primary purpose of the passport system was not to keep starving peasants from moving to cities. Instead Party leaders created it, at a moment of imminent food shortages, as an instrument to purge major cities of nonproductive people.[119] Politburo members expressly justified passportization as a way to rid Moscow, Leningrad, and other large cities of "superfluous people not involved in production or the work of institutions, as well as of kulak, criminal, and other antisocial elements hiding in the towns."[120] The decree itself required all citizens over age sixteen living in designated cities to be issued passports by the local police. "Persons not occupied in socially useful labor," "hidden kulaks," "criminals," and "other antisocial elements," were to be refused passports and expelled from the cities. Between January

117. Viola, *Unknown Gulag*, 102–3, 169. Already in 1930, Tolmachev was arguing that it would be better to release youth from the special settlements so as to remove them from the influence of their kulak parents; GARF f. 393, op. 43a, d. 1797, l. 120 ob.

118. *Sobranie zakonov i rasporiazhenii SSSR* 84 (1932), art. 516.

119. David L. Hoffmann, *Peasant Metropolis: Social Identities in Moscow, 1929–1941* (Ithaca, 1994), 52. See also Nathalie Moine, "Passeportisation, statistique des migrations et contrôle de l'identité sociale," *Cahiers du monde russe* 38:4 (October–December 1997): 587–600; Gijs Kessler, "The Passport System and State Control over Population Flows in the Soviet Union, 1932–1940," *Cahiers du monde russe* 42:2–4 (April–December 2001): 477–504.

120. As quoted in Kessler, "The Passport System," 482.

and August 1933, authorities expelled 65,904 people from Moscow and 79,261 from Leningrad.[121]

Once established, the passport system became an integral part of Soviet policing and purging. Local police departments set up passport offices that, along with regional passport centers and a security police central office, created card catalogues with a card to match every passport recipient and to record information on their previous residences, prior convictions, and so forth. Precinct police officers were supposed to gather additional information from doormen, shop personnel, waiters, and other service workers on people moving in and out of their neighborhoods, and then update card catalogues accordingly.[122] Police passport offices were also to register those without passports—kulaks and criminals—in order to identify and expel them. Between January and April 1933, police offices issued 6.6 million passports, and denied the passport applications of 265,000 people, including over 67,000 identified as former kulaks.[123] The passport system in theory provided a means to register all urban residents and expel those deemed socially harmful.

In practice the passport regime failed to operate in systematic fashion, as local police lacked the time or resources to maintain files comprehensively. Iagoda's vision of prophylactic policing based on a universal registration system was not realized, despite repeated orders to tighten the passport and residency permit systems.[124] Nonetheless, the passport system became a crucial component of mass policing operations, as the police carried out sweeps of urban areas to arrest those without passports. Often these sweeps targeted both social outcasts and class enemies—alcoholics, homeless people, petty thieves, and ex-convicts, as well as former NEPmen or kulaks who had escaped from special settlements. Police officials saw these sweeps coupled with the passport and residency permit systems as an effective way to remove dangerous segments from the urban population.[125] In Au-

121. *Sobranie zakonov i rasporiazhenii SSSR* 84 (1932), arts. 516, 517; Kessler, "The Passport System," 485.

122. GARF f. 5446, op. 15a, d. 130, l. 2.

123. V. Popov, "Pasportnaia sistema v SSSR (1932–1976)," *Sotsiologicheskie issledovaniia* 8 (1995): 11–14; Kessler, "The Passport System," 490; David R. Shearer, "Social Disorder, Mass Repression, and the NKVD during the 1930s," *Cahiers du monde russe* 42:2–4 (April–December 2001): 515; David Shearer, "Elements Near and Alien: Passportization, Policing, and Identity in the Stalinist State, 1933–1952," *Journal of Modern History* 76 (December 2004) 845.

124. GARF f. 5446, op. 150, d. 1130, l. 2.

125. David R. Shearer, *Policing Stalin's Socialism: Repressions and Social Order in the Soviet Union, 1924–1953* (New Haven, 2009), 169–80; Kessler, "The Passport System," 493.

gust 1933, Iagoda instituted special tribunals to review cases of passport violators. These tribunals, like those used during collectivization and subsequently during the mass operations, provided an extrajudicial sentencing mechanism to deport or incarcerate violators. Iagoda specified that former kulaks, people with no useful employment, and ex-convicts were to be exiled or deported to special settlements, while "criminals and other antisocial elements" were to be sent to labor camps.[126] The passport system soon became the basic method of urban policing, as the police arrested and sentenced petty criminals using passport tribunals rather than the regular court system. In addition the security police continued periodic sweeps to round up and expel former kulaks from passport regime cities, the number of which grew to thirty-seven by the mid-1930s.[127]

The Soviet passport system had some features in common with the tsarist internal passport system on which it was partially based. In fact, by the late nineteenth century systems to document identity had been developed in countries throughout Europe.[128] But internal passports did more than allow the Soviet government to keep tabs on the population and define citizenship. Both in its origins and as it evolved during the 1930s, the Soviet passport system served as a vital purging mechanism. In 1933 the Politburo ordered the security police to "establish order in the streets of Moscow and purge them of filth."[129] And police reports described socially marginal people as dirt "on the face of our cities," and exhorted authorities to make Soviet cities models of socialism by first removing the social trash from the streets and then cleansing the literal trash as well. In his 1935 report on crime, Iagoda highlighted passportization's role in cleaning up cities and making them "models of socialism."[130] As David Shearer concludes, passports were used to identify and extract groups deemed alien or harmful, and to distance them from the socialist core of the country (the major cities and industrial areas). Categorization of the population through pass-

126. GARF f. 5446, op. 150, d. 1130, l. 3; f. 9401, op. 12, d. 137, ll. 202–4.

127. Paul M. Hagenloh, "'Chekist in Essence, Chekist in Spirit': Regular and Political Police in the 1930s," *Cahiers du monde russe* 42:2–4 (April–December 2001): 469; Shearer, "Social Disorder," 521–22; Shearer, "Elements," 854.

128. See John Torpey, *The Invention of the Passport: Surveillance, Citizenship, and the State* (New York, 2000). On tsarist Russia, see Charles Steinwedel, "Making Social Groups, One Person at a Time: The Identity of Individuals by Estate, Religious Confession, and Ethnicity in Late Imperial Russia," *Documenting Individual Identity: The Development of State Practices in the Modern World*, ed. Jane Caplan and John Torpey (Princeton, 2001).

129. Hagenloh, "Chekist," 470.

130. Shearer, "Elements," 850, 855.

ports combined with the designation of passport regime areas created "a geographical mosaic of socialist and nonsocialist parts of the country. Officials could look at a map and cite statistics, as did Iagoda, to see visually the progress of constructing socialism in the country."[131] Although Party leaders continued to develop the positive aspects of building socialism (industrialization, health care, enlightenment), they increasingly emphasized social excision—the removal of "alien elements"—as an integral part of achieving socialism.

Excisionary violence, then, was central to Party leaders' attempt to transform the social order. To collectivize agriculture, they chose to "liquidate the kulaks," relying on preexisting practices of social categorization and social excision. It was an approach to socialist construction based as much on the removal of "class enemies" as on the creation of new economic structures. At the same time there was no careful plan for dekulakization, and the entire process was characterized by random dispossessions, ill-prepared deportations, and social chaos. Moreover, the labeling and dispossession of "kulaks" created a permanent mass of uprooted and stigmatized people. Party leaders responded to this crisis of their own making with new efforts at social categorization and control in the form of the internal passport system. Ultimately they launched an even more lethal campaign of state violence known as the mass operations.

The Mass Operations

Soviet state violence reached its apogee in the late 1930s. Of the 4 million sentences (including 800,000 executions) handed down by Soviet extrajudicial organs between 1921 and 1953, 1,575,000 (including 682,000 executions) were in 1937–38.[132] The number of Gulag prisoners increased from 965,000 in January 1935 to 1,930,000 by 1941, with an increase of 700,000 in 1937 alone.[133] This period was known to contemporaries as

---

131. Shearer, *Policing Stalin's Socialism*, 256.

132. Werth, "The Mechanism of a Mass Crime," 217. Werth notes that these figures do not include "non-ratified execution supplements"—people who died during preliminary investigations or under torture—and that if these were added then the estimated number of executions in 1937–1938 would rise to 800,000. See also N. Vert and S. V. Mironenko, eds., *Istoriia stalinskogo Gulaga: Konets 1920-kh—pervaia polovina 1950-kh godov. Sobranie dokumentov v 7-mi tomakh*, vol. 1: *Massovye repressii v SSSR* (Moscow, 2004).

133. Werth, "A State against Its People," 204. See also V. N. Zemskov, "Zakliuchennye v 30-e gody: Demograficheskii aspect," *Sotsiologicheskie issledovaniia* 7 (1996): 3.

the Ezhovshchina (the reign of Ezhov) and has been referred to by scholars as the "Great Terror." Both terms, however, are misnomers. Ezhovshchina implies that the state violence of this period was masterminded by Nikolai Ezhov, the head of the security police who replaced Iagoda in 1936, when in fact it was based on resolutions by the Politburo and carried out by Ezhov under Stalin's meticulous supervision.

The "Great Terror," a term popularized by Robert Conquest, implies that the purpose of the arrests and executions was to terrorize the population.[134] Such an idea fits with the totalitarian model's structural explanation for state violence, namely that the Soviet regime kept people in a state of fear and uncertainty through the random application of terror. Indeed Soviet leaders had no compunction about using terror, for they had burned villages, taken hostages, and carried out public executions during the Civil War.[135] But the state violence of the late 1930s was not random, and it was not intended to terrorize the population. The arrests and executions of the mass operations were conducted in secret, and their purpose was to eliminate enemies, not to frighten people into submission. In other words, these actions were not exemplary violence aimed at terrorizing the population. Instead they were forms of excisionary violence intended to eliminate segments of the population deemed alien or dangerous.[136]

What historians term the "Great Terror" was in fact a number of related yet discrete operations instigated by Stalin and his fellow leaders to strike down potential political opponents and fifth columnists in anticipation of the coming war.[137] Purges within the Communist Party claimed a large number of victims, including many of the "old Bolsheviks" who had been Party leaders since the Revolution. The security police also conducted

---

134. Robert Conquest, *The Great Terror* (New York, 1990).

135. On Stalin and Gorky's subsequent strictures against using the term terror, see Dariusz Tolczyk, *See No Evil: Literary Cover-ups and Discoveries of the Soviet Camp Experience* (New Haven, 1999).

136. As David Shearer writes, the purges were a terror for those victimized, and to insist on a precise label for the mass arrests and executions of 1937–1938 is not to relativize or minimize victims' suffering. See Shearer, *Policing Stalin's Socialism*, 286.

137. Sheila Fitzpatrick writes "that the events that we label 'The Great Purges' may be best understood not as a single phenomenon but as a number of related but discrete phenomena," and Nicolas Werth calls the Great Terror not a unitary process but rather "the convergence of several repressive lines." See Sheila Fitzpatrick, ed., *Stalinism: New Directions* (New York, 2000), 258; Werth, "The Mechanism of a Mass Crime," 219. See also Barry McLoughlin, "Mass Operations of the NKVD, 1937–1938," *Stalin's Terror: High Politics and Mass Repression in the Soviet Union*, ed. McLoughlin and Kevin McDermott (New York, 2003), 144.

purges of military officers, industrial leaders, particularly in the defense industry, and of government bureaucrats.[138] But the greatest number of victims in this period were not elites but common people, arrested either in the mass operations (which targeted a broad range of social and political outcasts) or in the national operations (which targeted members of diaspora national minorities, who were suspected of having ties or allegiances to foreign countries). My focus here will be on the mass operations and the national operations of 1937–38, both of which were predicated on social categorization and which relied on preexisting technologies of social excision.

To understand the character of the mass operations, we must first examine the establishment of a police monopoly over the use of state violence in the mid-1930s. During collectivization, local Party officials, urban activists, and poor peasants had played a leading role in dekulakization, and this decentralization of violence had been sanctioned by Party leaders. Beginning in 1933, Party leaders recentralized control over violence and placed it solely under the authority of the police.[139] Henceforth, campaigns to remove "anti-Soviet elements" were conducted not as movements that sought to enlist popular support, but rather as secret, controlled, police operations. Excisionary violence was no longer enacted by the military (as during the Civil War and 1920s) or by plenipotentiary groups (as during collectivization). It was now the sole domain of the security police, under the direction of Party leaders.

The Soviet police apparatus itself underwent several changes at this time. In 1930, the security police (OGPU) had gained control over the civil police (*militsiia*), as its leaders sought to create a more unified, systematic police force.[140] This reform transformed both the civil police and the security police. The civil police, previously a constable force under the jurisdiction of local government, became nationalized and politicized under the control of the security police apparatus. And the security police, previously charged with countering perceived threats to national security, became involved in combating petty crime, hooliganism, and the problem of

138. Khlevniuk, *History of the Gulag*, 142–43. In 1937 Georgii Malenkov prepared a list of over 1.5 million former Party members excluded since the early 1920s, and Stalin referred to this list at the February–March 1937 Central Committee plenum, where he warned of a "reserve" organizing force for enemies of the Soviet state; Shearer, *Policing Stalin's Socialism*, 314–15.

139. Shearer, *Policing Stalin's Socialism*, 13.

140. Hagenloh, "Chekist," 448. See also Paul Hagenloh, *Stalin's Police: Public Order and Mass Repression in the USSR, 1926–1941* (Baltimore, 2009).

homeless children.[141] This expansion of the purview of the security police meant that basic issues of public order now fell under its jurisdiction, and petty crime was increasingly treated as a security threat.

As a model of systematic policing, the leaders of the Soviet security police looked to contemporary European police forces that relied on regular contact between officers and the population in order to achieve more effective control. But this type of systematic policing required a stable population, and the Soviet industrialization and collectivization drives caused enormous social turmoil in the early 1930s.[142] Instead of methodical policing, Soviet authorities resorted to extrasystemic, extrajudicial methods of repression. As described above, periodic sweeps in conjunction with the passport system became the main form of urban policing. This approach tended to blur the distinction between social aliens and criminals, as security police officials ordered the compilation of lists of "counterrevolutionary, kulak, criminal, and other anti-Soviet elements."[143]

There were also ideological reasons that Soviet authorities increasingly conflated social aliens and criminals. Stalin and other Party leaders expected the attainment of socialism to resolve social problems. Under the limited capitalism of the New Economic Policy, Party officials had attributed crime and other social ills to the pernicious influence of capitalism. According to their line of thinking, the petty bourgeois milieu of NEPmen and kulaks spawned criminal behavior. With the abolition of the New Economic Policy, the collectivization of agriculture, and the establishment of a state-run economy, crime should have disappeared. Dekulakization had removed kulaks from villages and sent many of them to labor camps or special settlements to be reformed through hard labor. Yet far from disappearing, petty theft and other economic crimes actually increased during the 1930s (a product of the horrendous shortages triggered by the industrialization drive). Party leaders viewed the black market, speculation, and other forms of now illegal economic activity as a refusal on the part of some members of society to abide by the socialist order. In other words, they saw illegal trade and theft of state property not only as criminality but as political opposition. At the 1933 Central Committee plenum, Stalin

141. Shearer, *Policing Stalin's Socialism*, 6.
142. Peter Solomon describes how the criminal justice system, including basic legal procedures such as investigations and trials, virtually ceased functioning during collectivization. See Peter H. Solomon, *Soviet Criminal Justice under Stalin* (New York, 1996), 81–110.
143. Hagenloh, "Chekist," 467–68.

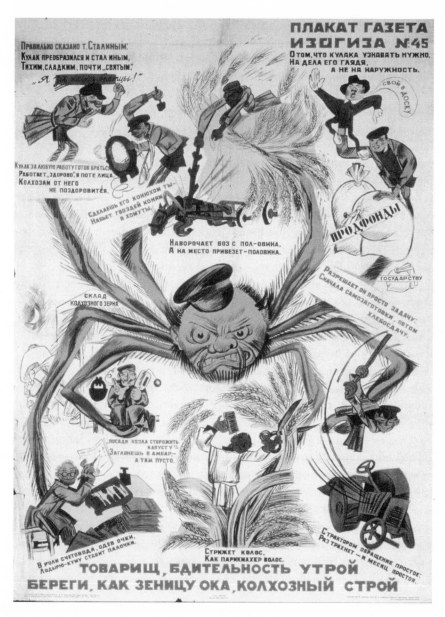

Fig. 15. Soviet poster showing kulak sabotage of collective farms, 1933. "Comrade, maintain vigilance. . . . Protect the collective farm as if it were something precious." Poster identification number RU/SU 1434, Poster Collection, Hoover Institution Archives.

stated that the theft of state or collective farm property was tantamount to "the undermining of the Soviet system."[144]

Iagoda further articulated these sentiments in a 1935 speech when he declared, "In our country—a country where the socialist order has triumphed completely, where there is no unemployment, where every citizen of the Soviet Union is presented with the complete opportunity to work and live honorably, any criminal act by its nature can be nothing other than a manifestation of class struggle." He went on to call hooligans, bandits, and robbers "counterrevolutionary."[145] The Commissariat of Justice began to prosecute cases of hooliganism more vigorously, imposing prison sentences on roughly 40 percent of those convicted, as government reports began to blame "declassified elements" and people of "petty bourgeois origin" for crime and hooliganism in cities.[146]

In this context it is not surprising that Soviet authorities began to refer to kulaks and criminals interchangeably. In fact, they assumed that most criminal activity was perpetrated by former kulaks. Party leaders were obsessed with the idea that former kulaks, having hidden their class origins, were infiltrating collective farms and industrial enterprises where they engaged in theft and sabotage. In 1933 Stalin focused on this new type of enemy—the hidden enemy—and warned that former kulaks had slipped into Soviet factories, institutions, and even the Communist Party.[147] The following year Iagoda cautioned that the "basic mass" of peasants arriving in cities on their own (that is, outside the parameters of official labor recruitment) were from "the class alien and criminal element," and he claimed that "the majority of kulaks, thieves, and other such types" already had false documents to circumvent the passport system.[148] In addition to revealing his fear of uncontrolled population movement, Iagoda's statement vividly demonstrates Party leaders' conflation of "kulaks" and "thieves."

Party leaders' belief that dekulakized peasants engaged in criminal and treasonous activities tells us more about their assumptions than about the behavior of the victims of dekulakization. However, they were not wrong to assume that many of those labeled kulaks tried to hide their

144. Stalin, *Sochineniia*, vol. 13 (Moscow, 1952), 209.

145. GARF f. 9401, op. 12, d. 135, document 119. My thanks to Paul Hagenloh for supplying me with this quotation.

146. GARF f. 8131 s.ch., op. 37, d. 48, ll. 185–86, 225; f. A-353, op. 10, d. 50, l. 24; Solomon, *Soviet Criminal Justice*, 225.

147. Stalin, *Sochineniia*, vol. 13, 207.

148. GARF f. 5446, op. 15a, d. 1175, ll. 8–9, as quoted in Shearer, "Elements," 863.

background and sought work in cities. Already in 1930 many peasants fearing dekulakization had liquidated their property and moved to cities, as numerous Party reports had noted.[149] "Third-category kulaks" who were dispossessed but not deported during dekulakization—some 2 million people—often had little choice but to flee to the cities.[150] In addition, of the 1.6 to 1.8 million people deported to special settlements in 1930 and 1931, hundreds of thousands had escaped while others had been officially rehabilitated and released by the mid-1930s.[151] Party leaders and local Soviet officials alike harbored considerable suspicion of former kulaks, in part because they feared reprisals for the violence they had perpetrated against them.[152] Dekulakization, far from resolving social tensions through the "liquidation of the kulaks as a class," had left a bitter legacy of distrust and hostility in Soviet society.

Following the "liquidation" of the bourgeois classes and the establishment of a noncapitalist economy, Party and police leaders saw themselves as entering a new era and facing a new type of enemy. Although open class warfare had ceased, remnants of the bourgeoisie engaged in quiet sabotage of the Soviet system, and this new kind of enemy required a new type of policing. In 1934 the Soviet government formed the All-Union Commissariat of Internal Affairs (Narodnyi Komissariat Vnutrennykh Del, or NKVD) to replace the OGPU. It had jurisdiction over both the civil police and the security police (now renamed the Main Administration of State Security (Glavnoe Upravlenenie Gosudarstvennoi Bezopastnosti, but often referred to simply as the NKVD).[153] As David Shearer explains, Iagoda oversaw the transformation of the police from "a weapon of revolutionary class war into an organ of public order." The resulting police structure combined the security and civil police together with carceral institutions "into a new policing empire."[154] Policing became more professionalized and state violence became even more centralized, bureaucratized, and secret. The new type of hidden enemy required systematic forms of policing,

149. RGASPI f. 17, op. 114, d. 314, l. 58; TsAOPIM f. 432, op. 1, d. 49, l. 107; f. 468, op. 1, d. 155, l. 207; f. 634, op. 1, d. 207, l. 60.

150. Hoffmann, *Peasant Metropolis*, 34–35.

151. Viola, *Unknown Gulag*, 161.

152. See, for example, local officials' vehement objections to the restoration of former kulaks' rights; GARF f. 3316, op. 40, d. 14, ll. 32–33, 56–58; d. 18, ll. 155–57; op. 41, d. 52, l. 59.

153. For further discussion, see Francesco Benvenuti, "The 'Reform' of the NKVD, 1934," *Europe-Asia Studies* 49:6 (1997): 1037–56.

154. Shearer, *Policing Stalin's Socialism*, 289.

and the NKVD relied on extensive card catalogues, which would be used during the mass operations of 1937–38 to identify and arrest "anti-Soviet elements."[155]

In the mid-1930s, Soviet authorities escalated their campaign against former kulaks and other socially marginal people.[156] In 1935, Iagoda and head of the procuracy Andrei Vyshinskii sent a directive to local police officials expanding repression against "socially harmful elements"—defined to include not only former kulaks and criminals but beggars, the unemployed, repeat offenders of the passport regime, and juveniles over age twelve caught in a criminal act.[157] This directive established extrajudicial police tribunals with the authority to sentence those convicted to five years in a labor camp. A report indicates that these police tribunals sentenced roughly 120,000 people in 1935 and another 141,000 in 1936.[158] Highlighting this campaign against "socially harmful elements," Paul Hagenloh writes that "by the mid-1930s, local police forces were conducting constant purges of their bailiwicks of marginals and criminals of all types," and he concludes that "a twisted but identifiable line of continuity in policing practices runs from the 1920s through the urban purges of 'harmful' elements in the mid-1930s up to the mass operations of 1937–38."[159]

Although longstanding practices of excisionary violence explain the method of the mass operations, we still need to consider why these mass arrests and executions occurred in 1937, and why, paradoxically, this upsurge in state violence coincided with steps toward democratization. Part of the domestic context for the mass operations was the issuance of a new constitution in 1936 and preparations for elections to the Supreme Soviet in 1937. In accordance with the purported attainment of socialism and the new economic and social structure of the country, Party leaders decided to issue a new constitution. Stalin publicly stated that in the time since the 1924 Constitution was written, the country had been transformed and a new constitution was necessary due to "the complete victory of the

155. Ibid., 8–9, 13, 351. See also David L. Hoffmann, *Stalinist Values: The Cultural Norms of Soviet Modernity* (Ithaca, 2003), 182.

156. On increasing arrests of "hooligans" by the security police, see RGASPI f. 17, op. 2, d. 597, ll. 9–12.

157. Shearer, "Social Disorder," 523–24.

158. Paul M. Hagenloh, "'Socially Harmful Elements' and the Great Terror," *Stalinism: New Directions*, ed. Sheila Fitzpatrick (New York, 2000), 292–93. See also Gabor T. Rittersporn, "Extrajudicial Repression and the Courts: Their Relationship in the 1930s," *Reforming Justice in Russia, 1864–1996: Power, Culture, and the Limits of Legal Order*, ed. Peter H. Solomon, Jr. (Armonk, N.Y., 1997), 207–27.

159. Hagenloh, "'Socially Harmful Elements,'" 287, 303.

socialist system in all spheres of the economy."[160] Commissar of Justice Nikolai Krylenko and other Soviet jurists further explained that the elimination of the exploiting classes and the establishment of the socialist order necessitated a new legal order.[161] Privately as well as publicly Party leaders stressed the attainment of socialism and the "new order of classes" as the reason for a new constitution.[162]

Whereas the 1918 and 1924 constitutions had disenfranchised "social aliens" (the former nobility, bourgeoisie, and petty bourgeoisie), the 1936 Constitution granted everyone the right to vote.[163] Party leaders' emphasis on social inclusion reflected their belief that with the era of class warfare over, all members of Soviet society could contribute to the socialist order. In his speech to the Eighth All-Union Congress of Soviets, Molotov pronounced that alien social origin no longer prevented people from loyally serving the Soviet government.[164] In keeping with their policy of social inclusiveness, Party leaders planned elections to the Supreme Soviet that would enfranchise the entire adult population. At the February-March 1937 Central Committee Plenum, Andrei Zhdanov announced that these elections would be contested elections with universal, equal, and direct suffrage, and he added that candidates could run without Party approval. And in June the Central Committee prescribed procedures for secret-ballot, multiple candidate elections.

Already during discussions of the 1936 Constitution, however, local Party officials voiced enormous concern over granting former kulaks, merchants, and priests voting rights, and they emphasized the danger these people continued to pose to the Soviet government.[165] Once election preparations were underway, local Party and security police officials began to warn

160. *Pravda,* November 26, 1936, 1–2. The Politburo first charged the Central Committee with drafting a new constitution in January 1935; RGASPI f. 17, op. 3, d. 958, l. 38.

161. N. V. Krylenko, *Stalinskaia konstitutsiia v voprosakh i otvetakh,* 2nd ed. (Moscow, 1937), 22; G. Amfiteatrov, "Proekt konstitutsii SSSR i grazhdanskii kodeks sotsialisticheskogo obshchestva," *Sovetskoe gosudarstvo* 4 (1936): 84.

162. GARF f. 3316, op. 40, d. 22, l. 4. Peter Solomon has highlighted the role of the 1936 Constitution in enhancing the legitimacy of the Soviet system in the eyes of both foreign and domestic observers; Solomon, *Soviet Criminal Justice,* 191–95.

163. *Istoriia sovetskoi konstitutsii: Sbornik dokumentov, 1917–1957* (Moscow, 1957), 85, 356–58; Ia. Berman, "Stalinskaia konstitutsiia i izbiratel'naia sistema," *Sovetskoe gosudarstvo* 5 (1936): 11; *Sovetskaia iustitsiia* 19 (1936): 6. For further discussion, see Golfo Alexopoulos, *Stalin's Outcasts: Aliens, Citizens, and the Soviet State, 1926–1936* (Ithaca, 2003).

164. *Pravda,* November 30, 1936, 2.

165. GARF f. 3316 s.ch., op. 64, d. 2005, l. 5; RGASPI f. 78, op. 1, d. 833, l. 23.

that former kulaks and priests were organizing for the elections, and that widespread peasant animosity toward the Party could mean that Communists would be voted out in favor of religious leaders.[166] One Party official in March 1937 stated, "The facts in our possession show that counterrevolutionary clergymen and sectarians are very actively preparing to submit their candidacies for the secret ballot."[167] On July 2, 1937, the same day that *Pravda* published rules for upcoming multicandidate elections to the Supreme Soviet, the Politburo ordered the security police to register all former kulaks and criminals in order to arrest those hostile to Soviet power.[168] Three months later, the Central Committee cancelled plans for multicandidate elections in favor of single-candidate elections with candidates chosen by the Party, but the effort to purge the population of "anti-Soviet elements" continued nonetheless in the form of the mass operations.[169]

Urgent warnings from local Party and police officials about the threat posed by former kulaks seemed to confirm what Stalin had cautioned at the 1933 Central Committee plenum, namely that "people from the past," (*byvshie liudi*) though too weak to openly defy Soviet power, had "wormed their way" back into Soviet society and would attempt to sabotage the system. Stalin concluded, "The destruction of classes is achieved not by the extinguishing of class struggle but by its strengthening."[170] The idea that progress toward socialism would provoke a sharpening of class struggle had long figured prominently in the thought of Party leaders, especially Stalin. Erik van Ree traces this idea to the writings of Georgii Plekhanov, who even prior to the Revolution argued that capitalists' realization that

166. Sheila Fitzpatrick, *Stalin's Peasants: Resistance and Survival in the Russian Village after Collectivization* (New York, 1994), 280–85; J. Arch Getty and Oleg V. Naumov, *The Road to Terror: Stalin and the Self-Destruction of the Bolsheviks, 1932–1939* (New Haven, 1999), 468.

167. RGASPI f. 17, op. 21, d. 2197, l. 78, as reprinted in Getty and Naumov, *Road to Terror*, 438–39.

168 J. Arch Getty, "'Excesses are not Permitted': Mass Terror and Stalinist Governance in the Late 1930s," *Russian Review* 61:1 (January 2002): 124–26. Getty concludes that Stalin gave local Party officials the authority to eliminate "dangerous elements" to ensure the election's outcome. Paul Hagenloh disputes Getty's argument, noting that contested elections were subsequently cancelled; Hagenloh, *Stalin's Police*, 285. Either way Party officials' warnings in advance of the elections contributed to the Stalinist leadership's perception of widespread internal opposition.

169. Priestland, *Stalinism and the Politics of Mobilization*, 387. David Shearer notes that the 1936 Constitution emboldened many former kulaks to demand the right to return to their native villages and reclaim their property—something that further alarmed Soviet authorities; Shearer, *Policing Stalin's Socialism*, 304–6.

170. Stalin, *Sochineniia*, vol. 13, 207, 211–12.

they were historically doomed might lead to "energy of resistance"—a term Lenin used during the Civil War to explain why class struggle was escalating after the establishment of the proletarian dictatorship.[171] Stalin frequently reiterated this theme in his speeches, declaring in 1928 "the inevitable sharpening of class struggle" and describing resistance to collectivization in 1930 as "the class struggle intensified."[172]

Party leaders' thinking was infused with a type of millenarianism—a belief they were moving toward the final stage of history in which all members of society would live in harmony under communism. But they did not envision progress toward communism as a placid endeavor. Instead they foresaw an ever-intensifying struggle that they would win only through the complete elimination of enemies. Collectivization and the abolition of private enterprise marked the advent of the socialist era, but opposition to the Soviet order continued anyway. In 1937 Stalin again warned that the Communist Party's successes would only make the remnants of the moribund classes fight back more desperately. He added that capitalist encirclement meant that the Soviet Union faced a very real threat from external enemies as well.[173]

Indeed, the other crucial factor behind the timing of the mass operations was the rising international threat. Soviet leaders were acutely aware of the ever-intensifying threat posed by Germany and Japan in the late 1930s. Barry McLoughlin notes that 1937 was a year of particularly ominous developments, with Germany's abrupt cessation of talks with Soviet diplomats in March followed by Japan's invasion of China proper in July, the combination of which made a two-front war appear to be a strong possibility.[174] Of course, leaders have a range of ways to respond to international threats, the most common of which are the buildup of military defenses and the negotiation of military alliances.[175] Stalin and his fellow leaders pursued both of these options, but they also strove to eliminate

171. van Ree, *The Political Thought of Joseph Stalin*, 114–15.

172. van Ree, *The Political Thought of Joseph Stalin*, 114; Michael Jakobson, *Origins of the Gulag: The Soviet Prison Camp System, 1917–1934* (Lexington, KY, 1993), 103. Other political and cultural leaders at the time sounded the same theme. See M. Gor'kii, "O solitere," *Nashi dostizheniia* 6 (June 1930): 3.

173. I. V. Stalin, *Sochineniia*, ed. Robert H. McNeal, vol. 1 [XIV] (Stanford, 1967), 194–95. From this point of view the Second World War was a battle Stalin and his fellow leaders fully expected; see Amir Weiner, *Making Sense of the War: The Second World War and the Fate of the Bolshevik Revolution* (Princeton, 2001).

174. McLoughlin, "Mass Operations," 142.

175. On the various types of military alliances and their functions, see Patricia A. Weitsman, *Dangerous Alliances: Proponents of Peace and Weapons of War* (Stanford, 2004).

internal enemies who represented potential fifth columnists in the event of war.[176]

Oleg Khlevniuk has argued that with war on the horizon Stalin sought to eliminate potential opposition within the country, and that this accounts for both the purges (within the Party, military, and industry) and the mass operations. In particular Khlevniuk emphasizes Stalin's awareness in early 1937 of rear-guard uprisings against the Republican government during the Spanish Civil War and his fear of similar rebellions within the Soviet Union in the event of war.[177] Beyond Stalin's awareness of events in Spain, his launching of the mass operations followed a well-established pattern of relying on excisionary violence to deal with perceived internal threats at a time of heightened external threat. This pattern dated from the Russian Civil War, when the combination of foreign intervention and counterrevolution endangered the existence of the nascent Soviet state.[178] Leaders of the security police who carried out summary executions and incarcerations during the Civil War took similar measures in subsequent years. During the 1927 War Scare, Evdokimov stepped up extrajudicial executions of alleged Whiteguardists arguing that it was "very important to destroy them," because they would be "a real force against us, in the event of an international conflict."[179] Stalin sanctioned these executions and ordered the mass arrests of Whiteguardists in response to the war scare.[180] Evdokimov and his close associates (Frinovskii, Vladimir Kurskii, Izrail' Dagin, Nikolai Nikolaev-Zhurid, and Aleksandr Minaev-Tsikanovskii) came to dominate the operational leadership of the security police when their ally Ezhov was appointed commissar of internal affairs in 1936. It was this group that directed the mass operations and national operations.[181]

---

176. The term *fifth columnists* comes from the Spanish Civil War, where Franco's forces surrounded Madrid with four columns of regular troops and then relied on a "fifth column" within the city to start an uprising and bring down the Republican government; Shearer, *Policing Stalin's Socialism*, 301.

177. Khlevniuk, "The Objectives of the Great Terror"; Khlevniuk, "Reasons for the 'Great Terror': The Foreign-Political Aspect."

178. The Civil War saw not only British, French, American, and Japanese intervention, but the Polish invasion of 1920, which allowed the White army to regroup and which undercut efforts to put down widespread peasant revolts. According to Stephen Wheatcroft, Soviet leaders throughout the 1920s and 1930s remained haunted by the specter of foreign invasion coupled with internal rebellion. Wheatcroft, "Agency and Terror," 25.

179. Wheatcroft, "Agency and Terror," 30.

180. Olga Velikanova, "Popular Defeatism and the First Wave of Stalin's Terror in 1927," Paper presented at the ICCEES World Conferernce, Stockholm (July 2010), 4–5.

181. Wheatcroft, "Agency and Terror," 39.

The immediate pretext for the mass operations came from the Western Siberian security police chief, S. N. Mironov. On June 17, 1937, Mironov reported on a vast counterrevolutionary organization made up primarily of exiled kulaks, who were allegedly spying for the Japanese and preparing for an armed overthrow of the Soviet government.[182] Noting the 208,400 exiled kulaks in Western Siberia, Mironov added that this area was overrun by large numbers of itinerants, gypsies, beggars, orphans, and criminals, and that together all these groups constituted a fifth column that would revolt against Soviet power in the increasingly likely event of war with Japan.[183] The way this report linked political conspiracy, foreign espionage, and socially marginal groups provided the justification for the mass operations.

On June 28, 1937, the Politburo adopted the following resolution, "On the uncovering of a counterrevolutionary, insurrectionary organization among deported kulaks in Western Siberia." The resolution declared, "We consider it necessary to apply the supreme penalty to all activists belonging to this insurrectionary organization of deported kulaks."[184] Four days later the Politburo passed another resolution stating, "It has been observed that a large number of former kulaks and criminals deported at one time from various regions to the North and to Siberian districts and then returning to their regions at the expiration of their period of exile are the chief instigators in all sorts of anti-Soviet crimes, including sabotage." The resolution went on to order the security police to register all kulaks and criminals that returned home "in order that the most hostile of them be forthwith arrested and executed by means of a troika [three-person tribunal] and that the remaining, less active but nevertheless hostile elements be listed and exiled to districts as indicated by the NKVD."[185]

In accordance with a telegram from Stalin, Ezhov immediately ordered regional security police chiefs to register all kulaks and criminals who had returned to their home territories, either on completing their sentences or because they had escaped from a labor camp or special settlement. He told them to complete two lists, one with the "most hostile elements," who were to be executed, and the other with "less active, but still hostile elements,"

---

182. *Tragediia* vol. 5 (book 1), 256–58.

183. See Shearer, "Elements," 856. The impetus for this report probably came from Moscow, given that the Politburo resolution quickly followed. My thanks to David Shearer for pointing out this fact.

184. TsKhSD f. 89, op. 43, d. 48, l. 1, as reprinted in Getty and Naumov, *Road to Terror*, 469.

185. Khlevniuk, *History of the Gulag*, 144.

who were to be exiled.[186] The figures submitted by regional security police chiefs in response would become the basis for arrest and execution quotas set by the Politburo for each region during the mass operations.

Security police Operational Order 00447, approved by the Politburo on July 31, 1937, launched the mass operations. Its preamble noted the presence of "former kulaks," "church officials and sectarians," "cadres of anti-Soviet political parties," "active members of bandit uprisings, Whites, members of punitive expeditions, repatriates," and "criminals...[including] horse and cattle thieves, recidivist thieves, robbers, and others," and it went on to state that "all of these anti-Soviet elements constitute the chief instigators of every kind of anti-Soviet crimes and sabotage."[187] The order dictated the execution of 75,950 people (those in the "most hostile" category) and the sentencing of 193,000 people (those classified as "less active, but still hostile") to eight to ten years in a labor camp. It provided arrest and execution quotas for each region of the country, and it authorized extrajudicial organs—special tribunals composed of the first Party secretary, the procurator, and the security police chief of each territorial unit—to convict and sentence those arrested.[188]

To carry out the arrests and executions ordered by the center, local security police relied on card catalogues they had compiled on "politically unreliable elements"—a fact that highlights the importance of social cataloguing to Soviet state violence. Begun in the 1920s, police card catalogues in every locality contained literally thousands of names by the 1930s.[189] To help compile these names, a staff of roughly seventy state archivists compiled card catalogues for the security police on people identified in the files of the White armies' military and civil institutions—research that produced lists of over 600,000 former Whites still living in the Soviet Union and now classified as "anti-Soviet elements."[190] Police card files often covered 10–15 percent or more of the adult population, and each person on file was placed in one of three categories with those deemed the greatest threat in the first category. Based on Order 00447, the local security police

186. *Tragediia*, vol. 5 (book 1), 319.

187. Getty and Naumov, *Road to Terror*, 473–74.

188. *Tragediia*, vol. 5 (book 1), 331; Getty and Naumov, *Road to Terror*, 473–79.

189. Cynthia V. Hooper, "Terror from Within: Participation and Coercion in Soviet Power, 1924–1964" (Ph.D. diss., Princeton University, 2003), 151–53.

190. V. E. Korneev and O. N. Kopylova, "Arkhivy na sluzhbe totalitarnogo gosudarstva," *Otechestvennye arkhivy* 3 (1992): 13–24.

arrested those in the first category and, if they did not meet their quota, some in the second category as well.[191]

The practice of cataloging the population, then, both reinforced Party and police officials' belief that enemies existed and provided a sociological tool for acting to eliminate those alleged enemies. Just as the card catalogues compiled in connection with the passport system showed the presence of former kulaks and other "socially harmful elements," security police card files seemed to confirm the existence of "hostile elements." In this sense, the fear of enemies and efforts to document their presence were mutually reinforcing, for the more Soviet authorities gathered statistics to identify a threat the more data they had confirming that threat. Of course, social cataloguing did not directly cause state violence. Governments in other countries also kept card catalogues on suspect populations without using such instruments to carry out mass arrests and executions. The French police, for example, maintained a card catalogue on all foreigners living in France, and by 1939 the catalogue had 1.6 million names on file.[192] But cataloguing former kulaks as "anti-Soviet elements" nonetheless helped enable the mass operations, by categorizing certain groups as socially dangerous and sanctioning their physical removal.

To argue that the mass operations were enabled by social cataloguing is not to say they were conducted as an orderly surgical operation on the body social. Some local security police organs overfulfilled their arrest and execution quotas, while others requested sizeable increases in their quotas—something that Order 00447 stated they could do.[193] The Politburo approved supplemental arrests and executions in January 1938, and between September and November 1938, special tribunals sentenced an additional 105,000 people, including 72,000 to death.[194] A subsequent report on the mass operation in Soviet Turkmeniia described how the local security police, having arrested all "anti-Soviet elements" on file, began

191. Zemskov, "Zakliuchennye," 7; McLoughlin, "Mass Operations," 126.
192. Hooper, "Terror from Within," 151–53. See also Clifford Rosenberg, "The Colonial Politics of Health Care Provision in Interwar Paris," *French Historical Studies* 27:3 (summer 2004): 653.
193. See the documents from local NKVD officials reprinted in Mark Iunge and Rol'f Binner, *Kak terror stal "Bol'shim": Sekretnyi prikaz no. 00447 i tekhnologiia ego ispolneniia* (Moscow, 2003), 102–4.
194. Getty and Naumov, *Road to Terror,* 518–19; Khlevniuk, *History of the Gulag,* 165.

mass roundups of innocent people at markets in order to fulfill quotas.[195] In other regions too the security police, having arrested most of the suspects on file, began to make arbitrary arrests.[196] In this sense, the mass operations as carried out were not a controlled and rational process.[197] Yet to conceive of and launch this type of mass excisionary undertaking required a conceptual framework based on social cataloguing and technologies of modern state violence.

It is also necessary to explain the lethality of the mass operations—why, in contrast to earlier episodes of state violence, a high percentage of its victims were not just deported but executed. As argued above, collectivization and the creation of a state-run economy meant that misconduct or opposition could no longer be blamed on the petty bourgeois milieu of the New Economic Policy. Following the purported attainment of socialism, those who were seen as disloyal or not contributing to the socialist order were labeled "socially harmful elements" or "anti-Soviet elements," terms that implied they were irredeemable.

Soviet leaders differed somewhat on whether former kulaks and criminals could be reformed and reintegrated into society. While Iagoda paid lip service to the ideal of rehabilitation in labor camps, he stressed that a majority of crimes were committed by recidivist criminals who were "socially harmful elements" that had to be permanently removed from society.[198] Here Iagoda was following the emphasis that criminologists placed on recidivists as the source of crime.[199] Vyshinskii, on the other hand, opposed Iagoda and, following the latter's removal in 1936, sought to revive policies of social reintegration of repeat offenders. Ezhov, while he supported

195. GARF f. 8131, op. 37, d. 145, ll. 49–84, as reprinted in Khlevniuk, *History of the Gulag,* 157–61.

196. McLoughlin, "Mass Operations," 127. Significantly, some security police officials—including those who had willingly arrested suspects listed in card files—objected to these mass roundups as arbitrary. They saw arrests based on card catalogues as legitimate and mass roundups as illegitimate. See Shearer, *Policing Stalin's Socialism,* 351.

197. Wendy Goldman has analyzed the frenetical spread of purges in factories and trade unions in this period; see Goldman, *Terror and Democracy.* For an analysis of state repression in this period with a focus on the victims, see Hiroaki Kuromiya, *The Voices of the Dead: Stalin's Great Terror in the 1930s* (New Haven, 2007).

198. See his 1936 report on crime in GARF f. 9401, op. 12, d. 135, doc. 31, ll. 3–4, as cited in Shearer, "Elements," 860.

199. Shearer, *Policing Stalin's Socialism,* 264–65. In contrast to Lombrosian ideas that portrayed recidivism as biologically determined, Iagoda and Russian criminologists such as M. N. Gernet saw recidivism as socially determined. See M. N. Gernet, *Moral'naia statistika: Ugolovnaia statistika i statistika samoubiistv; posobie dlia statistikov i kriminalistov* (Moscow, 1922).

Vyshinskii's programs, emphasized the danger posed by recidivist criminals and even proposed that their labor camp sentences be extended if they exhibited any tendencies toward disobedience or hooliganism.[200] More generally, Party and security police officials possessed enormous distrust for any person with a tainted past. In compiling lists of "anti-Soviet elements," the security police had subcategories for "former kulaks," "former officers (tsarist, White, Petliurist, and others)," "representatives of the tsarist administration, nobles, landowners, and merchants," and former members of "anti-Soviet political parties."[201]

In the minds of Soviet leaders, those who could not be reformed had to be eliminated entirely. Indeed the preamble to Order 00447 charged the security police with countering anti-Soviet elements "once and for all." Party and security police officials alike seemed to take this charge seriously. In response to the order, the Donets regional Party secretary spoke of cleansing the area completely of "kulaks, nationalists, and all other scum."[202] And in the midst of the mass operations, at a private banquet November 7, 1937, Stalin proposed the following toast: "Anyone who attempts to destroy the unity of the socialist state...is a sworn enemy of the state and of the peoples of the USSR. And we shall destroy any such enemy....To the final destruction of all enemies!"[203] With the purported attainment of socialism, Stalin and his fellow leaders sought complete social unity, to be realized if necessary by the ruthless elimination of any lingering dissension. The *Short Course* history of the Soviet Communist Party (1938) extolled the physical annihilation of elusive enemies as necessary for the purification of Soviet society.[204] Also crucial was the rising external threat that made war seem imminent and that seemed to justify lethal violence against potential fifth columnists. At the Eighteenth Party Congress in 1939, Stalin

200. Shearer, *Policing Stalin's Socialism*, 311. For an example of Ezhov warning against the release of criminals, see RGASPI f. 17, op. 2, d. 597, ll. 13–15.

201. Vladimir Khaustov, "Razvitie sovetskikh organov gosudarstvennoi bezopasnosti: 1917–1953 gg.," *Cahiers du monde russe* 42:2–4 (April–December 2001): 369–70.

202. Iunge and Binner, *Kak terror stal "Bol'shim,"* 23. Iunge and Binner emphasize that local security police saw "anti-Soviet elements" as omnipresent and understood the mass operations as a final battle to eliminate them.

203. A. G. Latyshev, "Riadom so Stalinym," *Sovershenno sekretno* 12 (1990): 19, as quoted in McDermott, *Stalin*, 88.

204. *History of the Communist Party of the Soviet Union (Bolsheviks): Short Course* (New York, 1939), 346–48. As Golfo Alexopoulos writes, the late 1930s saw "a campaign of expulsion with almost no possibility of redemption"; Alexopoulos, *Stalin's Outcasts*, 184. See also Marc Jansen and Nikita V. Petrov, *Stalin's Loyal Executioner: People's Commissar Nikolai Ezhov, 1895–1940* (Stanford, 2002).

proclaimed "that in case of war, our front and home front will be stronger than in any other country, due to our uniformity and internal unity."[205]

Stalin and his fellow leaders ordered the mass operations and bear responsibility for them. But to understand the social and ideological context in which they undertook mass arrests and executions, and to account for how they conceived of and carried out these operations, we must consider a confluence of other factors. The purported attainment of socialism laid the ideological groundwork for the mass operations. Continued resistance to the Soviet order by former "kulaks," "hooligans," black marketeers, and petty criminals provided the social context—a context largely created by Soviet policies.[206] Practically the groundwork for the mass operations was prepared by longstanding practices of excisionary violence, already well-established during the First World War and Civil War, and further enhanced by the growth of the Soviet security police and its efforts to catalogue the population. Indeed Party leaders came to see social excision as integral to the construction of a socialist order, first through dekulakization, later through the purging of urban areas, and then through the mass operations. Finally the timing of the mass operations was heavily influenced by rising international tensions and Soviet leaders' fear of a fifth column in the event of war. These tensions, as well as fears of espionage, were also central to the national operations.

The National Operations

Beginning soon after the mass operations and running concurrently with them were the so-called national operations—security police operations that targeted certain national minorities for deportations, arrests, and executions. Composed of several discrete police actions, the national operations singled out diaspora nationalities—that is, populations with a

205. *XVIII s"ezd Vsesoiuznoi kommunisticheskoi partii (b): 10–21 marta 1939 g.: Stenograficheskii otchet* (Moscow, 1939), 26–27. Kevin McDermott argues that Stalin sought to create a unitary, modernized, homogeneous communist utopia, but that he was continually frustrated by division, opposition, and social flux, all compounded by the threatening international situation; McDermott, *Stalin,* 89.

206. Indeed, as Lynne Viola argues, the enormous social upheaval and antagonism caused by collectivization lasted throughout the 1930s and triggered repeated attempts by Soviet authorities to exercise social control—through the internal passport system, police sweeps, and ultimately the mass operations; Viola, *Unknown Gulag,* 191. See also McLoughlin, "Mass Operations," 142.

homeland outside the Soviet Union—and were referred to as "the Polish operation," "the Latvian operation," and so forth. According to scholarly estimates, from August 1937 to November 1938, the security police arrested 335,500 people and executed 247,200 of them in the national operations. These figures compare with 767,400 convicted, of whom 386,800 were executed, in the mass operations.[207] Hence the national operations were nearly half the size of the mass operations, and in terms of the ratio of those executed they were even more lethal.

Ethnic conflict and unrest had been common throughout the 1920s, particularly in the Caucasus and Central Asia. During collectivization, peasant resistance was particularly fierce among some national minorities, including among ethnic Poles, Germans, Chechens, and Kurds.[208] Moreover, many Party leaders, including Stalin himself, had either come from ethnically mixed border regions, or had been involved in Soviet rule of the Caucasus and Central Asia during the 1920s.[209] So it is not surprising that they, like their tsarist predecessors, attached significance to nationality. But unlike tsarist practitioners of military statistics, Soviet authorities did not initially assume national minorities to be less politically reliable than ethnic Russians. Throughout the 1920s, Soviet nationality policy actively encouraged the recruitment of national minority elites into the Communist Party, the development of national minority cultures, and even the ethnographic delineation of national differences. Party leaders believed that fostering national minority identities and cultures would disarm nationalist separatism and help to propel ethnic groups along an evolutionary timeline toward socialism.[210]

The shift to "Soviet ethnic cleansing" in the late 1930s resulted both from developments in Soviet nationality policy and from growing concerns about national security. In 1935, Stalin hosted a highly publicized reception for Tajik and Turkmen collective farm peasants at the Kremlin. There he proclaimed that the attainment of socialism had made possible interethnic cooperation and harmony. He asserted that eighteen years of

207. Khlevniuk, *History of the Gulag,* 165; Martin, *Affirmative Action Empire,* 338.

208. Jörg Baberowski and Anselm Doering-Manteuffel, "Order through Terror: National Socialist Germany and the Stalinist Soviet Union as Multi-Ethnic Empires," *Beyond Totalitarianism: Stalinism and Nazism Compared,* ed. Michael Geyer and Sheila Fitzpatrick (New York, 2009), 208–10.

209. See Alfred J. Rieber, "Stalin: Man of the Borderlands," *American Historical Review* 106:5 (December 2001): 1651–91.

210. See Francine Hirsch, *Empire of Nations: Ethnographic Knowledge and the Making of the Soviet Union* (Ithaca, 2005); Martin, *Affirmative Action Empire.*

Soviet rule had overcome the harmful tsarist legacy of national minority distrust, and that now there existed "complete mutual trust" between Russians and national minorities, and that "the friendship between the peoples of the USSR," was "a great and serious achievement."[211]

Just as the purported attainment of socialism closed off possibilities for the redemption of former kulaks and criminals who refused to abide by the new socialist order, the alleged attainment of equality and harmony among nationalities led to more repressive policies toward national minorities who were seen as unwilling to join the "family of Soviet peoples." According to the internal logic of Soviet nationality policy, the fostering of national minority cultures followed by the repression of certain national minority groups was not contradictory. Those national minorities who, given the chance, had not become Soviet and instead harbored other allegiances had to be dealt with, either through deportations, incarcerations, or executions.[212]

Party leaders suspected the diaspora nationalities in particular of having alternate allegiances. During the 1920s, diaspora nationalities inside the Soviet Union presented the opportunity to use cross-border ethnic ties to project influence abroad and perhaps spread socialism. But by the 1930s, Party leaders began to fear influence flowing the other direction, for example from Poland to the Polish minority within the Soviet Union.[213] From an ideological standpoint, the cultures of diaspora nationalities also presented a problem. The Soviet government was not fully in control of these cultures. Stalin's prescription for national minority cultures—"national in form, socialist in content"—could be rigorously enforced within the country, given that Soviet censorship only sanctioned cultural expressions that supported socialism. But in capitalist countries, national culture could assume forms antithetical to Soviet socialism, and if spread to diaspora nationalities within the Soviet Union, bourgeois nationalism could undermine allegiance to the Soviet government. Some officials and ethnographers questioned whether these nationalities could become truly Soviet.[214]

Rising international tensions and in particular the threats from Germany and Japan made the problem of diaspora nationalities all the more urgent. Following Hitler's rise to power, a campaign in Germany to send

211. *Pravda*, December 6, 1935, 3.
212. Peter A. Blitstein, "Nation and Empire in Soviet History, 1917–1953," *Ab Imperio* 1 (2006): 214–15.
213. Martin, *Affirmative Action Empire*, 342. See also Kate Brown, *A Biography of No Place: From Ethnic Borderland to Soviet Heartland* (Cambridge, Mass., 2004).
214. Hirsch, *Empire of Nations*, 295.

"Brothers in Need" (ethnic Germans in the Soviet Union) aid in the form of food packages and foreign currency remittances seemed to confirm that diaspora nationalities could be wooed by hostile foreign governments. And following the German-Polish nonaggression pact of 1934, the Soviet government began to worry that allowing Soviet Poles to have Polish language instruction in schools and other forms of cultural expression might become a means for "Polish fascism" to build a base within the Soviet Union for future expansion.[215] More generally the rising international tensions in the second half of the 1930s made Party leaders increasingly fearful of foreign espionage carried out by members of diaspora nationalities, as well as increasingly vigilant about securing border regions of the country.

In 1935 and 1936, the Soviet government carried out a series of deportations from border regions. "Unreliable elements" numbering 41,650 people were deported from Ukrainian border zones to eastern Ukraine in March 1935, and of these roughly 60 percent were ethnic Poles and Germans. The same month Soviet officials deported approximately 30,000 Ingerian Finns from the border areas of Leningrad oblast and Karelia to Western Siberia and Central Asia.[216] Ukrainian officials reported that deportations "had not completely cleansed" the border zone and they received permission to deport more people—300 Polish households in the summer, 1,500 more in the fall, and in January 1936 15,000 German and Polish households, in the last case to Kazakhstan rather than eastern Ukraine. However, these deportations were not total, in the sense that they included about half of the German and Polish populations of the border region, and no Poles or Germans outside the border regions were deported.[217]

With the national operations of 1937–38, the security police began arrests and deportations that reached far beyond the border regions and included total deportations of national minorities. At the February-March 1937 Central Committee plenum, Stalin declared that "as long as there exists capitalist encirclement, we will have wreckers, spies, saboteurs and murderers sent into our hinterland by the agents of foreign states."[218] In July 1937, Ezhov ordered the security police to arrest all German nationals working in military plants and railroads. His order warned, "Recent operative and investigative materials have proven that the German General

215. Martin, *Affirmative Action Empire*, 328–29.
216. Pavel Polian, *Against Their Will: The History and Geography of Forced Migrations in the USSR*, trans. Anna Yastrzhembska (Budapest, 2004), 95.
217. Martin, *Affirmative Action Empire*, 330.
218. Stalin, *Sochineniia*, vol. 1 [XIV], 197.

Staff and the Gestapo are organizing broadscale espionage and subversive work at the most important, primarily defense, industrial enterprises by utilizing German nationals who have taken root there."[219]

The following month the Politburo approved security police Order 00485, entitled, "On the Liquidation of Polish Subversive Espionage Groups and Organizations of the POV [Polish Military Organization]." The order called for the arrest of all Polish political émigrés and refugees, as well as "the most active part of local anti-Soviet nationalist elements from the Polish national districts." In practice, by 1938, the security police were arresting Poles simply because of their nationality.[220] Local security police easily identified national minorities given that Soviet passports included each person's nationality, and once they had made arrests, the security police prepared lists of the accused with summaries of the cases against them. Order 00485 set up a new procedure that allowed a two-person tribunal (*dvoika*), composed of the regional security police chief and local procurator, to review these lists and pass sentences of either incarceration (five-ten years in a labor camp) or death. The sentences were then approved by Ezhov and Vyshinsky before being carried out.[221]

The Polish operation became something of a model for similar actions directed against other diaspora nationalities. A series of security police operations targeted, in addition to Poles and Germans, the following diaspora nationalities: Romanians, Latvians, Estonians, Finns, Greeks, Afghans, Iranians, Chinese, Bulgarians, and Macedonians. In addition the security police conducted a special operation against the so-called Kharbinians (*Kharbintsy*), primarily ethnic Russians who worked on the Chinese-Manchurian Railroad (headquartered in Kharbin but owned and operated by the Soviet government) and who returned to the Soviet Union after the railroad was sold to Manchukuo in 1935.[222] While 73.7 percent of the 335,500 people convicted in the national operations were executed, the rates of execution varied considerably by nationality, with very high execution rates in the Polish, Greek, Finnish, and Estonian operations,

219. Khlevniuk, *History of the Gulag*, 144–45.

220. Martin, *Affirmative Action Empire*, 337. For further discussion, see N. V. Petrov and A. B. Roginskii, "'Pol'skaia operatsiia' NKVD 1937–1938 gg.," *Repressii protiv poliakov i pol'skikh grazhdan*, ed. L. S. Eremira (Moscow, 1997), 22–43.

221. Khlevniuk, *History of the Gulag*, 146–47.

222. Ezhov's order stated that the overwhelming majority of Kharbinians "belong to the Japanese secret service, which sent them to the Soviet Union over the last several years" to work as "spies, terrorists and saboteurs." As quoted in McLoughlin, "Mass Operations," 122.

and much lower execution rates, for example, in the Afghan and Iranian operations. Overall the national operations accounted for about one-fifth of the total arrests and one-third of the total executions of the 1937–38 period.[223]

At the time of the national operations, the Soviet government also carried out additional deportations from border areas. In August 1937 the Soviet government and Party Central Committee issued a joint decree, "On the Eviction of the Korean Population of the Border Zones of the Far East Region." The decree justified this action as a means to prevent "the penetration of Japanese espionage" into the region. It ordered the entire Korean population deported, without any effort to determine which Koreans were involved in alleged espionage, and as such marked the first wholesale deportation of a national minority. The decree stipulated that deportees be sent to Kazakhstan and Uzbekistan, and it further noted that Koreans should not be prevented from leaving the country if they wished.[224] The last stipulation highlights a difference between the Korean and Polish operations. The decree on Koreans did not aver the presence of subversive groups (though the Soviet press at the time frequently portrayed Koreans and Chinese as Japanese agents), and instead cast the removal of Koreans as a preemptive move against Japanese espionage. Deportees were allowed to take livestock with them and received some compensation (on average 6,000 rubles per family) for property left behind. The security police deported roughly 74,500 ethnic Koreans in the first stage of this operation, and another 171,781 in the second stage. The Soviet government planned to resettle depopulated areas from which Koreans had been deported with demobilized Red Army veterans and Russian peasants.[225] This policy of deporting unreliable groups combined with resettlement of reliable populations again mirrored nineteenth-century tsarist policies of colonial conquest discussed above.

The Soviet government also deported "unreliable elements"—diaspora nationalities—from border zones of the Caucasus in 1937–38. A security police report described the deportation in late 1937 of 3,101 Kurds and 2,788 Armenians and Turks from the Caucasus to Kazakhstan. The report noted that the infrastructure for receiving deportees was extremely poor, so that in some cases deported families were deposited without shelter in

223. Khlevniuk, *History of the Gulag*, 146; Martin, *Affirmative Action Empire*, 338.
224. GARF f. 5446, op. 1v, d. 497, ll. 27–28, as reprinted in *Stalinskie deportatsii, 1928–1953*, comp. N. L. Povol' and M. Polian (Moscow, 2005), 83.
225. Polian, *Against Their Will*, 99–101.

barren areas.[226] In October 1938 a top secret government decree ordered the deportation of 2,000 Iranian families from border regions of Azerbaijan and provided for their resettlement, transportation of their livestock, and so forth, to Kazakhstan. One scholar places the total number of families deported to Kazakhstan at over 21,000 in 1937–38, though that figure includes some Koreans, as well as Iranians, Turks, Armenians, and Kurds.[227]

Security concerns were clearly paramount in the national operations and in national minority deportations from border zones. A January 1938 Politburo decree extending the national operations until mid-April called for "the destruction of espionage and sabotage contingents made up of Poles, Latvians, Germans, Estonians, Finns, Greeks, Iranians, *Kharbintsy*, Chinese, and Romanians." And security police documents referred to these operations as directed against "nationalities of foreign governments."[228] This language makes clear that, despite the fact that these diaspora nationalities had resided in the Russian Empire and Soviet Union for decades if not centuries, the security police regarded them as loyal to the nation-state of their nationality rather than to the Soviet Union. At the same time, the fact that the national operations also targeted Kharbinians—ethnic Russians who had worked on the Chinese-Manchurian Railroad—indicates that these repressions were not a product of Russian chauvinism.[229] In fact, the security police in the late 1930s kept close tabs on anyone, including many ethnic Russians, who had any sort of connection with foreign countries. Security police lists of potential spies included categories for "repatriates," "smugglers," "individuals who have foreign correspondence," and "Esperantists."[230]

The Soviet government's repression of diaspora nationalities brings up an important historical comparison—the similarities and differences between Soviet and Nazi state violence. In their broad outlines, the applications of violence by the Soviet and Nazi governments did have similarities. The

226. GARF f. 9479, op. 1, d. 55, ll. 24–28, as reprinted in *Stalinskie deportatsii*, 77.

227. Nikolai Bougai, *The Deportation of Peoples in the Soviet Union* (New York, 1996), 40–44.

228. Martin, *Affirmative Action Empire*, 337–38.

229. See ibid., 343.

230. Khaustov, "Razvitie sovetskikh organov," 370. Soviet leaders' fear of foreign spies, while vastly exaggerated, was not entirely unfounded. Germany, Japan, and Poland all conducted espionage in the Soviet Union, just as the Soviet government engaged in espionage and counterespionage against other countries. See Kuromiya, *The Voices of the Dead*, 131–32, 256.

leaders of both countries pursued revolutionary social change, articulated utopian goals, posited claims to history-making, and deployed violence on an unprecedented scale. Some of their techniques of state violence were also similar, in that Soviet and Nazi leaders both relied on social cataloguing, special police forces, and concentration camps. Soviet persecution of diaspora nationalities and "social aliens" parallels Nazi persecution of Jews, Roma, the mentally handicapped, homosexuals, and other socially marginalized groups.

But the differences between Soviet and Nazi state violence were equally significant. The Soviet government never engaged in industrial killing, nor did it attempt to exterminate an entire people, or for that matter an entire social class. Whereas the Nazis sought to exterminate all Jews and wipe the Jewish genome off the face of the earth—genocide in the true sense of the word—the Soviets executed only those ethnic Germans, Poles, and so forth whom they (summarily) convicted of espionage and sabotage.[231] They never exterminated entire nationalities, and even with the kulaks, who were to be "liquated as a class," they sought to reform the vast majority of them through dispossession and forced labor. In the comparatively few executions carried out during collectivization, and the far more numerous executions carried out during the mass operations, the Soviet security police killed only those who were seen as irredeemable.[232]

The differences between Soviet and Nazi state violence reflected fundamental ideological distinctions between the two regimes. Whereas Nazi ideology was racist and exclusionary, Soviet Marxism was universalist and presented proletarian revolution as a means to eliminate class divisions and achieve social unity. For the Soviets, unity did not mean racial purity or ethnic homogeneity. Soviet nationality policy even promoted the development of national minority cultures as a means to progress through and ultimately supersede the stage of nationalism to reach socialism and

231. For a discussion that applies the word *genocide* to the Soviet case but nonetheless points out the differences between Nazi and Soviet state violence, see Norman M. Naimark, *Stalin's Genocides* (Princeton, 2010), 122–28.

232. Some scholars have described Soviet state violence as an attempt to realize an idealized image of the politico-social body, of "the People-as-One." (Holquist, "State Violence as Technique," 133–34, 147; Claude Lefort, "The Image of the Body in Totalitarianism," in Lefort, *The Political Forms of Modern Society,* ed. John Thompson (Cambridge, 1986), 292–306). But Soviet leaders never espoused anything akin to the Nazi ideal of a racially pure, undifferentiated *volk.* They maintained that Soviet society under socialism was made up of three nonantagonistic classes (the intelligentsia, the proletariat, and the peasantry), and they celebrated the existence of numerous nationalities as part of the "brotherly union and great friendship of Soviet peoples."

ultimately communism. Whereas the Nazis saw national cultures as an expression of racial traits, the Soviets saw national cultures as part of the superstructure that reflected, and would evolve according to, economic development. Soviet ethnographers viewed Uzbek culture, for example, not as the product of primordial Uzbekness but rather as the result of the historical process of Uzbek economic development. Soviet officials moreover praised the intermarriage and intermixing of ethnic groups, as opposed to authorities in many countries (Germany, the United States, Britain, France, and so forth) who warned against miscegenation.[233] In contrast to the Nazi project, which was only for Germans or Aryans, the Soviet project was to include everyone. It was only those who, in the eyes of Soviet authorities, refused to abide by the Soviet order who were to be eliminated.

To further contextualize the differences in Soviet and Nazi ideology, it is worthwhile to highlight the social, political, and disciplinary contexts in which these ideologies took root. It was in the context of an underdeveloped society ruled by a despotic tsarist bureaucracy that some members of the Russian intelligentsia embraced Marxism and its vision of a classless society. And it was in this context that Russian disciplinary culture came to emphasize the role of the environment over genetics to account for the condition of the lower classes. Russian and later Soviet scientists argued that social conditions, not race, influenced physical development.[234] Moreover, the prerevolutionary Russian ideology of empire, with its focus on cultural borrowing and assimilation, differed dramatically from the ideas of racial superiority that underlay Western European empires. By contrast the roots of Nazi ideology may be traced to the sense in turn-of-the-century Germany of entering a period of unprecedented anxiety that prompted the invocation of physical strength and willpower to shield the German nation against degeneration. These ideas became magnified by defeat and humiliation in the First World War, when "the design of new social, political, and psychological fortifications" seemed essential for the sake of national survival.[235] Despite similarities of scale and technique, Stalinist and Nazi state violence therefore differed fundamentally in their origins and ideological orientation, as well as in the victims they targeted.

To conclude this discussion, I will return to the question of what caused Soviet state violence. The direct cause of state violence during the late

233. Hirsch, *Empire of Nations*, 252–54, 269.

234. Ibid., 257

235. Peter Fritzsche and Jochen Hellbeck, "The New Man in Stalinist Russia and Nazi Germany," *Beyond Totalitarianism*, 309.

1930s were decisions taken by the Stalinist leadership. Stalin and his fellow leaders ordered the arrests, executions, and deportations that took place during the mass operations and national operations. Their Manichean worldview, their mentality of capitalist encirclement, their belief that the building and defending of socialism could be accomplished only through the ruthless elimination of internal enemies—all of these features of the Stalinist leadership account for its use of state violence on a massive scale.[236] Rising international tensions and the existential threats posed by Germany and Japan were also crucial to the context in which Stalin and his fellow leaders launched these operations.

Beyond the direct causes of Soviet state violence were several conditions of possibility that I have sought to highlight. Rulers throughout history, including many Russian autocrats, have used large-scale violence in dealing with their people. But only in the modern era have governments "scientifically" categorized their populations and excised specific social groups. Social excision was predicated on a science of society and on the definition of a social field to which this science could be applied. Soviet state violence was not the product of Russian backwardness.[237] Instead it was based on a modern conception of society as an artifact to be categorized and sculpted through state intervention. Modern forms of social knowledge were therefore a necessary precondition for Soviet state violence in the forms it was practiced.

Social sciences were the major source of this knowledge, especially the disciplines of sociology, psychology, and criminology. By the turn of the century, psychologists and criminologists increasingly stressed the problem of social deviance and the need to eliminate it, through coercive rehabilitation if necessary. Soviet officials in turn focused particularly on the deviance of what they termed "people from the past" (*byvshie liudi*) and prescribed their removal from society, so as not to contaminate the socialist future with the capitalist past. Disciplinary knowledge thus fused with another necessary though insufficient condition of Soviet state violence—the millenarian thinking of Soviet leaders. Part of this thinking came from

236. As Lars Lih argues, Stalin genuinely believed that there were no objective obstacles to the construction of socialism in the Soviet Union and that setbacks were the work of hostile individuals intent on sabotaging the Soviet system. See Lars T. Lih, "Introduction," *Stalin's Letters to Molotov, 1925–1936*, ed. Lars T. Lih, Oleg V. Naumov, and Oleg V. Khlevniuk (New Haven, 1995), 11–14.

237. Ironically, though the aim of *The Black Book of Communism* is to condemn communism as an ideology, Courtois instead underscores Russian traditions of violence; Stéphane Courtois, "Conclusion: Why?" *Black Book*, 728–32.

Marxism and its emphasis on stages of historical development, but Stalin developed his own doctrine on the intensifying struggle with internal enemies. Once collectivization had been accomplished and a socialist economy created, the failure of some members of society to conform to the new order signaled continued opposition within the country. According to Stalin, this opposition reflected the desperate struggle of both internal and external opponents to sabotage the Soviet state as it became stronger.[238] The defense of revolutionary gains therefore necessitated the ruthless elimination of enemies. Stalin's was a particular type of millenarianism, one focused on uncovering and removing adversaries as the means to progress toward communism.

To act on these ideas, Soviet authorities required the means to neutralize alleged enemies. Technologies of excisionary violence were therefore another necessary precondition for the mass operations and national operations. Card files, passport regimes, a security police apparatus, and concentration camps provided the means to identify and remove those deemed socially harmful or politically disloyal. Technologies of social excision were not invented by the Bolsheviks but rather by European administrators, first in the context of colonial rule and then during the First World War. The Soviet system, born at the juncture of the First World War and the Russian Civil War, institutionalized total war practices as permanent features of Soviet governance.

Modern forms of social knowledge, a discourse on deviance that fused with Soviet leaders' millenarianism, and wartime technologies of social excision were therefore all necessary though insufficient conditions of Soviet state violence in the late 1930s. Party leaders chose to enact this violence in an atmosphere of extreme international threat and continued social upheaval, the latter a product of their own frenetic attempt to collectivize agriculture and industrialize the country. For them, the survival of socialism and progress toward communism depended on the elimination of opposition. Although their end goal of social harmony remained vague and elusive, their efforts to categorize and neutralize "anti-Soviet elements" became ever more concrete. And when the security of the Soviet state seemed increasingly endangered, Party leaders radically escalated their attempts to eradicate those they regarded as potential fifth-columnists in the event of war.

238. Stalin, *Sochineniia*, vol. 13, 211–12.

Conclusion

The Soviet case is frequently omitted from comparative historical analyses. Scholars tend to view the Soviet Union and its distinctive socioeconomic order as anomalous and therefore fundamentally incomparable to other countries. My examination of social policies, however, indicates the value of including the Soviet Union in such comparisons, as a means to highlight certain features of state interventionism and population management in the interwar period. In particular, the Soviet case illustrates the connection between welfare and warfare, and the fact that welfare programs at this time were intended primarily to safeguard human resources and fulfill a set of reciprocal obligations between the state and its citizens. The Soviet health care system demonstrates how the rise of social medicine led to state-administered public health initiatives, as well as providing an example of an authoritarian regime that adopted an environmentalist approach to maintaining its population's bodily well-being. Soviet reproductive policies show that even a government as committed to social renovation as the Soviet regime could reject eugenics for disciplinary and ideological reasons and could construct an essentialist gender order that nonetheless upheld women's place in the workforce. The Soviet government's extensive use of surveillance and propaganda confirms that in an era of mass politics, even authoritarian rulers felt compelled to monitor and influence people's thinking. And in the area of state violence, the Soviet case reveals the lethal potentialities of techniques of social excision, particularly when wielded by a revolutionary dictatorship intent on achieving social transformation and state security.

Placing Soviet history in an international context also provides new perspectives on the Soviet system and allows us to move beyond explanations that attribute all aspects of Soviet social intervention to socialist ideology.

Although Marxism-Leninism imparted to Party leaders both a set of social categories and a particular historical teleology, it did not provide a blueprint for their policies. It established a historical timeline along which humanity was to travel, but it did not dictate a precise roadmap or timetable. I differ from those who see socialist ideology as a single, concrete program that, when put into practice, led inexorably to Stalinism.[1] Often coupled with a reified view of socialist ideology is its portrayal as a doctrine "out of step with reality"—an artificial attempt to reorder human society.[2] My purpose in placing Soviet social policies in an international context is to illustrate that both the idea of social transformation and the technologies to pursue such a transformation in fact predated the Soviet system and were common to many ideologies and regimes of the twentieth century.

Soviet social intervention is best understood as one particular version of modern aspirations to fashion a rational social order, aspirations that emanated from the Enlightenment idea that the social world was neither preordained nor fixed but was instead of humankind's own making. From this realization followed a new conception of society as an artifact that could be studied and remade. Inspired by dramatic advances in natural science, specialists developed a range of social sciences to understand society with the aim of improving it. The emerging disciplines of social statistics, demography, sociology, psychology, and criminology categorized the population, identified social problems, and justified new technologies of social intervention. In the same spirit of rational reform there arose ideologies of social transformation, one of which was Marxism.

Marxist thought drew not only on Enlightenment rationalism but on nineteenth-century Romanticism. Romantic social thinkers hoped to recover the (mythic) social unity of the past—an organic unity they believed to have been destroyed by the bitter class antagonisms and alienation of the modern world. Marxism arose within this more general intellectual context and responded to the social problems arising from European industrialization.[3] Strongly influenced by the revolutions of 1848, Marx proposed a distinct solution—violent proletarian revolution to overthrow

1. Martin Malia, for example, refers to the suppression of private property, profit, and the market as "the instrumental program of integral socialism." Martin Malia, *The Soviet Tragedy: A History of Socialism in Russia, 1917–1991* (New York, 1994), 224.
2. Stéphane Courtois, "Conclusion: Why?" *The Black Book of Communism: Crime, Terror, Repression* (Cambridge, Mass., 1999), 737. Malia calls socialism "an effort to suppress the real world" (Malia, *Soviet Tragedy*, 225).
3. The class categories employed by Marx, for example, were not invented by him but rather adapted from social categories developed by nineteenth-century government

the capitalist system—but his writings were far from the only nineteenth-century ideology to put forward a program of radical social change. As Katerina Clark has underscored, there were a range of "Romantic Anti-capitalist" thinkers in nineteenth and early twentieth-century Europe who critiqued capitalism and contemplated ways to create a harmonious social order. These thinkers were primarily but not exclusively leftists and included not only Marxists but, among others, Max Weber and members of his Heidelberg circle.[4] Indeed, attempts to create new, more cooperative forms of social organization for the mass, industrial age extended beyond Marxist radicalism to include Fabian socialism, solidarism, and even strands of liberalism.

In early twentieth-century Russia, not only Marxists but reformers and radicals of all stripes believed that the social and political order needed to be fundamentally changed. Rather than seeing Marxism as artificially imported to Russia, we should ask why many members of the Russian intelligentsia embraced Marxism. The Russian intelligentsia, like their counterparts in other developing countries, aspired to modernize, educate, and uplift their country's overwhelmingly peasant population. Some were drawn not only to the revolutionary agenda of Marxism but its promise of modernization without the exploitation and alienation characteristic of industrial capitalism. Russian disciplinary culture and the ideas of non-Marxist professionals in many ways meshed with Marxism. Russian physicians, teachers, and social scientists, working in this context of underdevelopment, blamed the downtrodden condition of the masses on social and political conditions rather than biological inferiority, and they shared with Marxists an environmentalist belief that human malleability and uplift were possible given a new socioeconomic context.

After the Bolsheviks took power, non-Party specialists contributed substantially to Soviet social programs. Social statisticians provided the information through which Party leaders mapped their transformational ambitions. Zemstvo physicians initially condemned the Bolshevik seizure of power but nonetheless supported the Soviet approach to public health—social medicine with an emphasis on free, universal, preventative health care. Demographers and sexologists prescribed reproductive policies that privileged the reproductive needs of the state. Educators and Soviet officials

statisticians; Ian Hacking, "Biopower and the Avalanche of Printed Numbers," *Humanities in Society* 5:3–4 (1982): 280.

4. Katerina Clark, *Petersburg, Crucible of Cultural Revolution* (Cambridge, Mass., 1995), 16, 80.

together expanded enlightenment efforts to instill in peasants and workers not only literacy but an appreciation of art and literature.[5] Similarly, Party leaders relied heavily on non-Party ethnographers for knowledge of the peoples of the Soviet Union. These specialists, many of whom had studied in Western Europe, shared Party officials' faith in the transformative power of scientific government and helped formulate Soviet nationality policy—a policy based on concepts of historical progression common to both European anthropological theories and Marxism.[6]

Despite these points of cooperation, the relationship between Party leaders and non-Party specialists was fraught with tensions. As Yuri Slezkine argues, the Stalinist leadership assumed that the scientific truth of specialists would coincide with the Party truth upheld by Communists, but in fact these frequently diverged.[7] The Great Break of the late 1920s marked the point at which Party officials and Komsomol militants asserted the primacy of Party truth in all disciplines and persecuted "bourgeois specialists" who did not share their views. While non-Party professionals continued to play a prominent role in the production of knowledge, they had to subordinate their disciplines and institutions to the control of the Party.[8] The creation in the 1930s of a new Soviet intelligentsia, largely of working-class origin, seemed to resolve this tension by establishing a cadre of specialists grounded in both science and Party orthodoxy.[9] But professional expertise and the Party's charismatic authority continued to clash nonetheless: for example, during the Second World War when officers' professional training was belatedly recognized as more important than proletarian origin or Party loyalty.[10] Near the end of his life, Stalin made pronouncements in several fields (including economics and linguistics), whereby he sought to reassert the Party leadership's ultimate authority over social science. But

---

5. Members of the artistic avant-garde, though subsequently repressed by Soviet authorities, shared with them a belief in a totalistic artistic vision, contempt for commercialized culture, and the desire to erase distinctions between high and low art. See Boris Groys, *The Total Art of Stalinism: Avant-Garde, Aesthetic Dictatorship, and Beyond* (Princeton, 1992). On the role of the artistic intelligentsia in the formation of Stalinist culture, see also Clark, *Petersburg*, ix–x.

6. Francine Hirsch, *Empire of Nations: Ethnographic Knowledge and the Making of the Soviet Union* (Ithaca, 2005), 6–8.

7. Yuri Slezkine, *The Jewish Century* (Princeton, 2004), 306.

8. Hirsch, *Empire of Nations*, 12.

9. Sheila Fitzpatrick, "Stalin and the Making of a New Elite," *The Cultural Front: Power and Culture in Revolutionary Russia* (Ithaca, 1992).

10. Amir Weiner, *Making Sense of the War: The Second World War and the Fate of the Bolshevik Revolution* (Princeton, 2001), 43–45.

in the wake of his death and Khrushchev's de-Stalinization campaign, the pendulum swung back in favor of expertise, particularly given the importance of science during the Cold War.[11]

The strife between Party officials and non-Party specialists reflected a more general tension stemming from the fact that the Soviet system was not a technocracy. While relying heavily on social science in their effort to transform society, Stalin and his fellow leaders espoused a Prometheanism that sought to break the bounds of time and rationality in their rush to build socialism. This Promethean strain of Stalinism accounts for such contradictory features as the "bacchanalian planning" of the First Five-Year Plan (fantastic production targets presented as part of a scientific plan) and the persecution of the very economists and engineers so desperately needed to industrialize the country. The Stalinist leadership in fact vacillated between Prometheanism and technicism, though it swerved decisively toward the former during the First Five-Year Plan and again in the late 1930s. The massive use of state violence in 1937–38 also reflected the growing international threat and Stalin's doctrine that the struggle with enemies would intensify as the Soviet Union progressed to socialism and on toward communism.

Even given Marxism's historical teleology, Leninism's vanguardism, and Stalinism's ferocity in dealing with purported enemies, it is impossible to discern the genesis of the Soviet system solely from Communist Party ideology. As I have illustrated through comparative analysis, many of the practices we consider Soviet in fact originated prior to the October Revolution. Nineteenth-century specialists in Western Europe sought, through sociological study and programs of amelioration, to ensure the well-being of the body social. Professionals in Russia and other developing countries emulated these efforts while seeking their own paths to modernity, often emphasizing the role that a progressive state might play in directed social transformation. The First World War greatly accelerated state intervention in society, through state-administered public health programs, extensive surveillance networks, and technologies of social excision common to all combatant countries. In contrast to liberal democratic countries, which reestablished limits on these measures after the war, the Soviet state was formed at this moment of total war, and it institutionalized these practices as building blocks of the new order. Soviet leaders subsequently attached these methods to their agenda of social transformation, but they did not invent housing inspections, the perlustration of letters, propaganda techniques, or

11. Slezkine, *Jewish Century*, 331.

concentration camps. Such is not to imply that these preexisting practices were somehow nonideological, for they themselves developed in tandem with ambitions to reshape and mobilize societies. But, as I have shown, these ideas of social transformation extended far beyond Marxism-Leninism.

Aside from general economic prescriptions, Marxism offered little guidance on how to produce a socialist society, and in particular how to purge the vestiges of capitalism from the body social. Here the work of psychologists and criminologists, much of it predating the Revolution, provided a discriminatory framework for concretizing and neutralizing deviant constituencies.[12] When applied to the Soviet project, this framework targeted NEPmen, kulaks, and other "bourgeois elements." Party leaders used concentration camps (employed during the First World War to isolate "enemy aliens") to remove "class aliens" from society. But they also imbued preexisting technologies with new meaning. No longer were concentration camps merely sites where social aliens could be isolated—in their Soviet incarnation they became locations where class enemies could be rehabilitated through forced labor. Soviet officials and criminologists maintained that members of the bourgeoisie, dispossessed of the means of production and sent to labor camps, would have their consciousness transformed through the redemptive power of manual labor.

Even more generally we see that transformational ideologies and interventionist practices were mutually reinforcing. Social transformation was premised on a conception of human society as malleable and on technologies of social intervention. At the same time the goal of creating a new society in itself legitimated interventionist practices to realize that goal. Social intervention was not necessarily harmful in and of itself. As James Scott writes, "Where it animated plans in liberal parliamentary societies and where the planners therefore had to negotiate with organized citizens, it could spur reform." But when social intervention was combined with an authoritarian state "ready to use coercive power to bring high-modernist designs into being," then it could result in lethal state violence, particularly in times of war and revolution when civil society was prostrate and unable to resist.[13]

In the wake of the Soviet system's collapse, it is easy to forget that at one time Soviet socialism exerted enormous appeal, particularly during

12. Daniel Beer, *Renovating Russia: The Human Sciences and the Fate of Liberal Modernity, 1880–1930* (Ithaca, 2008), 203.
13. James Scott, *Seeing Like a State: How Certain Schemes to Improve the Human Condition Have Failed* (New Haven, 1998), 4–5.

the Great Depression and following the Soviet Union's defeat of Nazi Germany. At a time when liberal democratic systems seemed incapable of solving the crisis of capitalism, the Soviet regime succeeded beyond all others in mobilizing its human and natural resources, in creating a purposeful economic system, in establishing a supposedly collectivist society without class divisions or stratification. The Soviet system, moreover, provided for the welfare of workers, offered them free, universal health care and education, and guaranteed everyone a job as well as subsidized food and housing. The Soviet system's legitimacy rested in part on the fact that it carried out rapid industrialization, a process that involved extracting workers' labor under often horrendous conditions, in the name of the working class itself.

The Soviet regime proved equally effective at mobilizing for war with Nazi Germany. This effectiveness stemmed in part from the fact that the Soviet system was built on total war practices, which its leaders used not only to pursue socioeconomic transformation but to mobilize for national defense. Indeed, it institutionalized these practices through the creation of a state-run economy, a system of pervasive surveillance, and state violence in the form of large-scale deportations, incarcerations, and executions. Eventually, however, these centralized and coercive features of Soviet governance proved to be an enormous liability. Once its record of state violence became well known, the Soviet system was shown to have jeopardized rather than protected the well-being of the population. Stalinist deportations and executions, far from creating social harmony, left a legacy of hatred and distrust that the Soviet government would never escape. The planned economy, while effective in early stages of industrialization, proved unable to adjust to the postindustrial era. Government control of information and resources impeded innovation in the age of computers and telecommunications. Slowing economic growth threatened both military strength and the supply of consumer goods, a sector where the Soviet economy had never delivered on its promises of material abundance.

The Soviet system reflected the aspirations and practices of a particular historical moment, but by the late twentieth century, that moment had passed. No longer did people possess a limitless faith in social science and human progress. Social science was now subjected to critiques that called into question its objectivity and revealed the normative hierarchies on which it was often based. The role of the state, both in administering the economy and in reshaping society, came to be seen as inefficient or even dangerous. The consensus about the state's role in social amelioration similarly eroded, as the collapse of the Soviet system was only the most salient marker of the welfare state's decline that included Thatcherism,

Reaganism, and privatization in developing countries. The era of mass warfare had passed as well, as military planners became more concerned with the development of high-tech weaponry than with the fitness of the population.[14] And grand schemes of human transformation came to be seen as an evil rather than a good, in part because of the Soviet Union's own record of inflicting enormous human suffering.

14. See P. W. Singer, *Wired for War: The Robotics Revolution and Conflict in the Twenty-first Century* (New York, 2009).

Archives Consulted

Gosudarstvennyi Arkhiv Rossiiskoi Federatsii (GARF)

f. A-305 Vsesoiuznyi Pushkinskii komitet

f. A-353 Narkomiust RSFSR

f. A-413 Narkomsobes RSFSR

f. A-482 Narkomzdrav RSFSR

f. A-1795 Vserossiiskoe popechitel'stvo ob okhrane materinstva i mladenchestva

f. A-2306 Narkompros RSFSR

f. 130 Sovet narodnykh komissarov RSFSR

f. 393 Narkomat vnutrennykh del RSFSR

f. 3316 Tsentral'nyi ispolnitel'nyi komitet SSSR

f. 3931 Tsentral'nyi ispolnitel'nyi komitet Vserossiiskogo soiuza pomoshchi uvechnym voinam

f. 4085 Narkomat raboche-krest'ianskoi inspektsii RSFSR

f. 4100 Ministerstvo truda Vremennogo pravitel'stva

f. 4265 Tsentral'nyi statisticheskii komitet pri narodnom komissariate vnutrennykh del

f. 5446 Sovet narodnykh komissarov SSSR

f. 5451 Vsesoiuznyi tsentral'nyi sovet profsoiuzov

f. 5465 Tsentral'nyi komitet profsoiuzov meditsinskikh rabotnikov

f. 5469 Tsentral'nyi komitet soiuza rabochikh-metallistov

f. 5475 Tsentral'nyi komitet soiuza stroitelei

f. 5515 Narkomtrud SSSR

f. 5528 Tsentral'noe upravlenie sotsial'nogo strakhovaniia pri Narkomtruda

f. 6787 Ministerstvo gosudarstvennogo prizreniia Vremennogo pravitel'stva

f. 7062 Soiuznyi sovet sotsial'nogo strakhovaniia pri Narkomtrude

f. 7511 Komissiia sovetskogo kontrolia

f. 7576 Komitet po fizkul'ture i sportu

f. 7709 Tsentral'nyi komitet profsoiuza rabotnikov gosudarstvennykh uchrezhdenii

f. 7710 Tsentral'noe biuro fizkul'tury VTsSPS

f. 7897 Tsentral'nyi komitet profsoiuza kino-fotorabotnikov

f. 7952 Istoriia fabrik i zavodov
f. 8009 Narkomzdrav SSSR
f. 8131 Prokuratura SSSR
f. 9226 Glavnaia gosudarstvennaia sanitarnaia inspektsiia pri Narkomzdrave
f. 9401 Ministerstvo vnutrennykh del SSSR
f. 9479 Chetvertyi spetsial'nyi otdel ministerstva vnutrennykh del SSSR
f. 9492 Narkomiust SSSR
f. 9505 Tsentral'nyi komitet sotsial'no-politicheskogo prosveshcheniia Vremennogo pravitel'stva

Hoover Institution Archives

Nicolaevsky Collection
Poster Collection
Shishkin Collection

Public Record Office, UK (PRO)

CAB Cabinet
ED Board of Education
HLG Local Government Board
HO Home Office
Inter-Departmental Commission on Physical Deterioration
LAB Ministry of Labour
MH Ministry of Health
MUN Ministry of Munitions
RG Registrar General
Royal Commission on Physical Training
WO War Office

Rossiiskii Gosudarstvennyi Arkhiv Ekonomiki (RGAE)

f. 399 Sovet po izucheniiu proizvoditel'nykh sil pri Gosplane
f. 1562 Tsentral'noe statisticheskoe upravlenie
f. 4372 Gosplan
f. 7622 Glavnoe upravlenie avtotraktornoi promyshlennosti Narkomtiazhproma
f. 7733 Ministerstvo finansov
f. 7995 Narkomtiazhprom SSSR

Rossiiskii Gosudarstvennyi Arkhiv Sotsial'no-Politicheskoi Istorii (RGASPI)

f. 5 Sekretariat V. I. Lenina
f. 17 Tsentral'nyi komitet VKP(b)
f. 76 Lichnyi fond F. E. Dzerzhinskogo

f. 77 Lichnyi fond A. A. Zhdanova
f. 78 Lichnyi fond M. I. Kalinina
f. 85 Lichnyi fond G. K. Ordzhonikidze
f. 88 Lichnyi fond A. S. Shcherbakova
f. 89 Lichnyi fond E. M. Iaroslavskogo
f. 112 Politupravlenie Narkomzema
f. 477 Vosemnadtsatyi s"ezd VKP(b)
f. 558 Lichnyi fond I. V. Stalina
f. 607 Biuro po delam RSFSR pri TsK
f. 613 Tsentral'naia kontrol'naia komissiia
f. 616 Vysshaia shkola partiinykh organizatorov pri TsK
f. 619 Vysshaia shkola propagandistov
f. 623 Izdatel'stvo politicheskoi literatury TsK
f. 671 Lichnyi fond N. I. Ezhova

Rossiiskii Gosudarstvennyi Istoricheskii Arkhiv (RGIA)

f. 457 Osoboe soveshchanie dlia obsuzhdeniia i ob"edineniia po prodovol'stvennomu
    delu MZ
f. 1253 Verkhovnyi sud po prizreniiu semei lits, prizvannykh na voinu
f. 1282 Kantseliariia ministra vnutrennykh del
f. 1322 Osoboe soveshchanie po ustroistvu bezhentsev pri MVD

Tsentral'nyi Arkhiv Goroda Moskvy (TsAGM)

f. 126 Moskovskoe gosudarstvennoe upravlenie narodnogo-khoziaistvennogo ucheta
    Gosplana
f. 150 Moskovskii gorodskoi sovet
f. 176 Zavod Serp i molot
f. 214 Moskovskii gorodskoi komitet soiuza rabochikh mashinostroenia
f. 415 Avtozavod im. Stalina
f. 493 Prezidium Moskovskoi gorodskoi kollegii advokatov
f. 528 Glavnoe upravlenie narodnogo obrazovaniia Mosgorispolkoma
f. 552 Glavnoe upravlenie zdravookhraneniia Mosgorispolkoma
f. 819 Moskovskyi gorodskoi sud Verkhovnogo suda RSFSR
f. 901 Narodnyi sud Leninskogo raiona
f. 1289 Moskovskii komitet raboche-krest'ianskoi inspektsii
f. 2399 Rabochii fakul'tet im. Kirova Narkomtiazhproma
f. 2429 Upravlenie militsii goroda Moskvy

Tsentral'nyi Arkhiv Obshchestvenno-Politicheskoi Istorii Moskvy (TsAOPIM)

f. 3 Moskovskii oblastnoi komitet VKP(b)
f. 4 Moskovskii gorodskoi komitet VKP(b)

f. 69 Krasnopresnenskii raionnyi komitet VKP(b)

f. 80 Proletarskii raionnyi komitet VKP(b)

f. 262 Partiinaia organizatsiia Pervoi sittsenabivnoi fabriki

f. 429 Partiinaia organizatsiia zavoda Serp i molot

f. 432 Partiinaia organizatsiia zavoda Dinamo (im. Kirova)

f. 433 Partiinaia organizatsiia Pervogo gosudarstvennogo avtomobil'nogo zavoda (im. Stalina)

f. 459 Partorganizatsiia kommunisticheskogo universiteta im. Sverdlova

f. 468 Partiinaia organizatsiia Elektrozavoda (im. Kuibysheva)

f. 634 Moskovskii oblastnoi komitet VLKSM

f. 635 Moskovskii gorodskoi komitet VLKSM

f. 1934 Partorganizatsiia ministerstva prosveshcheniia RSFSR

f. 4083 Partorganizatsiia raionnogo otdela narodnogo obrazovaniia frunzenskogo raiona

Tsentr Khraneniia Dokumentov Molodezhnykh Organizatsii (TsKhDMO)

f. 1 Tsentral'nyi komitet Komsomola

Tsentr Khraneniia Sovremmenoi Dokumentatsii (TsKhSD)

f. 6 Komissiia partiinogo kontrol'ia

f. 89 Sud Kommunisticheskoi partii Sovetskogo Soiuza

Index

Note: Page numbers followed by *f* indicate figures.

OGPU (Unified State Political Administration), 202, 203, 264
  expansion of authority to public order and petty crime, 280–81
  mass operations against "socially harmful elements," 282–95
Operational Order 00447, of security police, 291–94
Operational Order 00485, of security police, 299
Ordzhonikidze, Grigorii (Sergo), 94, 109, 230
Osipov, Vladimir, 268
Ottoman Empire, 39, 40, 252–54, 256–57

Paris Commune, 244–46
Passportization, 241, 275–78
Patriotism, 10
  wartime propaganda and, 187–94
  youth organizations and, 120, 179
Pearson, Karl, 157
Peasant revolts, state violence against, 261–62
Pensions, as social welfare, 57, 62–63
Perlustration of letters, 183–85, 195–96, 205–6
Peter the Great, 20, 74
Peukert, Detlev, 28
Pharmacies, nationalization of, 81–82
Philanthropic organizations
  government takeover of, 29, 51–52
  reproductive policies, 171
  social welfare and, 37–38, 40–46
Physical culture, militarism and, 110–23, 118f, 121f, 122f
Pinard, Adolphe, 169
Pirogov Society, 75, 77, 84, 85
Pius XI, pope, 161
Plauzoles, Sicard de, 106
Plekhanov, Georgii, 287–88
Podvoiskii, Nikolai, 216
Poland, 107, 119, 251
Political enlightenment
  as goal of propaganda and literacy campaigns, 211–24, 214f, 223f
  in labor camps, 265
Politics, origins of state interventionist practices and, 9–10
Poovey, Mary, 22
Popov, P. I., 49
Popular sovereignty
  ideal of, 5–6
  mass politics and, 9
  New Soviet Person and, 224–25, 234
  social welfare origins and, 21–22, 34, 68

  surveillance and propaganda and, 181–82, 236–37
  see also Democratization
Population. *See Civilian population entries*
Portugal, 148
Postal censorship. *See* Perlustration of letters
Posters, patriotic and political, 191, 218–19
Prometheanism, 310
Pronatalism. *See* Reproductive policies
Propaganda. *See* Surveillance and propaganda
Provisional Government, 236
  social welfare and, 45–48, 49
  state interventionist practices and, 9–10
  surveillance and propaganda and, 186–87, 193–94, 196, 212–13, 215
Public health, 70–124, 121f, 306
  Commissariat of Health and centralized administration, 80–86, 83f
  international influences of Soviet care, 101–10
  physical culture and militarization, 110–23, 118f, 121f, 122f
  social hygiene and environmentalism, 86–101, 92f, 95f
  social medicine, body social, and epidemiology, 72–77
  World War I and state centralized administration, 77–80
Puericulture. *See* Infant care and childraising, state intervention in

Quetelet, Adolphe, 24–25, 31, 72, 157, 243

Rabkrin (Worker-Peasant Inspectorate), 209, 210
Racial pathology, Soviet medicine's avoidance of, 105
Ransel, David, 154–55
Rathbone, Eleanor, 144
Reading huts, 192, 213, 217, 219–20
Red Army
  public health and, 90, 115
  social welfare and, 48, 53–55
  state violence and, 258, 261–64, 300
  surveillance and propaganda and, 196, 198, 200, 212, 216–20
"Red Terror," 260
Ree, Erik van, 287–88
Reeducation, in labor camps, 265–67
Rein, G. E., 78–79
Reproductive policies, 125–80, 129f, 306
  birthrates and national power, 126–35
  concerns for women's reproductive health, 138–43
  eugenics movement and, 156–68